DOMESDAY BOOK

Herefordshire

History from the Sources

DOMESDAY BOOK

A Survey of the Counties of England

LIBER DE WINTONIA

Compiled by direction of

KING WILLIAM I

Winchester
1086

DOMESDAY BOOK

General editor

JOHN MORRIS

17

Herefordshire

edited by

Frank and Caroline Thorn

from a draft translation prepared by
Veronica Sankaran

PHILLIMORE
Chichester
1983

1983

Published by

PHILLIMORE & CO. LTD.,
London and Chichester

Head Office: Shopwyke Hall,
Chichester, Sussex, England

ISBN 0 85033 469 1 (case)
ISBN 0 85033 470 5 (limp)

Printed in Great Britain by
Titus Wilson & Son Ltd.,
Kendal

HEREFORDSHIRE

History from the Sources
General Editor: John Morris

The series aims to publish history
written directly from the sources
for all interested readers, both
specialists and others. The first
priority is to publish important
texts which should be widely
available, but are not.

DOMESDAY BOOK

The contents, with the folio on which each county begins, are:

Domesday Book is termed *Liber de Wintonia* (The Book of Winchester) in column 332c

INTRODUCTION

The Domesday Survey

In 1066 Duke William of Normandy conquered England. He was crowned King, and most of the lands of the English nobility were soon granted to his followers. Domesday Book was compiled 20 years later. The Saxon Chronicle records that in 1085

> at Gloucester at midwinter ... the King had deep speech with his counsellors ... and sent men all over England to each shire ... to find out ... what or how much each landholder held ... in land and livestock, and what it was worth ... The returns were brought to him.[1]

William was thorough. One of his Counsellors reports that he also sent a second set of Commissioners 'to shires they did not know, where they were themselves unknown, to check their predecessors' survey, and report culprits to the King.'[2]

The information was collected at Winchester, corrected, abridged, chiefly by omission of livestock and the 1066 population, and fair-copied by one writer into a single volume. Norfolk, Suffolk and Essex were copied, by several writers, into a second volume, unabridged, which states that 'the Survey was made in 1086'. The surveys of Durham and Northumberland, and of several towns, including London, were not transcribed, and most of Cumberland and Westmorland, not yet in England, was not surveyed. The whole undertaking was completed at speed, in less than 12 months, though the fair-copying of the main volume may have taken a little longer. Both volumes are now preserved at the Public Record Office. Some versions of regional returns also survive. One of them, from Ely Abbey,[3] copies out the Commissioners' brief. They were to ask

> The name of the place. Who held it, before 1066, and now?
> How many *hides*?[4] How many ploughs, both those in lordship and the men's?
> How many villagers, cottagers and slaves, how many free men and Freemen?[5]
> How much woodland, meadow and pasture? How many mills and fishponds?
> How much has been added or taken away? What the total value was and is?
> How much each free man or Freeman had or has? All threefold, before 1066,
> when King William gave it, and now; and if more can be had than at present?

The Ely volume also describes the procedure. The Commissioners took evidence on oath 'from the Sheriff; from all the barons and their Frenchmen; and from the whole Hundred, the priests, the reeves and six villagers from each village'. It also names four Frenchmen and four Englishmen from each Hundred, who were sworn to verify the detail.

The King wanted to know what he had, and who held it. The Commissioners therefore listed lands in dispute, for Domesday Book was not only a tax-assessment. To the King's grandson, Bishop Henry of Winchester, its purpose was that every 'man should know his right and not usurp another's'; and because it was the final authoritative register of rightful possession 'the natives called it Domesday Book, by analogy

---

[1] Before he left England for the last time, late in 1086. [2] Robert Losinga, Bishop of Hereford 1079-1095 (see *E.H.R.* 22, 1907, 74). [3] *Inquisitio Eliensis*, first paragraph. [4] A land unit, reckoned as 120 acres. [5] *Quot Sochemani.*

from the Day of Judgement'; that was why it was carefully arranged by Counties, and by landholders within Counties, 'numbered consecutively ... for easy reference'.[6]

Domesday Book describes Old English society under new management, in minute statistical detail. Foreign lords had taken over, but little else had yet changed. The chief landholders and those who held from them are named, and the rest of the population was counted. Most of them lived in villages, whose houses might be clustered together, or dispersed among their fields. Villages were grouped in administrative districts called Hundreds, which formed regions within Shires, or Counties, which survive today with minor boundary changes; the recent deformation of some ancient county identities is here disregarded, as are various short-lived modern changes. The local assemblies, though overshadowed by lords great and small, gave men a voice, which the Commissioners heeded. Very many holdings were described by the Norman term *manerium* (manor), greatly varied in size and structure, from tiny farmsteads to vast holdings; and many lords exercised their own jurisdiction and other rights, termed *soca*, whose meaning still eludes exact definition.

The Survey was unmatched in Europe for many centuries, the product of a sophisticated and experienced English administration, fully exploited by the Conqueror's commanding energy. But its unique assemblage of facts and figures has been hard to study, because the text has not been easily available, and abounds in technicalities. Investigation has therefore been chiefly confined to specialists; many questions cannot be tackled adequately without a cheap text and uniform translation available to a wider range of students, including local historians.

Previous Editions

The text has been printed once, in 1783, in an edition by Abraham Farley, probably of 1250 copies, at Government expense, said to have been £38,000; its preparation took 16 years. It was set in a specially designed type, here reproduced photographically, which was destroyed by fire in 1808. In 1811 and 1816 the Records Commissioners added an introduction, indices, and associated texts, edited by Sir Henry Ellis; and in 1861-1863 the Ordnance Survey issued zincograph facsimiles of the whole. Texts of individual counties have appeared since 1673, separate translations in the Victoria County Histories and elsewhere.

This Edition

Farley's text is used, because of its excellence, and because any worthy alternative would prove astronomically expensive. His text has been checked against the facsimile, and discrepancies observed have been verified against the manuscript, by the kindness of Miss Daphne Gifford of the Public Record Office. Farley's few errors are indicated in the notes.

[6]*Dialogus de Scaccario* 1,16.

The editor is responsible for the translation and lay-out. It aims at what the compiler would have written if his language had been modern English; though no translation can be exact, for even a simple word like 'free' nowadays means freedom from different restrictions. Bishop Henry emphasized that his grandfather preferred 'ordinary words'; the nearest ordinary modern English is therefore chosen whenever possible. Words that are now obsolete, or have changed their meaning, are avoided, but measurements have to be transliterated, since their extent is often unknown or arguable, and varied regionally. The terse inventory form of the original has been retained, as have the ambiguities of the Latin.

Modern English commands two main devices unknown to 11th century Latin, standardised punctuation and paragraphs; in the Latin, *ibi* ('there are') often does duty for a modern full stop, *et* ('and') for a comma or semi-colon. The entries normally answer the Commissioners' questions, arranged in five main groups, (i) the place and its holder, its hides, ploughs and lordship; (ii) people; (iii) resources; (iv) value; and (v) additional notes. The groups are usually given as separate paragraphs.

King William numbered chapters 'for easy reference', and sections within chapters are commonly marked, usually by initial capitals, often edged in red. They are here numbered. Maps, indices and an explanation of technical terms are also given. Later, it is hoped to publish analytical and explanatory volumes, and associated texts.

The editor is deeply indebted to the advice of many scholars, too numerous to name, and especially to the Public Record Office, and to the publisher's patience. The draft translations are the work of a team; they have been co-ordinated and corrected by the editor, and each has been checked by several people. It is therefore hoped that mistakes may be fewer than in versions published by single fallible individuals. But it would be Utopian to hope that the translation is altogether free from error; the editor would like to be informed of mistakes observed.

The maps are the work of John Moore, Frank Thorn and Jim Hardy.

The preparation of this volume has been greatly assisted by a generous grant from the Leverhulme Trust Fund.

This support, originally given to the late Dr. J. R. Morris, has been kindly extended to his successors. At the time of Dr. Morris's death in June 1977, he had completed volumes 2, 3, 11, 12, 19, 23, 24. He had more or less finished the preparation of volumes 13, 14, 20, 28. These and subsequent volumes in the series were brought out under the supervision of John Dodgson and Alison Hawkins, who have endeavoured to follow, as far as possible, the editorial principles established by John Morris.

Conventions

★ refers to note on discrepancy between MS and Farley text

[ ] enclose words omitted in the MS   ( ) enclose editorial explanation

IN HEREFORD CIVITATE TĒPORE REGIS EDWARDI

erant. c 7 iii. hões cōmanentes intus 7 extra murum.
7 habebant has fubterfcriptas confuetudines.
Siq̇s eoᵹ uoluiffet recedere de ciuitate: poterat conceffu
p̄pofiti domū fuā uendere alteri homini feruitiū debitū
inde facere uolenti. 7 habebat p̄pofit̕ terciū denariū huj̕
uenditionis. Q̇d fiq̇s pauptate fua non potuiffet feruitiū
facere: relinquebat fine p̄cio domū fuā præpofito. qui
ₚuidebat ne dom̕ uacua remaneret 7 né rex careret feruitio.
Intra murū ciuitatis unaquaqᵹ integra mafura reddeƀ
vii. den̕ 7 obolū. 7 iiii. denar̕ ad locandos caballos. 7 iii⁺.
diebᵹ in Augufto fecabat ad Maurdine. 7 una die ad fenū
c̄gregandū erat ubi uicecomes uolebat. Qui equū habeƀ:
ter in anno ₚgebat cū uicecomite ad placita 7 ad hundrez
ad Vrmelauia. Quando rex uenatui inftabat: de una
quaqᵹ domo ₚ confuetudinem ibat un̕ homo ad ftabilitio
nem in filua.
Alij hões n̄ hn̄tes integras mafuras: inuenieƀ jneuuardos
ad aulā. quando rex erat in ciuitate.
Burgenfis cū caballo feruiens: cū moriebat: habeƀ rex
equum 7 arma ejus. De eo qui equū n̄ habeƀ. fi moreret:
habeƀ rex aut. x. folid. aut terrā ejus cū domibᵹ.
Siq̇s morte præuen̕ non diuififfet quæ fua eran: rex
habeƀ om̄em ej̕ pecuniam. Has c̄fuetudines habebaȷ
in ciuitate habitantes: 7 alij fimilit̕ extra murū ma
nentes. nifi tantū q̇d integra mafura foris murū non
dabat nifi. iii. denar̕ 7 obolū. Aliæ c̄fuetudines. erant
c̄omunes. ʃ Cujcunqᵹ uxor braziabat intus 7 extra ciui
tatem: dabat. x. denarios ₚ confuetudinem.

HEREFORDSHIRE

[HEREFORDSHIRE CUSTOMS]

1   In the City of HEREFORD before 1066 there were 103 men dwelling inside and outside the wall; they had the customs mentioned below.

2   If any one of them wished to leave the City, he could sell his house with the reeve's consent to another man who was willing to perform the service owed from it, and the reeve had the third penny of this sale. But if anyone could not perform the service because of his poverty, he left his house without payment to the reeve who ensured that the house did not remain empty and that the King was not without service.

3   Within the city wall every whole dwelling paid 7½d, and 4d for the hire of horses, and on three days in August reaped at Marden, and on one day had to gather hay where the Sheriff wished. The owner of a horse went three times a year with the Sheriff to (hear) pleas and to (meetings of) the Hundreds at Wormelow (Tump). When the King was engaged in hunting, by custom one man from each and every house went to stall game in the woodland.

4   Other men who did not have whole dwellings provided escorts for the court when the King was in the City.

5   When a burgess who served with his horse died, the King had his horse and arms. If a man who did not have a horse died, the King either had 10s from him or his land with its houses. If anyone had not bequeathed his possessions because of untimely death, the King had all his property.

6   Those who lived in the City had these (same) customs, as did others likewise who lived outside the walls, except that a whole dwelling outside the wall only gave 3½d; the other customs were common (to both).

7   Any man's wife who brewed ale inside or outside the City gave 10d as a customary due.

Sex Fabri eraɴ in ciuitate. quifqᷱ eoᷱ de fua forgia redɗ

unū denaꝛ̉. ⁊ quifqᷱ eoᷱ facieƀ. cxx. ferra de ferro regis.

⁊ unicuiqᷱ eoᷱ dabanꞇ. iii. denarij ꝓ conſuetudinem. *inde*

⁊ iſti fabri ab omi alio ſeruitio erãt quieti.

Septē monetarij erant ibi. Vn ex his erat monetari epi. *b* *a* *ꝯc*

★ Quando moneta renouaꞇ̉ dabat quifqᷱ eoᷱ xviii.

foliɗ ꝓ cuneis recipiendis. ⁊ ex eo die quo redibant uſqᷱ

ad unū menſē̉ dabat q́fqᷱ eoᷱ regi. xx. foliɗ. ⁊ fimiliꞇ

habeƀ eꝑs de fuo monetario. xx. foliɗ.

Quando ueniebat rex in ciuitatē̉ quantū uoleƀ denaꝛ̉

faciebant ei monetarij. de argento ſcilicet regis.

⁊ hi. vii. habebant ſacã ⁊ focham fuã. ⌐mento.

Moriente aliq́ regis monetariỏ habeƀ rex. xx. foł de releua

Qɗ fi morereꞇ̉ non diuifo cenfu fuỏ rex habeƀ omem censū.

Si uicecomes iret in Wales cū exercitủ ibaɴ hi homines

cū eo. Qɗ fiq́s ire juſſus non ireꞇ̉ emdabat regi. xl. foliɗ.

In ipfa ciuitate habeƀ Herald. xxvii. burgenfes. eafdē *comes ꝯ*

cſuetudines hñtes quas ⁊ alij burgenfes.

De hac ciuitate reddeƀ ꝑpofit. xii. liƀ regi. ⁊ vi. liƀ comiti. *.E.* *heraldo.*

⁊ habeƀ in fuo cenfu fuꝑdiƈtas oms cſuetudines.

⌐Rex ů habeƀ in fuo dñio tres forisfaƈturas. hoc. ē pacē fuã

infraƈtã. ⁊ heinfarã. ⁊ foreſtellum.

Quicunqᷱ hoᷱ unū feciſſet̉ emdaƀ. c. foł regi cujcunqᷱ hō fuiſſet. *ꝯ*

Modo hꞃ rex ciuitatē Hereford in dñio. ⁊ anglici burgenfes

ibi manentes hñt fuas priores cſuetudines. Francig̉ ů burg̅fes

hñt q́etas ꝑ. xii. denaꝛ̉ oms forisfaƈturas fuas. ꝓter tres fuꝑdiƈtas.

Ħ eiuitas redɗ regi. lx. liƀ ad numerū. de candidis denarijs.

Inꞇ ciuitatē ⁊ xviii. Ꝏ qui in hereford redɗt firmas fuas̉ cōpu

tantur. ccc.xxxv. liƀ. ⁊ xviii. foł. exceptis placitis de hunɗ

ɫ⁊ de comitatu.

8 There were six smiths in the City; each of them paid 1d from his forge and each of them made 120 horseshoes from the King's iron; for these each of them was given 3d by custom; these smiths were exempt from every other service.

9 There were seven moneyers there. One of these was the Bishop's moneyer. When the coinage was renewed, each of them gave 18s for acquiring the dies, and after the day on which they returned, within one month, each of them gave 20s to the King, and the Bishop likewise had 20s from his moneyer. When the King came to the City, the moneyers made him as many pence as he wanted, that is from the King's silver. These seven had their own full jurisdiction. When any moneyer of the King died, the King had 20s in relief. But if he died without bequeathing his wealth, the King had all his wealth.

10 If the Sheriff went into Wales with an army, these men went with him. But if anyone was ordered to go and did not go, he paid a fine of 40s to the King.

11 In this City Earl Harold had 27 burgesses who had the same customs as the other burgesses.

12 The reeve paid £12 from this City to King Edward and £6 to Earl Harold, and he had all the above customary dues in his revenue.

13 The King had the three forfeitures in his lordship, that is breach of the peace, house-breaking and highway robbery. Anyone who committed one of these paid a fine of 100s to the King, no matter whose man he was.

14 Now the King has the City of Hereford in lordship, and the English burgesses who live there have their former customs. But the French burgesses have all their forfeitures discharged for 12d, except the three above.

15 This City pays the King £60 of blanched pence at face value. Between the City and 18 manors which pay their revenues in Hereford, £335 18s are accounted for, besides (revenue from) the pleas of the Hundreds and the County (courts).

IN ARCENEFELDE HABET REX tres æcclas. Preſbiteri

harū æcclarum ferunt legationes regis in Wales. 7 quiſq̃

eoꝛ cantat pro rege. 11 . miſſas una quaꝗ ebdomada.

Siquis coꝗ moritur: rex habet de eo . xx . ſol p̄ cſuetud.

Siꝗs Walenſiū furat hoēm aut feminā . equū . bouē . uel uaccā:

conuict̃ inde redd prius furtū. 7 dat . xx . ſolid p forisfactura.

De oue uero furata uel faſciculo manipuloꝛ: emdat . 11 . ſol.

Siꝗs occid hōem regis. 7 facit heinfaram . dat regi . xx . ſot

de ſolutione hominis. 7 de forisfactura . c . ſot . Si alicuj taini

hōem occiderit: dat . x . ſot dño hōis mortui.

Q̃d ſi Walenſis Walenſē occiderit: cgregant parentes

occiſi. 7 prædant eū qui occidit ejꝗ ꝓpinquos. 7 cōburunt

domos eoꝛ donec in craſtinū circa meridiē corp̄ mortui ſepeliat̃.

De hac p̄da h̄t rex tciā partē. illi ū totū aliud h̄nt quietū.

Aliter aut̃ qui domū incenderit. 7 inde accuſat fuerit: p. XL.

hōēs de defend. Q̃d ſi n̄ potuerit: xx . ſolid regi emdabit.

Siꝗs de cſuetudine ſextariū mellis celauerit: ꝓbat inde

p unꝗ ſextario redd quinꝗ. ſi tant̃ træ ten ut debeat dare.

Si uicecom euocat eos ad ſiremot: meliores ex eis . vi . aut

vii . uadunt cū eo . Qui uocat n̄ uadit: dat . 11 . ſot aut unū

bouē regi. 7 qui de hundret remanet: tantd p̄ſoluit.

Similit̃ emdat qui juſſus a uicecomite ſecū ire in Walis

non pgit . Nā ſi uicecom non uadit: nemo eoꝛ ibit.

1 In ARCHENFIELD the King has 3 churches. The priests of these churches bear the King's dispatches into Wales and each of them sings two masses each and every week for the King. If any one of them dies, the King has 20s from him by custom.

2 If any Welshman steals a man, a woman, a horse, an ox or a cow, when he is convicted of it, he first restores what he stole, and gives 20s in forfeiture; but for stealing a sheep or a bundle of sheaves he pays a fine of 2s.

3 If anyone kills one of the King's men or commits house-breaking, he gives the King 20s as payment for the man and 100s in forfeiture. If anyone has killed a thane's man, he gives 10s to the dead man's lord.

4 But if a Welshman has killed a Welshman, the relatives of the slain man gather and despoil the killer and his relatives and burn their houses until the body of the dead man is buried the next day about midday. The King has the third part of this plunder, but they have all the rest free.

5 Otherwise, a man who has burnt a house and is accused of it, proves his innocence through 40 men; but if he has been unable to, he will pay a fine of 20s to the King.

6 If anyone has concealed a sester of honey from the customary due and this is proved, he pays five (sesters) for one sester, if he holds as much land as ought to produce them.

7 If the Sheriff summons them to a meeting of the Shire, six or seven of the nobler ones of them go with him. A man who is called and does not go, gives 2s or 1 ox to the King; a man who stays away from the Hundred (meeting) pays as much.

8 Anyone who does not go when ordered by the Sheriff to go with him into Wales, is fined the same. But if the Sheriff does not go, none of them goes.

Cū exercitus in hostē ꝑgit: ipsi ꝑ consuetudinē faciunt
Auantwarde.7 in reuersione Redrewarde.
Hæ ↄ̄suetuđ erant Walensiū T.R.E. in *ARCENEFELDE*.
RISET de Walesređ regi. W. xl. lib̄.
De tra Calcebuef. hť rex. x. sol. ext firmā.

HIC ANNOTANT TERRAS TENENTES IN HEREFORDSCIRE.

.I. REX WILLELMVS. 7 IN ARCENEFELDE 7 IN WALIS.
.II. Eṗs de Hereford.
.III. Æccła de Cormelies.
.IIII. Eccła de Lire.
.V. Æccła de Glouuecestre.
.VI. Æccła Ś Guthlaci.
.VII. Nigel medicus.
.VIII Radulf de Todeni.
.IX. Radulfus de Mortemer.
.X. Rogerius de Laci.
.XI. Rogerius de Mucelgros.
.XII Robertus Gernon.
.XIII Henricus de Ferieres.
.XIIII Wiłłs de Scohies.
.XV. Wiłłs filius Baderon.
.XVI. Wiłłs filius Norman.
.XVII. Turstinus filius Rolf.
.XVIII. Albert Lothariensis.
.XIX. Alured de Merleberge.
.XX. Alured de Hispania.
.XXI. Ansfrid de Cormelies.
.XXII. Durand de Glouuecestre.
.XXIII Drogo filius Poinz.
.XXIIII. Osbern filius Ricardi.
.XXV Gislebertus filius Turold.
.XXVI Ilbertus filius Turold.
.XXVII Herman de Dreuues.
.XXVIII Hunfrid de Buiuile.
.XXIX Hugo Lasne.
.XXX. Vrso de abetoth.
.XXXI. Grifin
.XXXII Raẏnerius
.XXXIII Carbonel.
.XXXIIII. Vxor Radulfi capellani.
.XXXV. Stefanus.
.XXXVI Madoch. Edric. Elmer.

9 When the army advances on the enemy, these men by custom form the vanguard and on their return the rearguard.
These were the customs of the Welshmen in Archenfield before 1066.

10 Rhys of Wales pays King William £40.
From the land of *Calcebuef* the King has 10s in addition to the revenue.

LIST OF LANDHOLDERS IN HEREFORDSHIRE, ARCHENFIELD AND WALES

1 King William
2 The Bishop of Hereford
3 Cormeilles Church
4 Lyre Church
5 Gloucester Church
6 St. Guthlac's Church
7 Nigel the Doctor
8 Ralph of Tosny
9 Ralph of Mortimer
10 Roger of Lacy
11 Roger of Mussegros
12 Robert Gernon
13 Henry of Ferrers
14 William of Écouis
15 William son of Baderon
16 William son of Norman
17 Thurstan son of Rolf
18 Albert of Lorraine
19 Alfred of Marlborough
20 Alfred of 'Spain'
21 Ansfrid of Cormeilles
22 Durand of Gloucester
23 Drogo son of Poyntz
24 Osbern son of Richard
25 Gilbert son of Thorold
26 Ilbert son of Thorold
27 Herman of Dreux
[28] Humphrey of Bouville
29 Hugh Donkey
30 Urso of Abetot
31 Gruffydd
32 Rayner
33 Charbonnel
34 The Wife of Ralph the Chaplain
35 Stephen
36 Madog, Edric, Aelmer

TERRA REGIS.   *IN BROMESAIS HD̃.*

R̃ex. W. ten̅ *LINTVNE* . Rex Edw̅ tenuit . Ibi eran̅ . v . hidæ.

7 reddeb̅ quartā partē firmæ unius noctis . Modo . ē ualde

imminutū . Ibi ſunt in dñio . III . car̅ .7 x . uiłł 7 v . bord̅ cū . XII.

car̅ . Ibi . VI . ſerui .7 molin̅ de . VIII . denar̅.

Ibi . I . francig̅ ten̅ dimid̅ hidā . quæ reddeb̅ . IIII . ſoł . T.R.E.

Hoc ⋒ ſicuti . ē modo redd̅ . x . lib̅ de albis denar̅.

De hoc ⋒ ten̅ S MARIA de Cormelijs æccłam 7 p̅brm cū ſua

tra .7 totā decimā .7 uñ uiłłm cū una virg̅ terræ.

De ipſo ⋒ ten̅ Ansfrid̅ de cormelijs . II . hid̅ .7 IX . uiłł 7 IX . car̅.

7 Wiłłs . F . Baderon ten̅ unā virg̅ træ . quæ ibi jacuit . T.R.E.

⌐Ilbert uicecom̅ h̅t ad firmā ſuā de Arcenefeld c̅ſuetudines

om̅s mellis 7 ouiū . quæ huic ⋒ p̅tineb̅ T.R.E.

⌐Wiłłs . F . Normanni h̅t inde . VI . ſextaria mellis .7 VI . oues

cū agnis .7 XII . denarios.

IN GREITREWES HVND̃.

R̃ex ten̅ *LVCVORDNE* . Rex . E . tenuit . Ibi . IIII . hidæ.

In dñio ſunt . III . car̅ .7 IX . uiłł 7 III . bord̅ 7 uñ ſeruieꝗ̅ regis.

Int̅ om̅s h̅n̅t . x . car̅ . Ibi . III . ſerui .7 molin̅ de . x . ſolid̅.

‡   [7 unx un̅ | ci̅i̅ auri]   Hoc ⋒ redd̅ . x . lib̅ m̅ de alb̅ denar̅ ‡ T . R . E . n̅ fuit poſit

ad firmā .7 id̅o ignorat̅ quantū t̅c ualuit . ⌐ de cormelijs.

⌐Decimā huj̅ ⋒ 7 uñ uiłłm cū . I . uirg̅ træ h̅t S MARIA

⌐Vna ex his . IIII . hid̅ fuit 7 eſt in Reueland . Ibi ſunt . IIII.

bord̅ 7 una ancilla . cu . II . car̅ .7 ibi . II . molini de . xv . ſolid̅.

⌐De alijs . III . hid̅ poſuit Rad̅ de bernai . L . acras ad ſuū

Reueland .7 uñ bord̅ .7 molin̅ de . VII . ſolid̅.

Qd̅ habet uicecom̅ ad ſuū opus . ual̅ . LX . ſolid̅.

In BROMSASH Hundred

1 King William holds LINTON. King Edward held it. There were
   5 hides. It paid the fourth part of one night's revenue.
   Now it is extremely reduced. In lordship 3 ploughs;
       10 villagers and 5 smallholders with 12 ploughs.
       6 slaves; a mill at 8d.
       1 Frenchman who holds ½ hide which paid 4s before 1066.
   This manor, as it now is, pays £10 of white pence.
       Of this manor St. Mary's of Cormeilles holds the church, a
   priest with his land, and the whole tithe, and
       1 villager with 1 virgate of land.
       Ansfrid of Cormeilles holds 2 hides of this manor;
       9 villagers and 9 ploughs.
       William son of Baderon holds 1 virgate of land which lay there
   before 1066.
       Ilbert the Sheriff has in his revenue of Archenfield all the
   customary dues of honey and sheep which belonged to this
   manor before 1066.
       William son of Norman has from it 6 sesters of honey, 6 sheep
   with lambs and 12d.

The King holds
in GREYTREE Hundred

2 LUGWARDINE. King Edward held it. 4 hides. In lordship 3 ploughs;
       9 villagers, 3 smallholders and a servant of the King;
           between them they have 10 ploughs.
       3 slaves; a mill at 10s.
   This manor now pays £10 of white pence and one ounce of gold;
   before 1066 it was not put in the revenue and therefore its value
   then is not known.
       St. Mary's of Cormeilles has the tithe of this manor and
       1 villager with 1 virgate of land.
       One of these 4 hides was and is in the reeveland.
       4 smallholders and 1 female slave with 2 ploughs.
       2 mills at 15s.
       Ralph of Bernay put 50 acres from the other 3 hides in his
           reeveland;
       1 smallholder.
       A mill at 7s.
   Value of what the Sheriff has for his use, 60s.

Rex ten̄ *CHINGESTONE* . Rex . E . tenuit . Ibi . IIII . hidæ.
In dn̄io ſunt . II . hidæ una v̄ min̄ .7 ibi . ē una car̄ .7 alia
poſſet . ēē .7 VI . uilti cū p̄poſito 7 III . borđ 7 un̄ faƀ . Int oms
hn̄t . VI . car̄ . Ibi Silua nōe Triueline . nullā reddeɴ c̄ſu
etudinē niſi uenationē . Vilti T.R.E. ibi manentes . portaƀ
uenationē ad hereford . nec aliud ſeruitiū facieƀ . ut ſcira dicit.
Huj̄ m̄ decimā totā ten̄ S̄ MARIA de Cormelijs .7 un̄ uilt cū . I . virḡ
terræ . Ilƀt . F . turoldi ten̄ de hoc m̄ . II as . hidas . p̄ uno m̄.
Huic m̄ p̄tineƀ T.R.E. una pars træ *CHEWESHOPE* .7 c̄ſue
tudo de ea p̄geƀ in Chingeſtone . Roger de Laci ten̄ de rege.
Ad hoc m̄ appoſuit uicecom Tp̄r . W . comitis *WAPLEFORD*.
Hoc m̄ tenuit Aluuin̄ .7 poterat ire ad quē dn̄m uolebat.
Ibi . I . hida . Tra . II . car̄ . Ibi ſunt . II . uilti cū . I . car̄ .   ſ trem.
Tot̄ hoc ita c̄gregat̄ . redđ regi . L . ſot de candiđ den̄ 7 un̄ accipi

Rex ten̄ *MAVRDINE* . Rex . E . tenuit . Ibi plures hidæ
eraɴ . ſed ex his . II . tantm̄ geldaɴ . H̄ tra p̄ plures . ē diuiſa.
In dn̄io h̄t rex . III . car̄ .7 XXV . uilt 7 v . borđ .7 II . bouarii.
7 IIII . ſerui .7 IIII . coliƀti . Int oms hn̄t . XXI . car̄ . Ibi molin̄
de . XX . ſoliđ .7 XXV . ſtiches anguilt . Silua . redđ . XX . ſoliđ.
Ibi . ē piſcaria ſine cenſu . De ſalinis in Wich . IX . ſūmæ ſalis . aut
IX . denar̄ .7 adhuc . VIII . ſeruientes regis hn̄t . VII . car̄.
De hoc m̄ ten̄ Wilts . F . Norman . III . hiđ una v̄ min̄ .7 Norman porcari²
ten̄ dimiđ hiđ de hoc m̄ .7 comes W . poſuit foris de hoc m̄ unā v̄.
7 deđ cuidā burgſi de hereford .7 Anſchitil ten̄ . XL . ac̄s int
planā trā 7 p̄tū . quas p̄poſit regis . E . preſtauit ſuo parenti.
Terrā . W . ſilij Norman . tenuer̄ . III . Radcheniſt . nec poteraɴ
de hoc m̄ ſeparari . De mercede tre m̄ huj̄ . exeuɴ . IX . ſolidi.
T.R.E. reddeƀ . IX . liƀ de candiđ denar̄ . Modo ap̄pciat̄ . XVI . liƀ.

[? in STRETFORD Hundred]
3 KINGSTONE. King Edward held it. 4 hides. In lordship 2 hides,
   less 1 virgate. 1 plough there; another would be possible.
      6 villagers with a reeve; 3 smallholders and a smith;
         between them they have 6 ploughs.
   A wood named TREVILLE which pays no customary dues except
   hunting rights. The villagers who lived there before 1066
   carried (the produce of) the hunt to Hereford and did no other
   service, as the Shire states.
   St. Mary's of Cormeilles holds the whole tithe of this manor, and
   1 villager with 1 virgate of land.
   Ilbert son of Thorold holds 2 hides of this manor as one manor.
   Before 1066, 1 parcel of land, CUSOP, belonged to this manor;
   its customary dues went to Kingstone. Roger of Lacy holds
   from the King. The Sheriff placed WAPLEFORD in this manor in
   Earl William's time.
   Alwin held this manor; he could go to whichever lord he would.
   1 hide there. Land for 2 ploughs.
   2 villagers with 1 plough.
The whole of this, added together thus, pays the King 50s of
blanched pence and 1 hawk.

[in THORNLAW Hundred]
4 MARDEN. King Edward held it. There were many hides, but only
   2 of them pay tax. This land is divided between many (people).
   The King has 3 ploughs in lordship;
      25 villagers, 5 smallholders, 2 ploughmen, 4 slaves and
         4 freedmen; between them they have 21 ploughs.
      A mill at 20s and 25 sticks of eels; woodland which pays 20s.
         A fishery without dues; from the salt-houses in Droitwich,
         9 packloads of salt or 9d; further, 8 servants of the King
         have 7 ploughs.
   William son of Norman holds 3 hides, less 1 virgate, of this
   manor.
   Norman Pigman holds ½ hide of this manor.
   Earl William put 1 virgate outside this manor and gave it to a
   burgess of Hereford.
   Ansketel holds 40 acres, both open land and meadow, which
   King Edward's reeve leased to a relative of his.
   3 riding men held William son of Norman's land; they could
   not be separated from this manor.
   9s comes from the produce of this manor's land.
Before 1066 it paid £9 of blanched pence; now it is assessed at £16.

Rex ten *LENE*. Rex. E. tenuit. Ibi. xv. hidæ.

In dñio funt. v. car. 7 adhuc. iiii. car poſſ.ẽe. 7 xxi. uiłł 7 ix.

borđ cũ. xvii. car. Ibi. x. bouarij. 7 ii. ſerui. 7 vi. coliƀti.

Ibi. ii. molini de. xxvi. ſol 7 iiii. den. 7 qngent anguiłł.

De ſilua 7 paſtura. viii. ſoliđ. De cſuetudiñ 7 de molinis 7 uiłłis

7 coliƀtis exeunt. c. ſoliđ. v. ſoliđ min. exceptis Anguillis.

De hoc ᴔ ten Rađ de mortemer uñ mẽbrũ *MERESTONE*.

de. ii. hiđ. 7 Rog de Laci uñ ᴔ de. ii. hiđ nõe *HOPE*. 7 aliũ ᴔ

de. i. hida nõe *STRETE*. 7 tciũ ᴔ de. i. hida nõe *LAVTONE*.

Iſđ Rog ten dimiđ hiđ quã tenuit uñ porcarius. T.R.E.

Hanc trã deđ Wiłłs comes Walterio de Laci.

De eođ ᴔ ten Ilƀt. F. turoldi dimiđ virg quã tenuit. i. porcari.

H̃ tra uocat *ALAC*.

T.R.E. ualƀ. vi. liƀ. Modo. ẽ ad firmã p. xiii. liƀ. 7 iii. ſoliđ.

Rex ten *LENE*. Morcar comes tenuit. Ibi. xv. hidæ. *IN LENE HVND*.

In dñio funt.. iii. car. 7 xix. uiłł 7 ix. borđ. 7 ii. radchen

cũ. xvi. car. Ibi. vi. ſerui. 7 ii. ancillæ. 7 vi. coliƀti.

Ibi. ii. molini de. xxv. ſoliđ. Silua redđ. xl. denar.

Viłłi daɴ de cſuetudine. xiii. ſol 7 iiii. den. 7 coliƀti redđt

iii. ſext frumti 7 ordei. 7 ii. oues 7 dimiđ cũ agnis. 7 ii. den

7 uñ obolũ.

Hoꝝ. ii. ᴔ æcclas 7 pƀros 7 decimas. 7 duos uiłłos. ten Ꞩ MARIA

de cormelijs in elemoſina de rege.

T.R.E. ualƀ. vi. liƀ. Modo. xii. liƀ de candidis denar.

ppoſit huj ᴔ cſuetuđ habeƀ T.R.E. ut ueniente dña ſua

in ᴔ pſentaret ei. xviii. oras denar. ut ẽet ipſa læto animo,

7 dapifer 7 alij miniſtri habeƀ de eo. x. ſoliđ.

Rex ten *MERCHELAI*. Herald coñ tenuit. *IN WIMESTRVIL HĐ*.

Ibi. xvii. hidæ gelđ.

In dñio funt. iiii. car. 7 xxxvi. uiłł 7 x. borđ cũ. xl. car.

hi uiłłi araɴ 7 ſeminaɴ de ppo ſemine qt̃ xx. acras

[in HAZELTREE Hundred]

5 KINGSLAND. King Edward held it. 15 hides. In lordship 5 ploughs;   179 d
a further 3 ploughs possible.
 21 villagers and 9 smallholders with 17 ploughs. 10 ploughmen,
  2 slaves and 6 freedmen.
 2 mills at 26s 4d and 500 eels; from the woodland and pasture,
  8s; from customary dues, mills, villagers and freedmen come
  100s, less 5s, besides eels.
 Ralph of Mortimer holds one member of this manor,
 MERESTONE, at 2 hides. Roger of Lacy (holds) one manor at 2
 hides, named HOPLEYS (Green); another manor at 1 hide, named
 STREET; and a third manor at 1 hide, named LAWTON. Roger also
 holds ½ hide which a pigman held before 1066. Earl William
 gave this land to Walter of Lacy.
 Also of this manor Ilbert son of Thorold holds ½ virgate which
 a pigman held. This land is called ALAC.
Value before 1066 £6; now it is in the revenue at £13 3s.

in LENE Hundred

6 EARDISLAND. Earl Morcar held it. 15 hides. In lordship 3 ploughs;
 19 villagers, 9 smallholders and 2 riding men with 16 ploughs.
  6 male and 2 female slaves and 6 freedmen.
 2 mills at 25s; woodland which pays 40d.
 The villagers give 13s 4d as a customary due; the freedmen pay
 3 sesters of wheat and barley, 2½ sheep with lambs and 2½d.
 Of these two manors St. Mary's of Cormeilles holds in alms from
 the King the churches, priests and tithes and 2 villagers.
Value before 1066 £6; now £12 of blanched pence.
 Before 1066 the reeve of this manor had the custom that when
his lady came to the manor he presented to her 18 *ora* of pence
so that she might be happy. The steward and other officers had
10s from him.

in WINSTREE Hundred

7 (Much) MARCLE. Earl Harold held it. 17 hides which pay tax. ...
 In lordship 4 ploughs;
 36 villagers and 10 smallholders with 40 ploughs. These
  villagers plough and sow with their own seed 80 acres of

frumti.7 totid ad auenas p̄ter . ix . acras . Harū . vi . p̄tiñ

ad Willm . F . baderon . 7 iii . ad S̄ MARIA de Cormelijs.

In hoc m̄ . ē p̄pofit 7 uñ francig . 7 uñ radchen . Hi hn̄t

iii . car . Ibi . viii . ferui 7 uñ bouari . 7 vi . ancillæ.

Ibi moliñ nil redd nifi tant uictū ej qui eū cuftodit.

Ibi Silua redd . v . folid . qui dant ad Wich p . lx . mittis

falis . Ad Hereford fux̄ . iiii . burḡfes huic m̄ reddtes

xviii . focos carrucis.

De hoc m̄ eft una hida ad Turleftane . quæ T.R.E. reddeb

. l . maffas ferri . 7 vi . falmones . Modo . ē h̄ tra in forefta.

De ipfo m̄ ten uicecom̄ . i . hidā . 7 ibi ht̄ . ii . car.

In eod m̄ funt . lviii . acræ træ p̄jecte de filua . 7 p̄po

fitus 7 alij . ii . ho̅es ten plures ac̄s de ipfa tra.

S̄ MARIA de cormelijs ht̄ decimā huj m̄ . 7 pbrm

7 æcclam cū . i . uitto tenente . i . virg træ.   ⌐ HD.

T.R.E. ualb . xxx . lib . 7 modo tantd ualet. *IN BREMESSE*

R ex ten *CLIVE* . Herald tenuit . Ibi xiiii . hidæ 7 dimid cū

Bereuuicha nōe *WILTONE* . In dn̄io funt . iiii . car . 7 xx . uitti

7 p̄pofit 7 xi . bord cū . xvi . car . Ibi . vii . ferui . 7 v . ancillæ.

7 uñ bouarius . Ibi . ii . molini de . vi . folid . 7 pifcaria nil redd.

Ad hoc m̄ p̄tiñ tot Walenfes qui hn̄t . viii . car . 7 reddt . x.

fext mellis . 7 dimid . 7 vi . fot 7 v . den.   ⌐ cormelijs.

⌐ Huj m̄ æcclam . pbrm 7 decimā cū . i . uitto . ten S̄ MARIA de
⌐ De hoc m̄ . ē in forefta regis . W . tant træ . quæ T.R.E. reddeb

vi . fextar mellis . 7 vi . oues cū agnis.

⌐ De ifto m̄ ten Witts baderon . i . hid . 7 iii . uirg.

180 a 7 Godefrid ten . i . virg . Roger de Laci ten dimid pifcariā quæ

ptineb huic m̄ Tp̄r . R.E. 7 tc̄ ptineb ibidē . xxv . mittæ falis

de Wich . 7 ipfo tp̄r erant in ipfo m̄ duæ hidæ una v̄ min

quæ funt in *ASCIS* . Alured de merleberge ten modo.

Herald teneb qdo mortuus fuit . 7 fcira dicit qd de hoc m̄ fux̄.

Hoc m̄ redd . ix . lib 7 x . folid denarioʒ candidoʒ.

wheat and as many of oats, except for 9 acres: 6 of these belong to William son of Baderon, 3 to St. Mary's of Cormeilles.

In this manor is a reeve, 1 Frenchman and 1 riding man; they have 3 ploughs. 8 slaves, 1 ploughman and 6 female slaves.

A mill which pays nothing, except sustenance for its keeper. Woodland which pays 5s which are given to Droitwich for 60 measures of salt.

In Hereford are 4 burgesses who pay 18 ploughshares to this manor. 1 hide of this manor is at TURLESTANE; before 1066 it paid 50 lumps of iron and 6 salmon. This land is now in the Forest. The Sheriff holds 1 hide of this manor; he has 2 ploughs. Also in this manor are 58 acres of land, cleared, extracted from the woodland; the reeve and 2 other men hold many acres of this land.

St. Mary's of Cormeilles has the tithe of this manor, a priest and the church, with 1 villager who holds 1 virgate of land.

Value before 1066 £30; value now as much.

in BROMSASH Hundred

8 CLEEVE. Earl Harold held it. 14½ hides, with an outlier named WILTON. In lordship 4 ploughs;

20 villagers, a reeve, and 11 smallholders with 16 ploughs. 9 male and 5 female slaves and 1 ploughman.

2 mills at 6s; a fishery which pays nothing.

To this manor belong as many Welshmen as have 8 ploughs; they pay 10½ sesters of honey and 6s 5d.

St. Mary's of Cormeilles holds the church of this manor, a priest and the tithe, with 1 villager.

In King William's Forest there is as much land of this manor as paid 6 sesters of honey and 6 sheep with lambs before 1066.

Of this manor William Baderon holds 1 hide and 3 virgates; Godfrey holds 1 virgate.

Roger of Lacy holds ½ fishery which belonged to this manor before 1066; 25 measures of salt from Droitwich then belonged there also.

At that time there were in this manor 2 hides, less 1 virgate, which are in ASHE (Ingen). Alfred of Marlborough holds them now. Harold was holding them when he died. The Shire states that they are this manor's.

This manor pays £9 10s of blanched pence.

180 a

Rex ten STANFORD. Eddid regina tenuit. IN PLEGELIET IID.

Ibi . IIII . hidæ. In dñio funt . III . car . 7 IIII . uitt 7 II . borđ

cū . III . car . Ibi . VI . bouarii 7 IIII . ancillæ.

Ibi molin de . VI . foliđ . 7 I . porcari 7 I . uacarius.

Decimā huj M̄ cū . I . uitto . h̄t S MARIA de cormeliis.

T.R.E. ualb . c . fot . modo redđ . c . fot de alb denar.

Rex tenct LEOFMINSTRE . Eddiđ regina tenuit . cū . XVI.

mēbris . Luftone . Larpol . Elmodeftreu . Brumefelde.

Eftune . Stoctune . Stoca . Merfetone . Vptone . Hope . Bredege.

★ Lumtune . Cerleftreu . Lentehale . Gedeuen . Fernelau.

In hoc M̄ cū his mēbris eraȵ q̄ter XX . hidæ . 7 in dñio . XXX . car.

Ibi eraȵ . VIII . ppofiti 7 VIII . bedelli . 7 VIII . radcheniſt . 7 CC.

7 XXXVIII . uitti . 7 LXXV . borđ . 7 q̄t XX 7 II . int feruos 7 ancillas.

Hi oms fimul habeb . CC 7 XXX . car . Vitti arabaȵ . CXL.

acs træ dñi . 7 feminab de ppo femine frumti . 7 dab de cfuetuđ

XI . lib 7 LII . den . Radchen dabant . XIIII . fot 7 IIII . denar.

7 III . fext mett . 7 VIII . molini eraȵ de . LXXIII . foliđ . 7 XXX.

ftichas anguitt . Silua reddeb . XXIIII . fot 7 pafnagium.

Modo h̄t rex in hoc M̄ in dñio . LX . hidas . 7 XXIX . car.

7 VI . pbros . 7 VI . Radmans . 7 VII . ppofitos . 7 VII . bedellos.

7 CC 7 XXIIII . uitt . 7 q̄ter XX . 7 uñ borđ . 7 XXV . int feruos

7 ancillas . Int oms h̄nt . CC . 7 unā car.

Hi araȵ 7 feminaȵ de fuo frumto . CXXV . acs . 7 daȵ de cfuetuđ.

VII . lib 7 XIIII . fot 7 VIII . den 7 obolū . 7 XVII . fot ad pifces.

7 VIII . fot ad fal . 7 LXV . foliđ de melle . Ibi . VIII . molini de

centū 7 VIII . foliđ . 7 c . ftiches anguitt . x . min.

Silua . VI . leuū lḡ . 7 III . leuū lat . redđ XXII . fot . Ex his

dant . V . fot ad ligna emđa in Wich . 7 h̄ntur . XXX . mittæ falis

inde . Quifq̄ uitts h̄ns . x . porcos . dat uñ porcū de pafnagio.

De exfartis filuæ exeunt XVII . foliđ 7 IIII . denar . Ibi eft

airea accipitris.

in PLEGELGATE Hundred

9 STANFORD. Queen Edith held it. 4 hides. ... In lordship 3 ploughs;
4 villagers and 4 smallholders with 3 ploughs. 6 ploughmen
and 4 female slaves.
A mill at 6s; 1 pigman and 1 cowman.
St. Mary's of Cormeilles has the tithe of this manor, with
1 villager.
Value before 1066, 100s; now it pays 100s of white pence.

[manor of LEOMINSTER]
10a LEOMINSTER. Queen Edith held it, with 16 members: LUSTON,
YARPOLE, AYMESTREY, BRIMFIELD, ASHTON, STOCKTON, STOKE (Prior),
MARSTON (Stannett), UPTON, (Miles) HOPE, BRIERLEY, IVINGTON,
CHOLSTREY, LEINTHALL, EDWYN (Ralph) and FARLOW.
In this manor, with these members, were 80 hides. In lordship
30 ploughs.
There were 8 reeves, 8 beadles, 8 riding men, 238 villagers,
75 smallholders and 82 slaves, male and female; altogether
they had 230 ploughs.
The villagers ploughed 140 acres of the lord's land and sowed
it with their own wheat seed. They gave £11 and 52d in
customary dues.
The riding men gave 14s 4d and 3 sesters of honey.
There were 8 mills at 73s and 30 sticks of eels; the woodland
paid 24s and pasture dues.
In this manor the King now has in lordship 60 hides,
29 ploughs and
6 priests, 6 riders, 7 reeves, 7 beadles, 224 villagers, 81
smallholders and 25 slaves, male and female; between them
they have 201 ploughs.
These (men) plough and sow 125 acres with their own wheat.
In customary dues they give £7 14s 8½d, 17s for fish, 8s for
salt and 65s from honey.
8 mills at 108s and 100 sticks of eels, less 10; woodland 6
leagues long and 3 leagues wide which pays 22s. From these,
5s are given for buying timber in Droitwich, and 30 measures
of salt are had from there.
Each villager who has 10 pigs gives 1 pig in pasture dues.
From cleared woodland come 17s 4d. A hawk's eyrie there.

Ad hoc M̄ redd̄ Hugo . v . ſoł . Rog de Laci . vi . ſoł 7 viii . den̄.

Rad̄ de mortemer . xv . ſoł . Bernard . v . ſoł . Ilbt̄ . v . ſolid̄.

Osbn̄ . vi . ſoł 7 viii . den̄ . Godmund . v . ſoł . Goduin . xl . den̄.

Æluuard̄ . xl . den̄ . Semer . xl . den̄ . Vitard . iii . ſoł . Eluuard

xxx . den̄ . Briſmer . xx . den̄ . Eluard . xx . den̄.

In om̄i hoc redditu p̄ter anguiłł . cōputant̄ . xxiii . lib̄ 7 ii . ſolid̄.

Hoc M̄ eſt ad firmā de . lx . lib̄ . p̄ter uiċt̄u monialium.

Dicit comitat̄ q̄a ſi deliberat̄ eſſet hoc M̄ . ap̄ciari poſſet

ſexies xx . lib̄ . hoc eſt . cxx.

De quat̄ xx . hid̄ huj M̄ . ten̄ Vrſo de abetot . iii . hid̄ jn Gedeuen.

7 Rog de Laci . iii . hid̄ 7 dim̄ in HVBRE . 7 i . hid̄ 7 dim̄ jn Brochēm̄.

7 Rad̄ de mortemer . i . hid̄ jn Elmodeſtreu . 7 viii . hid̄ geld̄ jn Letehale.

7 Wiłłs . F . Norman dimid̄ hid̄ in LEGE . 7 unā hid̄ in Ettone.

In his ſunt . iii . car̄ . in dn̄io . 7 xi . uiłł 7 xxii . bord̄ 7 ii . p̄bri.

Int om̄s hn̄t . x . car̄ . 7 xvi . ſerui . 7 ii . molini de . xxiiii . ſolid̄.

Ad Letehale . ē ſilua . i . leuū iḡ . 7 una levv̄ lat̄.

Int tot̄ ualent hæ træ . xii . lib̄ 7 xi . ſoł.

Leuuin Latinarius ten̄ tant̄ de t̄ra Leofminſtre q̄d̄ uał . xxv . ſoł.

De t̄ra Rad̄ de mortemer in Elmodeſtreu . h̄t̄ S̄ Petrus . xv . ſoł.

Ad hoc M̄ ptineb̄ . ii . M̄ Stanford 7 Merchelai . T.R.E.

qui redd̄t m̄ regi . xxx . lib̄ . ut ſupius diċt̄u eſt.

180 b

Hæ Terræ Infra Scriptæ . Jacebaꝧ ad Leofminstre . T.R.E.

Hvgo ten̄ HETFELDE . Letſlede tenuit . Ibi . v . hidæ . Ex his gld̄b . ii . hid̄ 7 . i . ⁙

In dn̄io ſunt . iii . car̄ . Ibi p̄poſit̄ 7 ii . radchen̄ . 7 ii . francig

7 viii . bord̄ . cū . vi . car̄ 7 dim̄ . 7 adhuc . ii . hōes nil tenentes.

T.R.E . uałb̄ . iiii . lib̄ . modo . c . ſolid̄.

Osbern . F . Ricardi ten̄ WAPLETONE . de dono regis ut dicit.

Ipſe tenuit T.R.E . Ibi . ii . hidæ . geld̄ . Ibi . ē un radcheniſt̄

7 un uiłł 7 xxii . bord̄ . Int om̄s hn̄t . vi . car̄ . Valet . xx . ſoł.

Vrso de abetot ten̄ BVTERLEI . Chetel tenuit . Ibi . i . hida.

In dn̄io ſunt . ii . car̄ . 7 iiii . bord̄ cū . i . car̄ . 7 iiii . bouarii . Vał . xl . ſoł.

10b To this manor Hugh Donkey pays 5s; Roger of Lacy 6s 8d;
Ralph of Mortimer 15s; Bernard Beard 5s; Ilbert 5s; Osbern 6s 8d;
Godmund 5s; Godwin 40d; Alfward 40d; Saemer 40d; Widard 3s;
Alfward 30d; Brictmer 20d; Alfward 20d.
In all these payments £23 2s are reckoned, besides the eels.
This manor is at a revenue of £60, besides the supplies of the
nuns. The County states that if it were (properly) valued this
manor could be assessed at six times £20, that is (£)120.

10c Of the 80 hides of this manor Urso of Abetot holds 3 hides in
EDWYN (Ralph); Roger of Lacy 3½ hides in HUMBER and 1½ hides
in BROCKMANTON; Ralph of Mortimer 1 hide in AYMESTREY and
8 hides in LEINTHALL which pay tax; William son of Norman ½
hide in LYE and 1 hide in EYTON. In these, 3 ploughs in lordship;
11 villagers, 22 smallholders and 2 priests; between them they
have 10 ploughs; 16 slaves.
2 mills at 24s. At Leinthall woodland 1 league long and 1
league wide.
In total, value of these lands £12 11s.
Leofwin Latimer holds as much land in Leominster as is worth
25s.
St. Peter's has 15s from Ralph of Mortimer's land in Aymestrey.
Before 1066 two manors, Stanford and (Much) Marcle, belonged
to this manor; they now pay £30 to the King, as stated above.

THESE LANDS MENTIONED BELOW LAY IN   180 b
LEOMINSTER (LANDS) BEFORE 1066

11 Hugh Donkey holds HATFIELD. Leofled held it. 5 hides; of these,
2 hides and 1 virgate paid tax. In lordship 3 ploughs.
A reeve, 2 riding men, 2 Frenchmen and 8 smallholders with
6½ ploughs; a further 2 men who hold nothing.
Value before 1066 £4; now 100s.

12 Osbern son of Richard holds WAPLEY by the King's gift, as he
states. He held it himself before 1066. 2 hides which pay tax.
1 riding man, 1 villager and 22 smallholders; between them
they have 6 ploughs.
Value 20s.

13 Urso of Abetot holds BUTTERLEY. Ketel held it. 1 hide. In lordship
2 ploughs;
4 smallholders with 1 plough; 4 ploughmen.
Value 40s.

Abbatissa ten̄ *FENCOTE*.7 ipſa tenuit T.R.E.Ibi.1.hida liba.
7 IIII.uilti cū.II.car̄.

Rog de Laci ten̄ *HANTONE*.Bruning tenuit.Ibi dimid hida.
In dñio.ē.1.car̄.T.R.E.ualb.XL.ſol.modo.XXX.ſol.

Iſd Rog ten̄ *HANTONE*.7 Gisleb̄t de eo.Eduui tenuit.Ibi.II.
hidæ.In dñio ſunt.II.car̄.7 ppoſit.7 II.radchen̄.7 II.bord
çū.IIII.car̄.Valuit.XX.ſolid.modo.XL.ſolid.

Iſd Rog ten̄ *SARNESFELDE*.7 Godmund de eo.Seric tenuit.
Ibi.1.hida 7 dimid.In dñio.ē una car̄.7 X.bord cū.III.car̄.
Ibi.1.ſeruus.7 una ancilla.Ĥ tra fuit uuaſta.r̄a ual.XX.ſol.

Iſd Rog ten̄ *GADREDEHOPE*.7 Walter de eo.Æluuin̄ tenuit.
Ibi.1.hida 7 in dñio.1.car̄.Ibi.1.uilts 7 VII.bord cū.II.car̄.
Ibi.II.ſerui 7 II.ancillæ.7 adhuc.1.car̄ poteſt.ēe.Val.XXX.ſol.

Radvlf de Mortemer ten̄ *WIGHEMORE*.Eluuard tenuit.
Ibi dimid hida.Caſtellū *WIGEMORE* ſedet in ea.

Iſd Rad ten̄ *BROMEFELDE*.Erneſi tenuit.Ibi.III.uirg træ.
In dñio una car̄.7 II.ſerui.Val.VII.ſol 7 VI.den̄.

Radvlf de Todeni ten̄ *FORNE* de.1.hida 7 una v̄.7 *BRADE*
FELDE de.1.hida.7 *SARNESFELDE* de dimid hida.Drogo ten̄
de Rad.In dñio ſunt.III.car̄.7 II.uilt 7 v.bord 7 III.ſerui
7 II.ancillæ.7 III.bouarij.7 piſcaria redd ſexcent anguilt.
Valb.LV.ſol.Modo.LXXV.ſolid.Eluuard tenuit.

Iſd Rad ten̄ *ETONE*.7 Herbt de eo.Leuenot tenuit.Ibi
una hida 7 dimid.In dñio ſunt.II.car̄.7 III.uilt 7 IIII.bord
cū.IIII.car̄ 7 dimid.Valuit.XL.ſol.modo.LX.ſolid.

14 The Abbess holds FENCOTE. She held it herself before 1066.
1 free hide.
    4 villagers with 2 ploughs.
[Value ...]

15 Roger of Lacy holds HAMPTON (Wafre). Browning held it. ½ hide.
In lordship 1 plough.
Value before 1066, 40s; now 30s.

16 Roger also holds HAMPTON, and Gilbert from him. Edwy held it.
2 hides. In lordship 2 ploughs;
    A reeve, 2 riding men and 2 smallholders with 4 ploughs.
The value was 20s; now 40s.

17 Roger also holds SARNESFIELD, and Godmund from him. Saeric held it.
1½ hides. In lordship 1 plough;
    10 smallholders with 3 ploughs. 1 male and 1 female slave.
The land was waste. Value now 20s.

18 Roger also holds GATTERTOP, and Walter from him. Alwin held it.
1 hide. In lordship 1 plough.
    1 villager and 7 smallholders with 2 ploughs. 2 male and
      2 female slaves; 1 further plough possible.
Value 30s.

19 Ralph of Mortimer holds WIGMORE. Alfward held it. ½ hide.
Wigmore Castle is situated in it.

20 Ralph also holds BRIMFIELD. Ernsy held it. 3 virgates of land.
In lordship 1 plough; 2 slaves.
Value 7s 6d.

21 Ralph of Tosny holds FORD at 1 hide and 1 virgate; BROADFIELD
at 1 hide; and SARNESFIELD at ½ hide. Drogo holds from Ralph.
In lordship 3 ploughs;
    2 villagers, 5 smallholders, 3 male and 2 female slaves and
      3 ploughmen.
    A fishery which pays 600 eels.
The value was 55s; now 75s.
    Alfward held it.

22 Ralph also holds EATON, and Herbert from him. Leofnoth held it.
1½ hides. In lordship 2 ploughs;
    3 villagers and 4 smallholders with 4½ ploughs.
The value was 40s; now 60s.

Wills de Scohies ten RISEBERIE.7 Robt de co.Eduuin tenuit.

Ibi.ii.hidæ.7 in dñio.ii.car.7 i.uill 7 iiii.bord 7 iiii.ſerui.7 moliñ

de.iiii.ſol.Vills redd.x.den.Valb.xx.ſol.Modo.lx.ſolid.

Iſd Wills ten WAVERTVNE.7 Bernard de eo.Ibi.i.hida.In dñio

ſunt.ii.car.7 un uills cũ dim car.7 iiii.bouarii.Valuit 7 ual.xx.ſol.

Iſd Wills ten NEWENTONE.7 Bernard de eo.   ⌠ Vluuard tenuit.

Bruning tenuit.Ibi dimid hida.Ħ tra waſta.ē.

Iſd Wills ten DILGE.7 Ricard de eo.Elmer tenuit.Ibi.i.hida.

7 in dñio.i.car.7 un radchen cũ.i.car.Ibi.i.francig.7 iiii.bord.

redd.xxv.den.Ibi.ii.ſerui 7 una ancilla.Valb.v.ſol.m̃.xx.ſol.

Iſd Wills ten HETFELDE.7 Rad de eo.Elmer tenuit.Ibi dim

hida.7 in dñio.i.car.7 ii.ſerui.Valuit.lxv.den.Modo.viii.ſol.

Wills.F.Norman ten BRADEFORD.Leuenod tenuit.Ibi dim

hida.7 in dñio.i.car.7 ii.uilli 7 faber 7 v.bord cũ.ii.car.Ibi.ii.

ſerui.7 moliñ de.x.ſolid.7 piſcaria de q̇ngent anguill.Valuit.xx.ſol.

DROGO.F.ponz ten HANTONE.7 Stefan de.eo.   ⌠modo.xxx.

Ibi.i.hida.7 in dñio.i.car.7 i.bord cũ.i.car.7 moliñ de.xl.den.

Iſd Drogo ten HAMENES   ⌠ Edric tenuit.Val ſep.xx.ſolid.

7 Walter de eo.Erneſi tenuit.Ibi.i.hida.7 in dñio.ii.car.

7 ii.bord.7 iiii.ſerui.Valeb.xx.ſolid.modo.xl.denar plus

23 William of Écouis holds RISBURY, and Robert from him. Edwin
held it. 2 hides. In lordship 2 ploughs;
    1 villager, 3 smallholders and 4 slaves.
    A mill at 4s.
    The villager pays 10d.
The value was 20s; now 60s.

24 William also holds WHARTON, and Bernard from him. 1 hide.
In lordship 2 ploughs;
    1 villager with ½ plough; 4 ploughmen.
The value was and is 20s.
    Wulfward held it.

25 William also holds NEWTON, and Bernard from him. Browning
held it. ½ hide. This land is waste.

26 William also holds DILWYN, and Richard from him. Aelmer held it.
1 hide. In lordship 1 plough;
    1 riding man with 1 plough. 1 Frenchman and 4 smallholders
      who pay 25s. 2 male slaves, 1 female.
The value was 5s; now 20s.

27 William also holds HATFIELD, and Ralph from him. Aelmer held it.
½ hide. In lordship 1 plough; 2 slaves.
The value was 65d; now 8s.

28 William son of Norman holds BROADWARD. Leofnoth held it.
½ hide. In lordship 1 plough;
    2 villagers, a smith and 5 smallholders with 2 ploughs.
    2 slaves; a mill at 10s; a fishery at 500 eels.
The value was 20s; now 30[s].

29 Drogo son of Poyntz holds HAMPTON, and Stephen from him.
1 hide. In lordship 1 plough;
    1 smallholder with 1 plough.
    A mill at 40d.
    Edric held it.
Value always 20s.

30 Drogo also holds HAMNISH, and Walter from him. Ernsy held it.
1 hide. In lordship 2 ploughs;
    2 smallholders and 4 slaves.
The value was 20s; now 40d more.

Dvrand uicecom ten MICELTVNE.7 Bernard de eo.Eluric

tenuit.Ibi.i.hida 7 dimiđ.7 in dñio.i.car.7 ii.borđ 7 ii.ſerui.

Ilbertvs ten DILGE.Rauechetel tenuit./ Valuit.xx.ſoł.m̃.x.ſoł.

Ibi.ii.hidæ.7 In dñio.ii.car.7 viii.borđ cũ.iiii.car.Ibi.iiii.bouarii.

Valuit.xx.ſoliđ.Modo.xl.ſoliđ.

180 c

Iſđ Ilbt ten LVTELEI.Rauechetel tenuit.Ibi.ii.hidæ.7 in dñio

una car.Ibi p̄poſit 7 iiii.borđ.7 ii.bouarii.cũ.ii.car.

Valb.xl.ſoł.modo.xxx.ſoliđ.

Grifin puer ten ALAC.7 Goduin de eo.Eluuarđ tenuit.

Ibi.i.hida.7 in dñio.i.car.7 ii.ſerui.Valuit 7 uał.x.ſoliđ.

Iſđ Grifin ten dimiđ hiđ.7 Eluuarđ de eo.

Ibi ht.i.car cũ ſuis hominibʒ.Waſta fuit.Modo uał.xv.ſoł.

Lewin Latinari ten LARPOLE.Æluric teuuit.Ibi.i.uirg.

Waſta fuit.Modo ſunt.ii.borđ cũ.i.car.7 uał iii.ſoliđ.

Int tot ſunt.xxxii.hidæ.7 om̃s geldabant T.R.E.7 reddeb

c̃ſuetudiñe ad LEOFMINSTRE.

Qđ ten Hugo:reddeb.v.ſoł.Qđ Osbn:redđ.v.oras.

Qđ Vrſo ten:red.leb.xl.den.Qđ abbatiſſa:xl.den.

Qđ Rog de Laci:xiii.ſoł 7 iiii.den.7 de gablo:xxv.den.

Qđ Rađ de Mortemer.reddeb.l.denar.modo ñ reddit.

Qđ Rađ de Todeni:xi.ſoł 7 x.denar.

Qđ Wilłs de Scohies:xi.ſoł 7 x.den.7 ii.ſext mellis.

Qđ Wilłs.F.Normanni:xx.denar.

Qđ Drogo.F.ponz:viii.ſoliđ 7 viii.denar.

Qđ Durand uicecom:v.ſoł.Qđ Ilbert:v.ſoliđ.   ꝉ opant.

Qđ Grifin tenet:v.ſoliđ.Qđ Leuuin:x.den.7 ii.dies in ebda

31 Durand the Sheriff holds MIDDLETON (on the Hill), and Bernard
from him. Aelfric held it. 1½ hides. In lordship 1 plough;
    2 smallholders and 2 slaves.
The value was 20s; now 10s.

32 Ilbert holds DILWYN. Ravenkel held it. 2 hides. In lordship
2 ploughs;
    8 smallholders with 4 ploughs. 4 ploughmen.
The value was 20s; now 40s.

33 Ilbert also holds LUNTLEY. Ravenkel held it. 2 hides. In lordship   180 c
1 plough.
    A reeve, 4 smallholders and 2 ploughmen with 2 ploughs.
The value was 40s; now 30s.

34 Gruffydd Boy holds *ALAC*, and Godwin from him. Alfward held it.
1 hide. In lordship 1 plough; 2 slaves.
The value was and is 10s.

35 Gruffydd also holds ½ hide, and Alfward from him. With his men
he has 1 plough. It was waste. Value now 15s.

36 Leofwin Latimer holds YARPOLE. Aelfric held it. 1 virgate. It was
waste. Now there are
    2 smallholders with 1 plough.
Value 3s.

37 In total, 32 hides; they all paid tax before 1066 and paid
customary dues to LEOMINSTER.

38 What Hugh Donkey holds paid 5s. What Osbern (holds) paid
5 *ora*. What Urso holds paid 40d. What the Abbess (holds), 40d.
What Roger of Lacy (holds), 13s 4d and 25d from tribute. What
Ralph of Mortimer (holds) paid 50d; now it does not pay. What
Ralph of Tosny (holds), 11s 10d. What William of Écouis (holds),
11s 10d and 2 sesters of honey. What William son of Norman
(holds), 20d. What Drogo son of Poyntz (holds), 8s 8d. What
Durand the Sheriff (holds), 5s. What Ilbert (holds), 5s. What
Gruffydd holds, 5s, and what Leofwin (holds), 10d. They work
2 days a week.

Rex ten *Merlie*. Regina Eddid tenuit. Ibi. x. hidæ.

7 una v̅ træ. In dn̅io funt. viii. car. 7 xl.vii. uiłł 7 xvi. borđ

7 duo radmanni cu̅. xl.iii. car. Ibi molin de. viii. foliđ.

7 duo Gurgites redđt. ii. miłł 7 q̅ngent' anguiłł 7 v. ftiches.

Ibi p̅pofitus 7 bedellus hn̅t. ii. virg træ. 7 ii. car.

In Wireceftræ funt. iii. dom. redđ. xii. den.

Viłłi 7 borđ redđt. xii. foliđ p̅ pifce 7 p̅ lignis.

Hoc. M̅ reddit ad hereford. xxiiii. lib̅ den̅ de. xx. in ora.

7 xii. foliđ de Gerfumme.

Huj M̅ æcclam cu̅ tra ibi p̅tinente 7 cu̅ fua decima deđ

comes. W. S̅ MARIÆ de Cormeliis. 7 ii.uiłłos cu̅. ii. virg træ.

Ipfe comes deđ Radulfo de bernai. ii. radmans. 7 mifit

eos extra hoc M̅. cu̅ tra qua̅ teneb̅. Hi hn̅t. ii. car.

Ifđ comes deđ Droardo. i. uirg træ. qua̅ adhuc tenet.

★ Rex ten *Feccheha*. quinq̅ taini tenuer̅ *In Naisse Hd*

de Eduino comite. 7 potera̅ʒ ire cu̅ tra quo uoleb̅. 7 habeb̅

fub fe.iiii. milites. ita libos ut ipfi erant. Int om̅s era̅ʒ. xiii. car.

Ibi. x. hidæ. 7 in dn̅io. vi. car. 7 xxx. uiłłi 7 xi. borđ

7 p̅pofit 7 bedel. 7 molinari 7 faber. Int om̅s hn̅t. xviii. car.

Ibi. xii. ferui 7 v. ancillæ. 7 un radman tenet|hiđ 7 ii. part dimidiā

dimiđ hidæ 7 una̅ crofta. 7 h̅t. i. car. Ibi molin de. ii. fot.

In Wich. iiii. falinæ. Silua huj M̅ foris. e̅ miffa ad filua̅ regis.

7 una hida træ qua̅ Wiłłs com̅ deđ Gozclino uenatori.

Huj M̅ decima̅ 7 æcclam cu̅ pb̅ro 7 ii. uirg træ cu̅ uno uiłło

deđ. W. com̅ æcclæ S̅ MARIÆ.   car.

Walter de Laci deđ cuida̅ Hub̅to. i. hiđ ex dn̅ica tra. hic h̅t dim

In DODDINGTREE Hundred [WORCESTERSHIRE]

39 The King holds MARTLEY. Queen Edith held it. 10 hides and 1 virgate of land. In lordship 8 ploughs;

> 47 villagers, 16 smallholders and 2 riders with 43 ploughs.
> A mill at 8s; 2 weirs pay 2,500 eels and 5 sticks.
> A reeve and a beadle have 2 virgates of land; 2 ploughs.
> In Worcester 3 houses which pay 12d.
> The villagers and smallholders pay 12s in place of fish and timber.

This manor pays to Hereford £24 of pence at 20 to the *ora*, and 12s in gifts.

Earl William gave to St. Mary's of Cormeilles the church of this manor with the land belonging to it and its tithe, and 2 villagers with 2 virgates of land.

The Earl himself gave Ralph of Bernay 2 riders; he put them outside this manor, with the land they held; they have 2 ploughs.

The Earl also gave Druward 1 virgate of land, which he still holds.

In ESCH Hundred [WORCESTERSHIRE]

40 The King holds FECKENHAM. Five thanes held it from Earl Edwin; they could go where they would with the land. Under them they had 4 men-at-arms, as free as they were themselves; between them there were 13 ploughs. 10 hides. In lordship 6 ploughs;

> 30 villagers, 11 smallholders, a reeve, a beadle, a miller and a smith; between them they have 18 ploughs. 12 male and 5 female slaves. A rider holds ½ hide, 2 parts of ½ hide and 1 croft; he has 1 plough.
> A mill at 2s; in Droitwich 4 salt-houses; the woodland of this manor has been put outside, into the King's woodland, and ½ hide of land which Earl William gave to Jocelyn Hunter.

Earl William gave to St. Mary's Church the tithe of this manor and the church with a priest, and 2 virgates of land with 1 villager.

Walter of Lacy gave 1 hide out of the lordship land to one Hubert; he has ½ plough.

Rex ten *HALOEDE*. Siuuard tenuit. tein 7 cognat̃ regis. E.
Ibi. iii. hidæ. 7 in dñio. iii. car̃. 7 iiii. uilli 7 i. bord̃. 7 p̄pofit 7 bedel
cū. iii. car̃. 7 vi. int̃ feruos 7 ancill. Ibi. ē parcus ferarū. fed
mifsū eft ext̃ Ϻ cū tota filua. In Wich. iiii. falinæ. 7 uñ hoch.
In Wireceftre. i. dom̃ redd. ii. uomeres. 7 aliæ. ii. dom̃ p̃tiñ
ad Fecheha. nichil reddeb̃. 7 extra miffæ funt.
Hæc. ii. Ϻ reddt̃ ad hereford. xviii. lib̃ denar̃ de. x̃x̃. in ora.

180 d

IN GLOWECESTRE SCIRE.

Rex ten̄ *HANLIE*. Briƈtric tenuit. Ibi. iiii. hidæ. In dñio. ii. car̃.
7 xx. uilli 7 xvii. bord̃. 7 p̄pofit. Int̃ om̃s hñt. xvii. car̃ 7 dimiđ.
Ibi. ix. int̃ feruos 7 ancill. 7 vi. porcarii reddt̃ lx. porcos. 7 hñt
.iiii. car̃. Ibi molin̄ de. ii. folid. Silua. v. leug̃ int̃ long̃ 7 lat̃.
h̃ miffa. ē foris Ϻ. Ibi. ē airea Accipitris. Foreftari ten̄ dim̄ v̄ træ.
7 un uilts de Baldehalle redd̃ huic Ϻ. ii. oras denar̃.

Rex ten̄ *FORHELMENTONE*. Briƈtric tenuit.
Ibi. ix. hidæ. quæ geldb̃ p̃. iiii. hid̃. In dñio funt. iii. car̃. 7 vii.
uilti cū. v. car̃. Ibi. iiii. porc̃ cū. i. car̃. reddt̃. xxxv. porcos.
Silua h̃t. iii. lew int̃ long̃ 7 lat̃. In defenfo filuæ regis. ē. 7 ibi
airea Accepitris. 7 ii. hidæ 7 dimiđ. 7 Anfgot ten̄. iii. virg̃ træ.
Huj̃ Ϻ decimā cū. i. uilto 7 una v̄ træ. ten̄ S MARIA.

IN WIRECESTRE SCIRE.

Rex ten̄ *BISELIE*. Briƈtric tenuit. qui & emit illud a Liuingo
epo Wireceftre. iii. mark̃ auri. fimul 7 unā domū in Wireceftre
ciuitate. quæ reddit p annū markā argenti. 7 fimul. i. filuā
una leuua lg̃ 7 tntđ lat̃. Hoc totū ita emit 7 quiete tenuit:
ut inde non feruiret cuiquā homini.
In hoc Ϻ una hida. 7 in dñio funt. ii. car̃. 7 iiii. uilt 7 viii. bord̃
7 p̄pofiꞇ 7 bedell. Int̃ om̃s hñt. iiii. car̃. Ibi. viii. int̃ feruos
7 ancillas. 7 uaccarius 7 daia. Ibi foreftari ten̄ dim̄ v̄ terræ.

41 The King holds HOLLOW (Court). Siward, a thane and kinsman of
King Edward, held it. 3 hides. In lordship 3 ploughs;
>4 villagers, 1 smallholder, a reeve and a beadle with 3 ploughs.
>6 slaves, male and female.
>A park for wild animals, but it has been put outside the
>manor, with all the woodland; in Droitwich 4 salt-houses
>and 1 *hoch*; in Worcester 1 house which pays 2 ploughshares;
>another 2 houses which belong to Feckenham: they paid
>nothing and have been put outside (the manor).

These two manors pay to Hereford £18 of pence at 20 to the *ora*.

In GLOUCESTERSHIRE   180 d
42 The King holds HANLEY (Castle). Brictric held it. 4 hides.
In lordship 2 ploughs;
>20 villagers, 17 smallholders and a reeve; between them they
>have 17½ ploughs. 9 slaves, male and female; 6 pigmen pay
>60 pigs; they have 4 ploughs.
>A mill at 2s; woodland 5 leagues in both length and width: it
>has been put outside the manor. A hawk's eyrie there.
>A forester holds ½ virgate of land.
>A villager of 'Baldenhall' pays 2 *ora* of pence to this manor.

43 The King holds FORTHAMPTON. Brictric held it. 9 hides which paid
tax for 4 hides. In lordship 3 ploughs;
>7 villagers with 5 ploughs. 4 pigmen with 1 plough pay 35 pigs.
>The woodland has 3 leagues in both length and width: it is in
>the Enclosure of the King's woodland; a hawk's eyrie and
>2½ hides there.
>Ansgot holds 3 virgates of land.
>St. Mary's holds the tithe of this manor, with
>1 villager and 1 virgate of land.

In WORCESTERSHIRE
44 The King holds BUSHLEY. Brictric held it; he bought it from
Leofing Bishop of Worcester for 3 gold marks; also a house in
the City of Worcester which pays a silver mark a year; also a
wood 1 league long and as wide. He bought the whole of this
and held it exempt, so that he did not serve any man for it.
In this manor 1 hide. In lordship 2 ploughs;
>4 villagers, 8 smallholders, a reeve and a beadle; between them
>they have 4 ploughs. 8 slaves, male and female; a cowman
>and a dairymaid. A forester who holds ½ virgate of land.

In Lapvle . funt . III . Virg̃ trǣ quǣ jaceƀ in Langedune
Ⓜ Odonis comitis . Hanc t̃ra miſit Wiłłs comes in Biſelie.
Ibi . ẽ una cař . 7 un hõ monachoʒ ten unã v trǣ.

Wiłłs cõm miſit ext̃ ſuos Ⓜ . II . foreſtar . uñ de haulie 7 aliũ
de Biſelie . ̃ppt ſiluas cuſtodiendas.

Ꝛex ten̄ *Chonhelme* . Adelric tenuit f̃r Brictrec ep̃i.
Ibi . I . hida . 7 in dñio . I . cař . 7 VII . uiłłi 7 III . borđ cũ . IIII . cař
7 dimiđ . Ibi . I . porcari 7 II . bouarij . 7 daia . Silua . ẽ foris Ⓜ miſſa.
Wiłłs cõm deđ decimã huj Ⓜ S̃ MARIE de Lire . cũ . I . uiłło
qui ten̄ dimiđ virg̃ trǣ.

Herman ten̄ de hoc Ⓜ uñ uiłłm . qui h̃t dimiđ virg̃ trǣ.

Ꝛex ten̄ *Edresfelle* . Reinbald tenuit T.R.E. Comes. W.
excãƀiauit illud ab eo . Ibi . v . hidǣ . In dñio ſunt . III . cař.
7 XII . uiłłi 7 XIII . borđ cũ . XI . cař . Ibi . v . int̃ ſeruos 7 anciłł.
7 VI . bouarij . 7 molin̄ de . II . ſoł . Silua . II . leuũ l̃g . 7 tntđ lat.
H̃ ext̃ Ⓜ eſt miſſa . Anſgot hõ comitis . ten̄ dimiđ v trǣ.
7 Vluiet . I . hidã liberǣ trǣ.

S̃ca Maria h̃t ibi . I . uiłłm qui ten̄ unã v trǣ

Ꝛex ten̄ *Svchelie* . Eduin tenuit . Ibi . v . hidǣ . In dñio
ſunt . II . cař . 7 XXII . uiłłi 7 XXIIII . borđ cũ . XXVII . cař.
Ibi alii . x . borđ paupes . 7 molin̄ de . VI . ſoliđ . 7 cuſtos apiũ.
. XII . uaſculoʒ . Silua h̃t . v . leuũ int̃ long 7 lat . 7 piſcaria ibi.
In Wireceſtre . I . burg̃ſis . ſed nil redđ . Ibi molin̄ de . VI . ſoliđ.
Decimã huj uillǣ cũ . I . uiłło 7 dimiđ v terrǣ . ten̄ S̃ MARIA.
Ꝛoger deđ cuidã Ricardo dimiđ v trǣ . in ſolida liƀtate.
Hǣc . VI . Maner . redđt ad hereford de firma . L . libras.
7 XXV . ſoliđ de gerſũma.

In Castello Monemvde . h̃t Rex in dñio . IIII . cař . Wiłłs
. F . baderon cuſtodit eas . Qđ rex h̃t in hoc caſtello: ual . c . ſoliđ.

In PULL (Court) there are 3 virgates of land which lay in (the lands of) Longdon, a manor of Earl Oda. Earl William put this land in Bushley. 1 plough there. A man of the monks of Lyre holds 1 virgate of land.

Earl William put 2 foresters, one from Hanley (Castle), the other from Bushley, outside his manors to guard the woodlands.

45 The King holds QUEENHILL. Aethelric, brother of Bishop Brictric, held it. 1 hide. In lordship 1 plough;
 7 villagers and 3 smallholders with 4½ ploughs. 1 pigman,
  2 ploughmen and a dairymaid.
The woodland has been put outside the manor.
Earl William gave to St. Mary's of Lyre the tithe of this manor with 1 villager who holds ½ virgate of land.
Herman holds 1 villager of this manor who has ½ virgate of land.

46 The King holds ELDERSFIELD. Reinbald the Chancellor held it before 1066. Earl William exchanged it with him. 5 hides.
In lordship 3 ploughs;
 12 villagers and 13 smallholders with 11 ploughs. 5 slaves,
  male and female; 6 ploughmen.
A mill at 2s; woodland 2 leagues long and as wide: it has been put outside the manor.
Ansgot, Earl William's man, holds ½ virgate of land, Wulfgeat 1 hide of free land.
St. Mary's has 1 villager there who holds 1 virgate of land. ...

47 The King holds SUCKLEY. Earl Edwin held it. 5 hides. In lordship 2 ploughs;
 22 villagers and 24 smallholders with 27 ploughs. Another
  10 impoverished smallholders.
A mill at 6s; a keeper of 12 beehives; the woodland has 5 leagues in both length and width; a fishery there.
 In Worcester 1 burgess, but he pays nothing. A mill at 6s.
St. Mary's holds the tithe of this village, with 1 villager and ½ virgate of land.
Earl Roger gave ½ virgate of land in absolute freedom to one Richard.

These six manors pay to Hereford £50 in revenue and 25s in gifts.

[CASTLE]

48 In MONMOUTH CASTLE the King has 4 ploughs in lordship. William son of Baderon has charge of them.
Value of what the King has in this castle, 100s.

Ibi Witts h̄t . viii . car̄ in dn̄io . 7 plures poſſuꝗ . ee . Ibi ſuꝗ

Walenſes hn̄tes . xxiiii . . car̄ . redd̄t . xxxiii . ſextar̄ mellis.

7 ii . ſolid̄ . Ibi . xv . int̄ ſeruos 7 ancitt . 7 iii . molini de . xx . ſolid̄.

Milites huj Witti hn̄t . vii . car̄ . Qd̄ Witts ten̄ : uat . xxx . lib̄.

Huj caſtelli æcctam 7 om̄em decimā cū . ii . carucatis træ :

tenet S̄ Florentius de Salmur.

181 a

Īn *ARCENEFELDE* h̄t Rex : c . hōes . iiii . miꝗ . qui hn̄t

Lxxiii . car̄ cū ſuis hominib₂ . 7 dant de c̄ſuetudine

xli . ſextar̄ mellis . 7 xx . ſolid̄ . ꝓ ouib₂ quas ſoleb̄ dare.

7 x . ſolid̄ ꝓ fumagio . nec daꝗ geld̄ aut aliā c̄ſuetudin̄.

niſi qd̄ ꝑguꝗ in exercitu regis ſi juſſū eis fuerit

Si lib̄ hō ibi moritur : rex h̄t caballū ej cū armis.

De uitto cū morit̄ : h̄t rex . i . boue.

Rex Grifin 7 Blein Vaſtaueꝛ hanc trā T . R . E . 7 ideo

neſcit qualis eo tēpore fuerit.

LAGADEMAR ꝑtineb̄ ad Arcenefelde T . R . E . 7 ibi eraꝗ

iiii . carucatæ træ . Herman ten̄ hanc trā . 7 ibi . iii . bord̄

hn̄t . iii . boues.

Gisteb̄t . F . Turoldi ten̄ ibi uꝋ ꝏ . in quo ſunt . iiii . libi

hōes cū . iiii . car̄ . 7 redd̄t . iiii . ſext mellis . 7 xvi . denar̄

de c̄ſuetudine . De ead̄ Arcenefelde ten̄ Wereſtan

unā uillā . 7 ibi h̄t cū ſuis hōib₂ . vi . car̄ . 7 foreſta

redd̄ dimid̄ ſextar̄ mellis . 7 vi . denar̄.

ꝼFELDE.

HÆ VILLÆ VEL TERRÆ SUBSCRIPTÆ . SITÆ Svꝗ IN *FINE ARCENE*

Witts . F . Normanni ten̄ *CHIPEETE* . Cadiand tenuit T . R . E.

In dn̄io ſunt . iii . car̄ . 7 ii . ſerui 7 iiii . bouarii . 7 lvii . hōes

cū . xix . car̄ . 7 redd̄t . xv . ſextar̄ mellis . 7 x . ſolid̄ . nec daꝗ

aliud geld̄ . nec faciuꝗ ſeruitiū ꝑt exercitū . Vat . iiii . lib̄.

Iſd̄ . W . ten̄ *BAISSAN* . 7 Walter de eo . Mereuuin tenuit

de rege . E . In dn̄io ſunt . ii . car̄ . 7 xiiii . hōes cū . vii . car̄.

7 redd̄t . v . ſolid̄ de c̄ſuetud̄ .   Vat . xxx . ſolid̄.

William has 8 ploughs in lordship; more possible. There are
Welshmen there who have 24 ploughs; they pay 33 sesters of
honey and 2s.
15 slaves, male and female; 3 mills at 20s.
William's men-at-arms have 7 ploughs.
Value of what William holds £30.
St. Florent's of Saumur holds the church of this castle and all
the tithe, with 2 carucates of land.

49 In ARCHENFIELD the King has 100 men, less 4, who have 73   181 a
ploughs, with their men. In customary dues they give 41 sesters
of honey, 20s in place of the sheep which they used to give,
and 10s for hearth tax. They do not pay tax nor other customary
dues, except that they march in the King's army if they have
been ordered. If a free man dies there, the King has his horse
with his arms. The King has 1 ox from a villager when he dies.
King Gruffydd and Bleddyn laid this land waste before 1066;
therefore what it was like at that time is not known.

50 GARWAY belonged to Archenfield before 1066. There were 4
carucates of land there. Herman holds this land.
3 smallholders have 3 oxen.
[Value ...]

51 Gilbert son of Thorold holds a manor there, in which are
4 free men with 4 ploughs; they pay 4 sesters of honey
and 16d in customary dues.

52 Waerstan holds one village also of Archenfield. With his men he
has 6 ploughs. The Forest pays ½ sester of honey and 6d.

THESE VILLAGES OR LANDS MENTIONED BELOW
ARE SITUATED WITHIN ARCHENFIELD

53 William son of Norman holds KILPECK. Cadiand held it before
1066. In lordship 3 ploughs; 2 slaves;
4 ploughmen and 57 men with 19 ploughs; they pay 15 sesters
of honey and 10s; they do not pay any other tax nor do
service, except (in) the army.
Value £4.

54 William also holds BAYSHAM, and Walter from him. Merwin held it
from King Edward. In lordship 2 ploughs;
14 men with 7 ploughs; they pay 5s in customary dues.
Value 30s.

Isď.W.ten CAPE.⁊ Walt de eo.Rex.E.tenuit in dñio.

Ibi funt.v.Walenſes hñtes.v.caŕ.⁊ reddt.v.fext mellis.

⁊ v.oues cū agnis.⁊ x.denaŕ.　　　　Val xxx.foliđ.

Ibi.ē uñ Francig cū.1.caŕ.

Aᴸᴠʀᴇᴅ de Merleberge ten ELWISTONE.Herald com

tenuit.In dñio.ē una caŕ ⁊ dimiđ.⁊ pƀr.⁊ 111.uilĬ.⁊ 1111.

borđ ⁊ 1111.ſerui.cū.v.caŕ.⁊ daɴ.111.oues.Val xxx.foĬ.

Iſđ Alured ten Ascis.Waſt fuit T.R.E.Ibi.ē uñ hō

hñs caŕ ⁊ dimiđ.⁊ redđ de firma.x.foliđ.

Rᴏɢᴇʀ de Laci ten MAINAVRE.Coſtelin tenuit.T.R.E.

Nc filius ej ten de Roger.⁊ ibi funt.1111.caŕ.⁊ redđ.vi.

fextaŕ ṃellis ⁊ x.foliđ.　　　　　　Ϝmellis.

Ibi hΤ Roger unū Walensē.reddtē.v.foĬ.⁊ uñ fextaŕ

Iſđ Rog ten PENEBECDOC.⁊ Noui de eo.Iſđ tenuit T.R.E.

Ibi funt.1111.caŕ.ħ tra redđ.vi.fextaŕ melt ⁊ x.foliđ.

Gᴏᴅʀɪᴄ Mappeſone ten HVLLA.Taldus tenuit T.R.E.

In dñio funt.11.caŕ.⁊ 1111.bouarii.⁊ una Ancilla.Ibi.xii.

uilĬi.⁊ xii.borđ cū.xi.caŕ.⁊ reddt.xviii.fextaŕ mellis.

Ibi faber ⁊ piſcaria.　　　　　　Val.xL.foliđ.

　　　　　　　　　　IN WERMELAV HĐ.

Scs ᴘᴇᴛʀᴠs de Glouuec.ten WESTVODE.cap ⳩ huj.

Rex.E.tenuit.Ibi.vi.hidæ.Vna ex his hΤ Waliſca cſuetuđ.

⁊ aliæ Anglicā.In dñio.ē.1.caŕ.⁊ 11.borđ ⁊ 11.bouarij.

Ħ tra S Pᴇᴛʀɪ dat de firma.xxx.foliđ.Durand deđ æcclæ

p anima fŕis ſui Rogerij.

Huj ⳩ partē ten Roger de Laci ⁊ Odo de eo.WilĬs deđ ei. com

In dñio funt.11.caŕ.⁊ ix.borđ cū.11.caŕ.⁊ 11.ſerui.⁊ 11.bouarij.

Ibi.1.francig cū.11.borđ hñs.11.caŕ.　　　　Val.iii.liƀ.

181 a

55 William also holds (Kings) CAPLE, and Walter from him.
King Edward held it in lordship.
5 Welshmen who have 5 ploughs; they pay 5 sesters of honey,
5 sheep with lambs, and 10d.
Value 30s.
1 Frenchman with 1 plough.

56 Alfred of Marlborough holds PONTRILAS. Earl Harold held it.
In lordship 1½ ploughs;
A priest, 3 villagers, 4 smallholders and 4 slaves with
5 ploughs; they give 3 sheep.
Value 30s.

57 Alfred also holds ASHE (Ingen). It was waste before 1066.
1 man who has 1½ ploughs; he pays 10s in revenue.

58 Roger of Lacy holds BIRCH. Costelin held it before 1066. Now his
son holds from Roger. 4 ploughs there. He pays 6 sesters of
honey and 10s. Roger has 1 Welshman who pays 5s and 1 sester
of honey.

59 Roger also holds PENEBECDOC, and Novi from him. He also held it
before 1066. 4 ploughs there. This land pays 6 sesters of honey
and 10s.

60 Godric Mapson holds HOWLE (Hill). Taldus held it before 1066.
In lordship 2 ploughs; 4 ploughmen; 1 female slave.
12 villagers and 12 smallholders with 11 ploughs; they pay
18 sesters of honey. A smith.
A fishery.
Value 40s.

In WORMELOW Hundred
61 St. Peter's of Gloucester holds 'WESTWOOD', the head of this manor.
King Edward held it. 6 hides. One of these has Welsh customs,
the others English. In lordship 1 plough;
2 smallholders and 2 ploughmen.
This land of St. Peter's gives 30s in revenue.
Durand gave it to the church for the soul of his brother Roger.
Roger of Lacy holds part of this manor, and Odo from him.
Earl William gave it to him. In lordship 2 ploughs;
9 smallholders with 2 ploughs; 2 slaves and 2 ploughmen.
1 Frenchman with 2 smallholders; he has 2 ploughs.
Value £3.

Rad de Salceit ten parte ejđ m̃.7 hĩ trã ad.ii.car.

Ibi.ẽ.i.car.cũ.ii.bouarijs.7 uñ Walenſis hñs dimiđ car.

7 redd.i.ſextar mellis.　　　Val.xx.ſoliđ.

Radvlf de Todeni ten WESTEVDE.7 Wilts 7 Ilbt de eo.

Vlfac tenuit.Ibi.i.hida.7 in dñio.ii.car.7 uñ ſeruus.

7 iiii.borđ cũ.ii.car.　　　Val.xxx.ſoliđ.

Eccłam huj m̃ 7 pbrm 7 trã ad.i.car.ten S MARIA de Lira.

Rex hĩ in Herefordſcire.ix.m̃ waſta.de.xix.hidis.

De foreſtis quas ten Wilts filius Normanni.redđ.xv.lib regi.

IN HEZETRE HVND.

Rex ten BERCHELINCOPE.Sol tenuit.T.R.E.Ibi.ii.hidæ

Waſtæ fuer 7 ſunt.Tra.ẽ.iiii.car.

Rex ten RADDRENOVE.Herald tenuit.Ibi.xv.hidæ.Waſtæ

ſunt 7 fuer.Tra.ẽ.xxx.car.

★ Hugo dicit qđ.W.com hanc trã ſibi dedit.qdo deđ ei

tram Turchil anteceſſoris ſui.　IN ELSEDVNE HVND.

Rex ten WITENIE.Æluuard tenuit.T.R.E.7 poterat ire

quo uoleb.Ibi dimiđ hida gelđ.Waſta fuit 7 eſt.

Herald tenuit MATEVRDIN.m̃ de.ii.hiđ gelđ.parte huj

træ hĩ rex 7 waſta.ẽ 7 fuit.

Iſđ Herald tenuit HERDESLEGE.Ibi ſunt.ii.hidæ 7 dim waſtæ.

Iſđ Herald tenuit CICVVRDINE.Ibi.i.hida 7 iii.virg træ Waſtæ.

In Vlfelmeſtune.ii.hidæ.In Stiuingeurdin.i.hida.

In Hantinetune.iii.hidæ.In Burardeſtune.i.hida.

In Hergeſth.i.hida.In Brudeford.ii.hidæ.In Chingtune.ii.hidæ.

In Ruiſcop.iiii.hidæ.Has tras tenuit Herald.Modo hĩ rex.Waſtæ ſuꝑ.

In Hergeſt.iii.hidæ.In Beuretune.ii.hidæ.In Ruiſcop.i.hida.

H tria m̃ tenuit Rex.E.7 gelđ.Modo hĩ rex 7 Waſta ſuꝑ.

Ralph of Sacey also holds part of this manor; he has land 181 b for 2 ploughs. 1 plough there, with

2 ploughmen; 1 Welshman who has ½ plough and pays 1 sester of honey.

Value 20s.

62 Ralph of Tosny holds DEWSALL, and William and Ilbert from him. Wulfheah held it. 1 hide. In lordship 2 ploughs; 1 slave; 4 smallholders with 2 ploughs.
Value 30s.
St. Mary's of Lyre holds the church of this manor, a priest and land for 1 plough.

63 The King has in Herefordshire 9 waste manors at 19 hides. William son of Norman pays the King £15 from the Forests he holds.

In HAZELTREE Hundred

64 The King holds BURLINGJOBB. Sol held it before 1066. 2 hides. They were and are waste. Land for 4 ploughs.

65 The King holds (Old) RADNOR. Earl Harold held it. 15 hides. They were and are waste. Land for 30 ploughs. Hugh Donkey states that Earl William gave this land to him when he gave him the land of his predecessor Thorkell.

In ELSDON Hundred

66 The King holds WHITNEY. Alfward held it before 1066; he could go where he would. ½ hide which pays tax. It was and is waste.

67 Earl Harold held *MATEURDIN*, a manor at 2 hides which pays tax. The King has part of this land. It is and was waste.

68 Harold also held EARDISLEY. 2½ hides waste.

69 Harold also held CHICKWARD. 1 hide and 3 virgates of land, waste. In WELSON 2 hides. In CHICKWARD 1 hide. In HUNTINGTON 3 hides. In BOLLINGHAM 1 hide. In HERGEST 1 hide. In BREADWARD 2 hides. In KINGTON 4 hides. In RUSHOCK 4 hides. Earl Harold held these lands. Now the King has them; they are waste.

In HERGEST 3 hides. In BARTON 2 hides. In RUSHOCK 1 hide. King Edward held these three manors; they paid tax. Now the King has them; they are waste.

In *WENNETVNE* . ē una hida 7 dim̄ gelđ. *IN ELSEDVNE HĐ.*

Elgar 7 Aluuin tenuer̄ ꝑ . ıı . Ꝏ̃ . 7 poteraꝰ ire quo uolƀ.

Radulf' de bernai cū . eet uicecom . mifit has . ıı . tras injuſte

ad firmā de Leofminſtre . Ibi . ē una car̄ 7 dim̄ . Nil aliud.

T.R.E. Waſt fuit . Modo redđ . lxıı . den ad firmā regis.

In *RVEDENE* eſt . ı . hida gelđ . Grim *IN PLEGELIET HVNĐ.*

tenuit ꝑ Ꝏ̃ . 7 potuit ire quo uoluit . Ibi h̄t Grichetel . ı . car̄.

7 uñ borđ 7 uñ bouar̄ . Valuit xıı . ſoł . modo . x . ſoł ad firmā.

In *NIWARE* ſunt . ıı . hidæ 7 dimiđ . quæ *IN BREMESESE HĐ*

conuenieƀ 7 opabant̄ . ſed Roger̄ de piſtes T.W. comitis

diuertit illas ad Glouueceſtreſcire.

In *BROCOTE* ſunt . ıı . hidæ 7 dimiđ . Aluric 7 Eluuard 7 Bercſi

tenuer̄ ꝑ . ıı . Ꝏ̃ . Waſta fuer̄ 7 ſuꝰ adhuc in ſilua regis.

Ibiđ tenuit Briſtric uñ Ꝏ̃ de . ı . hida . 7 Goduin comes tenuit

STANTVN . uñ Ꝏ̃ de . ı . hida waſta fuer̄ 7 ſuꝰ adhuc in ſilua

In *GETVNE* tenuit WETMAN unā hiđ gelđ. ┌ regis.
camerario.

★ 7 poterat ire quo uolƀ . Hugo tenuit ad firmā de de Hunfrido.

7 reddeƀ . xxx . ſoliđ . 7 adhuc redđ tn̄tđ.

H̄ tra fuit tainland T.R.E. ſed poſtea c̄uerſa . ē in Reueland.

7 idō dn̄t legati regis . qđ ipſa tra 7 cenſus qui inde exit

furtim aufert̄ regi.

181 c

TERRA ÆCCLÆ DE HEREFORD.

.II. IN *HEREFORD PORT* T.R.E. habuit Walter' eꝑs . c.

maſuras as . ıı . min' . Qui maneƀ in eis: reddeƀ . c . ſoliđ . vı .

ſoliđ min' . Habebat q̄ iſđ eꝑs unū monetariū.

Quando Roƀt' uenit in epiſcopatu: inuenit . lx . maſuras.

Qui maneƀ in eis: reddeƀ . xlııı . ſoliđ 7 ıııı . denar̄.

Modo aꝑꝑicatū eſt . l . ſoliđ . ┌ 7 ita ſuꝰ adhuc.

Roƀt' eꝑs q̄do uenit ad epiſcopat: inuen̄ . xl . hiđ uaſtatas.

In ELSDON Hundred

70 In WOONTON 1½ hides which pay tax. Algar and Alwin held them
as two manors; they could go where they would. When Ralph of
Bernay was Sheriff he wrongfully included these two lands in the
revenue of Leominster. 1½ ploughs there; nothing else.
Before 1066 it was waste. Now it pays 62d into the King's revenue.

In PLEGELGATE Hundred

71 In ROWDEN 1 hide which pays tax. Grim held it as a manor; he
could go where he would. Grimketel has 1 plough and
   1 smallholder and 1 ploughman.
The value was 12s; now (it pays) 10s into the revenue.

In BROMSASH Hundred

72 In 'NEWARNE' 2½ hides which came to (Hundred) meetings and did
service (there), but in Earl William's time Roger of Pîtres transferred
them to Gloucestershire.

73 In REDBROOK 2½ hides. Aelfric, Alfward and Brictsi held them as
two manors. They were waste and are still in the King's wood.

74 There also Brictric held a manor at 1 hide and Earl Godwin held
STAUNTON, a manor at 1 hide. They were waste and are still in the
King's wood.

75 In YATTON Hwaetmann held 1 hide which paid tax; he could go
where he would. Hugh held it at a revenue from Humphrey the
Chamberlain; he paid 30s and still pays as much.
   This land was thaneland before 1066, but afterwards it was
changed to reeveland; therefore the King's Commissioners state
that this land and the dues which come from it are being
surreptitiously taken away from the King.

2   LAND OF THE CHURCH OF HEREFORD   181 c

1 In the town of HEREFORD before 1066 Bishop Walter had 100
dwellings, less 2. The men who lived in them paid 100s, less 6s.
The Bishop also had one moneyer. When Robert succeeded to
the Bishopric he found 60 dwellings. The men who lived in them
paid 43s 4d. Now it is assessed at 50s. When Bishop Robert
succeeded to the Bishopric he found 40 hides laid waste; they
are still thus.

Walteri eps habuit un͠ M͠ *DODELEGIE* . qd appciatu͠ . e̅

.XL . folid . 7 juxta illud jacet aliud M͠ . *STANE* . qd recte ptin

ad epifcopatu͠ . In his . II͠ . Maner͠ funt . x . hidæ . On͠s hæ hidæ

waftatæ fu͠ſ . 7 waftæ fuer͠ . pter una͠ hida in *DODELIGE* .

De his . IX . hid una pars in Caftellaria Aluredi Ewias .

7 altera pars in defenfione regis .

Iftæ hidæ geldab͠ cu͠ . W . epo͠ T.R.E . In Tedefthorne . II . hid

7 dimid . In Salberga dim͠ hida . In Ardefhope . III . virg͠ træ .

In Ach . una hida 7 una v͠ .

Hæ TERRÆ SVBTER SCRIPTÆ . Ptin ad Canonic de hereford .

In *LVLLEHA*̅ funt . VIII . hidæ geld͠ .   IN *STRADFORD HVND* .

In dn͠io . e̅ una car͠ . 7 XI . uiƚƚ 7 v . bord͠ cu͠ . XIII . car͠ . Ibi una

ancilla . 7 III . ac͠ p̅ti . 7 una car͠ plus poffet . ee͠ . in dn͠io

De hac tra ten͠ . II . clerici . II . hid 7 III . virg͠ . 7 un͠ miles . I . hida͠ .

hi hn͠t in dn͠io . II . car͠ . 7 XIII . uiƚƚ 7 II . bord͠ . cu͠ . VIII . car͠ .

T.R.E . uaftu͠ fuit . modo uaƚ x . liƀ

In *PRESTRETVNE* . funt . VI . hidæ geld͠ . In dn͠io . e̅ una car͠ .

7 IX . uiƚƚi 7 VIII . bord͠ cu͠ . VIII . car͠ 7 dimid . Ibi molin͠ de . II .

folid . Silua . I . leuu lg͠ . 7 dimid lat͠ . 7 una car͠ plus poffet in dn͠io . ee͠ .

De hac tra ten͠ . II . clerici . II . hid 7 dimid . 7 una hida . e̅ wafta .

hi hn͠t VII . uiƚƚos cu͠ . III . car͠ . Villani plus hn͠t car͠ qua͠ arabile͠ tra͠ .

. T.R.E . waftu͠ fuit . modo . c . folid .

In *TIBRINTINTVNE* . funt . VI . hidæ geld͠ . Ibi . e̅ una car͠ in dn͠io .

7 XVI . uiƚƚ 7 VI . bord͠ cu͠ . IX . car͠ . 7 una car͠ plus poffet . ee͠ . in dn͠io .

Ibi . III . ac͠ p̅ti . Silua . I . leuu lg͠ . 7 dimid leuu lat͠ .

T.R.E . uuaft erat . Modo uaƚ . III . liƀ .

In ipfo *HVND* ten͠ . I . radman . I . hid quæ . e̅ de Bertune cano-

nicoʒ . 7 geld͠ . 7 ibi . e̅ una car͠ in dn͠io .   Vaƚ . v . folid .

In *ETVNE* . funt . v . hidæ   In dn͠io funt . II . car͠ .

7 XII . uiƚƚi 7 VI . bord͠ cu͠ . VII . car͠ . Ibi . II . ferui . 7 molin͠

de . v . folid . 7 XII . ac͠ p̅ti . Silua . I . leuu lg͠ . 7 II . q̅ʒ lat͠ .

Vaƚ . IIII . liƀ .

2   Bishop Walter had one manor, DIDLEY, which is assessed at 40s. Next to it lies another manor, STANE, which rightly belongs to the Bishopric. In these two manors are 10 hides. All these hides have been laid waste; they were waste except for 1 hide in Didley. Of these 9 hides, one part is in Alfred's castlery of Ewyas (Harold), the other part in the King's Enclosure.

3   These hides paid tax with Bishop W(alter) before 1066: in TEDSTONE 2½ hides, in SAWBURY (Hill) ½ hide, in YARSOP 3 virgates of land, and in NOAKES 1 hide and 1 virgate.

**THESE LANDS MENTIONED BELOW BELONG TO
THE CANONS OF HEREFORD**

In STRETFORD Hundred

4   In LULHAM 8 hides which pay tax. In lordship 1 plough;
11 villagers and 5 smallholders with 13 ploughs.
1 female slave; meadow, 3 acres; 1 more plough would be possible in lordship. ...
Of this land 2 clerks hold 2 hides and 3 virgates and 1 man-at-arms 1 hide. They have 2 ploughs in lordship;
13 villagers and 2 smallholders with 8 ploughs.
Before 1066 it was waste. Value now £10.

5   In PRESTON (on Wye) 6 hides which pay tax. In lordship 1 plough;
9 villagers and 8 smallholders with 8½ ploughs.
A mill at 2s; woodland 1 league long and ½ wide; 1 more plough would be possible in lordship.
Of this land 2 clerks hold 2½ hides; 1 hide is waste. They have 7 villagers with 3 ploughs. The villagers have more ploughs than ploughable land.
Before 1066 it was waste. [Value] now 100s.

6   In TYBERTON 6 hides which pay tax. In lordship 1 plough;
16 villagers and 6 smallholders with 9 ploughs; 1 more plough would be possible in lordship.
Meadow, 3 acres; woodland 1 league long and ½ league wide.
Before 1066 it was waste. Value now £3.

7   In the same Hundred 1 rider holds 1 hide which is (part) of the canons' barton; it pays tax. 1 plough in lordship.
Value 5s.

8   In EATON (Bishop) 5 hides. ... In lordship 2 ploughs;
12 villagers and 6 smallholders with 7 ploughs.
2 slaves; a mill at 5s; meadow, 12 acres; woodland 1 league long and 2 furlongs wide.
Value £4.

Hoc M̄ tenuit Herald.7 Wiłłs deđ Walterio epo ꝓ tra

in qua mercatū.ē modo.7 ꝑ tribȝ hiđ de LIDENEGIE

In MEDELAGIE ſunt.III.hidæ.7 ptiñ ad Bertune epī.

In dñio.ē una car.7 VI.uiłłi cū.IIII.car.Ibi Silua

dimiđ leuu lḡ.7 una q̊ȝ lat.H̄ ſilua.ē in defenſu regis.

In eođ HVND teñ.II.libi.hões.IIII.hiđ.7 ptiñ ad Bertune

epī.In dñio hñt.I.car 7 dim.7 VI borđ eū.II.car.

Toť M̄ uał.c.ſolid.Tra milit.XV.ſolid 7 VIII.denar.

In BERTVNE ſunt.X.hidæ gelđ. IN DVNRE HVND.

In dñio.ē una car.7 uñ uiłłs 7 II.borđ.cū.I.car.Ibi una

ancilla.7 IIII.ač p̄ti.Siluā huj M̄ hť rex in ſuo dñio.

De hac tra teñ.IIII.clerici.IIII.hiđ 7 dimiđ.7 IIII.milit

teñ.V.hidas.Hi hñt in dñio.VII.car 7 dimiđ.7 XXII.

uiłłos.7 XII.borđ cū.X.car 7 dimiđ.Dimiđ hida.ē Waſta.

In dñio poſſent eſſe.II.car pluſquā ſunt.

T.R.E.Waſtū fuit.Modo uał.VII.lib.

181 d

In HAMME ſunt.VI.hidæ gelđ.In dñio ſunt.II.car.

7 XVI.uiłłi.7 p̄br 7 p̄poſitus 7 uñ francig.7 IIII.buri.

Int oms hñt.XX.car 7 dimiđ.Ibi.I.ſeruus.7 II.ancillæ.

7 X.ač p̄ti.Silua dimiđ leuu lḡ.7 tntđ laŧ.

Ad hoc M̄ ptiñ una æccła uocat LADGVERN.7 ibi ſu

.IIII.car.ſed ñ gelđ tra huj æcclæ.P̄br redđ.II.ſoł inde.

Hanc trā teñ Roger de Laci ſub epo.

Hoc M̄ tenuit Herald com injuſte.q̊a.ē de uiču cano

nicoȝ.Rex.W.reddiđ Walterio epo.

T.R.E.uałb.IX.lib.Modo.VIII.lib. IN KAGETREV HD.

In HOPE ſunt.XVI.hide gelđ.In dñio.ē una car.

7 alia poſſeŧ.ēe.7 XXXV.uiłłi 7 VII.borđ cū.XXXV.car.

Ibi.VIII.ač p̄ti.Silua.III.q̊ȝ lḡ.7 una q̊ȝ laŧ.

Earl Harold held this manor. Earl William gave it to Bishop Walter for land in which the market is now and for 3 hides of Lydney.

9 In MADLEY 3 hides ... ; they belong to the Bishop's barton. In lordship 1 plough;
6 villagers with 4 ploughs.
Woodland ½ league long and 1 furlong wide. This woodland is in the King's Enclosure.

10 In the same Hundred 2 free men hold 4 hides; they belong to the Bishop's barton. They have 1½ ploughs in lordship;
6 smallholders with 2 ploughs.
Value of the whole manor, 100s; of the men-at-arms' land, 15s 8d.

In DINEDOR Hundred
11 In 'BARTON' 10 hides which pay tax. In lordship 1 plough;
1 villager and 2 smallholders with 1 plough.
1 female slave; meadow, 4 acres. The King has the woodland of this manor in his lordship.
Of this land 4 clerks hold 4½ hides; 4 men-at-arms hold 5 hides.
They have 7½ ploughs in lordship and
22 villagers and 12 smallholders with 10½ ploughs.
½ hide is waste. 2 more ploughs would be possible in lordship than there are.
Before 1066 it was waste. Value now £7.

12 In HOLME (Lacy) 6 hides which pay tax. In lordship 2 ploughs;   181 d
16 villagers, a priest, a reeve, 1 Frenchman and 4 boors;
between them they have 20½ ploughs.
1 male and 2 female slaves; meadow, 10 acres; woodland ½ league long and as wide.
A church called LLANWARNE belongs to this manor. 3 ploughs there, but the land of this church does not pay tax. A priest pays 2s from it. Roger of Lacy holds this land under the Bishop. Earl Harold held this manor wrongfully because it is for the canons' supplies. King William restored it to Bishop Walter.
Value before 1066 £9; now £8.

In GREYTREE Hundred
13 In WOOLHOPE 16 hides which pay tax. In lordship 1 plough; another would be possible;
35 villagers and 7 smallholders with 35 ploughs.
Meadow, 8 acres; woodland 3 furlongs long and 1 furlong wide.

De hac tra ten.II.clerici.I.hid 7 una v.7 un miles
una hid 7 dimid.In dnio.e una car.7 v.uitti.7 IIII.
bord cu.IIII.car.Miles redd.v.solid canon S Albti.
T.R.E.ualb.XVI.lib.7 modo similit.

In *CAPEL*.sunt.v.hidæ geld.In dnio sunt.III.car.7 IX.uitt
7 un bord cu.VIII.car.Ibi.I.seruus 7 II.ancillæ.7 molinu
de.III.solid.7 VIII.ac pti.

T.R.E.ualb.XL.sot.7 post 7 modo. LX.solid.

In *CAPLEFORE*.sunt.v.hidæ anglicæ geld.7 III.hidæ Waliscæ
reddtes.VI.solid canon p annu.In.v.hid.e una car in dnio.
7 VIII.uitti cu.VII.car.7 III.ac pti.

T.R.E.ualb.LXX.sot.7 post 7 m tntd. *IN THORNLAV HD.*

In *PRESTETVNE*.sunt.IIII.hidæ.geld.Vna v 7 dimid.e wasta.
Duo canonici tenuer T.R.E.7 postea un cleric 7 un miles.
In dnio.IIII.car.7 v.uitti cu.IIII.car 7 dimid.Ibi.I.ancilla.
7 XX.ac pti.

T.R.E.ualb.LXV.sot.Modo.v.sot min.

In *WIDINGTVNE* sunt.VIII.hidæ geld.In dnio.e una car.
7 IIII.uitti 7 II.bord.cu.III.car.Ibi.II.ac pti.7 molin de.II.
solid.De isto M ten.III.clerici.IIII.hid.7 hnt in dnio.III.
car.7 VI.uitt 7 IIII.bord cu.VI.car.7 un seruu 7 II.ancillas.
7 VII.acs pti.

De eod M ten Moniales de hereford.II.hid.7 hnt ibi.I.car.
7 III.uitt cu.II.car 7 dimid.7 XIIII.acs pti.

Int totu ual 7 ualuit sep.VI.lib 7 v.solid.

In *VLLINGWIC* sunt.VI.hidæ.Ex his.III.hidæ geld.7 III.sun
wastæ.In dnio sunt.III.car.7 VIII.uitti 7 IIII.bord cu.VI.
car 7 dimid.Ibi.II.serui.7 pars salinæ in Wich.

T.R.E.7 post 7 modo.ual.c.solid.Vn miles epi ten de eo.

Of this land 2 clerks hold 1 hide and 1 virgate, and 1
man-at-arms 1½ hides. In lordship 1 plough;
5 villagers and 4 smallholders with 4 ploughs.
The man-at-arms pays 5s to the canons of St. Albert's.
Value before 1066 £16; now the same.

14 In (How) CAPLE 5 hides which pay tax. In lordship 3 ploughs;
9 villagers and 1 smallholder with 8 ploughs.
1 male and 2 female slaves; a mill at 3s; meadow, 8 acres.
Value before 1066, 40s; later and now, 60s.

15 In BROCKHAMPTON 5 English hides which pay tax, and 3 Welsh
hides which pay 6s a year to the canons. In the 5 hides 1 plough
in lordship;
8 villagers with 7 ploughs.
Meadow, 3 acres.
Value before 1066, 70s; later and now as much.

In THORNLAW Hundred
16 In PRESTON (Wynne) 4 hides which pay tax. 1½ virgates waste.
Two canons held it before 1066; later a clerk and a man-at-arms.
In lordship 4 ploughs;
5 villagers with 4½ ploughs.
1 female slave; meadow, 20 acres.
Value before 1066, 65s; now 5s less.

17 In WITHINGTON 8 hides which pay tax. In lordship 1 plough;
4 villagers and 2 smallholders with 3 ploughs.
Meadow, 2 acres; a mill at 2s.
3 clerks hold 4 hides of this manor; they have 3 ploughs
in lordship and
6 villagers and 4 smallholders with 6 ploughs; 1 male and
2 female slaves;
meadow, 7 acres.
The nuns of Hereford hold 2 hides also of this manor; they
have 1 plough there and
3 villagers with 2½ ploughs;
meadow, 14 acres.
In total, the value is and always was £6 5s.

18 In ULLINGSWICK 6 hides. Of these, 3 hides pay tax and 3 are waste.
In lordship 3 ploughs;
8 villagers and 4 smallholders with 6½ ploughs.
2 slaves; part of a salt-house in Droitwich.
Value before 1066, later and now, 100s.
One of the Bishop's men-at-arms holds from him.

In *DVNNINCTVNE* eſt.ı.hida gelđ. *IN WIMÉNDESTREV HĎ.*

In dñio.ē una caŕ.7 vı.uiłł 7 vı.borđ cū.vıı.caŕ.Ibi una

ancilla 7 vııı.a̋c p̃ti.

T.R.E.7 poſt 7 m̃.uał.xxv.ſoliđ.Vn̐ cleric̚ ep̄i ten̐ de eo.

In *MORTVNE* ſunt.ıııı.hidæ gelđ. *IN RADENELAV HVNĎ.*

In dñio ſunt.ııı.caŕ.7 ıı.uiłłi 7 un̐ borđ cū.ıı.caŕ.Ibi.ıııı.ſerui

7 vı.ancillæ.7 vıı.a̋c p̃ti.7 una ſalina in Wich.

T.R.E.7 poſt 7 modo.uał.c.ſoliđ.   *Ƭ HVNĎ.*

In *FROME* ſuꝗ.x.hidæȷ.Ex his.ıııı.hidæ jaceꝗ in *PLEGELGETE*
    geldantes.

In dñio eſt.ı.caŕ.7 xxıı.uiłłi 7 ıııı.borđ cū.xxı.caŕ.
                                            ti a

Ibi un̐ ſeruus.7 moliñ de.vııı.ſoliđ.7 vı.a̋c p̃ti.Silua nil redđ

De iſto m̃ ten̐.ıı.milit̚.ııı.hiđ.7 capellan̐ ep̄i.ı.hidā.

7 p̄br uillæ unā v̇ træ.Hi hñt.vı.caŕ.7 v.uiłłos 7 uā borđ.

cu̇.ıııı.caŕ.7 ııı.ſeruis.P̃poſit̚ uillæ h̄ṫ.ı.moliñ de.xxxıı.den.

T.R.E.7 poſt 7 modo.uał.x.lıɓ 7 xv.ſoliđ. *IN BROMESESCE HĎ.*

In *WIBOLDINGTVNE* ſunt.ııı.hidæ.quæ reɧte p̃tin̐ ad

epiſcopat̄.Waſtæ ſuꝗ 7 waſtæ fueŕ.Ibi.ē piſcaria.

In *WALECFORD* ſunt.vıı.hidæ gelđ.In dñio.ē una caŕ.
                     e
7 adhuc.ıı.poſſent.ēe.Ibi.vı.uiłłi 7 ıııı.borđ cū.v.caŕ.

Ibi.xıııı.a̋c p̃ti.7 ııı.haiæ.Viłłi redđt.x.ſ.ł ꝑ waſta tra.

In *ROSSE* ſunt.vıı.hidæ gelđ.In dñio.ē una caŕ.7 alia

poſſet.ēe.Ibi.xvııı.uiłłi 7 vı.borđ 7 p̄br cū.xxııı.caŕ.

Ibi.ııı.ſerui 7 moliñ de.vı.ſoliđ 7 vııı.den.7 xvı.a̋c p̃ti.

Silua.ē in defenſu regis.Viłłi redđt.xvııı.ſoł de cenſu.

In *VPTVNE* ſunt.vıı.hidæ gelđ.In dñio ſunt.ıı.caŕ.7 xvııı.

uiłłi 7 xı.borđ 7 ıı.buri.7 p̄br.Int̄ om̄s hñt.xxvııı.caŕ 7 dim̄.

In WINSTREE Hundred

19 In DONNINGTON 1 hide which pays tax. In lordship 1 plough;
6 villagers and 6 smallholders with 7 ploughs.
1 female slave; meadow, 8 acres.
Value before 1066, later and now, 25s.
One of the Bishop's clerks holds from him.

In RADLOW Hundred

20 In MORETON (Jeffries) 4 hides which pay tax. In lordship 3 ploughs;
2 villagers and 1 smallholder with 2 ploughs.
4 male and 6 female slaves; meadow, 7 acres; 1 salt-house
in Droitwich.
Value before 1066, later and now, 100s.

21 In (Bishops) FROME 10 hides which pay tax. Of these, 4 hides lie
in Plegelgate Hundred. In lordship 1 plough;
22 villagers and 4 smallholders with 21 ploughs.
1 slave; a mill at 8s; meadow, 6 acres; woodland which
pays nothing.
Of this manor 2 men-at-arms hold 3 hides; the Bishop's chaplain
1 hide; a priest of the village 1 virgate of land. They have
6 ploughs and
5 villagers and 1 smallholder with 4 ploughs and 3 slaves. 182 a
The reeve of the village has 1 mill at 32d.
Value before 1066, later and now £10 15s.

In BROMSASH Hundred

22 In 'WHIPPINGTON' 3 hides which rightly belong to the Bishopric.
They are waste and were waste. A fishery there.

23 In WALFORD 7 hides which pay tax. In lordship 1 plough; a further
2 would be possible.
6 villagers and 4 smallholders with 5 ploughs.
Meadow, 14 acres; 3 hedged enclosures.
The villagers pay 10s for the waste land.

24 In ROSS (on Wye) 7 hides which pay tax. In lordship 1 plough;
another would be possible.
18 villagers, 6 smallholders and a priest with 23 ploughs.
3 slaves; a mill at 6s 8d; meadow, 16 acres. The woodland
is in the King's Enclosure.
The villagers pay 18s in dues.

25 In UPTON (Bishop) 7 hides which pay tax. In lordship 2 ploughs;
18 villagers, 11 smallholders, 2 boors and a priest; between
them they have 28½ ploughs.

Ibi . v . ſerui . 7 iiii . aͨ p̃ti . 7 una Haia . 7 Silua nichil reddeɹꞩ.

Viłłi reddt . xx . ſoliđ p̃ cꝭſuetuđ.

H̄ tria m̃ Walforde 7 Roſſe 7 Vptune . ap̃pciata ſuɴͥ . xiiii . liƀ.

In LIEDEBERGE ſunt . v . hidæ . In dn̄io IN WIMVNDESTREV HD̄.

ſunt . ii . caꞅͬ . 7 x . uiłł 7 unꞛ burꞛ cꞛ . xi . caꞅͬ . Ibi molin̄ de . xxxii .

den̄ . 7 vii . aͨ p̃ti . Silua dimiđ leuu lg̃ . 7 dimiđ laꞅͭ . 7 nil redđ.

De hoc m̃ ten̄ p̃ƀr . ii . hiđ 7 dimiđ . 7 ii . milit̄ . i . hidā . 7 unͨ

radman . iii . virg . Hi hn̄t in dn̄io . x . caꞅͬ . 7 vii . borđ cꞛ alijs

hꝋiƀꝫ hn̄tibꝫ . viii . caꞅͬ . 7 pars ſalinæ In Wich.   ꟿualet.

T.R.E . ualƀ . x . liƀ . 7 poſt 7 modo . viii . liƀ . Qd p̃ƀr ten̄ꞏ l . ſoliđ

Dͨ iſto m̃ tenuit Herald coꝥ injuſte . i . hidā HASLES . 7 Godricͧ

de eo . Rex . W . reddiđ Walterio ep̃o . In dn̄io ſunt . iii . caꞅͬ.

7 iiii . uiłłi cꞛ . iii . caꞅͬ . 7 molin̄ de . ii . ſoliđ 7 vii . aͨ p̃ti.

T.R.E . 7 poſt 7 modo . uaꞅͭ . xxv . ſoliđ.

In ASTENOFRE ſunt . iiii . hidæ gelđ . In dn̄io ſunt . iii . caꞅͬ.

7 viii . uiłłi 7 vii . borđ cꞛ . xi . caꞅͬ . Ibi . vi . aͨ p̃ti . 7 ii . haiæ.

7 Silua quæ nil redđ . 7 pars ſalinæ in Wich . Silua . iiii . q̃ꝫ

lg̃ . 7 ii . laꞅͭ.

De iſto ten̄ꞅ . i . miles dimiđ hidā . 7 unͧ cem̄tarius dimiđ hiđ.

7 dimiđ virg . In dn̄io . i . caꞅͬ . 7 ii . borđ cꞛ aliđꝫ alijsꞏ iii . caꞅͬ.

T.R.E . 7 poſt 7 modo . uaꞅͭ . iiii . liƀ.

In BAGEBERGE ſunt . v . hidæ gelđ . In dn̄io ſunt . ii . caꞅͬ.

7 xvi . uiłłi 7 xiii . borđ cꞛ . xx . caꞅͬ . Ibi molin̄ de . xxxii . den̄ꞅ.

7 viii . aͨ p̃ti . 7 Silua nichil redđ . 7 Pars ſalinæ in Wich.

De iſto m̃ ten̄ꞅ . ii . milit̄ . i . hiđ 7 iii . virg . 7 ii . Radmanni

iii . virg꞊ꞅ 7 dimiđ . In dn̄io hn̄t hi . iiii . caꞅͬ . 7 hꝋcꞅs eoꝫ . vi . caꞅͬꞅ.

7 molinꞛ de . xvi . denaꞅͬ.

T.R.E . 7 poſt 7 modo . uaꞅͭ . viii . liƀ . v . ſoliđ minͧ.

5 slaves; meadow, 4 acres; 1 hedged enclosure; woodland
which pays nothing.
The villagers pay 20s in customary dues.

These three manors, Walford, Ross (on Wye) and Upton (Bishop)
are assessed at £14.

In WINSTREE Hundred
26 In LEDBURY 5 hides. In lordship 2 ploughs;
10 villagers and 1 boor with 11 ploughs.
A mill at 32d; meadow, 7 acres; woodland ½ league long
and ½ wide: it pays nothing.
Of this manor a priest holds 2½ hides; 2 men-at-arms 1 hide;
a rider 3 virgates. They have 10 ploughs in lordship;
7 smallholders with other men who have 8 ploughs.
Part of a salt-house in Droitwich.
Value before 1066 £10; later and now £8. Value of what the
priest holds, 50s.
Of this manor Earl Harold wrongfully held 1 hide, HAZLE, and
Godric from him. King William restored it to Bishop Walter.
In lordship 3 ploughs;
4 villagers with 3 ploughs.
A mill at 2s; meadow, 7 acres.
Value before 1066, later and now, 25s.

27 In EASTNOR 4 hides which pay tax. In lordship 3 ploughs;
8 villagers and 7 smallholders with 11 ploughs.
Meadow, 6 acres; 2 hedged enclosures; woodland which
pays nothing; part of a salt-house in Droitwich; woodland
4 furlongs long and 2 wide.
Of this (manor) a man-at-arms holds ½ hide; a mason ½ hide and
½ virgate. In lordship 1 plough;
2 smallholders, with some other men, 3 ploughs.
Value before 1066, later and now £4.

28 In 'BAGBURROW' 5 hides which pay tax. In lordship 2 ploughs;
16 villagers and 13 smallholders with 20 ploughs.
A mill at 32d; meadow, 8 acres; woodland which pays
nothing; part of a salt-house in Droitwich.
Of this manor 2 men-at-arms hold 1 hide and 3 virgates;
2 riders 3½ virgates. They have 4 ploughs in lordship; their
men 6 ploughs; a mill at 16d.
Value before 1066, later and now £8, less 5s.

In BOSEBERGE funt . vi . hidæ gelđ . In dñio . ii . caɼ . 7 xvii .

uitti 7 xvi . borđ 7 uñ burũ cũ . xxii . caɼ . Ibi . ii . ſerui . 7 moliñ

de . xxx . deñ . 7 viii . aĉ pti . 7 Silua nil redđ .

Prbr ten . i . hiđ 7 hĩ . i . caɼ .

T . R . E . 7 poſt 7 modo . uaɫ . vi . liƀ .

In CREDELAIE . funt . xii . hidæ . Vna ex his . ē waſta . Aliæ gelđ .

In dñio funt . iii . caɼ . 7 xxiii . uitti 7 iii . borđ 7 . vi . buri cũ . xxviii .

caɼ . Ibi . v . ſerui . 7 moliñ de . xxxii . deñ . 7 vii . aĉ pti . Silua

una leuú lḡ . 7 dim leuú laĩ . 7 nil redđ . Ibi . i . haia .

De hoc ꝏ ten pbr unā v̄ 7 dimiđ . 7 ꝑpoſit dimiđ hidā .

7 ii . milit . i . hiđ 7 unā v̄ 7 dimiđ . 7 un radman dimiđ hiđ .

Hi hñt in dñio . v . caɼ . 7 borđ eoɀ . vi . caɼ .

T . R . E . 7 poſt 7 modo . uaɫ . x . liƀ .

In COLEWELLE funt . iii . hidæ gelđ . 7 jaceɴ ad Credelaie .

In dñio funt . ii . caɼ . 7 viii . uitti 7 viii . borđ cũ . x . caɼ .

182 b

Ibi . vi . ſerui . 7 moliñ de . xvi . deñ . 7 viii . aĉ pti . 7 una Haia .

De hoc ꝏ ten . i . radman dimiđ hiđ . 7 ibi hĩ . i . caɼ .

T . R . E . 7 poſt 7 modo . uaɫ . lx . foliđ .

Hoc ꝏ tenuit Herald coñ injuſte . 7 Turmod de eo .

Rex . W . reddiđ Walterio epo .

In COTINGTVNE funt . iii . hidæ . Dimiđ hida . ē waſta . Aliæ

hidæ gelđ . In dñio funt . ii . caɼ . 7 vi . uitti . 7 un borđ cũ . vi . caɼ .

Ibi . i . radmann ten . i . hiđ . 7 hĩ . i . caɼ . Ibi . iii . aĉ pti . 7 Silua

nil redđ . Ad iſtud ꝏ ptin . iii . maſuræ . in Wireceſtre

reddt . xxx . denaɼ .

T . R . E . 7 poſt 7 modo . uaɫ . xlv . foliđ .

Hoc ꝏ tenuit Herald coñ injuſte . Rex . W . reddiđ Walterio epo .

In HANTVNE . funt . iiii . hidæ gelđ IN CVTETHORN HĐ .

In dñio funt . ii . caɼ . 7 vi . uitti 7 . v . borđ cũ . vii . caɼ . Ibi . ii . ancillæ .

7 ii . molini 7 dimiđ . de . xxxv . foliđ . 7 xxviii . aĉ pti .

29 In BOSBURY 6 hides which pay tax. In lordship 2 ploughs;
17 villagers, 16 smallholders and a boor with 22 ploughs.
2 slaves; a mill at 30d; meadow, 8 acres; woodland which
pays nothing. ...
A priest holds 1 hide and has 1 plough.
Value before 1066, later and now £6.

30 In CRADLEY 12 hides. One of them is waste; the others pay tax.
In lordship 3 ploughs;
23 villagers, 3 smallholders and 6 boors with 28 ploughs.
5 slaves; a mill at 32d; meadow, 7 acres; woodland 1 league
long and ½ league wide: it pays nothing. 1 hedged enclosure.
Of this manor a priest holds 1½ virgates; a reeve ½ hide; 2
men-at-arms 1 hide and 1½ virgates; a rider ½ hide. They
have 5 ploughs in lordship; their smallholders 6 ploughs.
Value before 1066, later and now £10.

31 In COLWALL 3 hides which pay tax. They lie in Cradley. In
lordship 2 ploughs;
8 villagers and 8 smallholders with 10 ploughs.
6 slaves; a mill at 16d; meadow, 8 acres; 1 hedged   182 b
enclosure.
A rider holds ½ hide of this manor; he has 1 plough there.
Value before 1066, later and now, 60s.
Earl Harold held this manor wrongfully, and Thormod from
him. King William restored it to Bishop Walter.

32 In CODDINGTON 3 hides. ½ hide is waste; the other hides pay tax.
In lordship 2 ploughs;
6 villagers and 1 smallholder with 6 ploughs. 1 rider holds 1
hide; he has 1 plough.
Meadow, 3 acres; woodland which pays nothing. 3 dwellings
in Worcester belong to this manor; they pay 30d.
Value before 1066, later and now, 45s.
Earl Harold held this manor wrongfully. King William restored
it to Bishop Walter.

In CUTSTHORN Hundred
33 In HAMPTON (Bishop) 4 hides which pay tax. In lordship 2 ploughs;
6 villagers and 5 smallholders with 7 ploughs.
2 female slaves; 2½ mills at 35s; meadow, 28 acres.

De isto M̃ ten uñ miles . III . virg̃ . 7 uñ radman . I . uirg̃ . 7 hñt
in dñio . III . car̃.

T.R.E. 7 poſt 7 modo . ual̃ . c . ſolid̃.

Hoc M̃ tenuit Herald com̃ injuſte . Rex . W . reddid̃ Walterio ep̃o.

In TOPESLAGE . eſt una hida geld̃ . In dñio ſuj̃ . II . car̃.

7 IIII . uiħi 7 VI . bord̃ cũ . II . car̃ . Ibi moliñ de . XX . ſolid̃.

7 XX . ac̃ pti . 7 Salina ad Wich . redd̃ . XVI . mittas ſalis.

Vñ francig̃ teñ iſtã hidã dimid̃ . 7 hẽ . I . car̃.

T.R.E. 7 poſt ualb̃ XL . ſol̃ . Modo . V . ſolid̃ plus.

In SCELWICHE . ſunt . II . hidæ geld̃ . In dñio . ẽ una car̃.

7 VI . uiħi 7 VI . bord̃ cũ . IIII . car̃ . Ibi una ancilla . 7 moliñ
de . XXX . ſolid̃ . 7 XVIII . ac̃ pti.

T.R.E. 7 poſt . ualb̃ . LX . ſolid̃ . Modo . c . ſolid̃.

In SCELWICHE ſunt . III . hidæ geld̃ . In dñio eſt una car̃.

7 V . uiħi cũ . III . car̃ . 7 ibi . I . francig̃ teñ dimid̃ hid̃ . 7 hẽ . I . car̃.
cũ . II . bord̃ . Ibi . VIII . ac̃ pti.

T.R.E. 7 poſt . ualb̃ . XXX . ſolid̃ . Modo . V . ſolid̃ plus.

In SVCWESSEN ſunt . II . hidæ geld̃ . In dñio eſt una car̃.

Vñ miles teñ ad firmã unã ex his hid̃ . p . VIII . ſolid̃.

T.R.E. 7 poſt 7 modo . ual̃ . XXIII . ſolid̃.

Hoc M̃ tenuit Herald com̃ injuſte . Rex . W . reddid̃ Walterio ep̃o.

In WERHAM ſunt . II . hidæ 7 dimid̃ . geld̃ . Ibi . VIII . uiħi
cu . IIII . car̃.   Val̃ 7 ualuit . XXX . ſolid̃.

In PEVNE ſunt XII . hidæ geld̃ . In dñio . ẽ una car̃.

7 XV . uiħi 7 X . bord̃ cũ . XVI . car̃ . Ibi uñ bedellus . 7 II . ancillæ.

7 II . ac̃ pti.

De tra huj M̃ ten . III . clerici epi . IIII . hid̃ 7 dimid̃ . 7 III . milit̃
teñ . III . hid̃ 7 dimid̃ . Hi hñt in dñio . VI . car̃ . 7 XIIII . uiħi

7 IX . bord̃ cũ . VI . car̃ . Ibi hñt . IIII . ſeruos . 7 moliñ de . XXXII.

T.R.E. 7 poſt 7 modo . ual̃ . XII . lib̃ 7 X . ſolid̃.   Ƭ denar̃.

Of this manor a man-at-arms holds 3 virgates; a rider 1 virgate; they have 3 ploughs in lordship.
Value before 1066, later and now, 100s.
Earl Harold held this manor wrongfully. King William restored it to Bishop Walter.

34 In TUPSLEY 1 hide which pays tax. In lordship 2 ploughs;
4 villagers and 6 smallholders with 2 ploughs.
A mill at 20s; meadow, 20 acres; a salt-house at Droitwich which pays 16 measures of salt.
A Frenchman holds half this hide; he has 1 plough.
Value before 1066 and later, 40s; now 5s more.

35 In SHELWICK 2 hides which pay tax. In lordship 1 plough;
6 villagers and 6 smallholders with 4 ploughs.
1 female slave; a mill at 30s; meadow, 18 acres.
Value before 1066 and later, 60s; now 100s.

36 In SHELWICK 3 hides which pay tax. In lordship 1 plough;
5 villagers with 3 ploughs. 1 Frenchman holds ½ hide; he has 1 plough with 2 smallholders.
Meadow, 8 acres.
Value before 1066 and later, 30s; now 5s more.

37 In SUGWAS 2 hides which pay tax. In lordship 1 plough. A man-at-arms holds one of these hides at a revenue of 8s.
Value before 1066, later and now, 23s.
Earl Harold held this manor wrongfully. King William restored it to Bishop Walter.

38 In WARHAM 2½ hides which pay tax.
8 villagers with 4 ploughs.
The value is and was 30s.

39 In (Canon) PYON 12 hides which pay tax. In lordship 1 plough;
15 villagers and 10 smallholders with 16 ploughs. 1 beadle; 2 female slaves.
Meadow, 2 acres.
Of this manor's land 3 of the Bishop's clerks hold 4½ hides; 3 men-at-arms hold 3½ hides; they have 6 ploughs in lordship.
14 villagers and 9 smallholders with 6 ploughs.
They have 4 slaves; a mill at 32d.
Value before 1066, later and now £12 10s.

In *HVNTENETVNE* . ſunt . x . hidæ . Ex his . iiii . ſunt waſtæ.

7 aliæ gelđ . In dñio . ē una car̕ . 7 v . uiłłi 7 iiii . borđ cū . vii . car̕.

Ibi . v . aͫc p̃ti . 7 adhuc . i . car̕ plus poſſet . ēē . in dñio.

De iſto ꝏ̃ teñ uñ clericus . ii . hiđ . 7 uñ miles . iii . hiđ.

In dñio hñt . ii . car̕ . 7 iii . borđ 7 uñ faber cū . i . car̕.

T.R.E. 7 poſt 7 modo . uał . iiii . liƀ.

In *HOLEMERE* . ē una hida gelđ . Ibi ſunt . iiii . uiłłi cū . iiii . car̕.

Vał 7 ualuit . x . ſoliđ.

In *MORTVNE* ſunt . iiii . hidæ . gelđ . Tres clerici teñ de eƥo.

7 hñt . iii . car̕ in dñio . 7 viii . uiłłos 7 iiii . borđ cū . ii . car̕ 7 dimiđ.

Ibi . iii . ſerui 7 ii . ancillæ . 7 moliñ de . iiii . ſoliđ . 7 xx . aͫc p̃ti.

T.R.E. ualƀ . iiii . liƀ . 7 poſt 7 modo . iii . liƀ.

182 c

In *PIFE* eſt una hida . gelđ . Ibi . i . car̕ 7 xvi . aͫc p̃ti . Vał . v . ſoł.

In *LEODE* ſunt . ii . hidæ gelđ . Ibi . i . car̕ 7 dimiđ in dñio

7 iii . uiłłi cū . iii . car̕ 7 dimiđ . Ibi . i . ancilla . 7 adhuc poſſet

ēē . in dñio dimiđ car̕ . Ibi . viii . aͫc p̃ti.

Vał 7 ualuit . xl . ſoliđ . Vñ miles teñ de eƥo. *IN STAPEL*

In *NORTVNE* . ſunt . vi . hidæ . gelđ . In dñio   ꝉ *HVND*.

ē una car̕ . 7 viii . uiłłi 7 iii . borđ cū . viii . car̕ 7 dimiđ.

Ibi . i . ancilla 7 una aͫc p̃ti . 7 ſilua redđ . ii . ſoliđ.

T.R.E. 7 poſt . ualƀ . lx . ſoliđ . Modo : c . ſoliđ.

In *MALVESHILLE* ſunt . v . hidæ gelđ . In dñio . ē una car̕

7 alia ocioſa . 7 ix . uiłłi 7 ƥpoſit 7 iiii . borđ cū . vi . car̕ 7 dim̕.

Ibi . i . ancilla 7 vi . aͫc p̃ti.

T.R.E. ualƀ . iii . liƀ . 7 poſt 7 modo . iiii . liƀ.

40   In HUNTINGTON 10 hides. Of these, 4 are waste; the others pay tax.
In lordship 1 plough;
> 5 villagers and 4 smallholders with 7 ploughs.
> Meadow, 5 acres; a further 1 more plough would be possible
>   in lordship.
> Of this manor a clerk holds 2 hides; a man-at-arms 3 hides;
> they have 2 ploughs in lordship.
> 3 smallholders and 1 smith with 1 plough.

Value before 1066, later and now £4.

41   In HOLMER 1 hide which pays tax.
> 4 villagers with 4 ploughs.

The value is and was 10s.

42   In MORETON (on Lugg) 4 hides which pay tax. Three clerks hold
from the Bishop; they have 3 ploughs in lordship and
> 8 villagers and 4 smallholders with 2½ ploughs.
> 3 male and 2 female slaves; a mill at 4s; meadow, 20 acres.

Value before 1066 £4; later and now £3.

43   In PIPE 1 hide which pays tax. 1 plough there.   182 c
> Meadow, 16 acres.

Value 5s.

44   In LYDE 2 hides which pay tax. 1½ ploughs in lordship;
> 3 villagers with 3½ ploughs. 1 female slave; a further ½
>   plough would be possible in lordship.
> Meadow, 8 acres.

The value is and was 40s.
> A man-at-arms holds from the Bishop.

In STAPLE Hundred

45   In NORTON (Canon) 6 hides which pay tax. In lordship 1 plough;
> 8 villagers and 3 smallholders with 8½ ploughs.
> 1 female slave; meadow, 1 acre; woodland which pays 2s.

Value before 1066 and later, 60s; now 100s.

46   In BISHOPSTONE 5 hides which pay tax. In lordship 1 plough;
another idle;
> 9 villagers, a reeve and 4 smallholders with 6½ ploughs.
> 1 female slave; meadow, 6 acres.

Value before 1066 £3; later and now £4.

In *WRMESLEV* . dimiđ hida . ē gelđ . Vñ miles ten̅ de ep̄o

7 hī . II . uiłłos cū . I . car̄.

T.R.E. 7 post 7 modo . ual . IIII . soł

In *BRICGE* sunt . V . hidæ gelđ . Vñ miles ten̅ de ep̄o .

In dñio sunt . II . car̄ . 7 IIII . uiłł cū . II . car̄ . 7 uñ alt miles

ten̅ ibi . I . hiđ . 7 hī . I . car̄ . 7 IIII . borđ cū . I . car̄ .

Ibi . I . seru 7 una ancilła . T.R.E. ualb . L . soł . Modo . LX . soł .

In *BROMGERBE* sunt XXX . hidæ .   *IN PLEGELGET HD̄.*

Ex his . III . hidæ suꝧ 7 fuer̄ waste . Aliæ gelđ . In dñio sunt

.V . car̄. 7 XLII . uiłłi 7 IX . borđ cū . XXXIX . car̄ . Ibi . VI . serui.

7 molin̄ de . X . soliđ . 7 XII . ac̄ p̄ti . Silua . ē ibi . nil redđ .

De hoc M ten̅ . III . miliꞇ ep̄i . IX . hiđ . 7 unā virg .

7 II . p̄bri . I . hiđ . 7 uñ capellan̅ . I . hiđ 7 III . virg . 7 p̄positꝰ

unā hiđ . 7 uñ Radman . I . hidā .

In dñio hn̅t . XI . car̄ 7 dimiđ . 7 hōes eoꝛ hn̅t XX . car̄ .

Vñ eoꝛ hī . II . seruos . 7 III . ac̄s p̄ti .

T.R.E. 7 post 7 modo . uał tot M . XLV . lib 7 X . soliđ .

In *COLLINTVNE* sunt . III . hidæ gelđ . In dñio suꝧ . III . car̄ .

7 II . uiłłi 7 IIII . borđ cū . II . car̄ 7 dimiđ . Ibi . II . ac̄ p̄ti .

T.R.E. 7 post 7 modo . uał . XXX . soliđ .

Hoc M 7 illud sup̄i scriptū *BRICGE* . tenuit Herald injuste .

★ Rex . W . redđiđ eos Walterio ep̄o . *IN WLFAGIE HD*

In *LVTELONHEREFORD* sunt . VII . hidæ . Tres ex his suꝧ

wastæ . aliæ gelđ . In dñio sunt . III . car̄ . 7 XVII . uiłłi 7 III .

borđ . cū . XI . car̄ . Ibi . II . ancillæ . 7 molin̄ de VI . soliđ

7 VIII . denar̄ . Ibi suꝧ . IIII . molini . quoꝛ medietas recte

p̄tin̅ ad p̄dictū M . Ibi . V . ac̄ p̄ti . 7 Silua . II . q̄ꝛ lg̅ .

7 dimiđ q̄ꝛ lar̅ . 7 nil redđ .

De hoc M ten̅ p̄br dim̄ hiđ . 7 uñ radman dimiđ hidā .

Ipsi hn̅t . III . car̄ .

T.R.E. ualb . C . soliđ . 7 post 7 modo . IIII . lib .

47 In WORMSLEY ½ hide which pays tax. A man-at-arms holds from
the Bishop; he has
   2 villagers with 1 plough.
Value before 1066, later and now, 4s.

48 In BRIDGE (Sollers) 5 hides which pay tax. A man-at-arms holds
from the Bishop. In lordship 2 ploughs;
   4 villagers with 2 ploughs.
   Another man-at-arms holds 1 hide there; he has 1 plough;
   4 smallholders with 1 plough. 1 male and 1 female slave.
Value before 1066, 50s; now 60s.

In PLEGELGATE Hundred
49 In BROMYARD 30 hides. Of these, 3 hides are and were waste;
the others pay tax. In lordship 5 ploughs;
   42 villagers and 9 smallholders with 39 ploughs.
   6 slaves; a mill at 10s; meadow, 12 acres; woodland there
     which pays nothing.
   Of this manor 3 of the Bishop's men-at-arms hold 9 hides and
   1 virgate; 2 priests 1 hide; a chaplain 1 hide and 3 virgates;
   a reeve 1 hide; a rider 1 hide. They have 11½ ploughs in
   lordship; their men have 20 ploughs. One of them has 2 slaves
   and 3 acres of meadow.
Value of the whole manor before 1066, later and now £45 10s.

50 In COLLINGTON 3 hides which pay tax. In lordship 3 ploughs;
   2 villagers and 4 smallholders with 2½ ploughs.
   Meadow, 2 acres.
Value before 1066, later and now, 30s.

Earl Harold wrongfully held this manor and that mentioned
above, Bridge (Sollers). King William restored them to Bishop
Walter.

In WOLPHY Hundred
51 In LITTLE HEREFORD 7 hides. Of these, 3 are waste; the others pay
tax. In lordship 3 ploughs;
   17 villagers and 3 smallholders with 11 ploughs.
   2 female slaves; a mill at 6s 8d. 4 mills there, half of which
     rightly belongs to the above manor. Meadow, 5 acres;
     woodland 2 furlongs long and ½ furlong wide: it pays
     nothing.
   Of this manor a priest holds ½ hide; a rider ½ hide; they have
   3 ploughs.
Value before 1066, 100s; later and now £4.

In *WINETVNE* .ē dimiđ hida   Hanc teñ uñ Ra̧dman.

7 ibi hŧ.ı.cař 7 ıı.uiłłos.   Vał 7 ualuit.v.ſol.

In *CRADENHILLE* ſunt.ıı.hidæ.   IN *CVTETHORN* HĐ.

Ibi.ıı.uiłłi cū.ı.cař.reddt.v.ſoliđ de cenſu.Vał.xx.ſoł.

In *MORE*.eſt una hida.quæ uał.v.ſoliđ. IN *STRADĒL* HĐ.

Ipſi canonici haɓ.ıııı.hiđ.Ibi.ııı.clerici hñt.ııı.uiłłos

cū.ıııı.cař.   Vał.xv..ſoliđ.

Ipſe eꝗs Walteri habuit .ı.hiđ Waleſcā.T.R.E.uaſtatā.

Ibi ſunt.ıı.cař in dñio.7 ııı.uiłłi 7 vı.borđ 7 ıı.alii hoēs

cū.vı.cař.   Vał.xL.ſoliđ.

Hui tr̄æ maxima pars.ē in defenſu regis.

182 d

Circa portā *HEREFORDIE* habuit Walŧ eꝗs tras T.R.E

quæ ñ geldaɓ.Ibi hŧ Roɓt eꝗs.ıııı.cař in dñio.7 ıı.uiłłos

7 v.buros cū.v.cař.7 dimiđ.Valuit xL.ſoł.modo.ıııı.liɓ.

De hac tra teñ.ıı.c̨apellani eꝗi aliꝗ partē.7 uñ miles.ı.hiđ.

hi hñt in dñio.vı.cař.7 uñ uiłłm 7 vı.borđ.7 ıı.ſeruos

7 ııı.ancillas.   Inŧ toŧ uał.Lx.vıı.ſoliđ.

INTER TOTŪ SVNT IN EPISCOPATV.CCC.HIDÆ.quāuis de

xxx.ııı.hiđ hoēs eꝗi rationē ñ dederint. IN *GREITREWES* HĐ.

Sc̄s PETRVS de hereford teñ *FROME*.Walter de Laci deđ æcclæ

c̄ceſſu.W.regis.Ibi.ı.hida 7 una v̄.7 gelđ.Eduuj cilt tenuit

7 poterat ire quo uoleɓ.In dñio.ē.ı.cař.7 ııı.uiłłi.7 ııı.borđ

cū.ıı.cař.Ibi.vıı.ſerui.

Valuit.xv.ſoliđ.Modo.xxx.ſoliđ.

52 In *WINETUNE* ½ hide. ... A rider holds this; he has 1 plough
there, and
    2 villagers.
The value is and was 5s.

In CUTSTHORN Hundred
53 In CREDENHILL 2 hides.
    2 villagers with 1 plough pay 5s in dues.
Value 20s.

In STRADDLE Hundred
54 In (The) MOOR 1 hide; value 5s.

55 The canons have 4 hides themselves. 3 clerks have
    3 villagers with 4 ploughs.
Value 15s.

56 Bishop Walter himself had 1 Welsh hide, laid waste before 1066.
2 ploughs in lordship;
    3 villagers, 6 smallholders and 2 other men with 6 ploughs.
Value 40s.
    The largest part of this land is in the King's Enclosure.

57 Around the town of HEREFORD Bishop Walter had lands before   182 d
1066 which did not pay tax. Bishop Robert has 4 ploughs
in lordship and
    2 villagers and 5 boors with 5½ ploughs.
The value was 40s; now £4.
    Two chaplains of the Bishop hold some part of this land;
a man-at-arms (holds) 1 hide; they have 6 ploughs in lordship and
    1 villager, 6 smallholders, 2 male and 3 female slaves.
In total, value 67s.

IN TOTAL THERE ARE 300 HIDES IN THE BISHOPRIC, although the
Bishop's men have given no account of 33 hides.

In GREYTREE Hundred
58 St. Peter's of Hereford holds (Priors) FROME. Walter of Lacy gave
it to the church with King William's consent. 1 hide and 1 virgate;
they pay tax. Edwy Young held it; he could go where he would.
In lordship 1 plough;
    3 villagers and 3 smallholders with 2 ploughs. 7 slaves.
The value was 15s; now 30s.

.III. TERRA ÆCCLÆ DE CORMELIJS. *IN BREMESESE HVND.*

Eccla S mariæ de Cormelijs ten̄.ii.hid in *CHINGESTVNE*.7 geld.

in Glouuecſcire 7 opant̄.ſed in iſto *HVND* ad placita c̄ueniuɴ q̄ ibi maneɴ.

ut rectū faciant 7 accipiant.   ECCLE DE LIRA.

.II. Eccla S marie DE LIRA h̄ dimid hid in *MERCHELAI.*

TERRA S petri DE GLOWEC. *IN BREMESSE HD.*

.V. Eccla S petri de Glouuec ten̄ *BRVNTVNE*.Ibi.ii.

hidæ.Vna geld.alia.ē liba á geldo 7 ab om̄i c̄ſuetudine.

In hac libera hida ſunt.iii.car̄ in dn̄io.7 v.uilti 7 v.bord.

cū.v.car̄.Ibi.xvi.ſerui.   Val.iiii.lib.

In altera hida.ē un̄ uilts 7 un̄ bord.cū.i.car̄.7 molin̄

de.viii.ſolid.   Val.x.ſolid.

Ipſa æccla ten̄ *LECCE*.dono Walterij de Łaci.Anſgot tenuit T.R.E.

Ibi.i.hid geld.Hic poterat ire quo uoleb.In dn̄io eſt.i.car̄.

7 ii.ſerui.7 un̄ bord.Val 7 ualuit.x.ſolid.Vna car̄ plus poteſt.ec̄.

TERRA SC̄I GVTHLACI. *IN BREMESSE HD.*

.VI. Eccla S GVTHLACI ten̄ *BRVNTVNE*.Ibi.i.hida geld.

Tra.ē.ii.car̄.Waſta fuit.7 ē.Tam̄ redd.v.ſolid. *IN GREITREV*

Ipſa æccla tenuit *DERMENTVNE*.7 Æſtan canon   *HVND.*

teneb.Ibi.i.hida geld.Walter ten̄ m̄ 7 h̄ ibi.i.car̄.7 un̄

bord 7 un̄ ſeruū.   Val 7 ualuit.x.ſolid.

3   LAND OF THE CHURCH OF CORMEILLES

In BROMSASH Hundred

1   St. Mary's Church of Cormeilles holds 2 hides in KINGSTONE; they pay tax and do service in Gloucestershire, but the men who live there come to pleas in this Hundred to give and receive right.

4   [LAND] OF THE CHURCH OF LYRE

[In WINSTREE Hundred]

1   St. Mary's Church of Lyre has ½ hide in (Much) MARCLE. [Value ...] .

5   LAND OF ST. PETER'S OF GLOUCESTER

In BROMSASH Hundred

1   St. Peter's Church of Gloucester holds BRAMPTON (Abbotts). 2 hides; 1 pays tax; the other is free from tax and from every customary due. In this free hide 3 ploughs in lordship;
     5 villagers and 5 smallholders with 5 ploughs. 16 slaves.
Value £4.
     In the other hide 1 villager and 1 smallholder with 1 plough.
     A mill at 8s.
Value 10s.

2   The Church itself holds LEA by gift of Walter of Lacy. Ansgot held it before 1066. 1 hide which pays tax. He could go where he would. In lordship 1 plough; 2 slaves;
     1 smallholder.
The value is and was 10s.
     1 more plough possible.

6   LAND OF ST. GUTHLAC'S

In BROMSASH Hundred

1   St. Guthlac's Church holds BRAMPTON (Abbotts). 1 hide which pays tax. Land for 2 ploughs.
It was and is waste. However it pays 5s.

In GREYTREE Hundred

2   The Church itself held DORMINGTON. Estan the canon held it. 1 hide which pays tax. Walter holds it now; he has 1 plough there and
     1 smallholder and 1 slave.
The value is and was 10s.

Ipſa æcclā teñ *HINETVNE*. Ibi . I . hida gelđ

In dñio . ē . I . car̄ . 7 IIII . uiłłi cũ . II . car̄ 7 dimiđ . Ibi . III . ſerui.

7 IIII . cot . 7 moliñ de . IIII . ſoliđ.   Val . xxv . ſot.

Ipſa æcclā teñ *TINGEHALLE*.   *IN TORNELAVVES HĐ.*

Ibi . I . hida gelđ . In dñio ſunt . II . car̄ . 7 IIII . uiłłi 7 I . borđ

cũ . II . car̄ . Ibi . v . ſerui.   Val 7 ualuit . xxx . ſoliđ.

✠ Ipſa æcclā teñ *FELTONE* . Ibi . III . hidæ . gelđ p̄t dim̄ hiđ.

In dñio ſunt . III . car̄ . 7 v . ſerui . 7 uñ borđ . Ibi . I . francigena

cũ . I . car̄ . redđ . vi . ſoliđ . Valuit . Lx . ſoliđ . Modo . xL . ſot.

Ipſa æcclā teñ *MOCHES* . Ibi . II . hiđ gelđ . *IN STRATFORD HĐ.*

Ibi ſunt . vi . uiłłi 7 III . borđ . cũ . IIII . car̄ . Ibi . I . franciḡ.

Val . xxx . ſoliđ.   *IN ELSEDVNE HVNĐ.*

Ipſa æcclā teñ *ELMELIE* . 7 de Laci Roger de ea . Ibi . IIII . hiđ gelđ.

T̄ra . ē . vIII . car̄ . Alteri uillæ hõēs laboran̄ in hac uilla.

7 reddt . xxxvII . ſoliđ 7 vIII . denar̄.

Ipſa æcclā teñ *MIDEVRDE* . 7 Drogo de ea . Ibi . I . hida gelđ.

In dñio . ē una car̄ . 7 II . bouarij 7 III . borđ cũ . I . car̄.

Val . x . ſoliđ.

Ipſa æcclā teñ *WITENIE* . 7 Herald de ea . Ibi . IIII . hidæ

gelđ . Waſtæ ſun̄ 7 fuer̄ . Tam̄ redđ . vi . ſoliđ.

✠ Ipſa æcclā teñ *HOPE* . Ibi . II . hidæ . Vna gelđ . alia non . In dñio ſun̄ . II.

car̄ . 7 uñ uiłł 7 II . borđ cũ . I . car̄ 7 dimiđ . Ibi . III . ſerui . Val . xxx . ſoliđ.

In *VLFEGIE HĐ* . habuit S̄ Gutłac . I . hiđ *WESTELET* . Vaſta fuit 7 eſt.

8ff

The Church itself holds
[in THORNLAW Hundred]
3 HINTON. 1 hide which pays tax. ... In lordship 1 plough;
4 villagers with 2½ ploughs. 3 slaves and 4 cottagers.
A mill at 4s.
Value 25s.

in THORNLAW Hundred
4 THINGHILL. 1 hide which pays tax. In lordship 2 ploughs;
4 villagers and 1 smallholder with 2 ploughs. 5 slaves.
The value is and was 30s.

↗ (6,5 is entered at the foot of col. 182d, directed to its proper place by transposition signs)

6 FELTON. 3 hides which pay tax, except for ½ hide. In lordship 3
ploughs; 5 slaves;
1 smallholder. 1 Frenchman with 1 plough who pays 6s.
The value was 60s; now 40s.

in STRETFORD Hundred
7 MOCCAS. 2 hides which pay tax.
6 villagers and 3 smallholders with 4 ploughs. 1 Frenchman.
Value 30s.

in ELSDON Hundred
8 ALMELEY. Roger of Lacy holds from it. 4 hides which pay tax.
Land for 8 ploughs. The men of another village work in this
village; they pay 37s 8d.

9 'MIDDLEWOOD'. Drogo holds from it. 1 hide which pays tax.
In lordship 1 plough;
2 ploughmen and 3 smallholders with 1 plough.
Value 10s.

10 WHITNEY. Harold holds from it. 4 hides which pay tax. They are
and were waste. However, they pay 6s.

(Misplaced entry, directed to its proper place by transposition signs)

↗5 The Church itself holds HOPE (under Dinmore). 2 hides; 1 pays
tax, the other does not. In lordship 2 ploughs;
1 villager and 2 smallholders with 1½ ploughs. 3 slaves.
Value 30s.

In WOLPHY Hundred
11 St. Guthlac's had 1 hide, WESTELET. It was and is waste.

a

.VII. TERRA NIGELLI MEDICI. IN GREITREWES HD.

De terra S Gvtlaci ten Nigellus BERTOLDESTREV.

Leflet tenuit. Ibi . ii . hidæ, una geldat teſte comitatu.

In dñio ſunt . iii . car . 7 iii . ſerui . 7 un ꝑpoſit cū . i . car.

Ibi ꝑtū.　　　　Tra . ē . iii . car.

Valeb . Lx . ſolid . Modo . L . ſolid.

Ad hoc ꝳ adjacet una Bereuuich . Lefled tenuit.

Ibi . ii . hidæ . una geld teſte comitatu . Ibi hт Nigellus

in dñio . ii . car . 7 ii . ſeruos . 7 i . bord . 7 un Radman cū tra

ſine car.　　　Val 7 ualuit . xL . ſolid . IN TORNELAVS

Iſd Nigel ten BOLELEI . 7 Radulf de eo.　　　ʃ HVND.

Leflet tenuit . Ibi . i . hida libera a geldo 7 regis ſeruitio.

In dñio ſunt . ii . car . 7 ii . bouarij . Tra . ē , iiii . car.

Valuit . xxv . ſolid . Modo . xx . ſolid.

Iſd Nigel ten SVTVNE . Leflet tenuit.

Ibi . ii . hidæ geld . In dñio . ē una car . 7 ii . bouar . 7 iiii .

bord 7 ii . cot cū . i . car . 7 un francig cū . i . car.

Ibi ꝑtū bob . 7 moliñ quē ten Hugo de Nigello . redd . viii .

ſolid . 7 viii . ſtiches anguill.

T.R.E , ualb . Lx . ſolid . 7 poſt . xxx . ſol . modo . ʹL . ſolid.

Hoc ꝳ tenuit Hugo tꝑr Willi

Iſd Nigel ten SVTVNE . Spirites tenuit . Ibi . i . hida geld.

Tra . ē . ii . car . In dñio ſunt . 7 iiii . ſerui . 7 un bord . 7 mo

linū de . x . ſolid 7 vii . ſtiches anguill . 7 ꝑtū bob . tant.

Val 7 ualuit . xxx . ſolid.

Iſd Nigel ten MAGE . Leflet tenuit de S Guthlaco.

Ibi . ii . hidæ geld.　　　Ibi ſunt . vii . uilli cū . v . car.

Valuit . xL . ſolid . modo . xxx.

a

In GREYTREE Hundred

1   Nigel the Doctor holds BARTESTREE from the land of St. Guthlac's. Leofled held it. 2 hides; 1 of them pays tax according to the testimony of the County (Court). In lordship 3 ploughs; 3 slaves; 1 reeve with 1 plough.
Meadow there. ... Land for 3 ploughs.
The value was 60s; now 50s.
An outlier is attached to this manor. Leofled held it. 2 hides; 1 of them pays tax according to the testimony of the County (Court). Nigel has 2 ploughs in lordship and 2 slaves and 1 smallholder and 1 rider with land without a plough.
The value is and was 40s.

Nigel also holds
in THORNLAW Hundred

2   BOWLEY. Ralph holds from him. Leofled held it. 1 hide free from tax and the King's service. In lordship 2 ploughs; 2 ploughmen. Land for 4 ploughs.
The value was 25s; now 20s.

3   SUTTON. Leofled held it. 2 hides which pay tax. In lordship 1 plough;
2 ploughmen, 4 smallholders and 2 cottagers with 1 plough; 1 Frenchman with 1 plough.
Meadow for the oxen; a mill which Hugh Donkey holds from Nigel pays 8s and 8 sticks of eels.
Value before 1066, 60s; later 30s; now 50s.
Hugh held this manor in William's time. ...

4   SUTTON. Spirtes the priest held it. 1 hide which pays tax. Land for 2 ploughs; they are in lordship; 4 slaves; 1 smallholder.
A mill at 10s and 7 sticks of eels; meadow only for the oxen.
The value is and was 30s.

5   MAUND. Leofled held it from St. Guthlac's. 2 hides which pay tax. ... 7 villagers with 5 ploughs.
The value was 40s; now 30[s].

Isd Nigell ten TINGEHELE.7 Goisfrid de eo. Spirtes
tenuit. Ibi. ı, hida ñ geld. In dñio sunt. ıı. car. 7 ıııı. serui.
Val 7 ualuit. xx. solid.   IN DUNRE HUND,

Isd Nigel ten MOCHES 7 Ansfrid de eo. Ernuin tenuit
de S Gutlaco. Ibi, e una hida. 7 in dñio. ı. car.
Val xv, solid.   IN PLEGELIET HD.

Isd Nigel ten COLGRE. Spirtes tenuit. Ibi, ııı. hidæ geld.
In dñio sunt. ııı. car. 7 vıı. serui, 7 ıı. bord. 7 un lib hõ cũ, ı,
car 7. ıı. bord.   Valuit. L. sot. modo. XL. sot.

Isd Nigel ten AWENEBURI. Spirtes tenuit. Ibi. vı, hidæ
geld.   In dñio sunt. ııı. car. 7 ıııı. serui. 7 xxıı. uitti
7 ıı. pbri 7 ı. bord cũ. xıı. car, Ibi molin nil redd
Val 7 ualuit, c, solid,

.VIII. ^{183 b} TERRA RADULFI DE TODENI,

R ADULFUS De Todeni ten castellũ de CLIFORD,
Witts com fecit illud in Wasta tra. quã teneb Bruning
T.R,E. Ibi ht Radulf tra ad. ııı, car. sed ñ est nisi. ı. car,
Istud castellũ. e de regno Angliæ, non subjacet alicui
hundret neq in csuetudine,
Gislebt uicecom ten illud ad firmã 7 burgũ, 7 car
De toto redd. LX. solid,
In hac castellaria ten Rogeri tra ad. ıııı. car,
7 Gislebt ad. xıı. car, 7 Drogo ad. v. car, 7 Herbt ad. ıı. car,
Hi hñt in dñio. ıx. car. 7 xvı. burgses, 7 xııı. bord.
7 v. uualenses. 7 vı. seruos. 7 ıııı, ancillas. 7 molin redd
ııı. modios annonæ. 7 ıııı, bouar ibi sunt, Hoes hñt, ııı. car.
Int tot qd hñt ual vııı. lib 7 v, sot.
Et isti 7 quicunq alij hñt aliqd ibi, de Radulfo ten. IN HEZETRE ^{HD.}
Isd Rad ten LEINE, 7 Scs Petrus de castellion de eo.
Elmar 7 Ulchete tenuer p. ıı. M, 7 poteraʒ ire quo uoleb,

6 THINGHILL. Geoffrey holds from him. Spirtes held it. 1 hide which does not pay tax. In lordship 2 ploughs; 4 slaves.
The value is and was 20s.

in DINEDOR Hundred
7 MOCCAS. Ansfrid holds from him. Ernwin held from St. Guthlac's. 1 hide. In lordship 1 plough.
Value 15s.

in PLEGELGATE Hundred
8 (Little) COWARNE. Spirtes held it. 3 hides which pay tax. In lordship 3 ploughs; 7 slaves;
2 smallholders and 1 free man with 1 plough; 2 smallholders.
The value was 50s; now 40s.

9 AVENBURY. Spirtes held it. 6 hides which pay tax. In lordship 3 ploughs; 4 slaves;
22 villagers, 2 priests and 1 smallholder with 12 ploughs.
A mill which pays nothing.
The value is and was 100s.

8   LAND OF RALPH OF TOSNY   183 b

[CASTLE]
1 Ralph of Tosny holds the castle of CLIFFORD. Earl William built it on waste land, which Browning held before 1066. Ralph has land there for 3 ploughs, but there is only 1 plough. This castle is in the kingdom of England and not subject to any Hundred or customary dues. Gilbert the Sheriff holds it at a revenue, both the Borough and the plough. ... From the whole he pays 60s.
In this castlery Roger holds land for 4 ploughs; Gilbert for 12 ploughs; Drogo for 5 ploughs; Herbert for 2 ploughs. They have 9 ploughs in lordship and
16 burgesses, 13 smallholders, 5 Welshmen, 6 male and 4 female slaves.
A mill which pays 3 measures of corn.
4 ploughmen there. The men have 3 ploughs.
In total, the value of what they have is £8 5s.
These men and whoever else has anything there, hold from Ralph.

Ralph also holds
in HAZELTREE Hundred
2 MONKLAND. St. Peter's of Castellion holds from him. Aelmer and Ulfketel held it as two manors; they could go where they would.

Ibi.v.hidæ gelđ. Vna ex his n̄ gelđb̄.q̇a in dn̄io erat.

Ibi ſunt.ıı.car̄,7 x.uiłłi 7 vııı.borđ cū.vıı.car̄,Ibi.ııı.ſerui.

7 un lib̄ bouarius.7 moliñ redđ.xı.ſoł,7 xxv.ſtiches anguiłł.

De p̃to.v.ſoł p̃t paſtū boum.

T.R,R,ualb̄.vı.lib̄.modo.vıı.lib̄.   *IN ELSEDVN HĎ.*

Iſđ Rađ ten̄ *WILLAVESLEGE.7 WIDFERDESTVNE*.Herald

tenuit.Ibi.ıııı.hiđ gelđ.In dn̄io ſunt,ıııı,car̄,7 xvıı.borđ

cū.ııı.car̄.7 ııı.libī hōes cū.ııı.car̄.Ibi.vııı,ſerui.

T.R.E.uuaſt erat.7 x.ſoł ualb̄.Modo.vıı.lib̄.

Iſđ Rađ ten̄ ibidē.ı.hiđ gelđ.Eluuard tenuit.7 poterat

ire quo uoleb̄.Vn̄ Walenſis ten̄ de Radulfo.7 ibi h̄t.vııı.

hōes hn̄tes.ı.car̄ 7 dimiđ.   Vał.xıı.ſoliđ.

Iſđ Rađ ten̄ *CHABENORE*.Ibi,ııı,hidæ *IN STRATFORD HĎ.*

gelđ.Ernui 7 Haduuiñ 7 Æluuard tenuer̄ ꝑ.ııı,Man̄.

In dn̄io ſunt,ıı.car̄.7 ıııı.uiłłi 7 vı.borđ 7 ı.fab̄ cū.ııı.car̄.

Ibi.vı.ſerui,7 p̃tū bobʒ tant̄.Silua ṇil redđ.7 adhuc.ııı.

car̄ plus ibi poſſent,ee.

In eađ uilla jacet tcia pars uni hidæ.7 ibi eſt.ı.car̄.

Tot̄ T.R.E,ualb̄,ıııı,lib̄ 7 x,ſoł.modo.cx.ſoł.

Iſđ Rađ ten̄ *MANITVNE*.7 Roger̄ de eo. *IN STÆPLESET HĎ.*

Herald tenuit.Ibi,v.hidæ gelđ.Ex his.ıı.teneb̄ Ælmar,

ꝑ M̄,7 poterat ire quo uoleb̄.

In dn̄io ſunt,ııı.car̄.7 v.uiłłi 7 vı.borđ cū.ııı.car̄.

T.R.E.ualb̄.ɪx.ſoliđ,modo.ıııı.lib̄. *IN DVNRE HĎ.*

Iſđ Rađ ten̄ *DVNRE*.7 Wiłłs 7 Iłłbt̄ fr̄ ej de eo.Godric

7 Vlfac tenuer̄ ꝑ.ıı.M̄,Ibi.vı.hidæ gelđ.

In dn̄io ſunt,ıı.car̄.7 xııı.uiłłi cū ꝑpoſito 7 v.borđ.cū.xıı.

car̄.Ibi.ıııı.bouarij 7 ııı.ancillæ.7 moliñ de.xxvııı.den̄.

Silua huj h̄t rex in dn̄io.In aqua ū̇ nemo piſcat̄ ſine lictia.

T.R.E.ualb̄ hi.ıı.M̄.vıı.lib̄ 7 v.ſoł,Modo ſimilit̄.

5 hides which pay tax. One of these did not pay tax because it
was in lordship. 2 ploughs there.
> 10 villagers and 8 smallholders with 7 ploughs. 3 slaves
> and 1 free ploughman.
> A mill which pays 11s and 25 sticks of eels. From the meadow
> 5s besides pasture for the oxen.

Value before 1066 £6; now £7.

in ELSDON Hundred

3 WILLERSLEY and WINFORTON. Earl Harold held them. 4 hides which
pay tax. In lordship 4 ploughs;
> 17 smallholders with 3 ploughs; 3 free men with 3 ploughs.
> 8 slaves.

Before 1066 it was waste and the value was 10s; now £7.

4 there also 1 hide which pays tax. Alfward held it; he could go
where he would. A Welshman holds from Ralph; he has there
> 8 men who have 1½ ploughs.

Value 12s.

in STRETFORD Hundred

5 CHADNOR. 3 hides which pay tax. Ernwy, Hadwin and Alfward
held it as three manors. In lordship 2 ploughs;
> 4 villagers, 6 smallholders and 1 smith with 3 ploughs.
> 6 slaves; meadow only for the oxen; woodland which pays
> nothing; a further 3 more ploughs would be possible there.
> In the same village lies the third part of 1 hide; 1 plough there.

Value of the whole before 1066 £4 10s; now 110s.

in STAPLE Hundred

6 MONNINGTON (on Wye). Roger holds from him. Earl Harold held it.
5 hides which pay tax. Of these, Aelmer held 2 as a manor; he
could go where he would. In lordship 3 ploughs;
> 5 villagers and 6 smallholders with 3 ploughs.

Value before 1066, 60s; now £4.

in DINEDOR Hundred

7 DINEDOR. William and his brother Ilbert hold from him. Godric
and Wulfheah held it as two manors. 6 hides which pay tax.
In lordship 2 ploughs;
> 13 villagers with a reeve and 5 smallholders with 12 ploughs.
> 4 ploughmen and 3 female slaves.
> A mill at 28d; the King has the woodland of this (manor) in
> lordship. No-one fishes in the river without permission.

Value of these two manors before 1066 £7 5s; now the same.

Iſd Raď ten *STOCHES*.Eddied tenuit. *IN RADELAV HĎ.*

7 poterat ire quo uolɓ.Ibi.ɪɪ.hidæ 7 una v̆ gelđ.

In dnio ſunt.ɪɪɪ.car.7 vɪ.uiłłi 7 v.borđ 7 ɪɪɪɪ.cot.cū.ɪɪɪɪ,

car.Ibi.vɪɪ.ſerui.7 adhuc.ɪ.car plus poſſet.c̄ɇ.ibi.

T.R.E.ualɓ.vɪ.liɓ.Modo.c.v.ſolid.

De hac tra deđ Raď dimiđ hidā cuidā ſuo miliṭi.

7 iđo ꝏ.min reddit.

Iſd Raď ten unā v̆|in *RADELAV HĎ.*7 Bȓ̄toalđ de eo.

Vluui tenuit,7 poterat ire quo uolɓ.II tra gelđ.*SPTVNE.*

Ibi.ē dimiđ car.7 un uiłłs 7 un borđ.   Val.ɪɪɪɪ.ſoł.

Iſd Raď ten *STOCHES*.Eddied tenuit.7 quó uolɓ ire poterat.

Ibi.ɪɪ.hidæ 7 dimiđ gelđ.In dnio ſunt.ɪɪ.car.7 vɪ.uiłłi 7 vɪ.

borđ 7 ɪɪ.pɓri cū.vɪɪ.car.Ibi.vɪɪ.ſerui.7 moliñ de.x.ſoliđ.

T.R.E.ualɓ.vɪɪ.liɓ.Modo.vɪ.liɓ.v.ſoł miñ.

.ɪX. TERRA RADVLFI DE MORTEMER *IN HEZETRE HVNĎ.*

RADVLFVS De Mortemer ten Caſtełłū *WIGEMORE.*

Wiłłs com fecit illud in Waſta tra quæ uocat *MERESTVN.*

quā teneɓ Gunuert T.R.E.Ibi.ɪɪ.hidæ gelđ.

In dnio h̄t Raď.ɪɪ.car.7 ɪɪɪɪ.ſeruos.

Burgū qđ ibi eſt.redđ.vɪɪ.liɓ.   *IN HEZETRE HVNĎ.*

Iſd Raď ten *DVNTVNE.*7 Oidelarđ de eo. Ælmar 7 Vlchet

tenueȓ ꝑ.ɪɪ.ꝏ.7 poterant ire quó uoleɓ.Ibi.ɪɪɪɪ.hidæ.

Duæ ex his n̄ gelđ.In dnio ſunt.ɪɪ.car.7 ɪɪɪ.uiłł 7 ɪɪɪ.borđ

cū dimiđ car.Ibi.vɪ.ſerui 7 piſcaria.Silua dimiđ leuū łg.

7 v.q̇ꝗ lat.Ibi ſunt.ɪɪ.haiæ.   Valɓ.xxx.ſoł.M tntđ.

Hanc tra deđ.W.com Turſtino flandrenſi.

in RADLOW Hundred

8   WESTHIDE. Edith held it; she could go where she would. 2 hides
and 1 virgate which pay tax. In lordship 3 ploughs;
>6 villagers, 5 smallholders and 4 cottagers with 4 ploughs.
>7 slaves; a further 1 more plough would be possible there.

Value before 1066 £6; now 105s.
>Ralph gave ½ hide of this land to one of his men-at-arms;
therefore the manor pays less.

9   in RADLOW Hundred 1 virgate of land. Brictwold the priest holds 183 c
from him. Wulfwy held it as a manor; he could go where he would.
This land pays tax; it is called ASHPERTON. ½ plough there;
>1 villager and 1 smallholder.

Value 4s.

10   STOKE (Edith). Edith held it; she could go where she would.
2½ hides which pay tax. In lordship 2 ploughs;
>6 villagers, 6 smallholders and 2 priests with 7 ploughs.
>7 slaves; a mill at 10s.

Value before 1066 £7; now £6, less 5s.

9   LAND OF RALPH OF MORTIMER

In HAZELTREE Hundred

1   Ralph of Mortimer holds WIGMORE Castle. Earl William built it on
waste land which is called MERESTUN, which Gunfrid held before
1066. 2 hides which pay tax. Ralph has 2 ploughs in lordship and
4 slaves.

The Borough which is there pays £7.

Ralph also holds
in HAZELTREE Hundred

2   DOWNTON (on the Rock). Odilard holds from him. Aelmer and
Ulfketel held it as two manors; they could go where they would.
4 hides; of these, 2 do not pay tax. In lordship 2 ploughs;
>3 villagers and 3 smallholders with ½ plough.
>6 slaves; a fishery; woodland ½ league long and 5 furlongs
>>wide. 2 hedged enclosures there.

The value was 30s; now as much.

Earl William gave this land to Thurstan of Flanders.

Ifd Rad ten *BORATVNE*. ^{Salvage}Edric tenuit. Ibi. III. hidæ 7 una v.

In dñio funt. III. car. 7 VII. uitl 7 IIII. bord, cū. III. car, Ibi, IX,

ferui. 7 paululū filuæ.

Val 7 ualuit. XL. folid.

Iíd Rad ten *HESINTVNE*. Quinq̖ hões tenuer ꝑ. III. ꝏ̄

Ibi. III. hidæ geld. In dñio funt. II. car. 7 V. uitli 7 II. bord cū. III.

car. Wafta fuit h̄ tra. Modo ual. XXX. folid.

Ifd Rad ten *ELINTVNE*. Edric tenuit. Ibi. II. hidæ.

In dñio funt. II. car. 7 VI. uitl 7 III. bord 7 II. Radchen. Int oms

hūt. III. car. Ibi. IIII. ferui. 7 II. quarent filuæ.

Valuit. XII. fot. modo. XX. folid.

Ifd Rad ten *LENHALE*. Azor tenuit. Ibi. II. hidæ geld.

In dñio funt. II. car. 7 VII. uitli 7 X. bord 7 II. radman. 7 un fab

cū. V. car int oms. Ibi. I. feruus. 7 III. bouarij libi.

T.R.E. ualb. XX. fot. modo. XL. folid.

Ifd Rad ten *LINTEHALE*. Eddied regina tenuit. Ibi. IIII.

hidæ geld. In dñio funt. III. car. 7 X. uitli 7 VII. bord 7 III.

radchen cū. VII. car. Ibi. VI. bouarij libi. 7 molin de. XXX.fot.

T.R.E. ualb. L. folid. Modo. C. folid.

Ifd Rad ten *LECWE*. Elfi tenuit. 7 poterat ire quo uolb.

Ibi dimid hida geld. Ibi h̄t. I. car cū. III. bord. 7 alia car

poffet. ee. Val 7 ualuit. V. folid.

Ifd Rad ten *CAMEHOP*. Elmar tenuit. 7 potuit ire quo uoluit.

Ibi. I. hida geld. In dñio eft. I. car. 7 VI. bord 7 faber cū. II. car.

Ibi. I. feruus. 7 un lib bouari. 7 paruula filua. Val. X. fot.

Ifd Rad ten *SCEPEDVNE*. Edict tenuit.

Ibi, IIII. hidæ geld. In dñio funt. III. car. 7 XX. uitli 7 XX. bord

7 un Radchen 7 un fab cū. IX. car. Ibi. VI. ferui. Siluæ. I. Leuua

int lḡ 7 lat. Valb. VI. lib. modo. VII. lib.

3   BURRINGTON. Edric the Wild held it. 3 hides and 1 virgate.
In lordship 3 ploughs;
    7 villagers and 4 smallholders with 3 ploughs.
    9 slaves; very little woodland.
The value is and was 40s.

4   ASTON. Five men held it as three manors. 3 hides which pay tax.
In lordship 2 ploughs;
    5 villagers and 2 smallholders with 3 ploughs.
This land was waste. Value now 30s.

5   ELTON. Edric held it. 2 hides. In lordship 2 ploughs;
    6 villagers, 3 smallholders and 2 riding men; between them
      they have 3 ploughs.
    4 slaves; woodland, 2 furlongs.
The value was 12s; now 20s.

6   LEINTHALL. Azor held it. 2 hides which pay tax.
In lordship 2 ploughs;
    7 villagers, 10 smallholders, 2 riders and 1 smith
      with 5 ploughs between them. 1 slave; 3 free ploughmen.
Value before 1066, 20s; now 40s.

7   LEINTHALL. Queen Edith held it. 4 hides which pay tax.
In lordship 3 ploughs;
    10 villagers, 7 smallholders and 3 riding men with 7 ploughs.
    6 free ploughmen; a mill at 30s.
Value before 1066, 50s; now 100s.

8   LYE. Alfsi held it; he could go where he would. ½ hide which pays
tax. He has 1 plough there, with
    3 smallholders; another plough would be possible.
The value is and was 5s.

9   COVENHOPE. Aelmer held it; he could go where he would. 1 hide
which pays tax. In lordship 1 plough;
    6 smallholders and a smith with 2 ploughs. 1 slave
      and 1 free ploughman.
    A very small wood.
Value 10s.

10   SHOBDON. Edith held it. ... 4 hides which pay tax. In lordship 3
ploughs;
    20 villagers, 20 smallholders, 1 riding man and 1 smith   183 d
      with 9 ploughs.
    6 slaves; woodland, 1 league in both length and width.
The value was £6; now £7.

Isd Rad ten STANTVNE. Edric tenuit. Ibi. ii. hidæ geld.
In dnio sunt. ii. car. 7 vi. uitti 7 iii. bord cu. iiii. car.
Wastu fuit. Modo ual. xl. solid.

Isd Rad ten LEIDECOTE. Bricsmar tenuit. 7 poterat ire
quo uoleb. Ibi. i. hida geld. Ibi maneǰ. iii. hntes. i. car.
7 alia car posset ibi. ee.   Val. x. solid 7 vi. denar.

Isd Rad ten In PELELEI. ii. hid. In ORTVNE. ii. hid. In MILDE
TVNE. iii. hid. In WESTVNE. ii. hid. Int tot. ix. hidæ suǰ
wastæ in marcha de Wales. Terra. e. xviii. car.

Septe ꝿ fuer. 7 qnq̨ taini tenuer.

Isd Rad ht. lvii. acs træ 7 tota silua in LEGA ꝿ Grifini.

Isd Rad ten ELBVRGELEGA. 7 Ricard   IN ELSEDVN HD.
de eo. Edric tenuit. 7 poterat ire quo uoleb. Ibi. i. hida geld.
In dnio sunt. ii. car. 7 iii. uitti 7 vi. bord cu. iiii. car.
Wast fuit. Modo ual. xxx. solid. IN STRATFORD HD.

Isd Rad ten BVRLEI. 7 Ricard de eo. Edric 7 Ruillic
7 Leuiet tenuer p. iii. ꝿ. 7 poterant ire quo uoleb.
Ibi. ii. hidæ 7 iii. virg træ. geld. In dnio sunt. ii. car.
7 iii. uitti 7 un radchen 7 i. bord cu. iii. car. Silua redd. ii. sol.
H tria ꝿ T.R.E. ualb. iiii. lib. Modo. l. solid.

Isd Rad ten BVRLEI 7 Ricard de eo. Grinchetel tenuit.
7 poterat ire q̨ uolb. Ibi dimid hida geld. In dnio. e dimid
car. 7 ii. serui.   Val 7 ualuit. iii. sol. IN PLEGELIET HD.

Isd Rad ten. ii. hid in VLFERLAV. Aluuin tenuit.
H tra geld. In dnio ht. i. car. 7 un uittm cu dim car.
7 adhuc. iii. car plus possunt. ee.   Val. x. solid.

Isd Rad ten ALRETVNE. Eddid tenuit. IN VLFEI HVND.
Ibi. iiii. hidæ geld. In dnio sunt. iiii. car. 7 xi. uitt 7 xv. bord.
7 pposit 7 un radman. Int oms. vii. car. Ibi. vi. serui. 7 v. bouarij.
7 un faber.

T.R.E. ualb. vii. lib. Modo. c. solid.

11 STAUNTON (on Arrow). Edric held it. 2 hides which pay tax.
In lordship 2 ploughs;
6 villagers and 3 smallholders with 4 ploughs.
It was waste. Value now 40s.

12 LEDICOT. Brictmer held it; he could go where he would. 1 hide
which pays tax.
3 [men?] live there who have 1 plough; another plough
would be possible there.
Value 10s 6d.

13 in PILLETH 2 hides; in HARPTON 2 hides; in MIDDLETON 3 hides;
in WESTON 2 hides.

In total 9 hides are waste in the Welsh March. Land for
18 ploughs. There were seven manors; five thanes held them.

14 Ralph also has 57 acres of land and all the woodland in
Gruffydd's manor of LYE.

Ralph also holds
in ELSDON Hundred
15 KINNERSLEY. Richard holds from him. Edric held it; he could go
where he would. 1 hide which pays tax. In lordship 2 ploughs;
3 villagers and 6 smallholders with 4 ploughs.
It was waste. Value now 30s.

in STRETFORD Hundred
16 BIRLEY. Richard holds from him. Edric, Ruillic and Leofgeat held
it as three manors; they could go where they would. 2 hides and
3 virgates of land which pay tax. In lordship 2 ploughs;
3 villagers, 1 riding man and 1 smallholder with 3 ploughs.
Woodland which pays 2s.
Value of these three manors before 1066 £4; now 50s.

17 BIRLEY. Richard holds from him. Grimketel held it; he could go
where he would. ½ hide which pays tax. In lordship ½ plough;
2 slaves.
The value is and was 3s.

in PLEGELGATE Hundred
18 in WOLFERLOW 2 hides. Alwin held them. This land pays tax.
He has 1 plough in lordship and
1 villager with ½ plough; a further 3 more ploughs possible.
Value 10s.

in WOLPHY Hundred
19 ORLETON. Edith held it. 4 hides which pay tax. In lordship
4 ploughs;
11 villagers, 15 smallholders, a reeve and 1 rider; between
them 7 ploughs. 6 slaves, 5 ploughmen and 1 smith.
Value before 1066 £7; now 100s.

.X. ITERRA ROGERIJ DE LACI. *IN CVTESTORN HĎ*

n Caſtellaria de *EWIAS* deđ Wiłłs com̄ WALTERIO

de Laci . IIII . carucatas trǽ waſtas.

R OGERIVS de Laci fili ej ten eas . 7 Wiłłs 7 Osbn̄ de eo.

In dn̄io hn̄t . II . caŕ . 7 IIII . Walenſes redđtes . II . ſextaŕ mellis,

7 hn̄t . I . caŕ . Ibi hn̄t . III . ſeruos 7 II . borđ . H̄ tra uał . xx . ſoł.

Iſđ Roḡ h̄t una tra *EWIAS* dicta in fine *EWIAS*.

h̄ tra n̄ ptin ad caſtellaria neq̷ ad *HVNĎ* . De hac tra

h̄t Roḡ . xv . ſextaŕ mellis . 7 xv . porc q̄do hōes ſunt ibi,

7 placita ſup̱ eos.

In Caſtellaria de *CLIFORD* ten iſđ Roger . IIII . caŕ trǽ.

Pat ej tenuit . Waſtǽ fueŕ 7 ſunt . *IN GRETREWES HĎ.*

Iſđ Roḡ ten *POTESLEPE* . 7 Wiłłs de eo . Thoſtin tenuit

Ibi . I . hida gelđ . In dn̄io ſunt . II . caŕ . 7 II . uiłłi 7 I . borđ

cū . II . caŕ . Ibi . II . ſerui .   Vał 7 ualuit . xx . ſoliđ.

Iſđ Roḡ ten *AGLE* . Sex libi hōes tenueŕ *IN TORNELAVS HĎ.*

p̱ . VI . M̃ . 7 poteraꝓ ire quó uoleƀ . Ibi . VII . hidǽ gelđ.

In dn̄io ſunt . II . caŕ . 7 VII . uiłł 7 x . borđ . 7 p̄poſit 7 faƀ

cū . IX . caŕ int om̄s . Ibi . XII . ſerui.

De hac tra deđ Walter de Laci Ꝭ petro de hereforđ

. II . caŕ trǽ . c̄ceſſu regis . W . 7 un̄ uiłł 7 un̄ borđ cū tra eoꝛ̷

Ibi ſunt in dn̄io . II . caŕ . 7 un uiłł 7 un borđ cū . I . caŕ,

7 un ſeru ibi .   Vał . xxv . ſoliđ.

Qđ Rogeri ten ꞈ LXXV . ſoliđ.

Tot T.R.E. ualƀ . VII . liƀ 7 xv . ſoł.

Iſđ Roger h̄t in Waia piſcaŕ quǽ ap̱ꝑciat . VI . liƀ,

7 Burgenſes q̃uos h̄t in hereforđ , redđt ei . xx . ſoliđ.

Iſđ Roḡ ten *MAGENE* . 7 Hugo de eo . Wonni tenuit

Ibi . I . hida gelđ . 7 una caŕ . ē in dn̄io 7 III . ſerui , ibi,

Valuit . xx . ſoł . 7 poſt . x . ſoł . Modo . xv . ſoliđ.

In CUTSTHORN Hundred

1   In the castlery of EWYAS (Harold) Earl William gave 4 carucates
of waste land to Walter of Lacy. Roger of Lacy his son holds
them, and William and Osbern from him. They have 2 ploughs
in lordship;
> 4 Welshmen who pay 2 sesters of honey; they have 1 plough.
> They have 3 slaves; 2 smallholders.

Value of this land 20s.

[In EWIAS]

2   Roger also has one land called LONGTOWN within the boundary of
Ewias. This land does not belong to the castlery nor to the
Hundred. From this land Roger has 15 sesters of honey, 15 pigs
when men are there and (administers) justice over them.

[CASTLERY]

3   In the castlery of CLIFFORD (Castle) Roger also holds 4 carucates
of land. His father held them. They were and are waste.

In GREYTREE Hundred

4   Roger also holds PUTLEY, and William from him. Tosti held it.
1 hide which pays tax. In lordship 2 ploughs;
> 2 villagers and 1 smallholder with 2 ploughs. 2 slaves.

The value is and was 20s.

In THORNLAW Hundred

5   Roger also holds OCLE (Pychard). Six free men held it as six
manors; they could go where they would. 7 hides which pay tax.
In lordship 2 ploughs;
> 7 villagers, 10 smallholders, a reeve and a smith with 9 ploughs
> between them. 12 slaves.
> Of this land Walter of Lacy gave 2 carucates of land to St.
> Peter's of Hereford with King William's consent, and 1 villager
> and 1 smallholder with their land. In lordship 2 ploughs;
> 1 villager and 1 smallholder with 1 plough; 1 slave there.

ᵏ   Value 25s. (Value of) what Roger holds, 75s. Value of the whole
before 1066 £7 15s.

(10,6 is entered at the foot of col. 184a, directed to its correct place by transposition signs)

7   Roger also has a fishery on the (River) Wye which is assessed
at £6. The burgesses he has in Hereford pay him 20s.

Roger also holds

8   MAUND. Hugh holds from him. Wonni held it. 1 hide which pays
tax. In lordship 1 plough; 3 slaves there.
The value was 20s; later 10s; now 15s.

Iſd Rog ten *BODEHÃ*.7 Herbt de eo.Eduui tenuit.

Ibi.ɪ.hida 7 dimiđ gelđ.In dñio ſunt.ɪɪ.caŕ.7 vɪ.uiłłi

7 ɪɪɪ.borđ 7 faƀ 7 bedellus.7 vɪ.cot cũ.vɪ.caŕ.Ibi.vɪ.

ſerui.7 moliñ de.xvɪ.ſoliđ.7 xxx.ſtiches Anguiłł.

Pratũ.ē boƀ tanŧ.T.R.E.ualƀ.ʟ.ſoliđ.Modo.ʟx.ſoł.

Iſd Rog ten in eođ *HVND* 7 Herbt de eo uñ ꝏ de una v.

Qđ tenuit Eduui cilt.cũ una caŕ.   Vał 7 ualuit.xxvɪ.deñ.

Iſd Rog ten unã hidã de firma *MAVRDINE*.ꝏ regis.

Ingelrann teñ de eo.In dñio ſunt.ɪɪ.caŕ.7 ɪɪɪɪ.uiłłi 7 ɪ.borđ

cũ.ɪɪ.caŕ.Ibi.ɪɪɪ.ſerui.

T.R.E 7 poſt ualƀ.xʟ.ſoł.Modo.ʟx.ſoliđ.Eduui tenuit.

Iſd Roger ten *WENETONE*.7 Geralđ de eo. *IN VLFEI HÐ.*

Erneuui tenuit.Ibi.ɪɪɪ.virg gelđ.7 ibi.ē una caŕ.

Valuit.vɪ.ſoliđ.Modo.ɪɪɪɪ.ſoliđ.

Iſd Roger ten *HED*.7 Geralđ de eo.Leuuiñ tenuit.

Ibi.ɪɪɪ.virg gelđ.   Vał.vɪ.ſoliđ.

Iſd Roger ten *PILLESDVNE*.7 Hugo de eo.Wluuard

tenuit.Ibi.ɪɪɪ.hidæ gelđ.In dñio ſunt.ɪɪ.caŕ.7 ɪɪɪ.borđ

cũ.ɪ.caŕ.7 un francig cũ.ɪ.caŕ 7.ɪɪ.borđ.Ibi.vɪɪɪ.ſerui.

T.R.E.ualƀ.xxx.ſoliđ.Modo.xʟ.ſoliđ.

Iſd Roger ten uñ ꝏ de.ɪ.hida 7 dimiđ gelđ.Eluuiñ

ten de eo.Pat huj tenuit Eduui.Ibi hŧ.ɪ.caŕ.7 ɪɪ.uiłłos

cũ dimiđ caŕ.Ibi.ɪɪɪ.ſerui.   Vał 7 ualuit.x.ſoliđ.

Ꝟ Iſd Rog ten *MAGGE*.7 Wiłłs de eo.Ailric tenuit.Ibi.ɪɪ.hidæ gelđ.

In dñio ſunt.ɪɪ.caŕ.7 v.ſerui.7 adhuc.ɪɪ.caŕ poſſunt ibi.ēē.

Valuit.xxx.ſoł.Modo.xxv.ſoliđ.

184 b

In Valle *STRADELEI* ten iſđ Rogeŕ Bachetune de.v.

hiđ.7 Wadetune de.ɪ.hida.ħ.ɪɪ.ꝏ ten Giſłeƀt de Rog.

Eduui 7 Aluuard tenueŕ has.vɪ.hiđ.7 waſtæ fueŕ.

In dñio.ē.ɪ.caŕ.7 un ſeruus.7 ɪɪɪ.Walenſes redđt.ɪɪɪ.ſexŧ

mellis.   Vał.ɪx.ſoliđ.

9 BODENHAM. Herbert holds from him. Edwy held it. 1½ hides which pay tax. In lordship 2 ploughs;
    6 villagers, 3 smallholders, a smith, a beadle and 6 cottagers with 6 ploughs.
    6 slaves; a mill at 16s and 30 sticks of eels; meadow only for the oxen.
Value before 1066, 50s; now 60s.

10 in the same Hundred one manor of 1 virgate which does not pay tax. Herbert holds from him. Edwy Young held it with 1 plough. The value is and was 26d.

11 one hide from the revenue of MARDEN, the King's manor. Ingelrann holds from him. In lordship 2 ploughs;
    4 villagers and 1 smallholder with 2 ploughs. 3 slaves.
Value before 1066 and later, 40s; now 60s.
    Edwy Young held it.

in WOLPHY Hundred
12 WOONTON. Gerald holds from him. Ernwy held it. 3 virgates which pay tax. 1 plough there.
The value was 6s; now 4s.

13 HEATH. Gerald holds from him. Leofwin held it. 3 virgates which pay tax.
Value 6s.

14 PUDLESTON. Hugh holds from him. Wulfward held it. 3 hides which pay tax. In lordship 2 ploughs;
    3 smallholders with 1 plough; 1 Frenchman with 1 plough;
    2 smallholders. 8 slaves.
Value before 1066, 30s; now 40s.

15 one manor of 1½ hides which pay tax. Alwin holds it from him; his father Edwy held it. He has 1 plough there and
    2 villagers with ½ plough. 3 slaves.
The value is and was 10s.

ƕ (*Misplaced entry, directed to its proper place by transposition signs*)
6 Roger also holds MAUND, and William from him. Alric held it. 2 hides which pay tax. In lordship 2 ploughs; 5 slaves; a further 2 ploughs possible there.
The value was 30s; now 25s.

16 In the GOLDEN VALLEY Roger also holds BACTON at 5 hides and   184 b
WADETUNE at 1 hide. Gilbert holds these two manors from Roger. Edwy and Alfward held these 6 hides; they were waste. In lordship 1 plough; 1 slave.
    3 Welshmen pay 3 sesters of honey.
Value 9s.

In ead ualle ten iſd Rog ELNODESTVNE . de . III . hiđ

7 Wilts ten de Rog . 7 hī . II . car in dīnio . 7 VI . borđ , Val . x . ſot .

Ibiđ ten iſd Roger 7 Walter de eo EDWARDESTVNE

de . I . hida . Waſt fuit . Modo ual . VIII . ſoliđ . IN DVNRE HĐ .

Iſd Rog ten BONINIOPE . Elnod tenuit de Joħe uicecom .

Ibi . II . hidæ geld . In dīnio . ē una car . 7 IIII . uilt 7 IIII . borđ

cū . II . car 7 dimiđ , Ibi . v . ſerui . 7 tcia pars . II . molinoʒ quæ

ual . XIIII . ſoliđ 7 VIII . den . Silua . ē in foreſta regis .

T . R . E . ualb . L . ſoliđ . Modo . tntđ .

Iſd Rog ten COBEWELLE . Aluuard tenuit 7 poterat ire

quo uolb . Ibi . I . hida geld . Girold ten de Rog . In dīnio hī . II .

car . 7 IIII . borđ cū . I . hida . 7 IX . int ſeruos 7 ancillas .

T . R . E . ualb . L . ſoliđ . Modo tntđ .

Iſd Rog ten MALFELLE . 7 Ingelrann đe eo . Eduui tenuit .

Ibi . II . hidæ geld . In dīnio ſunt . II . car . 7 v . borđ 7 faber . 7 II .

ſerui 7 ancilla .   De hac tra ten Leuuin . I . uirg de ipſo Rog .

T . R . E . ualb . xx . ſot . Modo . XLVI . ſoliđ .

Iſd Rog ten WEBETONE 7 Berner đe eo . Æluuard tenuit .

Ibi dimiđ hida Ibi . ē . I . car .   Val 7 ualuit . xv . ſot .

Iſd Rog ten WEBETONE . 7 Girald 7 Berner de eo . Eduui tenuit .

Ibi . II . hidæ 7 dimiđ .   Ibi ſunt . VII . borđ cū . III . car .

waſt fuit . Modo ual . x . ſoliđ .   IN CVTESTORNES HĐ .

Iſd Rog ten STRATONE . 7 Robt de eo . Eduui tenuit .

Ibi . II . hidæ 7 dimiđ geld . In dīnio ſunt . II . car . 7 un uilts

7 IX . borđ 7 IIII . bouarij . 7 II . radchen . Int oms hīt . III . car .

T . R . E . ualb . XL . ſoliđ . Modo . L . ſoliđ . Ibi moliñ de . XXXII . den .

Iſd Rog ten LVDE . 7 Rađ de eo . Turchil tenuit de Heraldo com

Ibi . II . hidæ geld . In dīnio . ē una car . 7 alia poteſt . eē . Ibi . III .

borđ 7 un lib ħo cū . II . car 7 dimiđ .

T . R . E . ualb . xx . ſoliđ . Modo . xxv . ſoliđ .

17 In the same valley Roger also holds ELNODESTUNE at 3 hides.
William holds from Roger; he has 2 ploughs in lordship;
  6 smallholders.
Value 10s.

18 There also Roger holds EDWARDESTUNE at 1 hide, and Walter from
him. It was waste. Value now 8s.

Roger also holds
in DINEDOR Hundred
19 BULLINGHOPE. Alnoth held it from John the Sheriff. 2 hides which
pay tax. In lordship 1 plough;
  4 villagers and 4 smallholders with 2½ ploughs.
  5 slaves; the third part of 2 mills which is worth 14s 8d.
    The woodland is in the King's Forest.
Value before 1066, 50s; now as much.

20 COBHALL. Alfward held it; he could go where he would. 1 hide
which pays tax. Gerald holds from Roger. He has 2 ploughs in
lordship;
  4 smallholders with 1 hide; 9 slaves, male and female.
Value before 1066, 50s; now as much.

21 MAWFIELD. Ingelrann holds from him. Edwy Young held it. 2 hides
which pay tax. In lordship 2 ploughs;
  5 smallholders, a smith, 2 male slaves and a female slave.
  Leofwin holds 1 virgate of this land from Roger himself.
Value before 1066, 20s; now 46s.

22 WEBTON. Berner holds from him. Alfward held it. ½ hide. ...
1 plough there.
The value is and was 15s.

23 WEBTON. Gerald and Berner hold from him. Edwy held it. 2½ hides. ...
  7 smallholders with 3 ploughs.
It was waste. Value now 10s.

in CUTSTHORN Hundred
24 STRETTON. Robert holds from him. Edwy Young held it. 2½ hides
which pay tax. In lordship 2 ploughs;
  1 villager, 9 smallholders, 4 ploughmen and 2 riding men;
    between them they have 3 ploughs.
Value before 1066, 40s; now 50s.
  A mill at 32d.

25 LYDE. Ralph holds from him. Thorkell held it from Earl Harold.
2 hides which pay tax. In lordship 1 plough; another possible.
  3 smallholders and 1 free man with 2½ ploughs.
Value before 1066, 20s; now 25s.

Iſd Rog̃ teñ *LVDE*.7 Rað de eo. Bruning tenuit. Ibi. I. hida.
In dñio ſunt. II. car̃.　　　　　　Valuit. XL. ſot. Modo: LX. ſot.

Iſd Rog̃ teñ *WESTVNE*. Gunuer tenuit *IN RADELAV H̃D*.
7 poterat ire quo uoleb. Ibi. VI. hidæ geld. In dñio ſunt. II. car̃.
7 IX. uilti 7 p̃r 7 II. borð cũ. IX. car̃. Ibi. VI. ſerui. 7 moliñ
de. X. ſolið. 7 p̃tũ bob.

T.R.E. ualb. C. ſot. 7 modo tñtð.

Iſd Rog̃ teñ *ARCHEL*. Archil tenuit tañ Heraldi. Ibi. II.
hidæ geld. In dñio ſunt. II. car̃. 7 VII. uilti 7 IIII. borð cũ. VII. car̃.
Ibi. VII. ſerui. 7 moliñ de. C. denar.

T.R.E. ualb. L. ſolið. Modo. tñtð.

Iſd Rog̃ teñ *NEREFRVM*. Toſti tenuit de Eddid regina.
Ibi. IIII. hidæ geld. In dñio ſunt. II. car̃. 7 VII. uilti 7 IIII.
borð 7 p̃poſit cũ. VIII. car̃. Ibi. X. ſerui. 7 moliñ de. VII. ſot
7 VI. deñ. 7 V. ſtiches anguilt.

T.R.E. ualb. LX. ſolið. Modo tñtð.

Iſd Rog̃ teñ *BRISMERFRVM*. Briſmer tenuit de Heraldo.
Ibi. V. hidæ geld. In dñio ſunt. III. car̃. 7 VII. uilti 7 p̃poſit
7 uñ lib hõ cũ. VII. car̃. Ibi. X. ſerui. 7 moliñ de. X. ſolið.

T.R.E. ualb. LXX. ſolið. Modo: LX. ſolið.

184 c

Iſd Rog̃ teñ *MVNESLAI*. 7 Rað de eo. Briſmar tenuit. 7 quo
uoleb ire poterat. Ibi. III. hidæ 7 una v̄ geld.　In dñio ſunt
. III. car̃. 7 XI. uilt 7 VII. borð cũ. IX. car̃.

T.R.E. ualb. LXX. ſot. Modo. LX. ſolið.

Iſd Rog̃ teñ *MERCHELAI*. 7 Odo de eo. Turchil tenuit
de Heraldo. Ibi. V. hidæ geld. In dñio. e una car̃. 7 X. uilti
7 IIII. borð cũ. X. car̃. Ibi. I. lib hõ 7 uñ radchen cũ car̃ 7 dim̃.
Ibi. V. ſerui. 7 moliñ redð annonā. Silua redð. XVII. deñ.

T.R.E. ualb. C. ſolið. Modo tñtð.

De ipſis. V. hið tenuit Ælric dimid p M̃. 7 poterat ire
quó uoleb. Modo teñ Odo cũ alia t̃ra. Vat 7 ualuit. VI. ſot.

184 b, c

26 LYDE. Ralph holds from him. Browning held it. 1 hide.
In lordship 2 ploughs.
The value was 40s; now 60s.

in RADLOW Hundred

27 WESTON (Beggard). Gunfrid held it; he could go where he would.
6 hides which pay tax. In lordship 2 ploughs;
9 villagers, a priest and 2 smallholders with 9 ploughs.
6 slaves; a mill at 10s; meadow for the oxen.
Value before 1066, 100s; now as much.

28 YARKHILL. Arkell, a thane of Earl Harold, held it. 2 hides which
pay tax. In lordship 2 ploughs;
7 villagers and 4 smallholders with 7 ploughs.
7 slaves; a mill at 100d.
Value before 1066, 50s; now as much.

29 (Halmonds) FROME. Tosti held it from Queen Edith. 4 hides
which pay tax. In lordship 2 ploughs;
7 villagers, 4 smallholders and a reeve with 8 ploughs.
10 slaves; a mill at 7s 6d and 5 sticks of eels.
Value before 1066, 60s; now as much.

30 (Castle) FROME. Brictmer held it from Earl Harold. 5 hides which
pay tax. In lordship 3 ploughs;
7 villagers, a reeve and 1 free man with 7 ploughs.
10 slaves; a mill at 10s.
Value before 1066, 70s; now 60s.

31 MUNSLEY. Ralph holds from him. Brictmer held it; he could go   184 c
where he would. 3 hides and 1 virgate which pay tax. In lordship
2 ploughs;
11 villagers and 7 smallholders with 9 ploughs.
Value before 1066, 70s; now 60s.

32 (Little) MARCLE. Odo holds from him. Thorkell held it from Earl
Harold. 5 hides which pay tax. In lordship 1 plough;
10 villagers and 4 smallholders with 10 ploughs. 1 free man
and 1 riding man with 1½ ploughs.
5 slaves; a mill which pays corn; woodland which pays 17d.
Value before 1066, 100s; now as much.
Of these 5 hides Alric held half as a manor; he could go where
he would. Odo now holds it with the other land.
The value is and was 6s.

Iſd Rog teń *FROME* .7 Girard de eo . Turchil tenuit.

Ibi.iiii. hidæ gelđ. In dńio ſunt.ii. caŕ.7 viii. uiłłi 7 ii.

borđ 7 p̄poſit cū. vii. caŕ. Ibi. vi. ſerui.7 moliń de . x . ſoł

7 x . denar.

T.R.E. ualb . lxx . ſol . Modo . iii . ſoliđ plus.

Iſd Rog teń *SBECH* .7 Odo de eo . Elmer 7 Aluric 7 Turchil

tenueŕ p . iii . ꝏ de heraldo .7 poterạ̃ ire quo uoleb.

Ibi. i . hida tant 7 gelđ . In dńio ſunt . iiii . caŕ .7 uń uiłłs

7 uń radchen cū. ii. caŕ.7 iii.anciłł.

T.R.E. ualb . xxviii . ſol . Modo t̄ntđ.

Iſd Rog teń *HIDE* .7 Tezeliń de eo . Oſgod tenuit.7 po

tuit ire quo uoluit . Ibi . i . hida gelđ . In dńio . ē una caŕ.

7 uń borđ 7 iiii . ſerui .   Vał 7 ualuit . v . ſoliđ.

Iſd Rog teń *TATINTVNE* .7 Anſfrid de eo . Elric tenuit.

7 q̊ uolb ire poterat . Ibi dimiđ hida gelđ . In dńio . ē una

caŕ.7 uń borđ 7 iii . ſerui . Valuit . v . ſoł . modo . vi . ſol.

★ Iſd Rog teń *LEDE* .7 S̄ Petrus de eo . dono patris ej.

7 c̄ceſſu . W . Regis . Turchil tenuit .7 potuit ire q̊ uoluit.

Ibi dimiđ hida gelđ . In dńio . ē . i . caŕ .7 viii . borđ hńt

ibi . i . caŕ . T.R.E. ualb . xx . ſoliđ . Modo tńtđ.

Iſd Rog teń *LEDE* . Turchil tenuit 7 quó uoluit ire potuit.

Ibi dimiđ hida gelđ . Tra . ē . i . caŕ . Waſta . ē . Vał . iiii . ſol.

✝ Iſd Rog teń *LAVTVNE* .7 uń Anglic *IN HEZETRE HD.*

de eo . Vluric tenuit . Ibi . i . hida gelđ . In dńio . ē . i . caŕ.

7 iii . borđ hńtes caŕ 7 dim . Ibi . iiii . ſerui.

T.R.E. ualb . xx . ſol . Modo tńtđ.

Iſd Rog teń *LESTRET* . Rex . E . tenuit . Ibi . i . hiđ . cuj

medietas erat in dńio regis 7 ñ gelđ . alia medietas gelđ.

Hanc trã de firma regis deđ . W . com̄ Ewen britoni.

Modo teń Wiłłs de Rog de Laci .7 ibi hŧ . iii . uiłłos.

T.R.E. ualb xx . ſoliđ . modo . xv . ſol.

184 c

33   (Canon) FROME. Gerard holds from him. Thorkell held it. 4 hides
which pay tax. In lordship 2 ploughs;
    8 villagers, 2 smallholders and a reeve with 7 ploughs.
    6 slaves; a mill at 10s 10d.
Value before 1066, 70s; now 3s more.

34   EVESBATCH. Odo holds from him. Aelmer, Aelfric and Thorkell
held it from Earl Harold as three manors; they could go where
they would. Only 1 hide; it pays tax. In lordship 4 ploughs;
    1 villager and 1 riding man with 2 ploughs; 3 female slaves.
Value before 1066, 28s; now as much.

35   MONKHIDE. Tesselin holds from him. Osgot held it; he could go
where he would. 1 hide which pays tax. In lordship 1 plough;
    1 smallholder and 4 slaves.
The value is and was 5s.

36   TARRINGTON. Ansfrid holds from him. Alric held it; he could go
where he would. ½ hide which pays tax. In lordship 1 plough;
    1 smallholder and 3 slaves.
The value was 5s; now 6s.

✠ 37   LEADON. St. Peter's holds from him by his father's gift, and with
King William's consent. Thorkell held it; he could go where he
would. ½ hide which pays tax. In lordship 1 plough.
    8 smallholders have 1 plough there.
Value before 1066, 20s; now as much.

38   LEADON. Thorkell held it; he could go where he would. ½ hide
which pays tax. Land for 1 plough. It is waste.
Value 4s.

Ψ   *(10,39 is entered at the foot of col. 184c, directed to its proper place by transposition signs)*

    in HAZELTREE Hundred

40   LAWTON. An Englishman holds from him. Wulfric held it. 1 hide
which pays tax. In lordship 1 plough;
    3 smallholders who have 1½ ploughs. 4 slaves.
Value before 1066, 20s; now as much.

41   STREET. King Edward held it. 1 hide, half of which was in the
King's lordship and did not pay tax; the other half paid tax.
Earl William gave this land from the King's revenue to Ewen the
Breton. Now William holds it from Roger of Lacy. He has
    3 villagers there.
Value before 1066, 20s; now 15s.

Iſd Rog ten *LIDECOTE*.7 Giſlebt de eo|Eiſlet tenuit. ibi.r.hid geld.

7 poterat ire q̃ uolḃ.In dñio.ē.ɪ.caŕ.7 uñ hō cū.ɪ.caŕ

Waſt fuit.Modo ual.x.ſolid. *IN ELSEDVNE HVND.*

Iſd Rog ten *HOPE*.7 Walter de eo.Vluric tenuit.Ibi.ɪɪ.

hidæ geld.Tra.ē.ɪɪɪɪ.caŕ.Ibi ſunt hōes reddtes.x.ſol 7 vɪɪɪ.

denaŕ p̄ ſuis hoſpitiis.Nil aliud ibi.ē.

Iſd Rog ten *LENEHALLE*.7 Walter de eo.Turchil tenuit de

heraldo.Ibi.v.hidæ geld.In dñio ſunt,ɪɪ.caŕ.7 ɪɪɪ.uiłł 7 xɪ.

borđ 7 ɪɪɪ.radchen.cū.v.caŕ.Ibi,v.int ſeruos 7 ancił.

7 de q̃bƷdā hōilƷ ibi hoſpitatis.hñt.c.deñ.q̄diu ipſi uoluerın̄.

T.R.E.ualḃ.ʟx.ſolid.Modo.ʟ.ſolid.

† Iſd Rog ten *MATMA*.7 OJo de eo.Mereuin tenuit tein̄ Odonis.7 n̄ poterat

recede ſine lictia dñi.Ibi dim̄ hida geld.Ibi.ē una caŕ.Val 7 ualuit.x.ſol.

184 d

Iſd Rog ten *WENNETVNE*.Elgaŕ tenuit 7 potuit ire q̃ uoluit.

Ibi.ɪ.hida geld.Nil.ē in dñio ſed.v.uiłłi hñt ibi caŕ 7 dim̄.

Valuit,ɪɪɪ.ſol 7 vɪɪɪ.den.m̄.ʟxɪɪɪɪ.den.

Iſd Rog ten *HERDESLEGE*.7 Robt de eo.Eduui tenuit.

H̃ tra n̄ geld neqƷ c̄ſuetuđ dat,nec in aliq̄ hunđ jacet.

In medio cujdā ſiluæ.ē poſita.7 ibi.ē dom̄ una defenſabił.

In dñio.ē una caŕ.7 ɪɪ.ſerui.7 uñ Walenſis redđ.ɪɪɪ.ſolid.

Iſd Rog ten *LETVNE*.7 Tezelin de eo.Eduui tenuit.

7 poterat ire quo uolḃ.Ibi.ɪɪɪ.hidæ geld.In dñio.ē una caŕ.

7 pḃr 7 vɪɪ.hoſpites cū.ɪ.caŕ redđt.v.ſolid.Ibi.ɪ.molin̄

nil redđ 7 ɪɪ.ſerui.Valuit.ɪɪ.ſol.Modo.xxx.ſolid.

42 LEDICOT. Gilbert holds from him. 1 hide which pays tax. Aelfled
held it; she could go where she would. In lordship 1 plough;
1 man with 1 plough.
It was waste. Value now 10s.

in ELSDON Hundred

43 HOPLEYS (Green). Walter holds from him. Wulfric held it. 2 hides
which pay tax. Land for 4 ploughs.
There are men who pay 10s 8d for their right to settle. Nothing
else is there.

44 LYONSHALL. Walter holds from him. Thorkell held from Earl
Harold. 5 hides which pay tax. In lordship 2 ploughs;
3 villagers, 11 smallholders and 3 riding men with 5 ploughs.
5 slaves, male and female.
From some men settled there 100d are given for as long as
they wish (to remain).
Value before 1066, 60s; now 50s.

(Misplaced entry, directed to its proper place by transposition signs)

Ψ39 MATHON. Odo holds from him. Merwin, a thane of Earl Oda, held
it; he could not withdraw without the lord's permission. ½ hide
which pays tax. 1 plough.
The value is and was 10s.

45 WOONTON. Algar held it; he could go where he would. 1 hide   184 d
which pays tax. Nothing in lordship, but
5 villagers have 1½ ploughs there.
The value was 3s 8d; now 64d.

46 EARDISLEY. Robert holds from him. Edwy held it. This land does
not pay tax, nor gives any customary dues, nor lies in any
Hundred. It is situated in the middle of a wood; a fortified house
is there. In lordship 1 plough; 2 slaves.
1 Welshman who pays 3s.
[Value ...]

47 LETTON. Tesselin holds from him. Edwy Young held it; he could
go where he would. 3 hides which pay tax. In lordship 1 plough.
A priest and 7 settlers with 1 plough pay 5s.
A mill which pays nothing; 2 slaves.
The value was 2s; now 30s.

Iſd Rog ten *WIRELAI*. Eduui tenuit. *IN STRADFORD HĎ*.

Ibi.III.hidæ 7 dimiđ.geldant.

In dñio ſunt.III.car.7 x.uiƚƚ 7 pƀr 7 ꝓpoſit 7 faƀ 7 v.borđ.

cũ.IX.car 7 dim.Ibi.XI.ſerui.7 Silua dimiđ leuu lg̃.

7.IIII.q̃ᷓ lat.Ibi.ẽ parcus.7 tra ad.I.car de Eſſarz.

redđ.XI.ſoƚ 7 IX.den.

Vnã ex iſtis uiƚƚ hƚ S Petrus dono Walterij de Laci.

T.R.E.ualƀ.c.ſoliđ.7 poſt.LX.ſoƚ.Modo: c.ſoliđ.

Iſd Rog ten *FERNEHALLE*. Eduui tenuit.Ibi.II.hidæ

gelđ.In dñio.ẽ.I.car.7 IX.uiƚƚ 7 III.borđ 7 uñ Radchen

ten dimiđ v.Int oms hñt.x.car.Ibi.III.ſerui.

Silua ibi dimiđ leuu lg̃ 7 IIII.q̃ᷓ lat.7 tra ad.I.car de

Eſſarz redđ.LIIII.denar.

T.R.E.ualƀ.LX.ſoliđ.Modo tñtđ.

Iſd Rog ten *PIONIE*.Rex.E.tenuit.Ibi.v.hidæ gelđ.

In dñio ſunt.II.car.7 VIII.uiƚƚi 7 III.borđ 7 pƀr 7 ꝓpoſit

7 uñ radchen.Inƚ oms hñt.IX.car.7 adhuc.IIII.plus.ẽe.

poſſent ibi.Ibi.IIII.ſerui.

De hac tra ten Grifin dimiđ hiđ.

7 Sc̃a *MARIA* de Cormelijs unã v.7 decimã uillæ.Vaƚ.XII.ſoƚ.

Toƚ Ꝏ T.R.E.ualƀ.IIII.liƀ.7 modo tñtđ.

Hanc trã tenuit Ewen brito de Wiƚƚo.Rex ũ.W.deđ Walterio de Laci.

Iſd Rog ten *BVRLEI*.7 Godmund de eo.Seric tenuit.

tein Heraldi.Ibi dimiđ hida ñ gelđ.In dñio ſunt.II.car.

7 VIII.borđ cũ.I.car.Ibi.IIII.ſerui 7 nil redđ ſilua

T.R.E.ualƀ.XXX.ſoliđ.Modo.XL.ſoliđ.

Iſd Rog ten *PLETVNE*.7 Osƀn de eo.Elnod tenuit.7 po

tuit ire quo uoluit.Ibi.II.partes uni hidæ.7 gelđ.

Tra.ẽ.II.car.Ibi.II.ſerui.7 nil plus.Vaƚ 7 ualuit.x.ſoƚ.

Iſd Rog ten *SVENESTVN*.7 Godmund de eo.Seric

tenuit.7 poterat ire q̃ uoƚƀ.Ibi.I.hida gelđ.In dñio nil.

in STRETFORD Hundred

48 WEOBLEY. Edwy Young held it. 3½ hides which pay tax.
In lordship 3 ploughs;
 10 villagers, a priest, a reeve, a smith and 5 smallholders
  with 9½ ploughs.
 11 slaves; woodland ½ league long and 4 furlongs wide. A park;
  land for 1 plough, cleared of wood, which pays 11s 9d.
 St. Peter's has one of these villagers by gift of Walter of Lacy.
Value before 1066, 100s; later 60s; now 100s.

49 FERNHILL. Edwy Young held it. 2 hides which pay tax.
In lordship 1 plough;
 9 villagers, 3 smallholders and 1 riding man hold ½ virgate;
  between them they have 10 ploughs.
 3 slaves; woodland ½ league long and 4 furlongs wide; land
  for 1 plough, cleared of wood, which pays 54d.
Value before 1066, 60s; now as much.

50 (Kings) PYON. King Edward held it. 5 hides which pay tax.
In lordship 2 ploughs;
 8 villagers, 3 smallholders, a priest, a reeve and 1 riding man;
  between them they have 9 ploughs; a further 4 more would
  be possible there. 4 slaves.
 Gruffydd holds ½ hide of this land.
 St. Mary's of Cormeilles (holds) 1 virgate and the tithe of the
 village.
Value 12s.
Value of the whole manor before 1066 £4; now as much.
 Ewen the Breton held this land from Earl William, but King
William gave it to Walter of Lacy.

51 BIRLEY. Godmund holds from him. Saeric, a thane of Earl Harold,
held it. ½ hide which does not pay tax. In lordship 2 ploughs;
 8 smallholders with 1 plough.
 4 slaves; woodland which pays nothing.
Value before 1066, 30s; now 40s.

52 ALTON. Osbern holds from him. Alnoth held it; he could go where
he would. Two parts of 1 hide; they pay tax. Land for 2 ploughs.
2 slaves. Nothing more.
The value is and was 10s.

53 SWANSTONE. Godmund holds from him. Saeric held it; he could go
where he would. 1 hide which pays tax. Nothing in lordship.

Tres uilli 7 III . bord hñt , II . caꝛ.

Valuit . x . folid . Modo . xv . folid . *IN STEPLESET HD.*

Iſd Rog ten *BROCHEBERIE* . 7 Robt de eo . Ernui tenuit
de Eduui . 7 ñ poterat ab eo recedere . Ibi . II . hidæ geld .
In dñio funt . II , caꝛ . 7 II . uilli 7 VI . bord 7 uñ liƀ hõ cũ
. III . caꝛ . Ibi . II . ſerui .

T.R.E , ualƀ . x . folid , modo . xx . folid .

Iſd Rog ten *STANDVNE* . 7 Leuric de eo . Ernui tenuit
de Eduui cilt . Ibi . II . hidæ geld . Ibi . ē dim caꝛ . 7 adhuc . I .
caꝛ poſſet , ēe , ibi . Ibi , II . uilli hñt . I . caꝛ . Val . v . folid .

Iſd Rog ten *MALVESELLE* . Elſlet tenuit de Heraldo .
Ibi . VIII , hidæ geld . In dñio funt . III . caꝛ . 7 q̃rta poſſet . ēe .
Ibi . x . uilli 7 p̃poſit . 7 . II . francig 7 uñ bord cũ . x . caꝛ .

T.R.E . ualƀ . VII . liƀ . 7 poſt . c . ſol . Modo . VIII . liƀ .

Iſd Rog ten *STANDVNE* . 7 Wilts de eo . Alric tenuit
7 poterat ire quo uolƀ . Ibi . IIII . hidæ geld . In dñio ſuꝰ . II . caꝛ .

185 a
7 III . uilli 7 IIII . bord cũ . I . caꝛ . 7 adhuc . III . caꝛ poſſeꝰ ibi . ēe .
Ibi . VII . ſerui . 7 Silua . I . leuu lg̃ . 7 dimid leuu lat .

Valuit . xxv . folid . Modo . xxx . folid .

Iſd Rog ten *LAVESOVRE* . 7 Robt de eo . Ludri tenuit tein
Algari . 7 poterat ire q̃ uolƀ . Ibi . v . hid geld . In dñio funt . II .
caꝛ . 7 VI . uilt 7 faber cũ . III . caꝛ . 7 uñ Radman redd . II . ſol .
Ibi . IIII . bouarij . 7 una ancilla .

T.R.E . ualƀ . xv . ſol . 7 poſt xxx . ſol . Modo . Lx . folid .

Iſd Rog ten *EDRESHOPE* . 7 Robt de eo . Eduui 7 Leuuin
7 Semar tenueꝛ . [p. III. Manˀ. 7 poteraꝰ ire q̃ uolƀ . Ibi . I . hida 7 dimid geld .
In dñio . ē . I . caꝛ . 7 uñ francig . cũ dimid caꝛ . 7 uñ ſeruus .
7 II . caꝛ plus poſſeꝰ ibi . ēe .

T.R.E . ualƀ . IIII . ſol . 7 poſt . xxx . ſol . Modo . xv . folid .

3 villagers and 3 smallholders have 2 ploughs.
The value was 10s; now 15s.

in STAPLE Hundred

54 BROBURY. Robert holds from him. Ernwy held from Edwy Young;
he could not withdraw from him. 2 hides which pay tax.
In lordship 2 ploughs;
    2 villagers, 6 smallholders and 1 free man with 3 ploughs.
      2 slaves.
Value before 1066, 10s; now 20s.

55 STAUNTON (on Wye). Leofric holds from him. Ernwy held from
Edwy Young. 2 hides which pay tax. ½ plough there; 1 further
plough would be possible there.
    2 villagers have 1 plough.
Value 5s.

56 MANSELL (Gamage). Aelfled held it from Earl Harold. 8 hides
which pay tax. In lordship 3 ploughs; a fourth would be possible.
    10 villagers, a reeve, 2 Frenchmen and 1 smallholder with
      10 ploughs.
Value before 1066 £7; later 100s; now £8.

57 STAUNTON (on Wye). William holds from him. Alric held it; he
could go where he would. 4 hides which pay tax. In lordship
2 ploughs;
    3 villagers and 4 smallholders with 1 plough; a further   185 a
      3 ploughs would be possible there.
    7 slaves; woodland 1 league long and ½ league wide.
The value was 25s; now 30s.

58 YAZOR. Robert holds from him. Ludric, a thane of Earl Algar,
held it; he could go where he would. 5 hides which pay tax.
In lordship 2 ploughs;
    6 villagers and a smith with 3 ploughs; 1 rider who pays 2s.
      4 ploughmen; 1 female slave.
Value before 1066, 15s; later 30s; now 60s.

59 YARSOP. Robert holds from him. Edwy, Leofwin and Saemer held
it as three manors; they could go where they would. 1½ hides
which pay tax. In lordship 1 plough;
    1 Frenchman with ½ plough; 1 slave; 2 more ploughs would be
      possible there.
Value before 1066, 4s; later 30s; now 15s.

Iſd Rog ten BVIFORD .7 Walter de eo. Ailuuard tenuit.

7 q̃ uoluit ire potuit. Ibi. v . hidæ geld̄. In dñio.ē. i. car̄.7 vi. uiłłi

7 iii. bord̄ cū. ii. car̄. Ibi. ii. ſerui 7 moliñ de. xx. ſolid̄.7 ii. car̄

plus poſſeɴ ibi. ēe.

T.R.E. ualb̄. xl. ſoł.7 poſt. lx. ſolid̄. Modo. c. ſolid̄.

Iſd Rog ten WERMESLAI.7 Leuric de eo. Eluui 7 Vlnod

tenuer̄ de eo . p. ii. m̃.7 poterãɴ ire quo uolb̄. Ibi. i. hida 7 una v̄

geld̄. In dñio.ē car̄ 7 dimid̄.7 ii. bord̄ 7 pbr cū car̄ 7 dimid̄.

7 adhuc. i. car̄ poteſt. ēe.

T.R.E. ualb̄ . x . ſolid . Modo. xv . ſolid .

Iſd Rog ten WERMESLAI. Haduic tenuit 7 q̃ uoluit ire

potuit. Ibi. i. uirg̃ træ ñ geld̄. Tra.ē. i. car̄.

Valuit. ii. ſoł. Modo. iii. ſolid̄   IN PLEGELIET HVND̄.

Iſd Rog ten STOCHES. Elmer tenuit.7 q̃ uolb̄ ire poterat.

Ibi . x . hidæ geld̄. In dñio ſunt. iii. car̄.7 xxii. uiłłi cū. vi. car̄

7 aliæ. vi. adhuc poſſent. ēe. Ibi. xi. ſerui.7 moliñ de. v. ſolid̄.

T.R.E. ualb̄. x. lib̄. Modo ſimilit̃

Iſd Rog ten COLINTVNE.7 Hugo de eo. Vluuard tenuit.

7 quo uolb̄ ire poterat. Ibi. ii. hidæ geld̄. In dñio.ē una car̄.

7 un uiłłs cū dimid̄ car̄. Ibi. ii. ſerui.   Vał 7 ualuit. xx. ſolid̄.

Iſd Rog ten SARGEBERIE.7 Hugo de eo. Wenric tenuit.

Ibi . ii . uirg̃ 7 dimid̄. Tra.ē. i. car̄. Waſta fuit.7 eſt.

Iſd Rog ten in VLFERLAV. vi . hid̄ geld̄.7 Hugo de eo.

Wiłłs cõm ded̄ Walterio patri ej. iiii. hid̄ 7 dimid̄.7 Rex.W.

ded̄ Rogerio hid̄ 7 dim̄. Hanc trā tenuit Aluuin T.R.E.

7 quo uolb̄ ire poterat.

In dñio ſunt. ii. car̄.7 vi. uiłłi cū. iii. car̄.7 adhuc. iii. aliæ

poſſunt. ēe. Ibi. iii. ſerui.

T.R.E. ualb̄. xl. ſoł. Modo. lxv. ſolid̄.

Iſd Rog ten FROME.7 Hugo de eo. Lepſi tenuit.7 quo

uolb̄ ire poterat. Ibi. i. hida geld̄. In dñio . ē una car̄.

60 BYFORD. Walter holds from him. Alfward held it; he could go where he would. 5 hides which pay tax. In lordship 1 plough;
  6 villagers and 3 smallholders with 2 ploughs.
  2 slaves; a mill at 20s; 4 more ploughs would be possible there.
Value before 1066, 40s; later 60s; now 100s.

61 WORMSLEY. Leofric holds from him. Alfwy and Wulfnoth held it from him as two manors; they could go where they would. 1 hide and 1 virgate which pay tax. In lordship 1½ ploughs;
  2 smallholders and a priest with 1½ ploughs; 1 further plough possible.
Value before 1066, 10s; now 15s.

62 WORMSLEY. Hadwic held it; he could go where he would. 1 virgate of land which does not pay tax. Land for 1 plough.
The value was 2s; now 3s.

in PLEGELGATE Hundred
63 STOKE (Lacy). Aelmer Young held it; he could go where he would. 10 hides which pay tax. In lordship 3 ploughs;
  22 villagers with 6 ploughs; a further 6 others would be possible.
  11 slaves; a mill at 5s.
Value before 1066 £10; now the same.

64 COLLINGTON. Hugh holds from him. Wulfward the priest held it; he could go where he would. 2 hides which pay tax. In lordship 1 plough;
  1 villager with ½ plough. 2 slaves.
The value is and was 20s.

65 SAWBURY (Hill). Hugh holds from him. Wynric held it. 2½ virgates. Land for 1 plough. It was and is waste.

66 in WOLFERLOW, 6 hides which pay tax. Hugh and Walter hold from him. Earl William gave 4½ hides to Walter his father, and King William gave 1½ hides to Roger. Alwin the Sheriff held this land before 1066; he could go where he would. In lordship 2 ploughs;
  6 villagers with 3 ploughs; a further 3 others possible. 3 slaves.
Value before 1066, 40s; now 65s.

67 (Bishops) FROME. Hugh holds from him. Leofsi held it; he could go where he would. 1 hide which pays tax. In lordship 1 plough;

7 III.uilti cū .I.car.Ibi.II.ferui.7 molin de.xxxII.denař.

T.R.E.ualb.xx.fot.Modo.xv.folid.

Iſd Rog ten *TETISTORP*.Ernefi tenuit.7 quo potuit ire

uoluit.Ibi.I.hida geld.In dnio funt.II.car.7 IIII.uilti

7 un bord cū.II.car.Ibi.VII.ferui.

T.R.E.ualb.xxx.fot.7 poſt.xv.fot.Modo.xx.folid.

Iſd Rog ten *BRIDENEBERIE*.Lepfi tenuit.7 quo uolb

ire poterat.Ibi.I.hida geld.In dnio.ē una car.7 IIII.uilti

cū.IIII.car.7 adhuc.III.car poſſeꝗ ibi.ee in dnio.Ibi.v.ferui.

T.R.E.ualb.xxx.fot.Modo.x.fot.Herman ten de Rog.

Iſd Rog ten *BVTRELIE*.7 Aluuin de eo.Eduui pat ej tenuit.

Ibi.III.hidæ 7 dimid.geld.In dnio.ē una car.7 IIII.uilti

7 VIII.bord cū.III.car.Ibi.v.ferui.7 molinū de.xvI.den.

T.R.E.ualb.xx.fot.Modo.xxx.folid.7 adhuc.I.car poſſet.ee.ibi.

185 b

Iſd Rog ten *MERSTVNE*.7 Godmund de eo.Seric pat

ej tenuit.7 quo uolb ire poterat.Ibi dimid hida geld.

Ibi.I.car 7 II.ferui.Valuit.IIII.fot.Modo.v.folid.

Iſd Rog ten *GRENEDENE*.7 Wilts de eo.Eduui tenuit.

7 Ordric p.II.Ꙏ.Ibi.IIII.hidæ geld.Tra.ē.VIII.car.

Nichil ibi habetur.

Iſd Rog ten *STANFORD*.7 Turſtin de eo.Eduui tenuit.

Ibi.I.hida geld.In dnio.ē una car.7 II.bouarij.7 I.bord.

Valuit.v.fot.Modo.x.folid.7 adhuc.I.car poſſet.ee.

Iſd Rog ten *CHIPELAI*.7 Edric de eo.Lepfi tenuit.7 quo

uoluit ire potuit.Ibi.I.hida geld.In dnio.ē una car.

7 un uilts 7 un bouar.cū.I.car.Ibi.III.ferui.

Valuit.v.folid.Modo.xII.folid.

Iſd Rog ten *HANLEI*.7 S Petrus in elemofina dono.Walt

de Laci.Elnod tenuit 7 quo uoluit ire potuit.Ibi

dimid hida geld.Ibi eſt.un uilts qui hf.I.car.

Valuit.vI.folid.Modo.vIII.folid.

3 villagers with 1 plough.
2 slaves; a mill at 32d.
Value before 1066, 20s; now 15s.

68 TEDSTONE. Ernsy held it; he could go where he would. 1 hide
which pays tax. In lordship 2 ploughs;
    4 villagers and 1 smallholder with 2 ploughs. 7 slaves.
Value before 1066, 30s; later 15s; now 20s.

69 BREDENBURY. Leofsi held it; he could go where he would. 1 hide
which pays tax. In lordship 1 plough;
    4 villagers with 4 ploughs; a further 3 ploughs would be
      possible there in lordship. 5 slaves.
Value before 1066, 30s; now 10s.
    Herman holds from Roger.

70 BUTTERLEY. Alwin holds from him. Edwy Young, his father, held
it. 3½ hides which pay tax. In lordship 1 plough;
    4 villagers and 8 smallholders with 3 ploughs.
    5 slaves; a mill at 16d.
Value before 1066, 20s; now 30s.
    1 further plough would be possible there.

71 MARSTON (Stannett). Godmund holds from him. Saeric, his father,   185 b
held it; he could go where he would. ½ hide which pays tax.
1 plough there; 2 slaves.
The value was 4s; now 5s.

72 GRENDON. William holds from him. Edwy held it, and Ordric, as
two manors. 4 hides which pay tax. Land for 8 ploughs.
Nothing is recorded there.

73 STANFORD. Thurstan holds from him. Edwy Young held it. 1 hide
which pays tax. In lordship 1 plough;
    2 ploughmen and 1 smallholder.
The value was 5s; now 10s.
    1 further plough would be possible.

74 'CUPLE'. Edric holds from him. Leofsi held it; he could go where
he would. 1 hide which pays tax. In lordship 1 plough;
    1 villager and 1 ploughman with 1 plough. 3 slaves.
The value was 5s; now 12s.

75 HANLEY. St. Peter's holds it in alms by gift of Walter of Lacy.
Alnoth held it; he could go where he would. ½ hide
which pays tax.
    1 villager who has 1 plough.
The value was 6s; now 8s.

.XI. **R**ERRA ROGERIJ DE MV.CELGROS *IN VLFEI HVND.*

ᴏɢᴇʀɪᴠꜱ de Micelgros teñ de rege *VPETONE.*
Archetel 7 Ergriḿ tenueꝛ ᵽ.ɪɪ.ᴍ̃.Ibi.ɪɪ.hidæ gelđ.
In dñio funt.ɪɪ.caꝛ.7 uñ francig̅ cū.ɪ.caꝛ.Ibi.ɪɪɪɪ.ſerui.
7 ɪɪ.borđ.   ValꝔ 7 uaꞁ.xxɪɪ.ſoliđ.
Íſđ Rog̃ teñ *LAST.*Archetel 7 Ergrim tenueꝛ ᵽ.ɪɪ.ᴍ̃.
Ibi.ɪ.hiđ.gelđ.   ValꝔ.ɪɪɪɪ.ſoꞁ.Modo wasꞇ.ē̃.

★ .XII. **R**ᴏᴛʙᴇʀꞇ Gernon teñ de rege *LARPOL*
ꜱᴄʀᴜᴘᴇ 9
Ricard tenuit.Ibi.ɪɪɪ.hidæ.gelđ.Ibi funt.ɪɪɪɪ.uiꞁꞁi
7 ᴠɪɪɪ.borđ.cū.ɪɪɪ.caꝛ.

T.R.E.ualꝔ.xxᴠ.ſoliđ.Modo.xx.ſoliđ. *IN CVTESTORN HĐ.*
Íſđ Roꝃt teñ.ᴠ.hiđ 7 dimiđ in caſtellaria de *AVRETONE.*
Ricard tenuit.H̃ ꞇra n̄ gelđ.In dñio funt.ᴠ.caꝛ.7 xxxɪɪɪɪ.
uiꞁꞁ 7 ᴠɪ.borđ 7 faꝔ cū.xᴠ.caꝛ.inꞇ oms 7 redđt.xx.ſoliđ.
Ibi.x.ſerui.7 moliñ redđ.ɪɪɪɪ.modios annonæ 7 xᴠ.ſtiches
anguiꞁꞁ.   T.R.E.7 poſt.7 modo.uaꞁ.ᴠɪɪ.liꝔ.

.XIII. **H**ᴇʀʀᴀ HENRICI DE FERIERES. *IN GREITREWES HĐ.*

ᴇɴʀɪᴄᴠꜱ de ferreres teñ *FROME.*Aluiet tenuit de Eſtano ᵉᵖᵒ
7 poterat ire quo uolꝔ.Ibi.ɪɪ.hidæ 7 una ᵛ gelđ.In dñio funt.ɪɪ.
caꝛ.7 ɪɪɪɪ.uiꞁꞁi 7 x.borđ cū.ɪɪ.caꝛ.7 uñ burḡſis in hereford
redđ.xɪɪ.denar.

T.R.E.7 poſt 7 modo.uaꞁ.ɪɪɪ.liꝔ. *IN CVTESTORN HVND.*
In Caſtellaria de *EWIAS* teñ Roger̃ de Henrico.ɪɪɪ.æcclas.7 pꝔrm.
7 xxxɪɪ.aꞔs ꞇræ.7 redđt.ɪɪ.ſexꞇ mellis.In caſtello h̃ꞇ.ɪɪ.maſuras.

11   LAND OF ROGER OF MUSSEGROS

In WOLPHY Hundred

1   Roger of Mussegros holds UPTON from the King. Arketel and
Arngrim held it as two manors. 2 hides which pay tax. In
lordship 2 ploughs;
> 1 Frenchman with 1 plough. 4 slaves; 2 smallholders.

The value was and is 22s.

2   Roger also holds LAYSTERS. Arketel and Arngrim held it as two
manors. 1 hide which pays tax.
The value was 4s. Now it is waste.

12   LAND OF ROBERT GERNON

In WOLPHY Hundred

1   Robert Gernon holds YARPOLE from the King. Richard Scrope
held it. 3 hides which pay tax.
> 4 villagers and 8 smallholders with 3 ploughs.

Value before 1066, 25s; now 20s.

In CUTSTHORN Hundred

2   Robert also holds 5½ hides in the castlery of (Richards) CASTLE.
Richard held it. This land does not pay tax. In lordship 5 ploughs;
> 34 villagers, 6 smallholders and a smith with 15 ploughs
> between them; they pay 20s.
> 10 slaves; a mill which pays 4 measures of corn and 15 sticks
> of eels.

Value before 1066, later and now £7.

13   LAND OF HENRY OF FERRERS

In GREYTREE Hundred

1   Henry of Ferrers holds (Priors) FROME. Alfgeat held it from
Bishop Aethelstan; he could go where he would. 2 hides and
1 virgate which pay tax. In lordship 2 ploughs;
> 4 villagers and 10 smallholders with 2 ploughs; 1 burgess
> in Hereford who pays 12d.

Value before 1066, later and now £3.

In CUTSTHORN Hundred

2   In the castlery of EWYAS (Harold) Roger holds from Henry
3 churches, a priest and 32 acres of land; they pay 2 sesters of
honey. In the castle he has 2 dwellings.

.XII. WTERRA WILLI DE SCOHIES

Wills De Scohies ten viii . carucatas træ In Caſtella

ria de *CARLION* .7 Turſtin ten de illo . Ibi hŧ in dnĩo unã

car .7 iii . Walenſes lege Walenſi uiuentes cū . iii . caŕ .7 ii .

borđ cū dim caŕ .7 reddŧ . iiii . ſextaŕ mellis . Ibi . ii . ſerui 7 una

ancilla .

Ħ ŧra waſta erat T.R.E.7 qdo Wills recep̃ . Modo ual . xl . ſoł .

Iſđ . Wills ten *MAGGA* . Eduin tenuit . IN *TORNELAVS* HĎ .

Ibi . i . hida gelđ .7 dimiđ n̄ gelđ . In dnĩo ſunt . ii . caŕ .7 ii . uilli

7 iii . borđ cū , ii . caŕ .7 iiii . ſerui .7 iii . cot .7 p̃tū bobʒ .

T.R.E.7 poſt ualuit . xl . ſoł . modo . v . ſoliđ plus .

Hoc ÇĐ calūniant̃ clerici S̃ Guthlaci .

Iſđ . W . ten *BRADEFORD* . Eduin tenuit . Ibi . ii . hidæ

gelđ . In dnĩo . ē una ćaŕ .7 iii . borđ cū dim caŕ .7 ii . ſerui .

7 faŧ .7 p̃tū bobʒ . Stefan ten de Willo .

T.R.E.ualb̃ . xl . ſoliđ 7 poſt . xx . ſoł . Modo . xxv . ſoliđ .

Iſđ W . ten in *NIWETVNE* . dimiđ hiđ gelđ

Bruns tenuit . Bernard ten de Willo . In dnĩo . ē . i . caŕ .

7 ii . uilli cū . i . caŕ .7 iiii . ſerui . Valuit . x . ſoł . Modo . xii . ſoł .

Iſđ . W . ten *CROFTA* .7 Bernard de eo . IN *VLFEI* HĎ .

Eduin tenuit . Ibi . i . hida gelđ . In dnĩo . ē . i . caŕ .7 ii . bouarij

7 un francig 7 iii . borđ cū . ii . caŕ . Valuit . xx . ſoł . Modo . xxv .

Iſđ . W . ten *POSCETENETVNE* .7 Rađ de eo In Valle

de Stratelei . Eduin tenuit . Ibi . ii . hidæ . In dnĩo . ē . i . caŕ .

7 ii . uilli cū . i . caŕ . Waſŧ fuit . Modo . v . ſoliđ .

[CASTLERY] ,

1   William of Écouis holds 8 carucates of land in the castlery of
CAERLEON. Thurstan holds from him. He has 1 plough in lordship;
    3 Welshmen who live under Welsh law, with 3 ploughs;
      2 smallholders with ½ plough; they pay 4 sesters of honey.
      2 male slaves, 1 female.
This land was waste before 1066, and when William acquired it.
Value now 40s.

William also holds
in THORNLAW Hundred

2   MAUND. Edwin held it. 1 hide which pays tax and ½ which does
not pay tax. In lordship 2 ploughs;
    2 villagers and 3 smallholders with 2 ploughs; 4 slaves;
      3 cottagers.
Meadow for the oxen.
Value before 1066 and later, 40s; now 5s more.
The clerks of St. Guthlac's claim this manor.

3   BROADWARD. Edwin held it. 2 hides which pay tax. In lordship
1 plough;
    3 smallholders with ½ plough; 2 slaves; a smith.
Meadow for the oxen.
Stephen holds from William.
Value before 1066, 40s; later 20s; now 25s.

4   in NEWTON ½ hide which pays tax. ... Brown held it. Bernard
holds from William. In lordship 1 plough;
    2 villagers with 1 plough; 4 slaves.
The value was 10s; now 12s.

in WOLPHY Hundred

5   CROFT. Bernard holds from him. Edwin held it. 1 hide which pays
tax. In lordship 1 plough;
    2 ploughmen, 1 Frenchman and 3 smallholders with 2 ploughs.
The value was 20s; now 25[s].

6   POSTON. Ralph holds from him. In the Golden Valley. Edwin
held it. 2 hides. In lordship 1 plough;
    2 villagers with 1 plough.
It was waste. [Value] now 5s.

Iſd.W.ten *Rviscop*.Herald tenuit. *In Elsedvn* HD.

Ibi.i.hida geld.Waſt fuit 7 eſt.Ibi.é una haia in una magna ſilua.

Iſd.W.ten *Dilven*.Eduin tenuit.7 potuit ire quo uoluit. Ibi.iii.hidæ geld.In dnio.é una car.7 viii.uilli 7 v.bord cũ.vii.car.7 adhuc.ii.car plus poſſeɴ.eé.Ibi.i.ancilla. T.R.E.ualb.iiii.lib.7 poſt 7 modo.lxxv.ſolid.

Iſd.W.ten in ipſa uilla.i.hidā geld.Ernui tenuit 7 potuit ire q̊ uoluit.Tra.é.iii.car.Ibi.é un uilłs 7 iii. bord.T.R.E.ualb.xxv.ſol.7 poſt.x.ſol.Modo.xv.ſolid.

Iſd.W.ten *Erdeshop*.Elmar *In Stepleset* HD.
tenuit.7 q̊ uolb ire poterat.Ibi.i.hida geld.In dnio ſunt ii.car.7 ii.bord cũ dimid car.7 ii.ſerui. T.R.E.ualb.xx.ſol.7 poſt.xv.Modo.xx.ſol.

Iſd.W.ten in ipſa uilla unā v̄ træ geld.Æluric tenuit 7 poterat ire q̊ uolb.Nil ibi.é.Tam ualuit 7 ual.iii.ſol.

Iſd.W.ten *Merstvne*.Eduin tenuit 7 q̊ uolb ire poterat. Ibi dim hida geld.In dnio.é una car.7 ii.ſerui. T.R.E.7 poſt.ualuit.iiii.ſol.Modo.vi.ſol.

.XV. W TERRA WILLI FILIJ BADERON.*In Bremesese* HD.
Wiłłs.F.Baderon ten *Hope*.Leuric 7 Edeulf tenueꝛ p.ii.M̃.Ibi.iiii.hidæ geld.Salomon ten de Wiłło. In dnio ſunt.ii.car.7 un uilłi 7 un bord cũ.i.car 7 dimid. T.R.E.ualb.xl.ſol.7 modo ſimilit.   ꝼtatu.
Tercia pars jacuit in æccła S̃ Petri de Glouuec.T.R.E.teſte comi
huj' Manerij
Iſd.W.ten *Rvvirdin*.7 Salomon de eo.Hadeuui tenuit. Ibi.iiii.hidæ geld.In dnio poſſeɴ.eé.iii.car.Ibi.é un bord 7 ii.uilłi 7 un Walenſis cũ.iii.car.Valuit 7 ual.xxx.ſolid.

in ELSDON Hundred
7 RUSHOCK. Earl Harold held it. 1 hide which pays tax.
It was and is waste.
A hedged enclosure there in a large wood.

8 DILWYN. Edwin held it; he could go where he would. 3 hides
which pay tax. In lordship 1 plough;
8 villagers and 5 smallholders with 7 ploughs; a further 2 more
ploughs would be possible. 1 female slave.
Value before 1066 £4; later and now 75s.

9 in this village 1 hide which pays tax. Ernwy held it; he could go
where he would. Land for 3 ploughs.
1 villager and 3 smallholders.
Value before 1066, 25s; later 10s; now 15s.

in STAPLE Hundred
10 YARSOP. Aelmer held it; he could go where he would. 1 hide
which pays tax. In lordship 2 ploughs;
2 smallholders with ½ plough; 2 slaves.
Value before 1066, 20s; later 15[s]; now 20s.

11 in this village 1 virgate of land which pays tax. Aelfric held it; he
could go where he would. Nothing there.
However, the value was and is 3s.

[in PLEGELGATE Hundred]
12 MARSTON (Stannett). Edwin held it; he could go where he would.
½ hide which pays tax. In lordship 1 plough; 2 slaves.
Value before 1066 and later, 4s; now 6s.

15   LAND OF WILLIAM SON OF BADERON

In BROMSASH Hundred
1 William son of Baderon holds HOPE (Mansell). Leofric and Edwulf
held it as two manors. 4 hides which pay tax. Solomon holds it
from William. In lordship 2 ploughs;
1 villager and 1 smallholder with 1½ ploughs.
Value before 1066, 40s; now the same.
A third part of this manor lay in (the lands of) St. Peter's
Church of Gloucester before 1066, according to the testimony of
the County.

William also holds
2 RUARDEAN. Solomon holds from him. Hadwic held it. 4 hides
which pay tax. 3 ploughs would be possible in lordship.
1 smallholder, 2 villagers and 1 Welshman with 3 ploughs.
The value was and is 30s.

Iſđ.W.ten unã v̄ træ de *LINTONE* Ⓜ regis. Lefstan tenuit
7 ñ poterat recedere á Ⓜ ipſo. Ibi.ē una car̄ 7 nil plus.

Val̄ 7 ualuit. iii . ſoliđ.

185 d

Iſđ.W.ten dimiđ hidã in *MERCHELAI* Ⓜ regis. *IN WIMVNDSKVIL ⌐HĎ.*

Iſđ.W.ten *BICRETVNE* .7 Goisfriđ de eo. Adulf tenuit.7 q̃ uolƀ
ire poterat. Ibi.1. hida gelđ. In dñio. ſunt. ii . car̄.7 ii . uil̃i cũ.1.
car̄.7 ii . borđ.7 iii . ſerui.

Valet 7 ualuit.xxx. ſoliđ.   *IN RADELAV HVNḎ.*

Iſđ.W.ten *STRATVNE*.Turchil tenuit de Heraldo.Ibi.iii.hidæ
7·dimiđ gelđ.In dñio ſunt. ii . car̄.7 vii . uil̃i 7 un̄ borđ cũ. vii .
car̄.7 iii . ſerui.7 xxx. ac̄ p̃ti.7 ii . molini de. vi . ſol̄ 7 viii .den.
T.R.E. ualƀ. ix . liƀ. Mòdo. vii . liƀ.

Iſđ.W.ten *WITEWICHE*.Turchil tenuit de heraldo com̃.
Ibi. ii . hidæ gelđ. In dñio ſunt. ii . car̄.7 un̄ uil̃s 7 ii .borđ
cũ..1. car̄.7 iii .ſerui.7 ii .ac̄ p̃ti.   Valuit 7 ual̄. xx .ſoliđ.

Iſđ.W.ten *SPERTVNE*. Wluui tenuit de Heraldo.7 poterat
ire q̃ uolƀ. Ibi. v .hidæ 7 dimiđ gelđ. In dñio ſunt. iiii . car̄.
7 vi . uil̃i 7 ii .borđ cũ. iii .car̄.7 xiii . ſerui.7 xx . ac̄ p̃ti. Siluæ
una leuua int̄ l̄g 7 lat̄.

T.R.E. ualƀ. cx . ſoliđ. modo. tntđ.

Iſđ.W . ten *WALESAPELDOR* .7 Gerald de eo. Vlmer hō Turchil tenuit.
7 poterat ire q̃ uolƀ. Ibi.1. hida 7 una v̄ gelđ. In dñio.ē una
car̄.7 ii .borđ 7 un̄ liƀ hō cũ.1.car̄.7 ii . ac̄ p̃ti.

T.R.E . ualƀ. xxv .ſol̄. Modo tntđ.

Iſđ.W . ten *MONESLAI*. Aluric tenuit.7 q̃ uoluit ire potuit.
Ibi.1. hida 7 dimiđ gelđ. In dñio.ē una car̄.7 iii . borđ.7 un̄ ſeru.
7 una car̄ plus poteſt ibi. ēe.

T.R.E. ualƀ. xxx .ſol̄.7 poſt 7 modo. xv . ſoliđ.

3 one virgate of land from LINTON, the King's manor. Leofstan
held it; he could not withdraw from this manor. 1 plough there;
nothing more.
The value is and was 3s.

in WINSTREE Hundred   185 d
4 ½ hide in (Much) MARCLE, the King's manor.

5 BICKERTON. Geoffrey holds from him. Adolf held it; he could go
where he would. 1 hide which pays tax. In lordship 2 ploughs;
    2 villagers with 1 plough; 2 smallholders and 3 slaves.
The value is and was 30s.

in RADLOW Hundred
6 STRETTON (Grandison). Thorkell held it from Earl Harold. 3½ hides
which pay tax. In lordship 2 ploughs;
    7 villagers and 1 smallholder with 7 ploughs; 3 slaves.
    Meadow, 30 acres; 2 mills at 6s 8d.
Value before 1066 £9; now £7.

7 WHITWICK. Thorkell held it from Earl Harold. 2 hides which pay
tax. In lordship 2 ploughs;
    1 villager and 2 smallholders with 1 plough; 3 slaves.
    Meadow, 2 acres.
The value was and is 20s.

8 ASHPERTON. Wulfwy held it from Earl Harold; he could go where
he would. 5½ hides which pay tax. In lordship 4 ploughs;
    6 villagers and 2 smallholders with 3 ploughs; 13 slaves.
    Meadow, 20 acres; woodland, 1 league in both length and width.
Value before 1066, 110s; now as much.

9 WALSOPTHORNE. Gerald holds from him. Thorkell, Wulfmer's man,
held it; he could go where he would. 1 hide and 1 virgate which
pay tax. In lordship 1 plough;
    2 smallholders and 1 free man with 1 plough.
    Meadow, 2 acres.
Value before 1066, 25s; now as much.

10 MUNSLEY. Aelfric held it; he could go where he would. 1½ hides;
they pay tax. In lordship 1 plough;
    3 smallholders and 1 slave; 1 more plough possible there.
Value before 1066, 30s; later and now 15s.

WITTS.F.Normanni ten͛ *MVLESLAGE*. Wade tenuit.

7 poterat ire q̃ uolb͛.Ibi.i.hida geld͛.In dñio.ē una car͛.7 vi.

bord͛ 7 un̉ feruus.7 dimid͛ car͛ plus poffet ibi.ēe.

Val 7 ualuit.x.folid͛. *IN PLEGELIET HVND.*

Iſd͛.W.ten͛ *HOPETVNE*.7 Richerỉ de eo.Brifmar tenuit

7 q̃ uolb͛ ire poterat.Ibi.i.hida 7 una v̉ geld͛.In dñio.ē una

car͛.7 iii.uitti 7 ii.bord͛ cū.iii.car͛.7 iiii.ferui.

T.R.E.ualb͛.xxx.fot.7 modo tntd͛. *IN TORNELAVS HD.*

Iſd͛.W.ten͛ *FENNE*.Steinulf tenuit.Ibi.i.hida 7 dimid͛ gld͛.

In dñio.ē una car͛.7 ii.uitt 7.vii.bord͛ cū.iii͛.car͛.7 ii̊.ferui.

T.R.E.ualb͛.xx.fot.Modo.xxx.folid͛.

Iſd͛.W.ten͛ *FERNE*.Duo Radmans tenuer͛.T.R.E.Ibi dimid͛

hida. In dñio funt.ii.car͛.7 un̉ uitts 7 ii.bord͛ cū.i.car͛.

7 iiii.ferui 7 una ancilla.Valuit.x.fot.Modo.xvi.fot.

H̄ duo ᴍ̃ adjacuer͛ ad firmā Maurdine ᴍ̃ regis.

TVRSTIN̉ filỉ Rolf ten͛ *ALWINTVNE*.Brictric.tenuit.T.R.E.

Ibi.vi.hidæ In dñio funt.ii.car͛.7 xii.uitti cū.ix.car͛.

7 reddt͛.xx.blomas ferri 7 viii.fextar͛ mellis.Ibi.v.ferui.

7 molin̄ de.xl.denar͛.

T.R.E.ualb͛.xx.fot.Modo.iiii.lib͛. *IN RADELAV HD.*

Iſd͛ Turſtin̉ ten͛ *MERCHELAI*.7 alt͛ Turſtin̉ de eo.Brictric

tenuit de Heraldo.7 poterat ire q̃ uolb͛.Ibi.iii.hidæ geld͛.

In dñio funt.ii.car͛.7 vii.uitti 7 iiii.bord͛ cū.viii.car͛.7 iiii.ferui.

T.R.E.7 poſt 7 modo.ual.lx.folid͛.

16   LAND OF WILLIAM SON OF NORMAN

In RADLOW Hundred
1 William son of Norman holds MUNSLEY. Wada held it; he could go
where he would. 1 hide which pays tax. In lordship 1 plough;
    6 smallholders and 1 slave; ½ plough more would be
      possible there.
The value is and was 10s.

In PLEGELGATE Hundred
2 William also holds HOPTON (Sollers), and Richere from him.
Brictmer held it; he could go where he would. 1 hide and 1
virgate which pay tax. In lordship 1 plough;
    3 villagers and 2 smallholders with 3 ploughs; 4 slaves.
Value before 1066, 30s; now as much.

In THORNLAW Hundred
3 William also holds VENNS (Green). Steinulf held it. 1½ hides
which pay tax. In lordship 1 plough;
    2 villagers and 7 smallholders with 3 ploughs; 2 slaves.
Value before 1066, 20s; now 30s.

4 William also holds (The) VERN. Two riders held it before 1066.
½ hide. ... In lordship 2 ploughs;
    1 villager and 2 smallholders with 1 plough; 4 male slaves,
      1 female.
The value was 10s; now 16s.

These two manors were attached to the revenue of Marden, the
King's manor.

17   LAND OF THURSTAN SON OF ROLF

In BROMSASH Hundred
1 Thurstan son of Rolf holds ALVINGTON. Brictric held it before
1066. 6 hides. ... In lordship 2 ploughs;
    12 villagers with 9 ploughs; they pay 20 blooms of iron
      and 8 sesters of honey.
    5 slaves; a mill at 40d.
Value before 1066, 20s; now £4.

In RADLOW Hundred
2 Thurstan also holds (Little) MARCLE, and another Thurstan from
him. Brictric held it from Earl Harold; he could go where he would.
3 hides which pay tax. In lordship 2 ploughs;
    7 villagers and 4 smallholders with 8 ploughs; 4 slaves.
Value before 1066, later and now, 60s.

.XVIİ ꞘTERRA ALBERTI LOTHAꞄ. *IN RADELAV HD̅.*

ALBERTVS Lothariensis teñ *LEDENE* . Eddied tenuit
soror Odon comit̓ . Ibi . ix . hidæ gelđ . In dñio sunt . ii . car̓ .
7 tcia posset . ee̅ . Ibi . xxxii . uilli 7 xiii . borđ cu̅ . xxxii . car̅ ;
Ibi . vi . serui . 7 moliñ de . xxxii . deñ .
T.R.E. ualb̅ . xiiii . lib̅ . Modo . xv . lib̅ .

.IX. ꞘTERRA ALVREDI DE MERLEBERGE.

ALVRED de Merleberge teñ Castellu̅ *EWIAS* . de W . rege;
Ipse Rex eni concessit ei tras quas Wills comes ei dederat .
qui hoc castellu̅ refirmauerat . hoc est . v . carucatas træ ibidẽ;
7 ad Manitone alias . v . carucatas . Terrã q̓q̔ Radulfi de
bernai c̅cessit ei rex . quæ ad castellu̅ ptinebat;
Ibi h̅t in dñio . ii . car̅ . 7 ix . Walenses cu̅ ; vi . car̅ . redđtes
vii . sextar mellis . 7 xii . borđ opantes una die ebdomađ .
Ibi . iiii . bouarij . 7 uñ h̅o redđ . vi . denar̓ .
Quinq̔ milites ej Ricard Gislebt Wills 7 Wills 7 Hernold
h̅nt . v . car̓ in dñio . 7 xii . borđ . 7 iii . piscarias ; 7 xx.ii . ac̅s p̓ti .
Duo alij Wills 7 Radulf teñ trã . ii . car̅ .
Turstin ten trã redđtẽ . xix . deñ . 7 Warneri trã de . v ; sol̅ .
Hi h̅nt . v . borđ .
Hoc castellu̅ *EWIAS* . ual̅ . x . lib̅ .

IN CVTESTORN HD̅.

Isđ Alured teñ *BVRGELLE* . Herald tenuit . Ibi . viii . hidæ
gelđ . In dñio sunt . ii . car̅ . 7 xvi . uilli 7 xix . borđ 7 pbr
cu̅ . xxiiii . car̅ . Ibi . iiii . serui . 7 moliñ de . xx . solid . 7 xxv .
stiches anguill . Silua redđ . iiii . solid . In Hereforđ . v . bur
genses redđt huic c̅o ; lii . denar̓ .
In ipso c̅o h̅nt . ii . milites . ii . car̅ . 7 ii . bouar̓ . 7 Godric qđa
tain h̅t . i . car̅ . 7 alt qđa h̅t uñ uillm .
T.R.E. ptineb huic c̅o tcius denari de duob̔ hund Strad
ford 7 Chistestornes ; Tc ualb̅ . xx . lib̅ . Modo . xv . lib̅ .

18   **LAND OF ALBERT OF LORRAINE**   186 a

In RADLOW Hundred

1   Albert of Lorraine holds UPLEADON. Edith sister of Earl Oda held it. 9 hides which pay tax. In lordship 2 ploughs; a third would be possible.

> 32 villagers and 13 smallholders with 32 ploughs.
> 6 slaves; a mill at 32d.

Value before 1066 £14; now £15.

[19]   LAND OF ALFRED OF MARLBOROUGH

[CASTLE]

1   Alfred of Marlborough holds the castle of EWYAS (Harold) from King William. The King himself granted him the lands which Earl William, who had refortified the castle, had given him; that is, 5 carucates of land in that place and 5 other carucates at MONNINGTON. The King also granted him the land of Ralph of Bernay which belonged to the castle. He has 2 ploughs in lordship;

> 9 Welshmen with 6 ploughs who pay 7 sesters of honey; 12 smallholders who work 1 day a week. 4 ploughmen; 1 man who pays 6d.
> Five men-at-arms of his, Richard, Gilbert, William, William, and Arnold, have 5 ploughs in lordship;
> 12 smallholders and
> 3 fisheries; meadow, 22 acres.

Two others, William and Ralph, hold land for 2 ploughs. Thurstan holds land which pays 19d; Warner land at 5s. They have 5 smallholders.

Value of this castle of Ewyas (Harold) £10.

Alfred also holds

in CUTSTHORN Hundred

2   BURGHILL. Earl Harold held it. 8 hides which pay tax.

In lordship 2 ploughs;

> 16 villagers, 19 smallholders and a priest with 24 ploughs.
> 4 slaves; a mill at 20s and 25 sticks of eels; woodland which pays 4s.
> 5 burgesses in Hereford pay 52d to this manor.

In this manor 2 men-at-arms have 2 ploughs; 2 ploughmen. Godric, a thane, has 1 plough; another man has 1 villager.

Before 1066 the third penny of the two Hundreds, Stretford and Cutsthorn, belonged to this manor. Value then £20; now £15.

Ise Alured ten *HOPE*.7 Ricard de eo .Herald tenuit.

Ibi.v.hidæ geld.In dnio funt.11.car 7 dimid.7 v11.uilli
7 pbr 7 xv.bord cu.v.car 7 dimid.Ibi.v.bouarij.

T.R.E.ualb.v111.lib.Modo: v1.lib.

H duo M tenuit Osbn auuncul Alueradi T.R.E.qdo Go
duin 7 Herald erant exulati. *IN VALLE STRADELIE.*

Ise Alured ten *MANETVNE*.Herald tenuit.Ibi.v.
hidæ Rad de Bernai inde abstulit.1.Hida injuste.

Ibi funt.111.francig cu.111.car.7 1x.bord.7 un radman
cu dimid car.   Wast fuit.Modo redd.xxx.solid.

Ise Alured ten *BROCHEVRDIE*.Herald tenuit.

Ibi.v.hidæ.   In dnio.e una car.7 v1.uilli 7 v1.bord
7 un ho.7 un Walenfis.Int oms hnt.111.car.7 111.serui.
Wast fuit.Modo ual.111.lib. *IN TORNELAVS HVND.*

Ise Alured ten un Maner de.xv.hid geld.7 filia ej de eo.
Ipse Alv tenuit T.R.E.In dnio funt.111.car.7 xx1.uills 7 1111.
bord.7 pbr cu æccla.7 faber.Int oms hnt.xx.car.Ibi.v1.serui
7 v1.bouarij.7 molin de.v.solid.

T.R.E.ualb.x1111.lib.modo.x.lib. *IN BREMESESE HVND*
Ise Alured ten *EDTVNE*.Herald tenuit.Ibi.11.hidæ 7 dim geld.
In dnio.e una car.7 1x.uill 7.v1.bord cu.v11.car.

T.R.E.ualb.L.solid.7 post 7 modo.xL.solid

Ise Alured ten *PENEBRVGE*.Herald tenuit.Ibi.x1.hidæ una
uirg min 7 geld.In dnio funt.111.car.7 xx.uilli 7 v11.bord
7 un radchen cu.x11.car.Ibi.111.serui.7 molin de.x.solid.
Silua ibi erat ad.cLx.porc si fructificasset.

186 b
Hoc M Penebruge caluniant canon S Guthlaci.7 dnt qd
Goduin 7 Herald filius ej abstuler injuste a sco Guthlaco.

T.R.E.ualb.xv1.lib.7 post fuit wast.modo ual:x.lib 7.x.sol.
Ise Alured ten *STRATFORD*.Herald tenuit. *IN STRATFORD HD.*
Ibi.11.hidæ geld.Gislebt ten de Turstino 7 Tursi de Aluredo.

3 BRINSOP. Richard holds from him. Earl Harold held it. 5 hides
  which pay tax. In lordship 2½ ploughs;
    7 villagers, a priest and 15 smallholders with 5½ ploughs.
      5 ploughmen.
  Value before 1066 £8; now £6.

Osbern uncle of Alfred held these two manors before 1066 after
Godwin and Harold had been exiled.

  in the GOLDEN VALLEY
4 MONNINGTON. Earl Harold held it. 5 hides. ... Ralph of Bernay
  took 1 hide wrongfully from it.
    3 Frenchmen with 3 ploughs; 9 smallholders and 1 rider
      with ½ plough.
  It was waste. Now it pays 30s.

5 BREDWARDINE. Earl Harold held it. 5 hides. ... In lordship 1 plough;
    6 villagers, 6 smallholders, 1 man and 1 Welshman; between
      them they have 3 ploughs; 3 slaves.
  It was waste. Value now £3.

  in THORNLAW Hundred
6 one manor at 15 hides which pay tax. His daughter holds from
  him. Alfred held it himself before 1066. In lordship 3 ploughs;
    21 villagers, 4 smallholders, a priest with a church, a smith;
      between them they have 20 ploughs. 6 slaves and 6
      ploughmen.
    A mill at 5s.
  Value before 1066 £14; now £10.

  in BROMSASH Hundred
7 (Hill of) EATON. Earl Harold held it. 2½ hides which pay tax.
  In lordship 1 plough;
    9 villagers and 6 smallholders with 7 ploughs.
  Value before 1066, 50s.; later and now, 40s.

  [? in ELSDON Hundred]
8 PEMBRIDGE. Earl Harold held it. 11 hides, less 1 virgate; they pay
  tax. In lordship 3 ploughs;
    20 villagers, 7 smallholders and 1 riding man with 12 ploughs.
    3 slaves; a mill at 10s. There was woodland there for 160
      pigs, if it had produced (mast).
    The Canons of St. Guthlac's claim this manor of Pembridge;   186 b
      they state that Earl Godwin and his son Harold wrongfully
      took it from St. Guthlac's.
  Value before 1066 £16; later it was waste; value now £10 10s.

  in STRETFORD Hundred
9 STRETFORD. Earl Harold held it. 2 hides which pay tax. Gilbert
  holds from Thurstan, and Thurstan from Alfred.

In dñio.ē una caŕ.7 uñ uitts 7 IIII . borđ cū dim̃ caŕ.7 III . caŕ

ibi poffeɴ . ee . Ibi . III . ſerui . 7 p̃tū redđ . III . ſot . Ibi ſilua.

T.R.E . ualƀ . xxx . ſot . Modo . xx . ſoliđ . IN RADELAV HĐ.

Iſđ Alured ten CᵛᵛRE . Herald tenuit . Ibi . xv . hidæ gelđ.

ſed rex . W . condonaū . vi . hiđ ꝗetas a geldo.

Hoc m̃ ten filia Aluredi Agnes uxor Turſtini de Wigemore.

In dñio ſunt . II . caŕ . 7 p̃br 7 p̃poſit 7 xxvi . uitti 7 vIII.

borđ . Int om̃s hn̄t . xxxII . caŕ . Ibi . IIII . ſerui . 7 faber.

7 p̃tū 7 ſilua nil redđt . 7 una hida de hac t̃ra jacet in ſilua

regis . Ad hoc m̃ ptineƀ t̃cius denari de . III . hunđ . T.R.E.

Modo abblaŧ eſt . Tc̃ ualƀ . xxv . liƀ . Modo . c . ſoliđ miñ.

TERRA ALVREDI HISPAÑ.   IN PLEGELIET HVND.

.XX. ALVRED de Hiſpania ten TORNEBERIE . Siuuard tenuit

7 quo uolƀ ire poterat . Ibi . vi . hidæ gelđ . In dñio ſunt . III . caŕ.

7 IIII . uitti 7 IIII . borđ cū . III . caŕ . Ibi . vi . ſerui . 7 II . caŕ plus

poſſent . ee . ibi.

T.R.E . ualƀ . vi . liƀ . 7 poſt . c . ſot . Modo : IIII . liƀ 7 x . ſoliđ.

Iſđ Alured ten in ead̃ uilla . I . hiđ . Leuric 7 Leuing 7 Ernui

tenueŕ p . III . m̃ . Waſta fuit ħ t̃ra . Ibi . ē dimiđ caŕ . 7 II.

uitti cū dim̃ caŕ . 7 una caŕ adhuc ibi poſſet . ee . ħ t̃ra gelđ.

Qui teneƀ poteraɴ ire ꝗ uolƀ . Valƀ xIII . ſot 7 IIII . denar.

Modo . II . ſoliđ.

TERRA ANSFRIDI DE CORMEL. IN RADELAV HVND.

.XXI. ANSFRID de Cormelijs ten TATINTVNE . Aluuold 7 Ernui

tenueŕ p . II . m̃ . 7 quo uolƀ ire poteraɴ . Ibi . III . hidæ gelđ.

In dñio ſunt . II . caŕ . 7 v . uitti 7 xII . borđ cū . Ix . caŕ . 7 alii

vIII . hoẽs ſunt ibi nil redđtes . 7 una caŕ adhuc poſſet . ee . ibi.

Ibi . IIII . ſerui 7 III . ancillæ.

T.R.E . ualƀ . cx . ſoliđ . 7 poſt . IIII . liƀ . Modo . vi . liƀ.

In lordship 1 plough;
> 1 villager and 4 smallholders with ½ plough; 3 ploughs
> would be possible there.
> 3 slaves; meadow which pays 3s. Woodland there.

Value before 1066, 30s; now 20s.

in RADLOW Hundred

10 (Much) COWARNE. Earl Harold held it. 15 hides which pay tax,
but King William granted 6 hides exempt from tax. Agnes daughter
of Alfred and wife of Thurstan of Wigmore holds this manor.
In lordship 2 ploughs;
> A priest, a reeve, 26 villagers and 8 smallholders; between
> them they have 32 ploughs. 4 slaves and a smith.
> Both the meadow and woodland pay nothing. 1 hide of this
> land lies in the King's wood.

Before 1066 the third penny of three Hundreds belonged to this
manor; now this has been removed. Value then £25; now 100s less.

20 # LAND OF ALFRED OF 'SPAIN'

In PLEGELGATE Hundred

1 Alfred of 'Spain' holds THORNBURY. Siward held it; he could go
where he would. 6 hides which pay tax. In lordship 3 ploughs;
> 4 villagers and 4 smallholders with 3 ploughs. 6 slaves;
> 2 more ploughs would be possible there.

Value before 1066 £6; later 100s; now £4 10s.

2 Alfred also holds 1 hide in the same village. Leofric, Leofing
and Ernwy held it as three manors. This land was waste.
½ plough there.
> 2 villagers with ½ plough; 1 further plough would be possible
> there.

This land pays tax. Those who held it could go where
they would.

The value was 13s 4d; now 2s.

21 # LAND OF ANSFRID OF CORMEILLES

In RADLOW Hundred

1 Ansfrid of Cormeilles holds TARRINGTON. Alfwold and Ernwy
held it as two manors; they could go where they would. 3 hides
which pay tax. In lordship 2 ploughs;
> 5 villagers and 12 smallholders with 9 ploughs. 8 other men
> there who pay nothing; 1 further plough would be possible
> there. 4 male and 3 female slaves.

Value before 1066, 110s; later £4; now £6.

Iſd Ansfrid ten̄ PICHESLEI. Turgar tenuit. 7 quo uolɓ
ire poterat. Ibi dimid̄ hida geld̄. In dn̄io eſt. 1. car̄. 7 11. liɓi
hōes 7 11. bord̄.

T.R.E. ualɓ. v111. ſolid̄. Modo. x. ſolid̄. IN BREMESESE HD̄.

Iſd Ansfrid ten̄ ESTVNE. 7 Godefrid de eo. Rex. E. tenuit.
Ibi. 11. hidæ geld̄. In dn̄io eſt. 1. car̄. 7 1111. uiłłi 7 1x. bord̄
cū. v111. car̄. 7 alij. v111. hōes nil reddtes. Ibi. 11. bouarij
7 molin̄ nil redd̄.

T.R.E. ualɓ. L. ſolid̄. Modo. c. ſolid̄. IN GREITREWES HD̄.

Iſd Ansfrid ten̄ HOPE. Hagene tenuit 7 potuit ire q̄ uoluit.
Ibi. v. hidæ geld̄. Ricard̄ ten̄ de Ansfr̄. 7 ht̄. 11. car̄ in dn̄io.
7 x1. ſeruos. Vn̄ miles ten̄ hid̄ 7 dimid̄. 7 ht̄ un̄a car̄
7 un̄ bord̄. 7 molin̄ de. v. ſolid̄. Tres car̄ plus ibi poſſeɴ. ēe.

T.R.E. ualɓ. 1111. liɓ. 7 poſt. 111. liɓ. Modo. 1111. liɓ ꝪHVND̄.

Iſd Ansfrid ten̄ AMBVRLEGE. 7 Ricard̄ de eo. IN TORNELAVS
Ibi. 1. hida geld̄. In dn̄io. ē. 1. car̄. 7 111. ſerui. 7 un̄ bord̄.
Valuit 7 ual. xx. ſolid̄.   IN DVNRE HVND̄.

Iſd Ansfrid ten̄ BONINHOPE. Reuer tenuit
Ibi. 11. hidæ.   In dn̄io. ē. 1. car̄. 7 111. uiłłi 7 v. bord̄ cū. 11.

★ car̄. 7 tcia pars duoꝗ molinoꝗ x1111. ſoł. 7 v111. denar̄
Silua. ē ibi. ſed poſita in foreſta regis.

Valuit. L. ſoł. Modo ſimilit̄.

186 c
Iſd Ansfrid ten̄ CLEVNGE. Herald̄ tenuit. IN STRATFORD HD̄.

★ Ibi ſt̄. v. hidæ geld̄. 7 In dn̄io. 11. car̄.   7 111. uiłłi
7 1111. bord̄. cū. 111. car̄. Ibi. 1111. bouarij. 7 Molin̄ de. v.
ſolid̄. Silua nil reddeꞩ. 7 ibi ē una hida waſtata.
De hac tra ten̄ Girard̄. 111. virḡ. 7 ht̄. dimid̄ car̄
cū uno hōe ſuo. Waſt fuit. Modo ual. Lxx. ſolid̄.

Ansfrid also holds

2 PIXLEY. Thorgar held it; he could go where he would. ½ hide which pays tax. In lordship 1 plough;
    2 free men and 2 smallholders.
Value before 1066, 8s; now 10s.

in BROMSASH Hundred

3 ASTON (Ingham). Godfrey holds from him. King Edward held it. 2 hides which pay tax. In lordship 1 plough;
    4 villagers and 9 smallholders with 8 ploughs; 8 other men who pay nothing. 2 ploughmen.
    A mill which pays nothing.
Value before 1066, 50s; now 100s.

in GREYTREE Hundred

4 (Sollers) HOPE. Hagen held it; he could go where he would. 5 hides which pay tax. Richard holds from Ansfrid. He has 2 ploughs in lordship and 11 slaves.
    A man-at-arms holds 1½ hides; he has 1 plough and 1 smallholder.
    A mill at 5s; 3 more ploughs would be possible there.
Value before 1066 £4; later £3; now £4.

in THORNLAW Hundred

5 AMBERLEY. Richard holds from him. 1 hide which pays tax. In lordship 1 plough; 3 slaves;
    1 smallholder.
The value was and is 20s.

in DINEDOR Hundred

6 BULLINGHOPE. Rever held it. ... 2 hides. ... In lordship 1 plough;
    3 villagers and 5 smallholders with 2 ploughs.
    The third part of 2 mills which pays 14s 8d; woodland there, but placed in the King's Forest.
The value was 50s; now the same.

in STRETFORD Hundred

186 c

7 CLEHONGER. Earl Harold held it. 5 hides which pay tax. In lordship 2 ploughs;
    3 villagers and 4 smallholders with 3 ploughs. 4 ploughmen.
    A mill at 5s; woodland which pays nothing; 1 hide laid waste.
    Gerard holds 3 virgates of this land; with 1 man of his he has ½ plough.
It was waste. Value now 70s.

TERRA DVRANDI DE GLOWEĊ. *IN RADELAV HD.*

DVRANDVS de Glouueċ teñ *SPERTVNE*. 7 Rädulf de eo. Ernui tenuit taiñ Heraldi 7 q̃ uolb ire poterat. Ibi. III. virg geld. In dñio funt. II. car. 7 II. bord. 7 IIII. ferui. 7 II. ancillæ.   Valuit 7 ual xx. folid.   HD.

Iſd Durand teñ *PANCHILLE*. 7 Bernard *IN BREMESESE* de eo. Gunner tenuit. 7 poterat ire q̃ uolb. Ibi. I. hida geld. Ibi. VI. bord hñt. III. car. Valuit 7 ual. VI. folid.

Iſd Durand teñ *WESTVNE*. 7 Bernard de eo. Gun ner p̃dict tenuit. Ibi. II. hidæ geld. Ibi. II. bord hñt unã car. 7 adhuc. III. car poſſunt. ẽe. Val 7 ualuit. II. fol.

Iſd Durand teñ *CALCHEBERGE*. 7 Bernard de eo. Iſd Gunuer tenuit. Ibi. I. hida geld. In dñio. ẽ una car. 7 uñ feruus.   Val 7 ualuit. LXIIII. denar.

Iſd Durand teñ *RECESFORD* 7 Walter *IN VLFEI HD.* nepos ej. 7 Widard de eis. Leuenot tenuit. Ibi hida 7 dimid geld. In dñio funt. II. car. 7 IIII. bord cũ. II. car. 7 v. ferui. 7 Silua nil redd. T.R.E. ualb. XL. folid. 7 poſt 7 modo: XXX. fol.

Iſd Durand 7 Walter nepos ej teñ *LAST*. 7 Bernard de eo. Godricus tenuit. Ibi. II. hidæ geld. Waſta. ẽ 7 fuit.

Iſd Durand teñ *TORCHESTONE IN STRATFORD HD.* 7 Bernard de eo. Robt. F. Wimarc tenuit. Ibi. III. hidæ geld. In dñio. ẽ una car. 7 III. uiłł cũ. II. car. Ibi. II. ferui. 7 uñ bord. Waſt fuit. Val. XL. folid.

Iſd Durand teñ *LVTELEI*. 7 Widard *IN CVTESTORN HD.* de eo. Reuer tenuit 7 Aluuiñ p̃. II. ω̃. Ibi. I. hida In dñio. ẽ una car. 7 II. bouarij. Hanc trã ded Rex. W. Rogerio de piſtes. Valb. XV. folid. Modo. X. folid.

22   LAND OF DURAND OF GLOUCESTER

In RADLOW Hundred

1   Durand of Gloucester holds ASHPERTON, and Ralph from him. Ernwy, a thane of Earl Harold, held it; he could go where he would. 3 virgates which pay tax. In lordship 2 ploughs;
    2 smallholders and 4 male and 2 female slaves.
The value was and is 20s.

In BROMSASH Hundred

2   Durand also holds PONTSHILL, and Bernard from him. Gunnar held it; he could go where he would. 1 hide which pays tax.
    6 smallholders have 3 ploughs.
The value was and is 6s.

3   Durand also holds WESTON (under Penyard), and Bernard from him. The said Gunnar held it. 2 hides which pay tax.
    2 smallholders have 1 plough; a further 3 ploughs possible.
The value is and was 4s.

4   Durand also holds COLDBOROUGH, and Bernard from him. Gunnar also held it. 1 hide which pays tax. In lordship 1 plough;
    1 slave.
The value is and was 64d.

In WOLPHY Hundred

5   Durand also holds ROCHFORD, and his nephew Walter too, and Widard from them. Leofnoth held it. 1½ hides which pay tax. In lordship 2 ploughs;
    4 smallholders with 2 ploughs; 5 slaves.
    Woodland which pays nothing.
Value before 1066, 40s; later and now, 30s.

6   Durand also, and his nephew Walter, hold LAYSTERS, and Bernard from him. Godric held it. 2 hides which pay tax.
It is and was waste.

In STRETFORD Hundred

7   Durand also holds THRUXTON, and Bernard from him. Robert son of Wymarc held it. 3 hides which pay tax. In lordship 1 plough;
    3 villagers with 2 ploughs. 2 slaves and 1 smallholder.
It was waste. Value (now) 40s.

In CUTSTHORN Hundred

8   Durand also holds LITLEY, and Widard from him. Rever held it, and Alwin, as two manors. 1 hide. ... In lordship 1 plough;
    2 ploughmen.
    King William gave this land to Roger of Pîtres.
The value was 15s; now 10s.

DTERRA DROGON FILIJ PONZ. *IN VLFEI HVND.*

ROGO filius Ponz ten RECESFORD . Wlmer

tenuit . Ibi . I . hida 7 una v geld . In dnio fuɴ . II.

car . 7 IIII . bord . cu . I . car . 7 VI . ferui.

T . R . E . ualb xxx . fot . Modo xxVIII . fot.

Ifd Drogo ten DODINTVNE . Herald tenuit . Ibi . VII . hide.

Ifd Drogo ten BVRCSTANESTVNE . Eduin 7 Elfild 7 Eluuard

tenuer ꝓ . III . Maner . Ibi . III . hidæ.

Ifd Drogo ten RVVENORE.

★ Ibi . e . I . hida . Ibi ht Drogo . IIII . car in dnio . 7 VII . uitt

7 II . bord cu . III . car . Ibi . IIII . ferui . 7 molin de . II.

folid . Ibi pbr 7 fab.   Vat . c . folid.

Ifd Drogo ten HANLIE . Leuing 7 Goduin 7 Eluuard te

nuer ꝓ . III . ꝏ . 7 poteraɴ ire quo uolb . Ibi . I . hida 7 una v

7 dim 7 geld . In dnio . e una car . 7 IIII . bord . cu . II . car.

7 tcia car poffet . ee . Ibi . I . feruus . 7 un burgfis de . IIII.

denar . Valuit . XIII . fot . Modo XII . fot . Adelelm ten.

Ifd Drogo ten MATME . Aluuard IN RADELAV HD

tenuit tein Odonis 7 n poterat recede fine licentia dni.

Ibi dimid hida geld . Adelelm ten 7 ht ibi . I . car.

Valuit . v . fot . 7 poft . IIII . fot . Modo . x . folid.

.XXIIII. **O**TERRA OSBERNI FILIJ RICARDI *IN HEZETRE HVND.*

SBERN filius Ricardi ten MILDETVNE . Ipfe tenuit T.R.E

Ibi . II . hidæ geld . In dnio . e una car . 7 VI . uitti cu . III . car.

Ibi . III . ferui . 7 un bord . Siluæ . IIII . qᷟ int lg 7 lat.

waftu fuit . Modo uat . xx . folid.

LAND OF DROGO SON OF POYNTZ

In WOLPHY Hundred

1 Drogo son of Poyntz holds ROCHFORD. Wulfmer held it. 1 hide
and 1 virgate which pay tax. In lordship 2 ploughs;
   4 smallholders with 1 plough; 6 slaves.
Value before 1066, 30s; now 28s.

Drogo also holds
[in the GOLDEN VALLEY]
2 DORSTONE. Earl Harold held it. 7 hides.
[Value ...]

3 *BURCSTANESTUNE*. Edwin, Alfhild and Alfward held it as three
manors. 3 hides. ...
[Value ...]

4 MYNYDDBRYDD. ... 1 hide. Drogo has 4 ploughs in lordship;
   7 villagers and 2 smallholders with 3 ploughs.
   4 slaves; a mill at 2s. A priest and a smith.
Value 100s.

in WINSTREE Hundred

5 'HANLEYS (End)'. Leofing, Godwin and Alfward held it as three
manors; they could go where they would. 1 hide and 1½ virgates;
they pay tax. In lordship 1 plough;
   4 smallholders with 2 ploughs; a third plough would be
     possible. 1 slave; 1 burgess at 4d.
The value was 13s; now 12s.
   Aethelhelm holds it.

in RADLOW Hundred

6 MATHON. Alfward, a thane of Earl Oda, held it; he could not
withdraw without the lord's permission. ½ hide which pays tax.
Aethelhelm holds it; he has 1 plough there.
The value was 5s; later 4s; now 10s.

LAND OF OSBERN SON OF RICHARD

In HAZELTREE Hundred

1 Osbern son of Richard holds MILTON. He held it himself before
1066. 2 hides which pay tax. In lordship 1 plough;
   6 villagers with 3 ploughs. 3 slaves and 1 smallholder.
   Woodland, 4 leagues in both length and width.
It was waste. Value now 20s.

Iſđ Osbn ten̄ *BOITVNE* . Ipſe tenuit T.R.E. Ibi . II . hidæ

In dn̄io . ē dimiđ car̄ . 7 IIII . uiłłi 7 II . borđ cū . II . car̄ . 7 aliæ . II .

poſſent . ēē . Ibi . ē uña broce . Valuit . XII . ſoł . Modo . XX . ſoł .

Iſđ Osbn ten̄ 7 tenuit *BRADELEGE* . de . I . hida .

7 *TITELEGE* de . III . hiđ . 7 *BRVNTVNE* de . I . hida .

7 *CHENILLE* de . II . hiđ . 7 *HERCOPE* de dimiđ hida .

7 *HERTVNE* de . III . hiđ . 7 *HECH* de . I . hida . 7 *CLATRETVNE*

de . II . hiđ . 7 *QVERENTVNE* de . I . hidā . 7 *DISCOTE*

de . III . hiđ . 7 *CASCOPE* de dimiđ hida .

In his . XI . M̄ eſt tra . XXXVI . car̄ . ſed Waſta fuit 7 eſt .

Nunꝗ geldauit . jacet in Marcha de Walis .

Iſđ Osbn ten̄ *LEGE* . 7 tenuit . Ibi . ē dimiđ hida . 7 poſſet

ēē . I . car̄ . Ibi . ē un̄ uiłłs tantūm̄ . Vał . V . ſoliđ .

In his waſtis tris excreuer̄ ſiluæ in quibƶ iſđ Osbnus

uenatione̅ exercet . 7 inde h̄t qđ cape poteſt . Nil aliud .

Iſđ Osbn ten̄ *TITELLEGE* . Herald tenuit . *IN ELSEDVNE HD̄* .

Tra . ē . VI . car̄ . Waſta fuit 7 ē . Eſt tam̄ ibi . I . haia in ſiluula .

In *NEVTONE* eſt ̃dimiđ hida quæ gelđ . *IN STRATFORD HD̄* .

7 una v̄ quæ n̄ gelđ . Seric tenuit ꝑ M̄ . 7 poterat ire quo

uolb̄ . Herbt habuit de Ricardo Scrupe .

In dn̄io ſunt . III . boues . 7 III . uiłłi 7 un̄ borđ cū . I . car̄ .

Valuit . XL . ſoł . Modo . XXIIII . ſoliđ . Vna car̄ poſſet ibi . ēē .

Iſđ Osbn ten̄ *STANTVNE* . 7 Drogo *IN STEPLESET HD̄* .

de eo . Saiffil tenuit 7 poterat ire quo uolb̄ . Ibi . IIII . hidæ

gelđ . In dn̄io ſunt . II . car̄ . 7 VI . uiłłi 7 IIII . borđ cū . IIII . car̄ .

Ibi . IIII . ſerui . Waſt fuit . Modo uał . LX . ſoliđ .

Iſđ Osbn ten̄ *BODEHA* 7 tenuit . *IN TORNELAVS HD̄* .

Ibi . I . hida 7 dimiđ gelđ . In dn̄io ſunt . III . car̄ . 7 VI . uiłłi

7 faþ 7 II . borđ 7 pþr 7 un̄ radman cū . VIII . car̄ int̄ om̄s .

T.R.E. ualb̄ . LX . ſoliđ . Modo . XLVIII . ſoliđ .

2 Osbern also holds BYTON. He held it himself before 1066. 2 hides.
... In lordship ½ plough;
    4 villagers and 2 smallholders with 2 ploughs; 2 others
      would be possible.
    1 water-meadow.
The value was 12s; now 20s.

3 Osbern also holds and held: BRADLEY at 1 hide; TITLEY at 3 hides;
(Little) BRAMPTON at 1 hide; KNILL at 2 hides; (Lower) HARPTON
at ½ hide; HARPTON at 3 hides; NASH at 1 hide; CLATTERBRUNE at
2 hides; *QUERENTUNE* at 1 hide; DISCOED at 3 hides; CASCOB at
½ hide.
    In these 11 manors is land for 36 ploughs, but it was and is
waste. It has never paid tax; it lies in the Welsh March.

4 Osbern also holds and held LYE. ½ hide. 1 plough would be
possible.
    1 villager only.
Value 5s.

5 On these waste lands have grown woods in which this Osbern goes
hunting and he has from them what he can catch. Nothing else.

In ELSDON Hundred
6 Osbern also holds TITLEY. Earl Harold held it. 3 hides which pay
tax. Land for 6 ploughs. It was and is waste. However,
    there is a hedged enclosure there in a little wood.

In STRETFORD Hundred
7 In NEWTON ½ hide which pays tax and 1 virgate which does not
pay tax. Saeric held it as a manor; he could go where he would.
Herbert had it from Richard Scrope. In lordship 3 oxen;
    3 villagers and 1 smallholder with 1 plough.
The value was 40s; now 24s.
    1 plough would be possible there.

In STAPLE Hundred
8 Osbern also holds STAUNTON (on Arrow), and Drogo from him.
Seisyll held it; he could go where he would. 4 hides which pay
tax. In lordship 2 ploughs;
    6 villagers and 4 smallholders with 4 ploughs. 4 slaves.
It was waste. Value now 60s.

In THORNLAW Hundred
9 Osbern also holds and held BODENHAM. 1½ hides which pay tax.
In lordship 3 ploughs;
    6 villagers, a smith, 2 smallholders, a priest and 1 rider
      with 8 ploughs between them.
Value before 1066, 60s; now 48s.

Isd Osbn ten *HVILECH* 7 tenuit. Ibi.i.hida geld. In dnio

est.i.car 7 dimid.7 iii.bord 7 ii.serui.

Valuit.xii.sol. Modo.viii.solid. *IN CVTESTORNES HD.*

Isd Osbn ten *LVDE*.7 Roger de eo. Saisi tenuit.

Ibi.ii.hidæ geld. In dnio sunt.ii.car.7 un uills 7 pposit

7 faber.cu.ii.car.

Valb.xxv.sol. Modo.xxx.solid.

Isd Osbn ten *LVDEFORDE*.Ibi.e una hida.7 in dnio.ii.car.

7 v.bord cu.i.car.7 molin de.vi.solid.   Val.xx.sol.

Isd Osbn ht.xxiii.hoes in castello *AVRETONE*.7 reddt

x.solid.   Val ei castellu hoc.xx.sol.

.XXV **G**TERRA GISLEBERTI FILIJ TVROLDI. *IN DVNRE HVND.*
ISLEBERT.F.Turoldi:ten *RETROWAS*.Siric tenuit.T.R.E.

Ibi.iiii.hidæ geld. In dnio sunt.ii.car.7 ii.uilli 7 iii.bord cu.ii.

car.T.R.E.ualb.vi.lib.Modo.iii.lib.Ibi fuer uilli cu.xiii.car.

Isd Gislebt ten *BONINHOPE*.Eduin tenuit.Ibi.ii.hidæ.

In dnio sunt.ii.car.7 iiii.uilli 7 iii.bord cu.ii.car.7 iiii.serui ibi.

7 tcia pars molini reddtis xiiii.sol 7 viii.denar.

Valuit.l.sol. Modo tntd.

187 a

Isd Gislebt ten *WILEHALLE*.Robt tenuit. *IN STRATFORD HD.*

Ibi.iii.hidæ.In dnio.e una car.7 alia posset.ee. Ibi.iii.uilli

7 iii.bord.7 ii.bouarij.cu.i.car.Picot ten de Gislebto.

Wast fuit.Modo ual.xxx.solid. *IN VALLE STRADELEI.*

Isd Gislebt ten *BECCE*.Eduin tenuit. Ibi.iii.hidæ.

Ibi sunt.viii.Walenses cu.ii.car.reddt un accipitre 7 ii.canes.

Isd Gislebt ten *MIDEWDE*.Herald tenuit.Ibi.ii.hidæ.

In WOLPHY Hundred
10 Osbern also holds and held WHYLE. 1 hide which pays tax.
In lordship 1½ ploughs;
    3 smallholders and 2 slaves.
The value was 12s; now 8s.

In CUTSTHORN Hundred
11 Osbern also holds LYDE, and Roger (of) Lacy from him. Seisyll
held it. 2 hides which pay tax. In lordship 2 ploughs;
    1 villager, a reeve and a smith with 2 ploughs.
The value was 25s; now 30s.

[In WOLPHY Hundred]
12 Osbern also holds LUDFORD. 1 hide. In lordship 2 ploughs;
    5 smallholders with 1 plough.
    A mill at 6s.
Value 20s.

13 Osbern also has 23 men in (Richards) CASTLE. They pay 10s.
Value to him of this castle, 20s.

25   LAND OF GILBERT SON OF THOROLD

In DINEDOR Hundred
1 Gilbert son of Thorold holds ROTHERWAS. Sigeric held it before
1066. 3 hides which pay tax. In lordship 2 ploughs;
    2 villagers and 3 smallholders with 2 ploughs.
Value before 1066 £6; now £3.
    There were 10 villagers with 13 ploughs.

Gilbert also holds
2 BULLINGHOPE. Edwin held it. 2 hides. In lordship 2 ploughs;
    4 villagers and 3 smallholders with 2 ploughs; 4 slaves there.
    The third part of a mill which pays 14s 8d.
The value was 50s; now as much.

in STRETFORD Hundred   187 a
3 WINNALL. Robert son of Wymarc held it. 3 hides. In lordship 1
plough; another would be possible.
    3 villagers, 3 smallholders and 2 ploughmen with 1 plough.
    Picot holds from Gilbert.
It was waste. Value now 30s.

in the GOLDEN VALLEY
4 (The) BAGE. Edwin held it. 3 hides. ...
    8 Welshmen with 2 ploughs; they pay 1 hawk and 2 dogs.

5 MIDDLEWOOD. Earl Harold held it. 2 hides.
    [Value ...]

Iſd Giſlebt ten *HAREWĐE* . Eduui tenuit . Ibi . iiii . hidæ.

Ħ tra in ſiluã . ẽ tota redacta . Waſta fuit 7 nil reddit.

IN VALLE STRADELĪE . POTERAN ARARE . C . 7 XII . CARVCÆ . 7 gelđ

IN PLEGELIET HĐ.

Iſd Giſlebt ten *CHETESTOR* . Ernui 7 Goduin tenue⁊ ᵱ . II . ᴔ .

7 poterant ire quo uolꝧ . Ibi . II . hidæ gelđ . In dñio ſunt . III . ca⁊ .

7 VII . uitti cũ . VII . ca⁊ . 7 adhuc . I . ca⁊ poſſet . ẽẽ . in dñio . Ibi . VI .

ſerui . 7 moliñ de . IIII . ſolid 7 dimiđ.

T.R.E . ualꝧ . L . ſolid . 7 poſt . XLV . ſoł . Modo . LXX . ſolid.

Iſd Giſlebt ten *WALELEGE* . Hèrald tenuit . *IN ELSEDVNE HĐ.*

Ibi ſunt . II . hidæ gelđ . Has Coñ Witts deđ Giſlebto ᵱ . IIII . hiđ.

Tra . ẽ . XII . ca⁊ . Ibi . ẽ dom deſenſabit . 7 Silua magna aduenanđ.

Waſt fuit . Modo uał . v . ſolid.

★ .XXV ⎫ TERRA ILBERTI FILIJ TVROLDI . *IN GREITREWES HĐ.*

ILBERTVS . F . Turoldi ten *FROME* . Wluuard tenuit

Ibi . I . hida 7 dimiđ .   In dñio . ẽ una ca⁊ . 7 II . uitti 7 VI .

borđ cũ . I . ca⁊ . 7 II . ſerui.

Valuit 7 uał . xxx . ſolid .   *IN DVNRE HVNĐ.*

Iſd Ilbt ten *CLEVNGE* . Leuenod tenuit . 7 poterat ire quo

uolꝧ . Ibi . I . hida gelđ . In dñio . ẽ una ca⁊ . 7 uñ uitts 7 IIII . borđ

cũ . II . ca⁊ . Ibi . II . bouarij .   Waſt fuit . m̃ uał . xxv . ſoł.

.XXVII . ⎫ TERRA HERMAN DE DREWES.

HERMAN de Dreuues ten de rege *MERSTONE* . Semar

7 Vluuin 7 Grim tenue⁊ ᵱ . III . ᴔ . 7 q̃ uolꝧ ire poterant.

Ibi . III . hidæ gelđ . In dñio eſt . I . ca⁊ . 7 III . radcheniſt.

7 VII . borđ cũ . I . ca⁊ . 7 adhuc . IIII . ca⁊ plus poſſeN ibi eſſe .

Ibi . II . ſerui . 7 Siluæ . v . q̃ʒ int l͡g 7 lat.

T.R.E . ualꝧ . xxxIIII . ſoł . 7 poſt . x . ſoł . modo . xx . ſolid.

6 HAREWOOD. Edwy held it. 4 hides. The whole of this land has been turned back into woodland.
It was waste and pays nothing.

7 In the GOLDEN VALLEY·112 ploughs could plough. 56 hides; they paid tax.

In PLEGELGATE Hundred

8 Gilbert also holds *CHETESTOR*. Ernwy and Godwin held it as two manors; they could go where they would. 2 hides which pay tax. In lordship 3 ploughs;
7 villagers with 7 ploughs; 1 further plough would be possible in lordship.
6 slaves; a mill at 4½s.
Value before 1066, 50s; later 45s; now 70s.

In ELSDON Hundred

9 Gilbert also holds AILEY. Earl Harold held it. 2 hides which pay tax. Earl William gave these to Gilbert (in exchange) for 4 hides. Land for 12 ploughs.
A fortified house there; a large wood for hunting.
It was waste. Value now 5s.

26 LAND OF ILBERT SON OF THOROLD

In GREYTREE Hundred

1 Ilbert son of Thorold holds (Priors) FROME. Wulfward held it. ...
1½ hides. ... In lordship 1 plough;
2 villagers and 6 smallholders with 1 plough; 2 slaves.
The value was and is 30s.

In DINEDOR Hundred

2 Ilbert also holds CLEHONGER. Leofnoth held it; he could go where he would. 1 hide which pays tax. In lordship 1 plough;
1 villager and 4 smallholders with 2 ploughs. 2 ploughmen.
It was waste. Value now 25s.

27 LAND OF HERMAN OF DREUX

[? In ELSDON Hundred]

1 Herman of Dreux holds MARSTON from the King. Saemer, Wulfwin and Grim held it as three manors; they could go where they would. 3 hides which pay tax. In lordship 1 plough;
3 riding men and 7 smallholders with 1 plough; a further 4 more ploughs would be possible there.
2 slaves; woodland, 5 furlongs in both length and width.
Value before 1066, 34s; later 10s; now 20s.

.XXV. ^{.III.} TERRA HVNFRIDI DE BVIVILE. *IN RADELAV HVND.*

Hvnfrid de Buiuile ten de rege *PICHESLEI* . Anfchil
tenuit hõ epi de Hereford.7 poterat ire quo uolb.

Ibi dimid hida geld . In dñio . ē una car.7 II . bord cũ . I . car.

Valuit 7 ualet . VIII . folid.

Ifd Hunfrid ten *MVLESLAGE* . Semar tenuit.7 q̃ uolb
ire poterat . Ibi . I . hida geld.

Valuit . XVI . folid. Modo funt ħ duo ℳ .p. xxx . fot. ad firmã.

XXIX. TERRA HVGONIS LASNE. *IN STEPLESET HD.*

Hvgo Lafne ten *CHENECESTRE* . Vluui cilt tenuit
7 poterat ire quo uolb . Ibi . IIII . hidæ geld . De hac tra emit
q̃dã Godric dimid hid de Vluuino fupdicto.7 tenuit .p ℳ.

In dñio ħt hugo . II . car.7 III . ferui .7 moliñ de . II . folid.

7 p̃dict Godric ħt ibi . I . car fub Hugone .7 dimid hidã.

De hac tra accõmodauit ifd hugo . I . hidã Witto comiti.

quã ifd cõm ded Mariadoc regi . Ibi ħt filius ej Grifin . II.

/bord.

187 b

T.R.E. ualb . LX fot. Modo . LXX . folid. Qd Grifin ten .'v. fot.

Ifd Hugo ten *HOPE* . Turchil tenuit ^{uuit} *IN GREITREWES HD.*

Ibi . XV . hidæ . Decē geld ^{ex his} . In dñio funt . III . car.7 XIIII.

uiħi 7 x . bord 7 II . pbri cũ æccła hñte dimid hidã træ.

Ibi p̃pofit.7 fab 7 capentari . Int oms hñt . XXV . car.

Ibi . XVIII . ferui.7 VIII . ancillæ.7 moliñ de . V . folid.

7 III . pifcarias reddtes . CCC . anguillas . De waftis tris.

ħt dñs . XII . fot 7 IIII . den.

Vn mēbrũ de hoc ℳ ded Hugo cuidã fuo militi . cũ . I . car.

T.R.E. ualb . XII . lib.7 poft . XV . lib . Modo . XVI . lib.

Ifd Hugo ten uñ ℳ de . I . hida ^{non} geld . *IN TORNELAVS HD.*

Leflet tenuit . In dñio funt . II . car.7 III . bord .7 IIII . feruos.

T.R.E. ualb . XXX . fot . modo . ^{ti} xx . folid.

187 a, b

28   LAND OF HUMPHREY OF BOUVILLE

In RADLOW Hundred
1   Humphrey of Bouville holds PIXLEY from the King. Askell, the
     Bishop of Hereford's man, held it; he could go where he would.
     ½ hide which pays tax. In lordship 1 plough;
         2 smallholders with 1 plough.
     The value was and is 8s.

2   Humphrey also holds MUNSLEY. Saemer held it; he could go where
     he would. 1 hide which pays tax.
     The value was 16s.

Now these two manors are at a revenue of 30s.

29   LAND OF HUGH DONKEY

In STAPLE Hundred
1   Hugh Donkey holds KENCHESTER. Wulfwy Young held it; he could
     go where he would. 4 hides which pay tax. One Godric bought
     ½ hide of this land from the said Wulfwy and held it as a manor.
     Hugh has 2 ploughs in lordship; 3 slaves.
         A mill at 2s.
         The said Godric has 1 plough there under Hugh and ½ hide.
     Hugh also leased 1 hide of this land to Earl William and this
     Earl gave it to King Maredudd. His son Gruffydd has
         2 smallholders there.
     Value before 1066, 60s; now 70s. [Value of] what Gruffydd   187 b
     holds, 5s.

     Hugh also holds
     in GREYTREE Hundred
2   FOWNHOPE. Thorkell White held it. 15 hides; 10 of them pay tax.
     In lordship 3 ploughs;
             14 villagers and 10 smallholders; 2 priests with a church which
                 has ½ hide of land. A reeve, a smith and a carpenter. Between
                 them they have 25 ploughs.
             18 male and 8 female slaves; a mill at 5s; 3 fisheries which pay
                 300 eels.
         The lord has 12s 4d from the waste lands.
         Hugh gave 1 member of this manor to a man-at-arms of his,
         with 1 plough.
     Value before 1066 £12; later £15; now £16.

     in THORNLAW Hundred
3   one manor at 1 hide which does not pay tax. Leofled held it.
     In lordship 2 ploughs;
         3 smallholders and 4 slaves.
     Value before 1066, 30s; now 20s.

Iſd Hugo ten uñ ꝫ̃ de . iii . virg geld . Leſlet tenuit.

Ibi fuer 7 ſunt . iii . radchen̄ cū . iii . car . 7 ſeruiuɴ̃ dño.

T . R . E . ualb̄ . xiii . ſot . Modo . x . ſolid.

Iſd Hugo ten SVDTVNE . Leſlet tenuit . Ibi . ii . hide ñ geld.

Ibi . ē un uitts 7 vi . bord cū . iii . car . 7 un franciᵹ cū . i.

car . Vat 7 ualuit . xxx . ſolid . IN VALLE STRATELIE.

Iſd Hugo ten BELTROV . Leſlet tenuit . Ibi dimid hida.

Iſd Hugo ten WLVETONE . Leſlet tenuit . Ibi . ii . hidæ

Hæ . ii . træ waſtæ fuer 7 ſuɴ̃.

Iſd Hugo ten WILMESTVNE . Leſlet tenuit . Ibi . v . hidæ.

In dñio ſunt . ii . car . 7 vii . uitti 7 ii . bord 7 fab̄ . 7 un radman

cū . ii . bord . Int oms hn̄t . ii . car 7 dim . Ibi . iiii . ſerui.

7 molin̄ de . iii . ſolid.

Waſt fuit . modo uat . xxx . ſolid.

Iſd Hugo ten ALMVNDESTVNE . Aluuard tenuit

Ibi . iii . hidæ . Ibi ſunt . ii . franciᵹ cū . ii . car . 7 pb̄r

cū æccta hn̄s dimid car . 7 iii . ſerui . 7 un bord . 7 ii . hoēs

reddt . viii . ſot . Waſt fuit . Modo . xx . ſot uat.

Iſd Hugo ten ALCAMESTVNE . Leſlet tenuit.

Ibi . i . hida . Waſta fuit 7 eſt . ſed tam redd . iii . ſot.

Iſd Hugo ten WALINTONE . Turchil IN CVTESTORNES HD.

tenuit . Ibi . v . hidæ geld . In dñio ſuɴ̃ . ii . car . Antea fuer . v . car.

7 ix . uitti 7 viii . bord . 7 pb̄r 7 ꝓpoſit 7 fab̄ 7 iiii . radchen

Int oms hn̄t . viii . car . Ibi . xi . ſerui . 7 ix . ancillæ . 7 ii . molini

de . xiii . ſolid . Ad Wich hr̄ . xvii . mittas ſat ꝑ . xxx . den.

T . R . E . ualb̄ . viii . lib̄ . Modo . vii . lib̄ . Plus eraɴ̃ ibi car quā nc ſuɴ̃.

Iſd Hugo ten CREDENELLE . Turchil tenuit . Ibi . ii . hidæ ñ geld.

In dñio ſunt . ii . car .   Valuit 7 uat . xxx . ſot.

Iſd Hugo ten STRATONE . Æluuard tenuit . Vitalis ten de hug.

Ibi dimid hida . In dñio . ē . i . car . 7 ii . ſerui . Vat 7 ualuit . x . ſot.

4 one manor at 3 virgates which pay tax. Leofled held it. There were and are
    3 riding men with 3 ploughs; they serve the lord.
Value before 1066, 13s; now 10s.

5 SUTTON. Leofled held it. 2 hides which do not pay tax.
    1 villager and 6 smallholders with 3 ploughs; 1 Frenchman
        with 1 plough.
The value is and was 30s.

in the GOLDEN VALLEY
6 *BELTROU*. Leofled held it. ½ hide.

7 *WLUETONE*. Leofled held it. 2 hides. ...

These two lands were and are waste.

8 WILMASTONE. Leofled held it. 5 hides. In lordship 2 ploughs;
    7 villagers, 2 smallholders, a smith and 1 rider with 2
        smallholders; between them they have 2½ ploughs.
    4 slaves; a mill at 3s.
It was waste. Value now 30s.

9 *ALMUNDESTUNE*. Alfward held it. 3 hides.
    2 Frenchmen with 2 ploughs; a priest with a church who has
        ½ plough; 3 slaves and 1 smallholder; 2 men pay 8s.
It was waste. Value now 20s.

10 *ALCAMESTUNE*. Leofled held it. 1 hide.
It was and is waste; but it pays 3s, however.

in CUTSTHORN Hundred
11 WELLINGTON. Thorkell White held it. 5 hides which pay tax.
In lordship 2 ploughs; previously there were 5 ploughs.
    9 villagers, 8 smallholders, a priest, a reeve, a smith and 4
        riding men; between them they have 8 ploughs.
    11 male and 9 female slaves; 2 mills at 13s.
    At Droitwich he has 17 measures of salt for 30d.
Value before 1066 £8; now £7.
    There were more ploughs there than there are now.

12 CREDENHILL. Thorkell held it. 2 hides which do not pay tax.
In lordship 2 ploughs.
The value was and is 30s.

13 STRETTON. Alfward held it. Vitalis holds from Hugh. ½ hide. ...
In lordship 1 plough; 2 slaves.
The value is and was 10s.

Iſđ Hugo dimiđ hidā in *WALINTONE*.7 Radulf⁹ de eo. Wluuin⁹

tenuit. Ibi.ē una car̃.Val̃ 7 ualuit.x.ſol̃. *IN RADELAV HĐ.*

Iſđ Hugo ten̋ *LINCVBE* Leſlet tenuit.Ibi.iii.virg̋

Tra.ē.i.car̃.   Valuit.ix.ſol̃.Modo.vii.ſoliđ.

Iſđ Hugo ten̋ *BERNOLDVNE*.Turchil tenuit. *IN HEZETRE HĐ.*

Ibi.ii.hidæ—Silua.ē ibi magna.ſed qtitas n̄ fuit diĉta.

Ibi.ē una haia.in qua qđ poteſt cape captat.Alia tra.ē waſta.

Iſđ Hugo ten̋ in *HERDESLEGE* dimiđ hiđ. *IN ELSEDVNE HĐ.*

geld.Herald tenuit.7 waſta fuit 7 eſt.

Iſđ Hugo ten̋.i.hiđ 7 i.v̋.frᴂin *CICVRDINE*.7 geld Herald tenuit

Comes.W.deđ ipſi Hugoni.Waſta erat 7 eſt.

Iſđ Hugo ten̋ *LEGE*.Leuiet tenuit.7 n̄ poterat recedē̋ ſine liĉtia

dñi ſui.Ibi dimiđ hida geld.Iſđ ten̋ q̇ tenuit.7 h̃t ibi.i.car̃.

Waſta fuit.Modo ual̃.x.ſol̃.   *IN SVLCET HVND.*

Iſđ Hugo ten̋ *ETONE*.Elric⁹ tenuit de ᵂⁱᵗᵉTurchil.Ibi dim hida.7 ii.hoēꝗ

hñtes.ii.car̃.7 redđ.ii.ſextar̃ meł̃.h̃ tra n̄ geld.

<h2>.XXX. ¹⁸⁷ᶜ VTERRA VRSONIS DE ABETOT. *IN PLEGELIET HĐ.*</h2>

Vrso de Abetot ten̋ *WIGETVNE*.Aluuin⁹ tenuit.7 q̇ uolɓ

ire poterat.Ibi.i.hida 7 una v̋.geld.Tra.ē.iiii.car̃.

Valuit.vi.ſol̃.modo.iii.ſol̃.

Hoc Ꟁ ten̋ Rog̋ de Laci p cābitionē de Vrſone.

<h2>.XXXI. GTERRA GRIFIN FILIJ MARIADOC. *IN ELSEDVN HĐ*</h2>

Grifin⁹.F.Mariadoc ten̋ de rege in *MATEVRDIN* tciā partē̋

de.ii.hiđ geld.com̄Herald tenuit.Com.W.deđ Mariadoc regi.

Waſt̋ fuit 7 eſt.ſed tam̄ ten̋ ibi Robt̋ de Grifino unā haiā.

14 Hugh also [holds] ½ hide in WELLINGTON, and Ralph from him.
Wulfwin held it. 1 plough there.
The value is and was 10s.

Hugh also holds
in RADLOW Hundred
15 *LINCUMBE.* Leofled held it. 3 virgates. ... Land for 1 plough.
The value was 9s; now 7s.

in HAZELTREE Hundred
16 'BERNALDESTON'. Thorkell held it. 2 hides.
A large wood there, but its size has not been stated.
There is a hedged enclosure in which he may keep what
he can catch.
The rest of the land is waste.

in ELSDON Hundred
17 in EARDISLEY ½ hide which pays tax. Earl Harold held it.
It was and is waste.

18 in CHICKWARD 1 hide and 1 virgate of land; they pay tax. Earl
Harold held them. Earl William gave them to Hugh himself.
It was and is waste.

19 *LEGE.* Leofgeat held it; he could not withdraw without his lord's
permission. ½ hide which pays tax. The same who held it, holds
it. He has 1 plough there.
It was waste. Value now 10s.

in SELLACK Hundred
20 STRANGFORD. Alric held it from Thorkell White. ½ hide.
2 men who have 2 ploughs and pay 2 sesters of honey.
The land does not pay tax.

30   LAND OF URSO OF ABETOT   187 c

In PLEGELGATE Hundred
1 Urso of Abetot holds WICTON. Alwin held it; he could go where
he would. 1 hide and 1 virgate which pay tax. Land for 4 ploughs.
The value was 6s; now 3s.
Roger of Lacy holds this manor by exchange from Urso.

31   LAND OF GRUFFYDD OF MAREDUDD

In ELSDON Hundred
1 Gruffydd son of Maredudd holds from the King in *MATEURDIN* the
third part of 2 hides which pay tax. Earl Harold held it. Earl
William gave it to King Maredudd. It was and is waste, but Robert
holds a hedged enclosure there from Gruffydd, however.

Iſd Grifin ten̅ *CVRDESLEGE*. Herald tenuit. Ibi . i . hida gelđ

T̅ra . e̅ . ii . car̅ . Waſta fuit 7 eſt . p̅t . iii . ac̅s t̅ræ nuꝑ ibi aratas.

Iſd Grifin ten̅ *BVNESVLLE*. Godric tenuit. *In STEPLESET H̅D*.

7 q̣ uolb̅ ire poterat . Ibi . i . hida gelđ . Ibi ſunt . iii . uiłł 7 un̊

borđ cu̅ . i . car̅ . 7 iii . car̅ poſſeɴ ibi . e̅e̅ . Valuit 7 uał . x . ſoł.

Iſd Grifin ten̅ *MALVESELLE* . Godric tenuit 7 q̣ uolb̅ ire

poterat . Ibi . iiii . hidæ gelđ . In dn̅io . e̅ una car̅ . 7 vi . uiłłi

7 iii . radmans cu̅ . ix . car̅ . 7 adhuc . iii . car̅ ibi poſſent . e̅e̅ .

Ibi . ii . ſerui.   Valuit . c . ſoł . Modo . x . ſoł min̊.

Iſd Grifin ten̊ *MALVESELLE* . Goduin 7 Vlchetel tenuer̅

ꝑ . ii . M̅ . 7 q̣ uolb̅ ire poteraɴ . Ibi . i . hida gelđ.

In dn̅io . e̅ una car̅ . 7 altera poſſet . e̅e̅ .

T.R.E. uałb̅ . xxx . ſolid . Modo . x . ſolid . *In PLEGELIET H̅D*.

Iſd Grifin ten̅ *STOCH* . Godric tenuit 7 potuit ire q̣ uoluit.

Ibi . i . hida gelđ . 7 una car̅ 7 vi . uiłł cu̅ . iii . car̅ . 7 iii . ſerui.

Valuit 7 uał . xxv . ſoł.   *In HEZETRE HVND*.

Iſd Grifin ten̅ *LEGE*. Ouen 7 Elmer tenuer̅ ꝑ . ii . M̅ . 7 waſti eraɴ.

Ibi . iii . hidæ|gelđ . Comes . W . deđ Mariadoc regi . Ibi ſunt . iiii . uiłłi

7 iii . borđ . cu̅ . ii . car̅ .   Vał . xv . ſoliđ . Siluā huj̊ M̅ cu̅ . lvii .

acris t̅ræ ten̅ Radulf de Mortemer . Rex . W . c̅donauit gelđ

regi Mariadoc 7 poſtea filio ej̊ .

RAŸNERIJ   *In PLEGELIET H̅D*.

.XXXII R̊aŸNER ten̅ de rege *MERSTVNE* . Ludi tenuit . 7 q̣ uolb̅

ire poterat . Ibi dim̅ hida gelđ . In dn̅io . e̅ una car̅ . cu̅ . i . borđ.

Valuit 7 uał . iiii . ſoł.

Gruffydd also holds

2 *CURDESLEGE.* Earl Harold held it. 1 hide which pays tax. Land for 2 ploughs. It was and is waste, except for 3 acres of land recently ploughed there.

in STAPLE Hundred

3 BUNSHILL. Godric held it; he could go where he would. 1 hide which pays tax.
   3 villagers and 1 smallholder with 1 plough; 3 ploughs would be possible there.
The value was and is 10s.

4 MANSELL (Lacy). Godric held it; he could go where he would. 4 hides which pay tax. In lordship 1 plough;
   6 villagers and 3 riders with 9 ploughs; a further 3 ploughs would be possible there. 2 slaves.
The value was 100s; now 10s less.

5 MANSELL (Lacy). Godwin and Ulfketel held it as two manors; they could go where they would. 1 hide which pays tax. In lordship 1 plough; another would be possible.
Value before 1066, 30s; now 10s.

in PLEGELGATE Hundred

6 STOKE (Bliss). Godric held it; he could go where he would. 1 hide which pays tax. 1 plough.
   6 villagers with 3 ploughs; 3 slaves.
The value was and is 25s.

in HAZELTREE Hundred

7 LYE. Owen and Aelmer held it as two manors. They were waste. 3 hides which do not pay tax. Earl William gave them to King Maredudd.
   4 villagers and 3 smallholders with 2 ploughs.
Value 15s.
   Ralph of Mortimer holds the woodland of this manor with 57 acres of land.
   King William granted the tax to King Maredudd, and later to his son.

32   [LAND] OF RAYNER

In PLEGELGATE Hundred

1 Rayner Carpenter holds MARSTON (Stannett) from the King. Ludi held it; he could go where he would. ½ hide which pays tax. In lordship 1 plough, with
   1 smallholder.
The value was and is 4s.

.XXXIII. Carbonel teñ de rege *Lacre*. Colegrim tenuit. 7 quo

uolɓ ire poterat. Ibi. i. hida gelđ. 7 dimiđ car̃. 7 ii. uiłłi cũ

una car̃. Valuit. xxx. fol. 7 poft. xx. fol. Modo. xxiiii. foliđ.

.XXXII. Uxor Radulfi ^capellani teñ *Erdesope* de rege. *In Stepleset hđ.*

Oruenot tenuit. 7 non poterat difcedere a fuo dño. Ibi. iii. v̄ træ

gelđ. Ibi. ii. ferui 7 iiii. animalia. Valuit. viii. foliđ. Modo. xii. fol.

★ In *Rvedene* teñ eađ mulier cũ filio fuo Waltero dim̃ hiđ gelđ.

Wafta. ē. 7 tam̃ redđ. ii. fol. Aueue tenuit 7 ualɓ. iiii. foliđ.

.XXXV. Siefan teñ de rege in *Mavrdine*. i. virg̃ *In Tornelavs hđ.*

træ. Aluuard tenuit ꝓ ꝏ de rege. E. In dñio hf. i. car̃. 7 iii.

borđ 7 iiii. feruos.   Valuit 7 ual. x. foliđ. *In Radelav hđ.*

.vi.
.XXX. Madoc teñ de rege *Spertvne*. Godric tenuit. Ibi. i. hida

gelđ. 7 una car̃ in dñio. 7 ii. ferui. 7 uñ uiłłs 7 uñ borđ. cũ. i. car̃.

Valuit 7 ual. xv. foliđ.   *In Vlfei hvnd*

Edric teñ de rege *Last*. 7 ipfe tenuit de rege. E. Ibi. i. hida

7 dimiđ gelđ. Tc ualɓ. xv. fol. modo. ē waft. *In ipso hvnđ.*

Elmer teñ de rege dimiđ hiđ. Ipfe tenuit de rege. E. 7 gelđɓ.

Valet. x. denar̃.

33 [LAND OF CHARBONNEL]

[In PLEGELGATE Hundred]

1 Charbonnel holds NOAKES from the King. Colgrim held it; he
could go where he would. 1 hide which pays tax. ½ plough.
2 villagers with 1 plough.
The value was 30s; later 20s; now 24s.

34 [LAND OF RALPH THE CHAPLAIN'S WIFE]

In STAPLE Hundred

1 Ralph the Chaplain's wife holds YARSOP from the King. Wulfnoth
held it; he could not leave his lord. 3 virgates of land which
pay tax.
2 slaves; 4 cattle.
The value was 8s; now 12s.

In PLEGELGATE Hundred

2 In ROWDEN this woman with her son Walter holds ½ hide which
pays tax. It is waste; however, it pays 2s. Aelfeva held it.
The value was 3s.

35 [LAND OF STEPHEN]

In THORNLAW Hundred

1 Stephen holds 1 virgate of land in MARDEN from the King. Alfward
held it as a manor from King Edward. In lordship he has 1
plough and
3 smallholders and 4 slaves.
The value was and is 10s.

36 [LAND OF MADOG, EDRIC AND AELMER]

In RADLOW Hundred

1 Madog holds ASHPERTON from the King. Godric held it. 1 hide
which pays tax. In lordship 1 plough; 2 slaves;
1 villager and 1 smallholder with 1 plough.
The value was and is 15s.

In WOLPHY Hundred

2 Edric holds LAYSTERS from the King. He held it himself from King
Edward. 1½ hides which pay tax.
Value then 15s. Now it is waste.

In this Hundred

3 Aelmer holds ½ hide from the King. He held it himself from King
Edward; it paid tax.
Value 10d.

HOLDINGS IN HEREFORDSHIRE IN 1086, ENTERED ELSEWHERE IN THE SURVEY

The Latin text of these entries is given in the county volumes concerned

In the GLOUCESTERSHIRE folios

1   LAND OF THE KING   162 d

E1   [In WESTBURY Hundred]   163 a
  11   In WESTBURY (on Severn) 30 hides. King Edward had 5 ploughs
       in lordship, and
         32 villagers and 15 smallholders with 28 ploughs. 1 slave.
       Before 1066 this manor paid one night's revenue; likewise for
       4 years after 1066.
         Later 6 hides in KYRE were taken from this manor and in
       CLIFTON (on Teme) 10 hides; in NEWENT and KINGSTONE 8 hides;
       in EDVIN (Loach) 1 hide. The Abbot of Cormeilles, Osbern
       and William sons of Richard now hold these lands; however,
       the Sheriff finds the whole revenue from the remainder. The
       men of the County state, however, that the fir-wood lay in
       Westbury in King Edward's revenue.

E2 34   Also in the manor of TEWKESBURY there belonged 4 hides not   163 c
       in lordship; they are in HANLEY (Castle). Before 1066 2
       ploughs in lordship;
         40 villagers and smallholders; 8 slaves, male and female.
         A mill at 16d; woodland in which there is a hedged
           enclosure.
       This land was Earl William's; now it is in the King's revenue
       in Hereford.
       Value before 1066 £15; now £10.

E3 35   In FORTHAMPTON 9 hides belonged to this manor. 2 ploughs in
       lordship;
         20 villagers and smallholders; 6 slaves, male and female.
         Woodland.
       Value before 1066 £10; now £8.

       Earl William held these two lands; they paid tax with Tewkesbury.

In the WORCESTERSHIRE folios

1   LAND OF THE KING   172 b

E4 1b   Before 1066 SUCKLEY, a manor of 5 hides, belonged to this
       manor, but Earl William took it away from here and placed it
       in the revenue of Hereford.
         In total, it paid £18 in revenue before 1066. Urso the Sheriff
       paid £24 by weight, so long as he had the woodland.

9   LAND OF ST. MARY'S OF PERSHORE   175 b

E5   In DODDINGTREE Hundred   175 c

6a The Church held MATHON itself. 5 hides, but it does not pay tax except for 3. 1 of these 5 hides lies in Herefordshire, in Radlow Hundred. Two riders hold it. The County of Worcester adjudged it for the use of St. Mary's of Pershore; it belongs to the above manor.

6b Also in this manor, 2 ploughs in lordship;
6 villagers, 20 smallholders and 1 smith with 12 ploughs.
A mill at 30d.
The value was £9; now 100s.

6c Urso holds 3 virgates of this manor. He has 1 plough.
A priest, 1 villager, 3 smallholders and a reeve; between them they have 3 ploughs.
Value 20s.
Walter Ponther holds 1 virgate also of this land, but the whole of it is waste. Value 5s.

18   LAND OF ROGER OF LACY   176 c

E6   [In CLENT Hundred]

6 Roger also holds ½ hide in DROITWICH. Aelfric Mapson held it.
11 burgesses and
1½ salt-houses; they pay 32½ measures.
This manor belongs to his manor of Hereford.

[X]   [ADDENDUM]   178 a

E7   In ESCH Hundred

2 lie 10 hides in FECKENHAM and 3 hides in HOLLOW (Court).
They are entered in the return for Hereford.

E8   In DODDINGTREE Hundred

3 lie 13 hides of MARTLEY and 5 hides of SUCKLEY; they hold pleas and pay tax here. They pay their revenue to Hereford and are entered in the King's return.

In the SHROPSHIRE folios

4   LAND OF EARL ROGER   253 b

E9   In CONDERTREE Hundred   259 d

28,5 Widard has one manor, FARLOW, at 1 hide and 3 virgates of land. It lies in LEOMINSTER, the King's manor in Herefordshire, and is assessed there. He holds it from the King.

E

HOLDINGS OUTSIDE HEREFORDSHIRE IN 1086, LATER TRANSFERRED TO THE COUNTY

Noted here to complete the description of the modern County.
See Notes to this County, and county volume referred to for full text.

In the SHROPSHIRE folios

CITY OF SHREWSBURY

252 a

ES 1	C 10	LEINTWARDINE	

LAND OF EARL ROGER

253 b

ES 2	4,20,20	LEINTWARDINE	258 b
ES 3	4,20,26	ADLEY	258 c

LAND OF RALPH OF MORTIMER

260 a

ES 4	6,11	LEINTWARDINE	260 b
ES 5	6,12	'STANWAY'	
ES 6	6,13	ADFORTON	
ES 7	6,14	LINGEN	
ES 8	6,15	SHIRLEY	
ES 9	6,16	LYE	
ES 10	6,17	*TUMBELAWE*	
ES 11	6,18	LETTON	
ES 12	6,19	WALFORD	
ES 13	6,20	WALFORD	
ES 14	6,21	BUCKTON	260 c
ES 15	6,23	BRAMPTON (Bryan)	
ES 16	6,24	PEDWARDINE	
ES 17	6,25	PEDWARDINE	
ES 18	6,26	PEDWARDINE	
ES 19	6,27	ADLEY	
ES 20	6,33	ADLEY	

In the WORCESTERSHIRE folios

LAND OF THE BISHOP OF BAYEUX

176 a

EW 1	11,1	ACTON (Beauchamp)	

LAND OF OSBERN SON OF RICHARD

176 c

EW 2	19,11	EDVIN (Loach)	176 d

(For Mathon, see E 5 above)

NOTES ON THE TEXT AND TRANSLATION
including:

Introductory Notes

1. The Welsh Border and Herefordshire, Geography
2. The Welsh Border and Herefordshire, History
3. Castles
4. The County Boundary
5. Herefordshire Domesday
6. Places
7. The Hundreds
8. Forest

Index of Persons

Index of Places

Maps and Map Keys

Systems of Reference

Technical Terms

NOTES ON THE TEXT AND TRANSLATION

BIBLIOGRAPHY and ABBREVIATIONS used in the Notes

AN ... Anglo-Norman

Anderson ... O. S. Anderson *The English Hundred Names*, Lund 1934 (Lunds Universitets Årsskrift N.F. Avd. 1 Bd. 30 Nr. i).

Annales Cambriae ... John Williams ab Ithel (ed.) *Annales Cambriae*, Rolls Series No. 20, London 1860.

ASC ... *The Anglo-Saxon Chronicle* (translated G. N. Garmonsway), London 1960.

Baddeley (HePN) ... W. St. Clair Baddeley *Herefordshire Place-Names* in TBGAS xxxix (1916) pp. 87–200.

Bannister (HEH) ... A. T. Bannister *The History of Ewias Harold, its Castle, Priory and Church*, Hereford 1902.

Bannister (MOH) ... A. T. Bannister *Memorials of Old Herefordshire*, Hereford 1904.

Bannister (PNHe) ... A. T. Bannister *The Place-Names of Herefordshire, their Origin and Development*, Hereford 1916.

Bardsley ... C. W. Bardsley *A Dictionary of English and Welsh Surnames*, London 1901.

Bateson ... M. Bateson *The Laws of Breteuil* in EHR xv (1900) pp. 73–78, 302–318, 496–523, 754–757; EHR xvi (1901) pp. 92–110, 332–345.

BCS ... W. de Gray Birch (ed.) *Cartularium Saxonicum*, 4 vols. with index, London 1885–1899, reprinted 1964.

BGAS ... Bristol and Gloucestershire Archaeological Society.

Book of Llan Dâv ... J. G. Evans (ed.) *The Text of the Book of Llan Dâv reproduced from the Gwysaney Manuscript*, Old Welsh Texts iv, Oxford 1893, reprinted Aberystwyth 1980.

Bosworth and Toller ... J. Bosworth and T. Northcote Toller *An Anglo-Saxon Dictionary*, Oxford 1882. Supplement by Toller (1921); Revised and Enlarged Addenda by A. Campbell (1972).

Brenhinedd y Saesson ... T. Jones (ed.) *Brenhinedd y Saesson*, Cardiff 1971.

Brut ... T. Jones (ed.) *Brut y Tywysogyon or The Chronicle of the Princes*, Board of Celtic Studies of the University of Wales, History and Law Series, vi (1941); xi (1952); xvi (1955).

Bryant ... A. Bryant *Map of the County of Hereford*, 1835.

Cal Inq PM ... *Calendar of Inquisitions Post Mortem* (HMSO State Papers).

Charles (A and B) ... B. G. Charles *The Welsh, their Language and Place-names in Archenfield and Oswestry; Angles and Britons*, O'Donnell Lectures, Cardiff 1963.

CL ... Classical Latin.

Colvin ... H. M. Colvin *Holme Lacy* in *Medieval Studies presented to Rose Graham* (V. Ruffer and A. J. Taylor eds.), Oxford 1950 pp. 15–40.

CRHC ... W. W. Capes (ed.) *Charters and Records of Hereford Cathedral*, Hereford 1908.

Dauzat ... A. Dauzat *Dictionnaire Étymologique des Noms de Famille et Prénoms de France* (édition revue et augmentée par Marie-Thérèse Morlet), Paris 1951.

DB ... Domesday Book.

DB 1–4 ... Domesday Book, associated texts, introduction and indices published by the Record Commission, London 1783–1816.

DBH ... V. H. Galbraith and J. Tait (eds.) *Herefordshire Domesday*, Pipe Roll Society lxiii (new series xxv), London 1950. (References are to the pages of the transcription not to the facing pages of the MS.)

DEPN ... E. Ekwall *The Concise Oxford Dictionary of English Placenames*, 4th edition, Oxford 1960.

DG ... H. C. Darby and G. R. Versey *Domesday Gazetteer*, Cambridge 1975.

DGM ... H. C. Darby and I. B. Terrett *The Domesday Geography of Midland England*, 2nd edition, Cambridge 1971.

Douglas (AW) ... D. C. Douglas *The Ancestors of William Fitz Osbern* in EHR lix (1944) pp. 62–79.

Douglas (WC) ... D. C. Douglas *William the Conqueror*, London 1964.

Du ... Dutch.

Ducange ... G. A. L. Henschel (ed.) *Glossarium Mediae et Infimae Latinitatis*, Niort and London 1884–7.

Duncumb ... J. Duncumb and continuators *Collections towards the History and Antiquities of the County of Hereford*, Hereford 1804–1897.

EcHR ... Economic History Review.

ECWM ... H. P. R. Finberg (ed.) *The Early Charters of the West Midlands*, Leicester 1961.

Edwards ... J. G. Edwards *The Normans and the Welsh March*, Proceedings of the British Academy xlii (1956) pp. 155–177.

EHR ... English Historical Review.

Ekwall (Studies) ... E. Ekwall *Studies on English Place-Names*, Stockholm 1936.

El(s) ... Element(s).

Ellis ... H. Ellis *A General Introduction to Domesday Book*, 2 vols., 1833 (reprint 1971).

Ellis (DTG) ... C. S. Ellis *On the landholders of Gloucestershire named in Domesday Book* in TBGAS iv (1879–1880) pp. 86–198.

EPNS ... English Place-Name Society. References are to the County Survey stated.

Exon ... *Liber Exoniensis* in DB 4 (DB 3 in certain bindings); see above.

FA ... *Inquisitions and Assessments relating to Feudal Aids with other analogous Documents preserved in the Public Records Office, AD 1284–1431*, HMSO 1899–1920, 6 vols.

Farley ... Abraham Farley, editor of DB 1, see above.

Fees ... *Book of Fees (Testa de Nevill)*, 3 vols., HMSO 1920–31.

von Feilitzen (CGPN) ... O. von Feilitzen *Some Continental Germanic Personal Names*, in A. Brown and P. Foote (eds.) *Early English and Norse Studies*, London 1963.

Fellows-Jensen ... G. Fellows-Jensen *Scandinavian Personal Names in Lincolnshire and Yorkshire*, Copenhagen 1968.

Finberg (GS) ... H. P. R. Finberg (ed.) *Gloucestershire Studies*, Leicester 1957.

Finn ... R. Welldon Finn *An Introduction to Domesday Book*, London 1963.

Florence of Worcester ... B. Thorpe (ed.) *Florentius Wigorniensis Chronicon ex Chronicis*, 2 vols., London 1848–9.

Forssner ... T. Forssner *Continental-Germanic Personal Names in England in Old and Middle English Times*, Uppsala 1916.

Fox ... Sir C. F. Fox *Offa's Dyke: a Field Survey of the Western Frontier Works of Mercia in the Seventh and Eighth Centuries A.D.*, London 1955.

Freeman ... E. A. Freeman *The History of the Norman Conquest of England*, 6 vols., Oxford 1867–79.

Galbraith (DB) ... V. H. Galbraith *Domesday Book: its Place in Administrative History*, Oxford 1974.

Galbraith (MDB) ... V. H. Galbraith *The Making of Domesday Book*, Oxford 1961.

GR ... Grid Reference.

Guéry ... C. Guéry *Histoire de L'Abbaye de Lyre*, Evreux 1917.

Harmer ... F. E. Harmer *Anglo-Saxon Writs*, Manchester 1952.

Harvey ... S. Harvey *Royal Revenue and Domesday Terminology* in EcHR (2nd Series) xx (1967) pp. 221–228.

HBC ... Sir F. M. Powicke and E. B. Fryde (eds.) *Handbook of British Chronology*, Royal Historical Society, Second Edition, London 1961.

Hearne ... see Hemming.

Hemming ... Thomas Hearne (ed.) *Hemingi Chartularium Ecclesiae Wigorniensis*, 2 vols., Oxford 1723.

History of St. Peter's, Gloucester ... W. H. Hart (ed.) *Historia et Cartularium Monasterii Sancti Petri Gloucestriae*, 3 vols., Rolls Series No. 33, London 1863-1867.

IN ... *Nonarum Inquisitiones in Curia Scaccarii tempore regis Edwardi III*, Record Commission, London 1807.

J.F. ... John Freeman, see Acknowledgements below.

J.McN.D. ... John McN. Dodgson, see Acknowledgements below.

Jönsjö ... Jan Jönsjö *Studies on Middle English Nicknames 1: Compounds*, Lund 1979, Lund Studies in English no. 55.

Kemp ... B. R. Kemp *The Monastic Dean of Leominster* in EHR lxxxiii (1968) pp. 505-515.

Lennard ... R. Lennard *Rural England: 1086–1135*, Oxford 1959.

LG ... Low German.

L Lat ... Late Latin.

Little Domesday ... Essex, Norfolk and Suffolk in DB 2 (see above).

Lloyd ... Sir J. E. Lloyd *Wales and the Coming of the Normans*, Transactions of the Honourable Society of Cymmrodorion (1899–1900) pp. 122–179.

Lloyd (History) ... Sir J. E. Lloyd *A History of Wales from the earliest Times to the Edwardian Conquest*, 2 vols., London 1911.

LSR ... R. E. Glasscock (ed.) *The Lay Subsidy of 1334*, British Academy Records of Social and Economic History, new Series II, London 1975.

Maitland (DBB) ... F. W. Maitland *Domesday Book and Beyond*, Cambridge 1897.

Marchegay ... P. Marchegay (ed.) *Chartes Anciennes du Prieuré de Monmouth en Angleterre*, Les Roches-Baritaud 1879.

Marshall ... G. Marshall *The Norman Occupation of the Lands of the Golden Valley, Ewyas and Clifford and their Motte and Bailey Castles* in TWNFC (1936–38) pp. 141–158.

MCGB ... C. R. C. Davis *Medieval Cartularies of Great Britain*, London 1958.

MDu ... Middle Dutch.

ME ... Middle English.

ML ... Medieval Latin.
Mod.E. ... Modern English.
Mod.Fr. ... Modern French.
Mod.G. ... Modern German.
Mod.W. ... Modern Welsh.
Mon. Ang. ... W. Dugdale *Monasticon Anglicanum*, 6 vols. in 8, London 1817-30.
MS ... Manuscript.
MW ... Middle Welsh.
Nelson ... L. H. Nelson *The Normans in South Wales 1070–1171*, Austin and London 1966.
ODan ... Old Danish.
OE ... Old English.
OEB ... G. Tengvik *Old English Bynames*, Uppsala 1938 (Nomina Germanica 4).
OED ... *Oxford English Dictionary* (formerly the *New English Dictionary*, 10 vols., Oxford 1884–1921), 12 vols., Oxford 1933; micrographic reprint in 2 vols., 1977.
OFr ... Old French.
OG ... Old German.
OHG ... Old High German.
ON ... Old Norse.
Orderic Vitalis ... A. Le Prévost (ed.) *Historia Ecclesiastica*, 5 vols., Paris 1838–1855. A new edition edited by M. Chibnall has recently been completed (6 vols., Oxford 1969 on). References are to the old edition.
OS ... Ordnance Survey. First Edition Maps (early 19th century) were reprinted Newton Abbot 1969 on.
OScand ... Old Scandinavian.
OW ... Old Welsh.
PNDB ... O. von Feilitzen *Pre-Conquest Personal Names of Domesday Book*, Uppsala 1937 (Nomina Germanica 3).
PNE ... A. H. Smith *English Place-Name Elements*, pt. i EPNS vol. 25; pt. ii EPNS vol. 26, Cambridge 1956.
Rawlinson ... R. Rawlinson *The History and Antiquities of the City and Cathedral Church of Hereford*, 1717.
RBE ... H. Hall (ed.) *The Red Book of the Exchequer*, Rolls Series No. 99, 3 vols., London 1896.
RCHM ... Royal Commission on Historical Monuments, England. *An Inventory of the Historical Monuments in Herefordshire*, 3 vols., London 1931–4.
Reaney ... P. H. Reaney *Dictionary of British Surnames*, 2nd edition, London 1976.
Rectitudines ... *Rectitudines Singularum Personarum* in F. Liebermann *Die Gesetze der Angelsachsen* 1, Halle 1903, translated in part in D. C. Douglas (ed.) *English Historical Documents* vol. 2 no. 172 (London 1968).
Redin ... M. Redin *Studies on Uncompounded Personal Names in Old English*, Uppsala 1919.
Regesta ... H. W. C. Davis, C. Johnson and H. A. Cronne (eds.) *Regesta Regum Anglo-Normannorum* vol. i, Oxford 1913; vol. ii, Oxford 1956.
Lord Rennell (ADG) ... Lord Rennell of Rodd *Aids to the Domesday Geography of North-West Hereford*, Geographical Journal cxx (1954) pp. 458–467.
Lord Rennell (DM) ... Lord Rennell of Rodd *The Domesday Manors in the Hundreds of Hezetre and Elsedune in Herefordshire* in *Herefordshire, its Natural History, Archaeology and History; Chapters written to celebrate the Centenary of the Woolhope Naturalists' Field Club*, Gloucester 1954, reprinted East Ardsley 1971 (Ch. xi pp. 130–158).
Lord Rennell (LL) ... Lord Rennell of Rodd *The Land of Lene* in I. Ll. Foster and A. Alcock (eds.) *Culture and Environment* Ch. 12 pp. 303–326, London 1963.
Lord Rennell (VM) ... Lord Rennell of Rodd *Valley on the March, a History of a Group of Manors on the Herefordshire March of Wales*, London 1958.
RH ... *Rotuli Hundredorum*, Record Commission 1812–18, 2 vols.
RMLWL ... R. E. Latham *Revised Medieval Latin Word-list*, London 1965.
Robertson ... A. J. Robertson *Anglo-Saxon Charters*, Cambridge 1939, 2nd edition, 1956.
Round (CDF) ... J. H. Round *Calendar of Documents preserved in France*, vol. i 918–1206, London 1899 (HMSO State Papers).
Round (FE) ... J. H. Round *Feudal England*, London 1909.
Round (GM) ... J. H. Round *Geoffrey de Mandeville*, London 1892.
Sawyer (1) ... P. H. Sawyer *Anglo-Saxon Charters: An Annotated List and Bibliography*, London 1968.
Sawyer (2) ... P. H. Sawyer *The 'Original Returns' and Domesday Book* in EHR lxx (1955) pp. 177–197.
Searle ... W. G. Searle *Onomasticon Anglo-Saxonicum*, Cambridge 1897.
Taylor (GS) ... C. S. Taylor *The Origin of the Mercian Shires* in Finberg (GS) pp. 17–51.

TBGAS ... Transactions of the Bristol and Gloucestershire Archaeological Society.
TE ... *Taxatio Ecclesiastica of Pope Nicholas IV*, Record Commission, London 1802.
TRHS ... Transactions of the Royal Historical Society.
TWNFC ... Transactions of the Woolhope Naturalists' Field Club.
VCH ... The Victoria History of the Counties of England. DB is translated with an introduction by
J. H. Round in Herefordshire vol. i (1908) pp. 263-345. References are to this volume unless
otherwise stated.
Vinogradoff ... P. Vinogradoff *English Society in the Eleventh Century*, Oxford 1908.
Walker (CEH) ... D. Walker *Charters of the Earldom of Hereford 1095-1201*, Camden Miscellany
vol. xxii (4th Series vol. i), Royal Historical Society, London 1964 pp. 1-75.
Walker (GL) ... D. Walker *A note on Gruffydd ap Llewelyn (1039-1063)*, Welsh History Review i
(1960) pp. 83-94.
Walker (HEH) ... D. Walker *The 'Honours' of the Earls of Hereford in the Twelfth Century* in
TBGAS lxxix pt. ii (1960).
Walker (NC) ... D. Walker *The Norman Conquerors*, Swansea 1977.
Walker (NS) ... D. Walker *The Norman Settlement in Wales*, Proceedings of the Battle Abbey
Conference (1978) pp. 131-143.
Walker (Register) ... D. Walker *A Register of the Churches of the Monastery of St. Peter's,
Gloucester* in *An Ecclesiastical Miscellany*, BGAS Records vol. xi (1976).
Walker (WL) ... D. Walker *The Descent of Westwood in Llanwarne in the Eleventh and Twelfth
Centuries* in TWNFC vol. 36 (1958-60) pp. 191-195.
Walker (WO) ... D. Walker *William Fitz Osbern and the Norman Settlement in Herefordshire* in
TWNFC vol. 39 (1967-69) pp. 402-412.
Wightman (LF) ... W. E. Wightman *The Lacy Family in England and Normandy 1066-1194*,
Oxford 1966.
Wightman (PE) ... *The Palatine Earldom of William Fitz Osbern in Gloucestershire and
Worcestershire (1066-1071)* in EHR lxxvii (1962) pp. 6-17.

Acknowledgements

The County Editors are very grateful to John Dodgson who is supervising the publication of this
series and to John Freeman, both of whom have read through the draft notes and saved them from
errors and infelicities. John Dodgson (abbreviated J.McN.D.) has in particular made important
contributions to place-name and personal name notes, while John Freeman (J.F.) has no less
generously allowed the incorporation of material from his unpublished M.A. Dissertation 'Some
Herefordshire Place-Names in Domesday Book, with Special Reference to Anglo-Norman Influence'.

Miss Daphne Gifford of the Public Record Office has kindly allowed Caroline Thorn to consult
the manuscript of Domesday Book and has tirelessly answered many written queries.

The editors also wish to thank Mr. R. J. H. Hill, Reference Librarian of the Hereford Library,
and the Staff of the Hereford Record Office, among them particularly Mr. J. S. Williams for help
with *Winetune* (2,52) and 'Cuple' (10,74); also Mr. Warren Skidmore of Akron, U.S.A., for
information concerning the Honour of Ewyas Harold and the Scudamore family included in the
notes at 1,56 and 10,16-18; and especially Mr. J. D. Foy for proof reading.

This edition had already been prepared for the press when Mr. Coplestone-Crow of Birmingham
most generously made available to the editors the results of his many years of study of Domesday
and the later descent of Herefordshire manors. His care for detail and intimate knowledge of the
County have helped to amplify and sharpen a number of the notes.

Introductory Notes

1 THE WELSH BORDER AND HEREFORDSHIRE: Geography

English penetration of Wales and Welsh counter-attacks involved centuries of border warfare, that
continued after the date of Domesday. Offa, King of Mercia (757-796), had erected a great
earthwork to define the limits of his kingdom and it is instructive to compare Offa's Dyke both
with the boundary of the modern County and with the pattern of English settlement recorded in
Domesday. In the north, the Dyke (whose course, sometimes conjectural, sometimes incomplete,
is marked on the maps of this volume) ran southwards across the highland of Clun Forest (now in
Shropshire), passed through Knighton, cut across modern Radnorshire and entered Herefordshire
near Knill, striking south-east past Lyonshall, Weobley and Mansell Gamage to join the Wye near

Bridge Sollers. From here Offa's boundary followed the river Wye; sometimes, especially in the south of the County and in Gloucestershire, a dyke stood proud on the crags to the east of the river. The fortification has been studied in detail by Sir Cyril Fox (see Bibliography).

By the time of the Domesday Survey, the English had made striking gains: almost the whole of Elsdon Hundred and half of Staple lie west of the Dyke and north of the Wye, while Domesday records south and west of the Wye the English Hundreds of Wormelow, Dinedor and the southern portion of Stretford, together with the Welsh districts of Ewias and Archenfield which were progressively coming under Norman influence.

The Domesday boundary corresponds in general to that of the modern County, except in the north-west where DB records a number of villages — Weston, Pilleth, Cascob, Discoed, Clatterbrune. Harpton, Old Radnor and Burlingjobb — lying to the west of the modern County and in some cases west of Offa's Dyke, in what was until 1974 Radnorshire. These form a wedge-shaped projection from Herefordshire up the valleys of the Lugg and Hindwell rivers that drain Radnor Forest, where the territory of the diocese of Hereford still projects into that of St. David's. In the same area, Litton, not mentioned in DB, to the west of Discoed, was a detached part of Herefordshire until modern times.

These border lands seem to have seen some of the bitterest contests with the Welsh: almost all the villages were waste in 1066 and 1086. With the exception of Old Radnor and Burlingjobb, Domesday expressly places them on the 'Welsh March' together with Bradley, Little Brampton, Lower Harpton, Knill and Middleton (9,13. 24,3) which have remained in England. Old Radnor and Burlingjobb should no doubt be similarly designated.

Domesday, however, records a subtler distinction in these border lands. Areas of long-standing English settlement, however devastated, are assessed in hides and virgates, the 5-hide unit being often apparent; but newly acquired areas — Ewias, Archenfield and lands associated with castles (Introductory Note 3) — are assessed in terms of plough-lands or carucates (1,48 note). Thus all the areas beyond Offa's Dyke and north of the Wye are hidated, even those later in Radnorshire, as are the Hundreds of Dinedor, Stretford and Wormelow, south of the Wye. The same applies to the Golden or Dore Valley, even though much of it was waste and its frontier position vulnerable, as indicated by the presence of castles north and south at Clifford and Ewyas Harold (Introductory Note 3).

Except in the area of Hay on Wye and Clifford, little is recorded in DB on the west bank of the river Dore (although the Golden Valley contains eight so far unidentified places). The land rose westwards from the valley floor and will have touched the ill-defined boundary with Ewias, part of a Welsh cantref, on the point of being acquired by the Normans. Ewyas Harold castle, built on unhidated land probably gained from the Welsh under King Edward the Confessor, will have supervised the occupation of Ewias. Beyond it, land 'not in the castlery nor in the Hundred' had been granted to Roger of Lacy; here his descendants were to build the castle of Ewias Lacy (now Longtown 10,2) as part of the Norman advance to the Black Mountains. Land within the mountains was no doubt soon acquired by the Lacy family for here they founded Llanthony priory, in an area that was later in Monmouthshire. However, a detached strip, Ffwddog, stretching down into the valleys of the Grwyne Fawr and Afon Honddu rivers from the mountain ridge to the west of Llanthony, remained in Herefordshire until the nineteenth century.

Apart from this one entry relating to Ewias (10,2), DB says nothing about the area, although early in King William's reign the land began to come, like Gwent, under Norman influence, since the Book of Llan Dâv (p. 278) records *Riderch* (Rhydderch son of Caradoc of Gwynllwg, died 1076) ruling over Ewias and Gwent Is Coed and 'serving King William'. The area remained in a Welsh diocese, first of Llandaff, then of St. David's until 1852.

The second Welsh district, or commote, Archenfield, was part of the same cantref, for RBE (p. 761) records *Talegard, Hereging, Ewias, Strediu, i cantref*, that is 'Talgarth, Archenfield (Welsh *Ergyng*), Ewias and Crickhowell (formed) one cantref'. Archenfield lay south of Dinedor and Stretford Hundreds, between the rivers Wye and Monnow, and in 1086 was still a semi-autonomous Welsh district with its own customs. Its major part is not surveyed in detail; indeed only Garway is entered for the whole of its southern half. This is because the district as a whole, though subject to the English since the time of King Edward, was under Welsh law, dues being given by Welsh custom, that is in money or renders of sheep or honey (see A 1-10. 1,49-60).

The lands that are surveyed in detail in DB within Archenfield are those acquired by the English before 1066, mostly in the centre and north, Normans having here succeeded the English lords. Yet even here the assessment is in terms of plough-lands, not hides, and the land is not part of the Hundredal organisation of the County. The Welsh lands, churches and clergy of Archenfield are surveyed in the Book of Llan Dâv pp. 275-278.

Penetration of the district west of the river Wye had probably begun with the establishment of the 'Hundred' of Wormelow, a composite manor measured in hides (1,61-62), and the 'Hundred' of Sellack in the lower loop of a pronounced 'S'-bend in the river (29,20 note). Moreover, the royal manor of Cleeve (1,8) had acquired a number of hidated members on the Welsh bank of the Wye, and Linton (1,1) received dues from Archenfield. Conversely, Archenfield extended east of the Wye to include Kings Caple (1,8 and 1,55 notes) in the upper loop of the same 'S'-bend, and Howle Hill (1,60). Under King Edward, the English interest in the area seems to have provoked the anger of Bleddyn and the Welsh King Gruffydd who laid it waste (1,49 note). Archenfield remained in the Welsh diocese of Llandaff until 1131.

South of Archenfield and of the modern county boundary lay the Welsh district of Gwent. Strong castles had been established at Monmouth and Caerleon under King William, and land measured in carucates was being awarded to Norman tenants between the Wye and the Usk, as well as beyond the latter, as part of Gloucestershire (DB Glos. W 1-19 cols. 162 a,b). This area was later to form the County of Monmouth.

By no means all the Herefordshire land of 1086 was productive: Welsh incursions in the time of both Edward and William had devastated large areas. The great majority of lands in Hazeltree and Elsdon Hundreds and in the Golden Valley are recorded as waste or partially waste before 1066, together with some lands on the north and east boundaries of Archenfield and in the north-east of the County. By 1086, the number of wholly waste manors had diminished and was practically confined to the border lands in Hazeltree and north Elsdon Hundreds, but conversely the 1086 value clauses reveal a larger number of partially waste manors elsewhere in the County. In such cases, the reference to the 1066 position had perhaps been omitted; see DGM pp. 94-98 and maps pp. 96-97.

Welshmen were not confined to Welsh areas in 1086: they are found in the Golden Valley, at Eardisley in Elsdon Hundred and at Cleeve in Bromsash. Welsh renders of sheep and honey are generally found within Archenfield or just over its borders (DGM p. 75). Hides having Welsh rather than English customs are found at 'Westwood' (1,61); Brockhampton (2,15) and in the Golden Valley (2,56).

2 THE WELSH BORDER AND HEREFORDSHIRE: History

The known history of the Welsh border in the eleventh century explains many of the entries in DB. In 1086 the County still bore the scars of forty years of turbulence featuring on the one hand the rise of powerful figures in Wales who overran and amalgamated Welsh kingdoms and on the other the ambitions of Kings Edward and William and the Norman families that they established on the border.

Ever since Offa had constructed his Dyke in the eighth century, periods of peace, such as when King Athelstan (927-939) received homage from Welsh princes at Hereford, alternated with times of border raiding and warfare. In the mid-eleventh century the major Welsh figure was Gruffydd ap Llywelyn ap Seisyll, ruler of Gwynedd from 1039 and of Powys probably from the same date. By 1044, after a long campaign, he had dislodged from the kingdom of Deheubarth in the south King Hywel ab Edwin and his successor Gruffydd ap Rhydderch ab Iestyn. He had already, in 1039, attacked a Mercian army at Rhyd y Groes ar Hafren, a ford near Welshpool, and there killed Edwin, brother of Earl Leofric of Mercia.

By 1042 responsibility for the English frontier had passed to Earl Swein, Godwin's eldest son. In 1046, by invading South Wales, he helped Gruffydd ap Llywelyn resist Gruffydd ap Rhydderch's attempt to restore himself to the kingdom of Deheubarth. It was on his return from this campaign that Swein made Edith, Abbess of Leominster, his mistress (1,10a note).

Gruffydd ap Rhydderch soon counter-attacked and in 1047 seems to have ambushed Gruffydd ap Llywelyn and restored himself to Deheubarth, driving his rival back to his northern kingdoms.

The southern Gruffydd had greater ambitions. In 1049, allied with Danish pirates, he attacked Gwent Is Coed, which since 1043 had been ruled by Cadwgan of the house of Morgannwg.

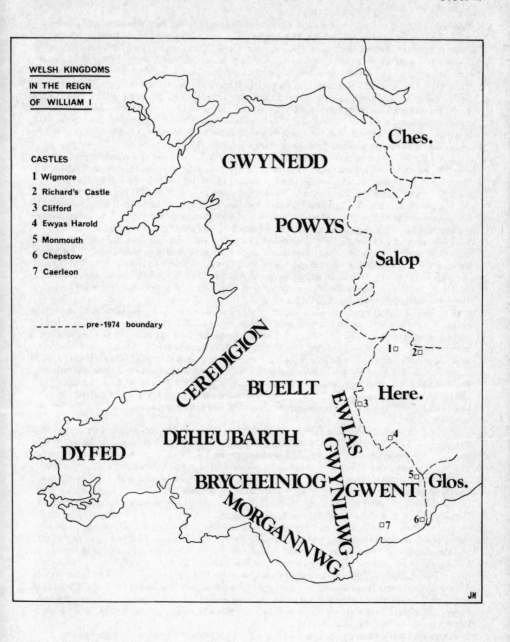

WELSH KINGDOMS
IN THE REIGN
OF WILLIAM I

CASTLES
1 Wigmore
2 Richard's Castle
3 Clifford
4 Ewyas Harold
5 Monmouth
6 Chepstow
7 Caerleon

------- pre-1974 boundary

Ches.

GWYNEDD

POWYS

Salop

CEREDIGION

BUELLT

Here.

DEHEUBARTH

DYFED

BRYCHEINIOG

EWIAS

GWYNLLWG

GWENT Glos.

MORGANNWG

JH

Gruffydd's expedition took him into the Forest of Dean and to the English manor of Tidenham lying on the west bank of the Severn. The English response, consisting of men from Hereford and Gloucester led by Aldred (Bishop of Worcester since 1047), was surprised and defeated.

This reverse, and the frequent border raids of both Kings Gruffydd, seem to have led to a new frontier policy on the part of the English king, Edward the Confessor (1042–1066): Earl Swein was replaced by an Anglo-Norman, Earl Ralph (the Timid) of Mantes, son of Count Drogo of the Vexin and of King Edward's sister, Goda. At the same time, the first Normans, such men as Osbern Pentecost and Richard Scrope, were probably settled on the frontier, and at least one castle was erected — Pentecost Castle, predecessor of Ewyas Harold (19,1 note). This castle was intended to be unwelcome to the Welsh, but the Anglo-Saxon Chronicle ('E' Version) vividly recalls the injuries and insults that the 'Frenchmen' also heaped on the English king's men in the area.

These border arrangements were soon tested, for in 1052, Gruffydd ap Llywelyn, probably invading from the north, harried the County as far as Leominster and was resisted by English and 'Frenchmen from the Castle'. Then in 1053, the other Gruffydd — Gruffydd ap Rhydderch — made an attack on the English manor of Westbury on Severn (GR SO 7113) killing the border guards. Two years later Gruffydd ap Llywelyn had Gruffydd ap Rhydderch murdered and was at last able to secure Deheubarth. Moreover in 1055, the turbulence of the English earls played into his hands. Algar, Earl of East Anglia and son of Earl Leofric (see 10,58 note), was banished by King Edward and fled first to Ireland whence he returned with a Danish fleet and then sought help from Gruffydd. The English, under Earl Ralph, opposed him, but being ordered to fight on horseback contrary to custom, they were quickly routed. The Welsh swept to Hereford, sacked the city and plundered the Cathedral. It was probably at this time that Archenfield was devastated by Gruffydd and his successor Bleddyn, angered that it was already under some form of English control or friendly to the English (1,49 note).

Earl Harold mobilised the English response to avenge the ravaging: in the same year, levies were assembled at Gloucester and with them he penetrated into Wales, pitching his camp *ultra Straddele*, that is, beyond the river Dore (2,54 note), but no success is reported and he seems to have given more thought to defence, fortifying the city of Hereford against further attacks, and to peace which was made with Gruffydd at a meeting at *Biligesleagea*, probably 'Billingsley' (1st edition OS one-inch map, GR SO 5333) near Bolstone in Archenfield. Earl Algar was recalled and reinstated. But the peace was short, for Aethelstan, Bishop of Hereford (who died in 1056), had been succeeded as Bishop by a soldier, Leofgar, who wasted no time in invading Wales and attacking Gruffydd above Glasbury. In the encounter, Gruffydd was victorious, killing both the Bishop and Alnoth the Sheriff.

As a result, Earls Leofric and Harold (the latter having formally succeeded Earl Ralph as Earl of Hereford on Ralph's death in 1057) with Bishop Aldred (now since 1056 Bishop of Hereford as well as of Worcester) came to make peace with Gruffydd. The Welsh King may well have been allowed to retain some of his conquests and in addition he was granted by King Edward land that had belonged to the Bishop of Chester (DB Cheshire B 7 col. 263a) and may possibly be the Gruffydd who administered land in Gwent under King William (DB Glos. W 4 col. 162a). He married Aldith daughter of Earl Algar at about this time (see DB Warwicks 6,5; she later married Harold) and swore to be a faithful under-king to Edward.

Peace followed, punctuated in 1058 by the second exile of Earl Algar and his reappearance in alliance with Gruffydd and Magnus son of Harold Hardrada of Norway. Gruffydd also proceeded to extend his power into Wales, attempting to control Gwent and Morgannwg, ruled over by Meurig ab Hywel and his son Cadwgan. On the death of the former, c.1060, Gruffydd finally seized Gwent. Then in 1062, Gruffydd again renewed his devastations in England and in reply, the following year, Earls Harold and Tosti attacked Wales simultaneously by land and sea. They failed to capture Gruffydd at Rhuddlan, but he was driven beyond his own kingdoms of Gwynedd and Powys and killed by his own men. The men of Gwent and Morgannwg had probably sided with Harold against him in the final conflict.

Although Gruffydd's devastations had left scars deep into Herefordshire and Shropshire, his death changed the political geography of Wales, and his empire was dismembered. His kingdoms of Gwynedd and Powys fell to his step-brothers Bleddyn (died 1075) and Rhiwallon (died c.1070), the sons of Cyfyn ap Gwerstan by Angharad the widow of Llywelyn ap Seisyll; Deheubarth returned to a nephew of Hywel ab Edwin named Maredudd ab Owain ab Edwin, the King Maredudd (father of another Gruffydd) of Domesday. Cadwgan ap Meurig regained Morgannwg and Caradoc son of Gruffydd ap Rhydderch succeeded to Gwynllwg and upper Gwent.

At first these kings ruled as clients of King Edward and it was probably during this period that the English penetration of Archenfield was intensified, and the first moves were made into Gwent.

But the frontier was not to be secured so easily. In 1065 Caradoc ap Gruffydd ap Rhydderch suddenly fell on an English party under Earl Harold that was establishing a toe-hold in Gwent by building a hunting lodge at Portskewett (GR ST 5088) on the banks of the Severn, west of the Wye. Further north, Edric the Wild, nephew of Edric Streona (see 9,3 note), in alliance with Kings Bleddyn and Rhiwallon, invaded Herefordshire and devastated the land as far south as the river Lugg, although repeatedly attacked by Richard Scrope. Again in 1069, Edric, now joined by Earl Edwin of Mercia and his brother Earl Morcar in alliance with King Bleddyn, revolted against King William. Although Edwin soon made his peace, the rest laid siege to Shrewsbury Castle.

The siege was relieved by William son of Osbern, one of the men whom King William speedily appointed to hold the troublesome frontier. In the north, the Norman king appointed Gherbod, his Flemish supporter, as Earl of Chester, rapidly succeeded by Hugh of Avranches. The earldom of Shrewsbury and the middle March were entrusted to Roger of Montgomery; the long southern frontier, where Wales marched with Herefordshire and Gloucestershire, was given to William son of Osbern.

William's value to his master is shown in his dual appointment to the Isle of Wight (Orderic Vitalis ii p. 218) and to the Welsh Border. Like his northern neighbour, Earl Roger, he was a palatine Earl, acting with royal authority on the Welsh border: he is found administering the royal manors of Herefordshire and granting their tithes, churches and small pieces of their lands to his monastic foundations at Lyre and Cormeilles in Normandy. It is he who received the revenues of the City of Hereford in the King's place and granted land directly to his followers and supporters: Ralph of Bernay (sometime Sheriff of Herefordshire), Thurstan of Flanders, Alfred of Marlborough, Walter of Lacy, Gilbert son of Thorold, Ewen the Breton, Hugh Donkey and Ansfrid of Cormeilles.

His short tenure of office and the fact that his son rebelled and forfeited his lands have obscured much of the detail of his authority and acts; but his palatine power extended into Gloucestershire, and perhaps in an attenuated form into Worcestershire. Thus he held Gloucester city; he is found active in Gwent in the extreme south of Wales, where the frontier touches Gloucestershire, allocating 50 carucates of land to Ralph of Limesy and building Chepstow Castle (DB Glos. W 16. S 1. cols. 162b, 162a); he administered or held royal land in Gloucestershire and drew the revenues of Worcestershire and Gloucestershire manors into Herefordshire (1,39–47).

His brief rule, terminated by his death abroad in 1071, was active. Three aspects are worthy of note. Firstly, he constructed castles (see Introductory Note 3 below), those at Clifford, Wigmore, Chepstow and Monmouth being certainly due to him. He also refortified Ewyas Harold (19,1 note).

Secondly, he established on the frontier families who were to be the bulwark against the Welsh: the Lacys, the Cliffords and the Mortimers, who could count on the support of an earlier generation of Normans such as Richard Scrope and his son Osbern, and Alfred of Marlborough, settled there by King Edward, and of the French burgesses whom he welcomed to Hereford and to whom he gave the customs of his own city of Breteuil (C 14 note).

Thirdly, his policy was aggressive: he moved into Brycheiniog and Gwent in South Wales attacking Maredudd ab Owain and his brother Rhys of Deheubarth and Cadwgan ap Meurig of Morgannwg. With the advance came territorial gains and a treaty. Gwent was overrun and given, then or later, a new castle at Caerleon on its western edge. By 1086 it was, like Archenfield, still partly Welsh, with a number of villages administered by Welsh reeves (DB Glos. W 2. col. 162a), and partly in the hands of Norman holders.

The treaty was with Maredudd ab Owain who seems to have allowed the English conquest of Gwent and to have been rewarded by the grant of lands in England, most of them later held by his son Gruffydd (DB Herefords. 29,1. Ch. 31).

Earl William's death, his son's revolt and the fact that no new Earl was created slowed the Norman advance on the southern March and the next major thrust (into Ewias and on into mid-Wales) was only beginning in 1086.

Within Wales, however, matters did not remain static. Caradoc ap Gruffydd ap Rhydderch, ruler of Gwynllwg, and his son Rhydderch, who held some of his lands as under-king, had not submitted to Earl William. In c.1071, with Norman help, they slew Maredudd ab Owain on the banks of the river Rhymney and soon moved into Morgannwg displacing Cadwgan ap Meurig. Deheubarth was briefly ruled by Maredudd's brother Rhys ab Owain, then from 1078 by Rhys ap Tewdwr. Rhys was under constant pressure from Cadwgan, and meanwhile the men of the Earl of Shrewsbury had in 1073–4 ravaged Ceredigion on his northern border. In 1081 Rhys fled to St. Davids and there he seems to have met King William who led an expedition into Wales 'and set many free'. Whatever William's objective, religious or political, he seems to have returned to England having made peace with Rhys; the latter's annual payment is recorded in Domesday (A 10). Rhys, in alliance with Gruffydd ap Cynan the deposed ruler of Gwynedd, proceeded to defeat Caradoc at Mynydd Carn.

The peace that followed allowed the frontier to be consolidated. Many of the men enfeoffed by Earl William had their lands confirmed by King William and are found as tenants-in-chief in Domesday. The Golden Valley and the Hundreds of Elsdon and Hazeltree begin to recover. Roger of Lacy is found in DB inviting settlers on to wasted land (10,43 note).

During this period, major advances into Wales were made from Cheshire and Shropshire (see Introduction to the Shropshire volume of this series); but even in the south the lull was temporary. In 1088 Bernard of Neufmarché began the conquest of Brycheiniog. In 1091, Rhys killed Gruffydd son of Maredudd ab Owain at Llan Dudoch as he attempted to recover the throne of Deheubarth. Then in 1093 Rhys himself was killed after attacking some Normans engaged in fortress building in Brycheiniog. At the same time, Roger of Montgomery was conquering Ceredigion and Dyfed while Glamorgan was falling to Roger son of Hamo. The result was the establishment within Wales of a network of Norman castles and of the first Marcher lordships.

(The main Welsh sources for the period are the *Brut y Tywysogyon*, the Book of Llan Dâv, the *Annales Cambriae* and the *Brenhinedd y Saesson*. Important English or Norman sources are the Anglo-Saxon Chronicle, Florence of Worcester (who expands the account of the Anglo-Saxon Chronicle) and Orderic Vitalis. Good modern studies are Edwards, Lloyd, Nelson and Walker (NC and NS; the former has a useful bibliography), and the 'Introduction to the Domesday Survey' and 'Political History' of Herefordshire in VCH i. There are valuable articles by Douglas (AW), Wightman (PE) and Walker (WO) on William son of Osbern; see also Round in FE pp. 320–326. Lloyd's article 'Wales and the Coming of the Normans' cited in the Bibliography contains a fuller version of material later incorporated in his 'History of Wales' and an appendix giving parallel texts of the *Annales Cambriae* for the period. A useful historical map is provided by W. Rees *A Map of South Wales and the Border in the Fourteenth Century*, Cardiff 1933.)

3 CASTLES
The erection of castles was an essential part of the Norman defensive plan. At least one, probably Ewyas Harold (19,1 note below), and possibly a second, Richards Castle, had been built by Norman settlers under Edward the Confessor, while most of the remaining castles noticed in DB·Herefordshire are due to Earl William.

Castles were a useful springboard for attacks launched into enemy territory; they provided a safe retreat in the case of invasions such as had earlier ravaged the County; they could supervise strategically important passes, valley-junctions, river-crossings or roads, and a chain of them could be used as bases from which to patrol a frontier or to consolidate newly-won territory.

Five castles, Wigmore (9,1), Richards Castle (24,13), Clifford Castle (8,1), Ewyas Harold (19,1) and Monmouth (1,48), are mentioned in DB, and the existence of Caerleon (14,1) is implied though only its 'castlery' is surveyed. Chepstow Castle, also built by Earl William, is described in DB Gloucestershire (S 1. col. 162a). Of the six castles mentioned or implied in DB Herefordshire, all except the two northernmost (Wigmore and Richards Castle) and Chepstow in the south lie on a line that marks approximately the boundary of land held in 1086.

From the detail that DB supplies, some major facts and differences emerge. Firstly, the castles were differently placed in relation to the county boundary. Some, such as Richards Castle, Clifford and Wigmore, were built on land long settled by the English. At Wigmore the land is hidated; the castlery of Richards Castle (and probably the castle itself) was measured in hides (12,2), while for Clifford a TRE holder is given. Moreover, Wigmore is included in the text under a normal Hundred heading and one should probably be supplied for Richards Castle (24,13 note). These two castles thus fell, like Dudley Castle in Worcestershire, within the normal Hundredal organisation of the

County. The land of Clifford Castle, on the other hand, is explicitly said to be not subject to any Hundred or customary due, although 'in the Kingdom of England'.

Other castles were built on or over the border in unhidated land. Ewyas Harold, if correctly identified with Pentecost Castle (19,1 note), was built on land seized by the English before 1066 but not hidated. The remaining castles, Monmouth and Caerleon, were beyond the English border and lay in land that had been Welsh in Edward the Confessor's reign. They were erected under King William to complete the conquest of Gwent and the consolidation of Archenfield. Earl William is said by DB to have built Clifford and Wigmore and to have refortified Ewyas Harold. The Gloucestershire folios record his construction of Chepstow Castle and there is other evidence that he built that at Monmouth (1,48 note).

Secondly, except in the case of Wigmore and Richards Castle, castle land is measured not in hides but in 'carucates', or, in an alternative expression, as "land for so many ploughs". This team-land formula is found in association with the hide in the south-western counties, but is used on its own of land newly acquired by the Normans (as in DB Glos. W 6–19. col. 162b) or of land not liable to a tax assessment (see 1,48 and 7,2 notes).

Thirdly, the growth of a borough appurtenant to a castle can be seen in the mention of a *burgus* or burgesses at Clifford and Wigmore and of 'dwellings' (*mansurae* C 3 note) at Ewyas Harold (13,2).

Fourthly, most castles had land subject to them: Monmouth (1,48), Clifford (8,1 and 10,3), Caerleon (14,1), Ewyas Harold (2,2. 10,1. 13,2), and Richards Castle (12,2). In the case of all except the first, the land is described as in a 'castlery' (*castellaria*). The word is rare in DB, being used of Hastings, Richmond, Montgomery and Dudley Castles, and, in the form *castellatio*, of Lewes. It refers to land rather like the outlier of a manor, administered directly by the castle (see VCH i pp. 272–3). While some castlery land, like some castles, lay outside the Hundred, that of Ewyas Harold and of Richards Castle is said to lie in Cutsthorn Hundred. These castles lay on opposite sides of Herefordshire, and Cutsthorn Hundred lay midway between, but adjacent to neither. The land of Dudley Castle at Bellington in Worcestershire (23,14) is nine miles away from the castle and there is strategic sense in a frontier area in having castlery land on which the castle might be dependent for food and supplies away from the border that was liable to be pillaged. The concept of land dependent on the castle, but remote from it, is one way of explaining why Caerleon's castlery is entered in the Herefordshire folios, rather than in those for Gloucestershire, and why the land is said to be waste TRE, probably before the English had penetrated as far as the Usk (see Note 2 above and 14,1 note below).

On the other hand, the land in the castlery of Ewyas Harold has Welsh customs (10,1–2. 13,2) suggesting proximity to the border, and land at Didley and *Stane* (2,2) is said to have been taken into this castlery, thus locating it near the castle. This implies either the existence of a detached part of Cutsthorn Hundred or a purely notional arrangement 'to make up the Hundred' as is found in the addition of lands to Fishborough Hundred in Worcestershire (DB Worcs. 10,2).

In 1086 the castles will have been of varying strategic value. At the northern end, Wigmore Castle stood well back from the frontier, in this case the boundary between Shropshire and Wales, but it guarded the major north-south Roman road and could oversee the confluence of the rivers Teme and Clun where they descend from the Welsh highlands. This was an area of Herefordshire and Shropshire heavily laid waste, probably by the Welsh incursion of 1052 which nearly reached Leominster, and by the raid of Edric the Wild in 1067 (maps in DGM pp. 96–7; 146–8).

Richards Castle stood on the south-eastern edge of the same devastated area. In 1086, as south-western Shropshire recovered, its military value will have been replaced by Wigmore and probably for this reason it is not described in detail, nor at the head of a chapter. Since it is held by Osbern, whose father Richard Scrope had come to England under the Confessor, it is possible that it was erected before 1066, as a part of the stabilising and reconstruction of the area after the Welsh invasion of 1052 and to prevent further penetration down the Teme should the Welsh overrun the Long Mynd and Wenlock Edge in Shropshire.

Clifford Castle on the other hand was a site of major importance. Lying on the line of Offa's Dyke, it blocked the important valley of the Wye and its tributaries where they entered Herefordshire from the directions of Brecon and Builth. In conjunction with Ewyas Harold it could ensure that the area between the Black Mountains and the Golden Valley was peaceful.

Ewyas Harold at the confluence of the Dore and Monnow rivers blocked another major invasion route up the valley from Abergavenny. The conquest of the Welsh commote of Ewias was already in prospect and Roger of Lacy's holding at Ewias Lacy (10,2; now Longtown), which did not belong to the castlery nor to the Hundred, represents the earliest steps towards the erection of a castle and of the Norman push into mid-Wales.

Monmouth Castle at the junction of the Wye and Monnow, constructed on the Welsh side of both, will have served the conquest of Gwent and the consolidation of Archenfield and will have helped resist ravages of the type inflicted by Bleddyn and King Gruffydd before 1066 (1,49 note). In the south, Caerleon would also help the settlement of Gwent and it stood in the way of any Welsh army attempting to attack from the flat land of Glamorgan. Its construction under Earl William or soon after will have demoted Chepstow Castle to a secondary defence.

The long gap between Wigmore and Clifford Castles was partly filled by two *domus defensabiles* near Eardisley (10,46. 25,9) and there may well have been other similar arrangements not mentioned in DB. The major penetration of Wales under William Rufus blocked other gaps, for instance at Brecon and Abergavenny.

The Herefordshire castles are usefully surveyed in RCHM iii pp. lxii–lxiii.

4 THE COUNTY BOUNDARY

Discussion of the complexities of the Welsh border (Note 1 above) has not taken into account the relationship of Herefordshire to other English counties in 1086 and later.

Whereas the shires in the southern part of the country were formed at an early date, all those south of the Thames being mentioned in the Parker MS of the Anglo-Saxon Chronicle before 892, the Mercian shires are not recorded therein before the early eleventh century, mostly before 1016, although by chance the first mention of Herefordshire is in 1048. In fact, the shires between the Thames and the Humber were artificially created units, apparently of 1200 hides, or multiples, mapped out for the provision of men and ships in order to expel the Danes in the early 11th century. This regular pattern stands out clearly in the County Hidage (see Maitland DBB p. 456) and seems to have been the work of Edric Streona, ealdorman of Mercia (see Taylor GS pp. 17-51).

Even in 1086, however, the boundary between Herefordshire and Gloucestershire had not been finally established. In the south, the area between the rivers Leadon and Wye and Severn and Wye, including the Forest of Dean, seems initially to have been in Herefordshire, the first boundary with Gloucestershire being the line of Bishop Aethelstan's Survey (Pembroke College MS 302, see ECWM pp. 225-227), that is, the limit of Herefordshire diocese. Before 1086 the Forest of Dean and some Hundreds had been transferred into Gloucestershire, and the whole was finally joined to Gloucestershire for secular purposes by the twelfth century, although ecclesiastically the parishes remained in Hereford diocese until 1542. This much is clear, even though there is some confusion about which Upleadon is meant by Hemming when he records it as lying in Herefordshire (10,5 note).

By 1086, some places in this area were in Gloucestershire, leaving Alvington in the south as a detached part of Herefordshire. The process continued and by the twelfth century 'Newarne', Redbrook, Ruardean, Staunton and 'Whippington' had been transferred fully into Gloucestershire. Domesday records some transfers as incomplete: 'Newarne' (1,72) had been transferred into Gloucestershire where it remained, though it is listed in the Herefordshire folios, while Kingstone (3,1) is said to pay tax and do service in Gloucestershire, but to come to meetings in Bromsash Hundred in Herefordshire. Kingstone in fact has remained in Herefordshire.

In this area of the County, a much later change has affected Lea, the southern half of which (Lower Lea) was transferred from Gloucestershire to Herefordshire in 1844.

Minor changes have also been made on the southern boundary where Archenfield touched Monmouthshire. Here, four places — Welsh Bicknor (an outlier of Monmouthshire within Herefordshire until 1845), Ganarew, Llanrothal and Tregate, all in the Welsh Commote of Monmouth in the Middle Ages — were probably among the unnamed villages of Gwent Is Coed mentioned in DB Glos. (W 2 note). They are now in Herefordshire.

In the north-west corner of the County, the boundary between Herefordshire and Shropshire was probably at first the river Lugg (although Cascob, later in Radnorshire, was surveyed in both counties). It then perhaps followed the tributary of the Lugg north of Aymestrey, skirting Lower Lye (see 1,10c note on Lye), then crossing north of Wigmore to follow the Roman road or the

Clun river, but passing to the east of Leintwardine. Shortly after the date of DB this area came into the Marcher lordship of the Mortimers, based on Wigmore, and a dozen places (S 1–12 in the map key) that were surveyed under Shropshire in 1086 (most held then by Ralph of Mortimer) were drawn into Herefordshire and were fully incorporated by the 14th century. They later formed part of the Hundred of Wigmore (see Note 7 below).

Nineteenth and twentieth century Boundary Orders have made further changes to the County. The Herefordshire boundary with Shropshire south of Ludlow was probably in 1086 marked by the river Teme. Before the 19th century part of Ludford was already in Shropshire and in 1901 the rest of the parish, together with Ashford Bowdler (not mentioned in DB) and a part of Richards Castle (12,2 note), was transferred to Shropshire. Farlow, a detached part of Herefordshire in 1086, was transferred to Shropshire in 1844.

On the boundary with Worcestershire, Rochford was transferred from Herefordshire in 1837 and Stoke Bliss in 1897. These two villages will, in 1086, have nearly severed from Worcestershire a part of Doddingtree Hundred which may originally have been in Herefordshire (see DB Worcs. Appendix I). Part of the Worcestershire villages of Hanley Child and Hanley William was probably in Herefordshire in 1086 (10,75 note below).

Transferred from Worcestershire to Herefordshire were Edvin Loach (formerly a detached portion of Worcestershire) in 1893, Acton Beauchamp in 1897 and in the same year a part of Mathon, the rest of the village having been in Herefordshire in 1086 (see 10,39 note below).

Even where the later changes are well documented, the 1086 county boundary is still unclear at some points: in the region of Hanley where it touched Worcestershire on the southern edge of Mathon (10,39 note); in the Forest of Dean where it bordered Gloucestershire and in the area south of Ledbury. Here the 1086 boundary skirting the Gloucestershire manors of Preston and Dymock seems to have severed Much Marcle, *Turlestane*, and Bickerton from the rest of the Winstree Hundred.

5 HEREFORDSHIRE DOMESDAY

Domesday Book continued to be used as a source-book for the taxability and tenure of land for the next three centuries (see Galbraith in DBH pp. xxiv–xxviii and in his DB pp. 100–122). Its use in Chancery and Exchequer administration as well as by local county officials led to the production of a number of subsidiary volumes: the commonest are abbreviations, either of the whole, such as the official Breviate (Public Record Office E 36/284) which was probably based on a lost original and of which there are two copies (Public Record Office E 164/1 and British Library MS Arundel 153); or of parts such as Bath B (see Appendix II of the Somerset volume in this series); the survey of Worcester Church lands (discussed as Worcs. B in Appendix V of the Worcestershire volume); the abbreviation of DB Worcs. Chs. 2–8 (Evesham C in the Worcestershire volume App. IV); the 12th century survey of Kent (British Library MS Cotton Vitellius C 8), and Evesham M (see the Gloucestershire volume). Such abbreviations normally give the place-name, the DB holder (sometimes updated), the hidage and state whether the hides are taxed.

Herefordshire is unique in having a 12th century copy of the whole of DB for the County. It is found in Balliol MS 350 folios 1–42, of which the last four contain related but later surveys. The majority of the MS is, like DB itself, in the 'Curial' script taught in the royal *scriptorium*. One folio containing 2,17 (part) to 2,33 (part) is missing. Herefordshire Domesday (here referred to as DBH) has been edited by V. H. Galbraith and J. Tait for the Pipe Roll Society with pages of MS facsimile facing a transcription and with notes at the end.

Apart from a free treatment of proper names, a procedure shared with the abbreviations of DB, as well as some minor errors and corrections to DB and the omission of chapter headings, DBH is a faithful transcript of Domesday Book for Herefordshire. It contains the Hundred heads from DB but makes no attempt to supply them when they are missing. It probably dates from c.1160–c.1170, and is part of the revival of the Chancery and Exchequer under Henry II following the turbulence of Stephen's reign. It was possibly the work of Thomas Brown who held a post at the Exchequer and had Herefordshire connections.

Its interest to the student of Domesday lies in its marginal additions. These are in both red and black ink and in a number of hands and begin at the time when the body of the MS was written, continuing for some years, though none is certainly later than c.1200. These marginalia usually give the hidage, sometimes discrepant with DB, the place-name and the 12th century holder. The place-names are especially valuable, often differing from the spellings of DB and of the text of DBH itself and being in a more recognisably 'English' form. They sometimes distinguish places of the same name by an additional name (e.g., Halmonds Frome and Castle Frome 10,29-30); or specify more closely a particular holding (Bishopstone for 'Mansell' in 2,46) or give a location or an alternative name for a lost place (Westhide for *Lincumbe* 29,15). Sometimes a name is supplied for an unnamed DB holding (Pencombe 19,6) or for a member or unnamed part of a holding ('Wormington' 1,61).

The 12th century holders have not been added systematically, but are present for about a third of the entries. In some cases, these men have named the village, as in Stoke Bliss (31,6) from *G. de Blez*; sometimes the tenant's name bridges the gap between DB and the earliest Feodaries, thus helping to trace the descent of DB holdings. These additions, corrections or clarifications are recorded in the notes below.

Some miscellaneous surveys are included in the MS with DBH. Of these, two are important for the study of DB. Folio 40r (= p. 77) contains a list of the total hides belonging to individual DB holders (similar to Worcs. D, discussed in App. V of the Worcestershire volume); in some cases the names of the holders have been updated to take account of changes of tenure to *c*.1107-1128. The second survey on folios 40v-41r (= pp. 78-79) is a later list of lands (the place-names and hidages and much of the order taken from DB) and tenants, probably compiled before 1139.

6 PLACES

The identification of many Herefordshire places is less secure than in some other counties. The evolution of the place-names has not yet been subjected to the exhaustive study of an EPNS volume and no further volumes of VCH have yet been published to trace the descent of DB holdings. Earlier surveys lack rigour; for instance, Bannister's volume on place-names is lacking in examples and can seriously mislead in its treatment of villages of the same name, such as Pembridge, Hinton, Marston, which occur in different parts of the County. The work of Lord Rennell of Rodd is helpful, but some of his methods of identification (discussed in ADG), for example from the presumed route of the DB Commissioners or surveyors from village to village, or from modern evidence of the extent of arable land in a given holding, are not convincing. Owing to this and the lack of early feudal evidence for the Welsh Marches area, there is an unusually large number of places unidentified in Herefordshire.

These difficulties are compounded by the usual problems of DB: the absence of Hundred headings in some parts of the text; the fact that the same DB form (e.g., *Mildetune; Hope*) can be represented by different modern names (Milton, Middleton; Hope, Hopleys Green, Brinsop, Miles Hope etc.); while *Frome, Hantone, Estune, Merstone* may each be one of several modern Fromes, Hamptons, Astons or Marstons scattered over the County. Moreover DB spellings, where they can be checked against the marginal name-forms in DBH, sometimes appear confused or corrupt.

On the other hand, considerable help can be derived from the Hundred heads that do exist in the text, from DBH and from the great 1243 survey of lands contained in the Book of Fees. With these sources of help for example, the eight occurrences of *Frome* in DB can be satisfactorily divided between five modern villages in two Hundreds.

The notes in the present edition do not aim to be exhaustive, but to provide supporting evidence for new identifications or for those which might otherwise be reasonably disputed.

Several adjacent modern villages, now distinguished by affixes such as East and West, Upper and Lower, share the same DB form, and if they existed as separate villages in 1086, this is rarely evidenced (*Nerefrum* and *Brismerfrum*, 10,29-30, being exceptional). They are not normally distinguished here in text and index and, in such cases, the Grid Reference refers to the larger village. Where these modern separate villages can be traced from individual DB holdings, this fact is recorded in the Notes below. On the other hand the affixes are included where two places of the same basic name are in different parts of the County. Thus Marston (Stannett) appears as a distinction from Marston in Pembridge; but Grendon Bishop and Grendon Warren which are adjacent appear simply as Grendon in the text.

Many changes have been made in identifications since the publication of VCH, mainly as a result of the appearance of DBH, and the table below sets out the major differences between VCH, DG and this edition. The identifications cited are those of the VCH translation, not the notes. Differentiation of adjacent places of the same basic name is ignored as are variant spellings and alternative forms (Eaton Episcopi for Eaton Bishops). Places within inverted commas are identifiable but now lost: that is, places no longer appearing on modern maps or only represented there by a wood, field or hill name. A dash indicates that a place has not been identified.

Column Ref.	Chapter & Section	DB form	VCH	DG	This Edition
179 d	1,5	*Merestone*	? Marston	–	as DG
179 d	1,5	*Hope*	–	Hopley's (Green)	as DG
179 d	1,6	*Lene*	Kingsland	Eardisland	as DG
180 a	1,10a	*Mersetone*	Marston	–	Marston (Stannett)
180 b	1,12	*Wapletone*	–	Wapley	as DG
180 b	1,15-16) 1,29)	*Hantone*	Hampton (in Docklow) or Hampton (in Hope under Dinmore)	1,15 Hampton (Wafre) 1,16;29 Hampton (in Hope under Dinmore)	as DG as DG
181 a	1,50	*Lagademar*	–	Garway	as DG
181 a	1,56	*Elwistone*	Helvistone Wood (in Harewood)	Elvastone	Pontrilas
181 a	1,58	*Mainaure*	? Mainoaks (nr. Huntsham)	*Mainaure* (in Birch)	Birch
181 b	1,62	*Westeude*	? Dewsall	–	as VCH
181 b	1,69	*Stiuingeurdin*	? 'Strangward' (Strongwood)	Chickward	as DG
181 b	1,69	*Burardestune*	Burton	Bollingham	as DG
181 b	1,69	*Beuretune*	Burton	Barton	as DG
181 b	1,72	*Niware*	? Huntsham	Newerne	'Newarne'
181 b	1,73	*Brocote*	–	–	Redbrook
181 b	1,75	*Getune*	? Gayton (nr. Ross)	Yatton	as DG
181 c	2,3	*Salberga*	–	Sawbury (Hill)	as DG
181 c	2,3	*Ach*	–	–	Noakes
181 c	2,11	*Bertune*	Burton (in Holme Lacy)	as VCH	'Barton' (in Hereford)
181 d	2,15	*Capelfore*	'Caple' (Foraway Farm in How Caple)	Brockhampton	as DG
182 a	2,22	*Wiboldingtune*	Whittington	as VCH	'Whippington'
182 a	2,28	*Bageberge*	? Backbury (nr. Mordiford)	as VCH	'Bagburrow'
182 c	2,46	*Malveshille*	? Mansell	Mansell (Gamage and Lacy)	Bishopstone
182 c	2,52	*Winetune*	Winnington	–	as DG
182 c	2,54	*More*	Moore (near Hereford)	(The) Moor	as DG
182 d	4,1	*Merchelai*	? Little Marcle	Much Marcle	as DG
182 d	6,1	*Bruntune*	Brampton (in Madley)	Brampton Abbotts	as DG
182 d	6,3	*Hinetune*	Hinton (in Peterchurch)	as VCH	Hinton (in Felton)
182 d	6,9	*Mideurde*	–	Middlewood (in Winforton)	as DG
183 a	7,8	*Colgre*	? Cold Green (in Bosbury)	Little Cowarne	as DG
183 d	9,13	*Ortune*	? Orleton	Harpton	as DG
183 d	9,13	*Mildetune*	Milton (in Pembridge)	as VCH	Middleton (in Lower Harpton)

Note 6

Column Ref.	Chapter & Section	DB form	VCH	DG	This Edition
183 d	9,13	*Westune*	Weston (in Pembridge)	as VCH	Weston (in Llangunllo)
183 d	9,15	*Elburgelega*	–	Kinnersley	as DG
184 b	10,17	*Elnodestune*	? 'Elston Bridge'	as VCH	*Elnodestune*
184 b	10,29	*Nerefrum*	? Castle Frome	Halmonds Frome	as DG
184 b	10,30	*Brismerfrum*	? Halmond Frome	Castle Frome	as DG
184 c	10,33	*Frome*	Frome	Canon Frome	as DG
184 c	10,35	*Hide*	Hide	Westhide	Monkhide
184 c	10,37-38	*Lede*	Leadon (in Bishops Frome)	Upleadon	as VCH
184 c	10,43	*Hope*	Hope	Hopley's Green	as DG
184 d	10,52	*Pletune*	–	as VCH	Alton
184 d	10,56	*Malveselle*	Mansell Lacy	Mansell (Lacy and Gamage)	Mansell (Gamage)
185 a	10,63	*Stoches*	Stoke Prior	Stoke Lacy	as DG
185 a	10,67	*Frome*	Frome	Bishops Frome	as DG
185 b	10,71	*Merstune*	Marston (Chapel)	Marston (Stannett)	as DG
185 b	10,75	*Hanlei*	Hanley's End	as VCH	Hanley (Child and William)
185 c	14,12	*Merstune*	Marston	Marston (in Pembridge)	Marston (Stannett)
185 d	16,4	*Ferne*	Ferne	(The) Vern	as DG
185 d	17,1	*Alwintune*	? Alton Court (in Ross)	Alvington	as DG
185 d	17,2	*Merchelai*	Much Marcle	Little Marcle	as DG
186 a	18,1	*Ledene*	Leadon (in Bishops Frome)	Upleadon	as DG
186 a	19,5	*Brocheurdie*	–	Bredwardine	as DG
186 a	19,8	*Penebruge*	Pembridge (nr. Skenfrith)	Pembridge (nr. Leominster)	as DG
186 c	22,4	*Calcheberge*	–	Coldborough	as DG
186 c	22,7	*Torchestone*	Dorstone	Thruxton	as DG
186 c	23,2	*Dodintune*	? Downton	Dorstone	as DG
186 c	23,3	*Burcstanestune*	? Burrington	–	as DG
186 c	23,4	*Ruuenore*	–	–	Mynyddbrydd
186 c	23,5	*Hanlie*	–	–	'Hanleys (End)'
186 d	24,3	*Bradelege*	? Broadheath	Bradley	as DG
186 d	24,3	*Hercope*	–	(Lower) Harpton	as DG
186 d	24,3	*Hech*	–	Nash	as DG
186 d	24,3	*Clatretune*	–	Clatterbrune	as DG
186 d	24,7	*Neutone*	Newton (nr. Bredwardine)	Newton (nr. Clifford)	Newton (nr. Weobley)
186 d	24,8	*Stantune*	Staunton on Wye	as VCH	Staunton on Arrow
187 a	27,1	*Merstone*	Marston	–	Marston (near Pembridge)
187 b	29,10	*Alcamestune*	? Chanstone	–	as DG
187 b	29,16	*Bernoldune*	–	–	'Bernaldeston'
187 b	29,20	*Etone*	? Eaton (in Foy)	–	Strangford
187 b	29,20	*Sulcet* (Hundred)	–	–	Sellack (Hundred)
187 c	30,1	*Wigetune*	Wigton (= Wickton near Hope under Dinmore)	as VCH	Wicton (in Bredenbury)

Column Ref.	Chapter & Section	DB form	VCH	DG	This Edition
187 c	31,2	*Curdeslege*	? Kinnersley	–	as DG
187 c	31,4-5	*Malveselle*	Mansell (Gamage)	Mansell (Gamage and Lacy)	Mansell (Lacy)
187 c	31,6	*Stoch*	Stoke (? Prior)	Stoke (Bliss)	as DG
187 c	32,1	*Merstune*	Marston	–	Marston (Stannett)
187 c	33,1	*Lacre*	–	–	Noakes

7 THE HUNDREDS

The Domesday pattern of Hundreds differed both from the medieval Hundredal arrangement of the County as represented in the *Nomina Villarum* of 1316 (FA ii pp. 382-390) and the later organisation that survived into the nineteenth century.

The 1086 County contained two Welsh areas (Ewias and Archenfield) only partially incorporated; the scattered 'Hundred' of Leominster, ecclesiastical in origin and akin to those found in Worcestershire, Gloucestershire and elsewhere (1,10a note); Stretford Hundred divided into two portions, and two manors Kingsland and Wormelow counted as Hundreds (1,5;61-62). The remaining thirteen Hundreds were of the normal compact type. *Sulcet* Hundred, if correctly identified with Sellack, will have been a third example of a manor regarded as a Hundred (29,20 note).

The Hundredal rubrication is generally full and reliable, but requires some supplementing, especially at the beginning and ends of chapters and in the *Terra Regis*. In some counties, e.g., Buckinghamshire, Hundreds are consistently entered in the same order in each fief (see Sawyer (2)). This is not the case in Herefordshire although a number of chapters contain sufficiently similar patterns for deductions to be made about omitted Hundred heads.

Hundred boundaries, since they do not often coincide with the later limits, are in most cases uncertain. To assist future reconstruction, place-names that appear immediately beneath a Hundred head or are otherwise explicitly stated by the text of DB to be in a particular Hundred, are starred in the map keys of this edition.

Although the pattern of Hundreds is in essence a simple one, it has some unusual features. A *Tragetreu* Hundred occurs once in the text, apparently in error for Greytree (2,13 note). Secondly, in Chs. 9 and 24 a number of places are said to be 'in the Welsh March'. In each case, these fall in the middle of a list of Hazeltree Hundred places and are assumed to be a part of that Hundred, though they are here separately indicated on the maps and in the map keys. Thirdly, the Golden Valley lands, which appear to have amounted to 56 hides (25,7 note) are only once said to constitute a Hundred (2,54). Their western boundary with the Welsh district of Ewias was probably ill-defined in 1086 and is still more difficult to determine because of the number of lands there that have not yet been identified. Some lands in the north-east corner of this Hundred lay rather in the Wye valley than in the Dore (Golden) Valley. Because of the absence of Hundred headings, it is not clear in which Hundred Marston (in Pembridge) and Pembridge itself lay; consequently the boundary between Elsdon and Hazeltree Hundreds is uncertain (19,8 note).

The isolated portions of Leominster 'Hundred' in the northern part of the County intrude into a number of ordinary Hundreds; thus Dilwyn is separated from Elsdon Hundred by Luntley; the two parts of Wolphy Hundred by Brimfield, Upton, Ashton and Middleton, while Broadward (if correctly identified, see 1,28 note) is separated from Thornlaw Hundred by a group of Leominster places. As with the ecclesiastical Hundreds in the southern part of Worcestershire, the lands that formed the 150 or so hides of Leominster manor may have been withdrawn from a number of original compact "territorial" Hundreds, thus disrupting their arrangement. In cases where a village was divided between Leominster and another holder, the latter parts are all in a 'territorial' Hundred: *Alac*, Leinthall, Lye, *Merestone* (Wigmore Castle), Dilwyn, Newton, Upton, Butterley, Broadward, Yarpole and a 'Marston' (probably Marston Stannett, 1,10a note) are all divided in this way.

Some villages are also split between territorial Hundreds: Bishops Frome between Radlow and Plegelgate; Titley between Hazeltree and Elsdon; Clehonger and Moccas between Stretford and Dinedor (although the latter may be an error, 7,7 note). Westhide is divided between Radlow and Thornlaw (29,4 note).

The medieval pattern of Hundreds, as represented by the 13th century surveys in the Book of Fees and the Feudal Aids, is different in many respects. Greytree and Bromsash Hundreds had merged to form the enlarged Hundred of Greytree; Cutsthorn and Staple Hundreds joined to form Grimsworth; from the northern half of Stretford and parts of Hazeltree and Elsdon with the manor-Hundred of *Lene* (1,5) was formed a greater Stretford Hundred. Dinedor, the southern part of Stretford Hundred and some Golden Valley villages were taken into Webtree Hundred, while Radlow was enlarged by the addition of Winstree. Plegelgate and Thornlaw Hundreds, with a few border villages from Radlow became Broxash Hundred; while Archenfield became an English Hundred incorporating Wormelow and named variously Archenfield or Wormelow Hundred. Wolphy and the scattered 'Hundred' of Leominster remained largely unaltered at this period.

During this time, the Marcher lords had full control of their lands which do not, as a result, appear in the feodaries. For this reason, parts of Elsdon and Hazeltree Hundreds and of the Golden Valley as well as the whole of Ewias are not surveyed. Their return to the County administration in the 16th century led to further changes: the creation of a Hundred of Ewias Lacy, which included the DB village of Cusop; the incorporation of the whole Dore (Golden) Valley in Webtree Hundred and the formation of a new Hundred of Huntington to receive a number of places that had been in Elsdon Hundred, such as Eardisley, Harpton, Huntington, Kington, Whitney, Willersley and Winforton, together with Lower Harpton from Hazeltree Hundred. A new Hundred of Wigmore was also made to include most places formerly in Hazeltree Hundred added to lands transferred from Leintwardine Hundred in Shropshire (Introductory Note 4). Finally, Leominster Hundred lost some of its outlying portions to the Hundreds in which they lay geographically, and its core was merged with Wolphy Hundred.

The Herefordshire Hundred names are usefully surveyed in Anderson. Some of the DB names continued as those of later Hundreds, for example Radlow, Greytree and Wolphy; but as a result of the mergers and reorganisation detailed above, a number of the names did not survive until recent times. Some of these are represented by surviving place-names and present no difficulty, this being the case with Elsdon, Dinedor, Stretford and Bromsash Hundreds. Others have long disappeared both as Hundred names and as place-names. Because their DB forms often differ, modern compromise names have been adopted in this edition as follows: Cutsthorn (DB *Cutethorn, Cutestorn, Cutestornes*); Hazeltree (DB *Hezetre*); Thornlaw (DB *Thornlau, Tornelauues, Tornelaus*); Staple (DB *Stapel, Staepleset, Stepleset*); Plegelgate (DB *Plegeliet, Plegelgete, Plegelget*); Winstree (DB *Wimestruil, Wimundestreu*).

8 FOREST

The word derives from ML *foresta*, from CL *foris* 'outside', meaning land, not necessarily wooded, beyond the bounds of the manor or village. Forests are in no sense surveyed in themselves in DB, there being only two cases in Herefordshire where they are mentioned separately from a manor: at 1,52 referring to a render of honey and money from the Forest of Archenfield and at 1,63 in connection with the forests, also in Archenfield, held by William son of Norman. In all other cases, forests are mentioned because they have encroached on the arable or the woodland properly belonging to a manor.

The King regarded *foresta* as his preserve for hunting, and most of the land removed from manors is said to be *in silva* or *in foresta* or *in defenso* (with variants, see 1,43 note) *regis*. Even where *regis* is not included, it is probably implied. The entries relating to Worcestershire and Gloucestershire lands (1,40-43;45-46) have more elaborate formulae such as *silva ... foris est missa ad silvam regis* (1,40) or *parcus ferarum ... missus extra manerium cum tota silva* (1,41).

In Herefordshire, forest is mentioned or implied in the following entries (asterisks indicate that it is specifically designated royal forest): *Turlestane* 1,7; *Cleeve 1,8; *Redbrook 1,73; *Staunton 1,74; *Didley and *Stane* 2,2; *Madley 2,9; *'Barton' 2,11; *Ross on Wye 2,24; *an unnamed place in the Golden Valley 2,56; *Dinedor 8,7; *Bullinghope 10,19 and 21,6; *Much Cowarne 19,10. Plotted on a map, these places fall into distinct groups: Ross, Cleeve, Staunton and Redbrook lie in what is still today the Forest of Dean; Didley and *Stane* are part of Treville Wood mentioned in 1,3; while 'Barton', Dinedor and Bullinghope and the entries at 1,52 and 1,63 (see above) imply the existence of a great forest in Northern Archenfield, probably a branch of the Forest of Dean. Another branch extended to the river Teme and incorporated Malvern Chase, at the southern end of which lay *Turlestane*. The woods of Madley and Much Cowarne seem to have been isolated from the main forests, although the former, together with the unnamed Golden Valley land, might have been part of Treville Wood. The existence of other forest, especially that of Malvern Chase, is implied by the mention of 'hays', that is, hedged enclosures for capturing game (2,33 note).

Wild woodland is sometimes difficult to distinguish from forest: woodland is said to have established itself on eleven waste manors in Hazeltree Hundred and Osbern son of Richard Scrope hunts there (24,5). Land at Harewood (25,6) in Clifford had similarly reverted to woodland, but there is no mention of hunting.

NOTES

The Manuscript is written on leaves, or folios, of parchment (sheepskin), measuring about 15 by 11 ins. (38 by 28 cm.), on both sides. On each side, or page, are two columns, making four to each folio. The folios were numbered in the 17th century and the four columns of each are here lettered a, b, c, d. The Manuscript emphasises words and usually distinguishes chapters and sections by the use of red ink. Underlining in the MS indicates deletion.

Herefordshire seems to have caused the scribe a great deal of difficulty. It is a poorly executed county with much compression, insertions in the margin and at the foot of columns, and a great many blank spaces left, both in the body of an entry (see the recurring spaces left after *hida*; 1,9 note) and between entries (as between 1,38 and 1,39) and at the end of chapters (almost half a column after Ch. 9). It would seem that the scribe began to write up the county before all the material was available. He miscalculated the amount of space needed for several fiefs when planning the layout of the folios, as for example on folio 185a,b where he left about 16 lines at the end of Ch. 10 and then had to squeeze in Ch. 13 at the foot of the column, presumably because he had already begun work on Ch. 14 on the reverse of the folio; (13,2 is below the bottom marginal ruling which is not clear from Farley who prints a smaller gap between Chs. 10 and 11.) There are a great many erasures and corrections, some neatly executed, others badly, some obviously done at the time of writing, others when the scribe came to check the work; not all of them are mentioned in the notes below. The parchment is thin and almost transparent in several places, and rough in many others, which adds to the difficulty in ascertaining which was the original reading and which the correction. The scribe is genuinely careless in some places, briefly omitting details in an entry, so that the word order or grammar is unusual (see 14,6. 22,8. 10,72).

Farley also seems to have encountered difficulties in his transcription of Herefordshire; he makes over a dozen mistakes (though some of them are probably printers' errors), ranging from capitals for lower-case letters and vice versa to the more serious letter and figure errors and omissions, which are noted below.

Because of the poor quality of the parchment and the faintness of some of the ink, the facsimile has failed to reproduce several abbreviation signs and letters, noted below.

When Latin is quoted in the notes below, words are extended only where there is no reasonable doubt. The Anglo-Saxon þ and ð are reproduced as *th*, except in 31,1 note where the distinction is important.

References to other DB counties are to the chapter and sections of volumes in the present series.

Notes follow the correct order of the text, ignoring displacements, thus 6,5 follows 6,4, not 6,10.

HEREFORDSHIRE. *Herefordscire* written in red above both columns on folio 179a,b and 180 a,b and at the head of the list of landholders on 179b; abbreviated *Heref'scire* above folios 179c,d and 180c,d-187c,d. Col. 187d is blank.

C 1   THE CITY. Latin *civitas*; at 2,1 the OE term *port* 'town, market-town' is preferred. See 2,57 note.
       THE CUSTOMS MENTIONED BELOW. *Consuetudo* has a general sense 'custom, habit' and a specific one 'customary due or payment'. It is here rendered by 'custom' whenever a payment is not involved or the case is unclear (as at 1,61 'Welsh customs').

C 2   REEVE'S CONSENT. On the reeve as a subordinate of the Sheriff, see W. A. Morris 'The Office of Sheriff in the Early Norman Period' pp. 157-8 in EHR xxxiii (1918). See also 1,3 note below.
       LEFT HIS HOUSE ... TO THE REEVE. From this it would appear that house ownership was dependent on ability to perform service.

C 3   WHOLE DWELLING. *Integra*, contrasting with *wasta* 'derelict', such dwellings paying no dues (see DB Wilts. M 2). The 'dwellings', *ma(n)surae*, are probably houses, but the word can denote a group of buildings or even a house-plot or plots; see DB Wilts. M 1 (col. 64c) 'In ... Malmesbury ... 25 dwellings (*masuras*) in which are houses (*domus*)'. See also DB Somerset 26,6 General note, Ellis i p. 244 and RMLWL s.v. *mansa*.
       PAID 7½d. DB uses the old English currency system which lasted for a thousand years until 1971. The pound contained 20 shillings, each of 12 pence, abbreviated £(ibrae), s(olidi) and d(enarii). DB often expresses sums above a shilling in pence (e.g., 52d in 1,10a instead of 4s 4d) and above a pound in shillings (e.g., 75s instead of £3 15s in 10,5).

HIRE OF HORSES. *Caballos* 'riding horses', 'war horses'. No distinction is probably intended between them and the classical *equus* as both appear in this entry and in C 5. However, see DB Somerset Exon. Notes 8,5 where *roncinos* 'cobs' is glossed above *caballos*. In some instances, therefore, ML *caballus* may be reflecting OE *capel*, ON *kapall* 'a nag'.

REAPED. *Secabat*, singular, to agree with *masura*, although the occupants of the dwelling are meant.

ON THREE DAYS IN AUGUST. Cf. DB Worcs. 19,12 where 13 burgesses in Droitwich had to reap for 2 days in August and March on Osbern son of Richard's manor of Wychbold.

MARDEN. The King's manor (1,4) was evidently large, although no hidage is given for it.

WHERE THE SHERIFF WISHED. *Ubi* can be translated either by 'where' or by 'when'. It is not certain whether a place or a time is meant here.

(MEETINGS OF) THE HUNDREDS. That is, to the Hundred courts.

WORMELOW (TUMP). Wormelow Hundred occurs at 1,61 as an 'English' area projecting into the Welsh district of Archenfield. It would be a natural point for the English and Welsh of South Herefordshire to meet; see A 7 note.

TO STALL GAME. *ad stabilitionem*. The practice is mentioned in DB Berks. B 11 (col. 56c) *ad stabilitionem uenationis*, a fine being payable if a man did not go. In DB Shrops. C 3 (col. 252a) the Sheriff sent 36 men on foot to stall game. The method was to drive deer and other game from all sides into the centre of a gradually contracting circle of men, where, presumably, there would be a pen or stall in which to trap the animals; see Ellis i p. 111. In DB Cheshire R1,40a (col. 269d) a cognate word *stabilitura* seems to imply an enclosure formed of nets or fences, similar in purpose to a 'hay' (2,23 note).

C 4   ESCORTS. *jneuuardos*, also *inward*, *inguard(us)* elsewhere in DB. They were armed and mounted men detailed to guard the King. The obligation to provide *inward* (frequently coupled with *auera* 'cartage'; see especially DB Cambs. and Herts. *passim*) was often commuted to a money payment; see DB Herts. 1,6 note.

C 5   WHEN A BURGESS ... DIED. See C 9 note below on 'relief'.

     PROPERTY. *Pecuniam*. In DB *pecunia* normally means 'cattle, livestock', its original Latin meaning (from *pecus* 'flock, herd'). However, it can also mean 'resources', 'money', 'goods', as in the similar list of customary dues in DB Cheshire R1,40g (col. 269d).

C 6   THESE (SAME) CUSTOMS. The ones mentioned in C 2–5.

C 9   ONE OF THESE WAS THE BISHOP'S MONEYER. The letters *b, a, c* are interlined over the first letters of *erat monetari' epi*, presumably to correct the word order to read *Un' ex his monetari' erat epi*.

     WAS RENEWED. In the MS *renouabat̄* (= *renouabatur*, the imperfect passive); Farley misprints *renouat̄* (= *renouatur*, the present passive).

     DIES. Latin *cunei*. Similar arrangements are found in DB Worcs. C 1 (col. 172a) and Shrops. C 10 (col. 252a).

     AFTER THE DAY ... WITHIN ONE MONTH ... KING. Each moneyer had a month in which to pay the King 20s, the month beginning on the day he returned home. Likewise in DB Dorset B 1–4 (col. 75a), each moneyer had to pay the King 20s whenever the coinage was changed (*uertebatur*) and in Shrops. C 11 (col. 252a) each of the 3 moneyers in Shrewsbury paid the King 20s on the 15th day.

     RETURNED. That is, from London where the dies were collected. DB Worcs. C 1 (col. 172a) records that each moneyer paid 20s at London for receiving coinage dies.

     FULL JURISDICTION. See Technical Terms and Maitland DBB pp. 80–107.

     20s IN RELIEF. *releuamentum* or *releuatio* was similar to the OE *heregeatu*, ME *heriot*; a form of death-duty, payable by an heir on taking up his inheritance. Originally the heriot and the 'relief' were payments in horses and arms, but like many other customary dues in kind they came to be commuted for payments in money; in C 5 above both forms of payment appear. See 1,49 below; DB Notts. S 3 note; Ellis i p. 269ff; Freeman V App. Note II.

C 10   INTO WALES WITH AN ARMY. The Welsh of Archenfield were bound by a similar custom, see A 8 and 1,49 below. There was a like custom in Shrewsbury (DB Shrops. C 4, col. 252a), and in Worcester (DB Worcs. C 5, col. 172a).

C 11   EARL HAROLD. Son of Earl Godwin and brother of Queen Edith (1,9 note); King of England from 6th January to 14th October 1066. William the Conqueror did not recognise his title to the crown, hence he is referred to as 'Earl' throughout DB. He was Earl of East Anglia (1045), received half of Swein's earldom (1046), was Earl of the West Saxons on his father's death in 1053, and Earl of Hereford (1058). These customs will equally have applied to the time when he was Earl of Hereford where he had large holdings of land and conducted war against the Welsh (see Introductory Note 2).

C 12   £12 ... TO KING EDWARD AND £6 TO EARL HAROLD. The division of a Borough's total revenues between the King and the Earl at a rate of two-thirds to one-third was a common one; see DB Staffs. B 12 (col. 246a), Cheshire C 2; 22 (cols. 262c,d), Shrops. C 12 (col. 252a) etc. For the third penny of the pleas of a county or of a Hundred, which is quite different, see 19,2 note below. See also Round GM pp. 287–296 and in EHR xxxiv (1919) pp. 62–64.

C 13   BREACH OF THE PEACE ... FINE OF 100s. In DB Worcs. C 4 (col. 172a) and Shrops. C 2 (col. 252a), the fine of 100s was payable if the peace 'given by the Sheriff' was broken; if the peace 'given by the King' was broken the culprit was made an outlaw.
HOUSE-BREAKING. *Heinfaram* (for *Hem-, Heim-*), accusative, 'breaking into a house' or 'breach of the peace within a house' (late OE *heimfare*, ON *heimför*, ME *hamfare*); see Harmer pp. 167, 319, also pp. 79–80 s.v. *hamsocn*.
HIGHWAY ROBBERY. *Forestellum*, 'waylaying' or 'ambushing', OE *foresteall*; see Harmer p. 81.

C 14   FRENCH BURGESSES. Earl William (see 1,3 note) modelled the customs of his French burgesses on those of his Norman Borough of Breteuil; see the article by Bateson. Cf. DB Cheshire FT 2,19 (col. 269b) where the burgesses of Rhuddlan Castle paid only a 12d fine for every crime other than homicide, theft and premeditated breaking and entering.
DISCHARGED. *Quietas*, commonly in DB meaning 'exempt from tax' (as in 19,10) or 'immune from dues or service' (see 1,44); or, as here, 'quit, settled, discharged'. See RMLWL s.v. *quietantia* and DB Worcs. 2,74 note.

C 15   BLANCHED PENCE AT FACE VALUE. Or 'white' or 'dealbated', *albas, candidas* or *blancas* in DB. A sample of coin was melted as a test for the presence of alloy or baser metal. Money could also be said to be blanched when, without a test by fire, a standard deduction was made to compensate for clipping or alloying; see *Dialogus de Scaccario* (ed. C. Johnson 1950) p. 125, and 1,6 note on *ora*. 'At face value' *ad numerum* contrasts with *ad pensum*, or *ad peis*, 'by weight'.
18 MANORS. The manors that pay their *firma* at Hereford form the first main block of Chapter 1 (see Ch. 1 note below). There appear to be 19 manors (i.e., 1,1–10;39–47) but it is possible that 1,40–41 were counted as one manor since their payments are combined.
WHICH PAY. *Qui* is an error for *quae*, referring to the neuter plural *maneria*. See also last note to 1,10c and penultimate notes to 1,44 and 31,7.
£335. In the MS there is a black ink spot written diagonally above the dot after *ccc*; the spot and the dot are reproduced in the facsimile rather like a *i*, making the amount of pounds seem to be *cccixxxv lib'*. Had the scribe needed to insert a *i* after the *ccc* (so that the amount was £301(+)35), there was room.

A   ARCHENFIELD. A Welsh area lying between the Wye and the Monnow; it fell into English hands before 1066 and was partially incorporated into England, part remaining with Welsh customs; see Introductory Note 1 and 1,49 note. Similar customs for Archenfield are given in 1,49.

A 1   BEAR THE KING'S DISPATCHES INTO WALES. *ferunt legationes regis in Wales*: possibly 'accompany or conduct the King's embassies into Wales'.

A 2   A BUNDLE OF SHEAVES. *Manipulus* from Latin *manus* 'a hand, a handful' has a number of derived meanings. A common ML sense is 'a vestment' or 'maniple', see RMLWL s.v. and Ducange which defines: *una e vestibus ecclesiasticis quae et sudarium appellatur, quam in bracchio sinistro deferunt sacerdotes*, 'an ecclesiastical vestment, also called a *sudarium* worn by priests on their left arms'. A common CL sense is 'sheaf', 'bundle of wheat, corn or barley' which seems appropriate to the context here. In DB Derbys. B 13 the burgesses of Derby pay 12 thraves (*trabes*) of corn, a thrave containing 12 sheaves. A similar sense may be intended here.

A 3   20s AS PAYMENT FOR THE MAN. Presumably because the King has lost the service of the dead man. Similarly for the thane's man.

A 5   PROVES HIS INNOCENCE. In the MS *se defend*; Farley misprints *de defend*.
40 MEN. That is, 40 men who were prepared to swear that he was guiltless.

A 6   CONCEALED. *celauerit*; the meaning here is 'kept back', 'not paid'.
A SESTER OF HONEY. Together with sheep or pig rents, honey is a normal customary due in the Welsh areas of Herefordshire (see Introductory Note 1 above). The sester (Latin *sextarium*) is a measure, both liquid and dry, of uncertain and probably variable size (see DB Glos. G 1 and 19,2). It was reckoned at 32 oz. for honey; see R. E. Zupko *A Dictionary of English Weights and Measures from Anglo-Saxon Times to the Nineteenth Century* (Univ. of Wisconsin Press 1968) p. 155.

A 7   IF THE SHERIFF SUMMONS THEM. For the judicial, military and financial duties of the Sheriff at this period, as well as the depredations many Sheriffs carried out, see W. A. Morris p. 158ff. in EHR xxxiii (1918).
MEETING OF THE SHIRE. Perhaps at Wormelow Tump (C 3 note); possibly in Hereford.

A 8   BUT IF THE SHERIFF. An adversative force seems required for *nam* here, although it usually means 'for'.

A 9   CUSTOMS OF THE WELSHMEN. The sentence summarises what has gone before, section A 10 being an addition.

A 10   RHYS OF WALES. *Riset* appears to represent the OFr diminutive *-et*, suffixed to OW *Ris*, Modern Welsh *Rhys*. The man is probably Rhys ap Tewdwr who ruled Deheubarth from *c*.1078. He was driven from his Kingdom in 1081 by Caradoc ap Gruffydd ap Rhydderch and took refuge in Saint Davids. Thereafter, with Norman help and allied with Gruffydd ap Cynan, the deposed ruler of Gwynedd, he consolidated his position in Deheubarth. He seems to have become an ally of King William, Deheubarth being perhaps regarded as his fief from which he rendered the customary due mentioned in DB here. Norman frontier policy soon changed, and in 1093 Rhys was killed while attacking a party of Normans engaged in fortress building in Brycheiniog; (see Introductory Note 2).
CALCEBUEF. Perhaps a surname, although the person is unknown. The second element is perhaps OFr *boef*, *buef* (Modern French *boeuf*) 'beef' 'ox'; the first element perhaps a verb. Similar words are *Escorceboef*, *Grindebofe*, see Jönsjö pp. 85, 105 and Dauzat p. 232. A Philip with the surname *Chaucebof*, *Chacebeof* or *Causebuf* is found in connection with several Devonshire manors in the 13th century, Fees pp. 265, 612, 1371. The context, however, really requires a Welsh ruler or kingdom. Mr. Coplestone-Crow points out that *Calcebuef* might be a corruption of *Kenthlebiac*. This name occurs in the total of a list of Welsh cantrefs in RBE p. 762 and refers to the eastern part of Buellt lying 'between the Severn and the Wye': *summa xlviii cantredi, exceptis xi cantredis de Pois et vii cantredis inter Sabrinam et Gwaiam; et excepto Buhelt inter Sabrinam et Wayam — in tempore Ris filii Oeni vocata fuit Kenthlebiac*. The figure *vii* should probably be corrected to *iii* and refers to the cantrefs of *Elfael*, *Maelienydd* and *Gwerthrynion* which occupied approximately the area of modern Radnorshire. *Kenthlebiac* occurs as *Cinlipiuc* or *Cinloipiauc* in Nennius and is derived from the personal name *Cynllib*, a by-form of Saint Cynllo. *Ris filius Oeni* must be Rhys ab Owain, brother of Maredudd ab Owain whom he succeeded as King of Deheubarth (*c*.1078). Both were defeated during the campaigns of Earl William in 1067-71 (see Introductory Note 2). If *Calcebuef* is *Kenthlebiac*, it was probably conquered but not occupied by Earl William and was in 1086 continuing to pay tribute to the English King. English settlement was already beginning in the area: a number of the manors recorded by DB as 'in the Welsh March' lay within the area of *Kenthlebiac*.

L   NOTES CONCERNING MAJOR LANDHOLDERS are to be found at the head of their individual chapters. Notes referring to other individuals are under their first occurrence in the text.

L 2   THE BISHOP OF HEREFORD. Ch. 2 is headed 'Land of the Church of Hereford'.

L 5   GLOUCESTER CHURCH. The Church of St. Peter, Gloucester, in Ch. 5.

L [28] THE CHAPTER is wrongly numbered 27 here.

L 31   GRUFFYDD. Gruffydd son of Maredudd at the head of Ch. 31.

Ch.[1] THE MS, followed by Farley, does not give a number to Ch. 1, as happens in several DB counties.
THE CHAPTER falls into a number of distinct blocks:
1,1-47: manors that pay their *firma* in Hereford (see C 15 note). Among them are the great manor of Leominster (1,10-38) and a number of manors in Gloucestershire or Worcestershire (1,39-47) drawn into Herefordshire by Earl William.
1,48: Monmouth Castle.
1,49-60: Lands within Archenfield mostly held from the King by major tenants who have separate chapters elsewhere in the Herefordshire survey.
1,61-75: Land of the King in various Hundreds, mostly on the Welsh border, not contributing to the *firma* of Hereford.

1,1   IN BROMSASH HUNDRED. The name of the meeting-place is now represented by Bromsash in Linton parish (GR SO 6424), '*Brēme*'s ash-tree'.
5 HIDES. The hide was a unit of land measurement, either of productivity or of extent or of tax liability, and contained 4 virgates. Administrators attempted to standardise the hide at 120 acres, but incomplete revision and special local reductions left hides of widely differing extents in different areas; see Dr. J. Morris in DB Sussex Appendix. Within the 1086 county of Herefordshire the hidation of areas that had long been under English rule contrasts with

areas that are recently acquired from the Welsh, measured in terms of ploughlands (*carucatae*). 'Welsh' hides are also found in Herefordshire (1,61. 2,15;56) where Welshmen have settled on areas of English hidation and have been granted their customs. See Introductory Note 1.

ONE NIGHT'S REVENUE. Many royal manors (especially in the south-west) had to pay this revenue, which took the place of the normal tax payment. Originally this meant the amount of food needed to support the King and his household for one night. By the 11th century these food rents were generally commuted, though apparently not in the case of Glos. (see DB Glos. 1,9;11;13) nor of Dorset (see DB Dorset 1,2-6). Before 1066 £80 was a probable figure for one night's revenue, of which a quarter was paid here; after 1066 £100 is a likely amount. See R. L. Poole *The Exchequer in the Twelfth Century* (Oxford 1912) p. 29. Manors often combined to provide this rent; see DB Somerset General Notes 1,2. Latin *firma* here represents OE *feorm* 'a food rent'. See 'In his revenue' note below for different meanings of *firma*.

A MILL AT 8d. In the MS and Farley *denar*; the facsimile does not reproduce the abbreviation mark, although it is quite clear.

OF WHITE PENCE. See C 15 note above.

ST. MARY'S OF CORMEILLES. See Ch. 3 note. The Church held Kingstone (3,1) which may have been adjacent to this holding.

1 VILLAGER WITH 1 VIRGATE OF LAND. In the MS and Farley *virg*́; the facsimile does not reproduce the abbreviation mark, although it is quite clear.

ANSFRID OF CORMEILLES HOLDS 2 HIDES. In 21,3 Ansfrid holds 2 hides at Aston (Ingham) in this Hundred and they had been held before 1066 by King Edward. The same land may be meant although details differ.

WILLIAM SON OF BADERON HOLDS 1 VIRGATE. The land reappears in his fief at 15,3.

IN HIS REVENUE. Latin *firma*, OE *feorm*. The word is used in several related senses in DB. Apart from the *firma unius noctis* (1,1 note above), it generally refers to a fixed-sum payment or agreed rent, unaffected by changes in value. Depending on the verb or preposition employed, it refers either to the sum received by the King or a noble for his revenue, or the whole revenue itself (e.g., 1,70 *misit ad firmam*; 16,4 *adiacuerunt ad firmam*; 1,70 *reddit lxii denarios ad firmam regis*) or to the type of payment (e.g., 1,75 *Hugo tenuit ad firmam de Hunfrido*; 28,2 *sunt haec duo maneria pro xxx solidis ad firmam*). The first sense is especially common in the case of royal manors in Herefordshire, 18 of them contributing to a single *firma* (C 15); the appropriate translation is 'put, lie, pay, belong in the (King's) revenue'. The second group of examples shows the manner of payment 'at farm' or 'at a (fixed) revenue'. In some phrases, especially involving the verb *ponere* and *ad firmam*, it is not always clear whether movement of money into a central 'revenue' or the 'farming' of a manor is implied, e.g., 1,5 *modo est ad firmam pro xiii libris et iii solidis*: 'now it is in the (royal) revenue at £13 3s' or 'now it is at a (fixed) revenue for £13 3s'. See also 1,2 note on 'Put in the revenue'.

ARCHENFIELD ... HONEY AND SHEEP. Archenfield (1,49-60 note and Introductory Note 1) lay between the rivers Wye and Monnow. Linton, like Cleeve (1,8), lay on its borders and seems to have served as a collecting point for the typical Welsh sheep and honey renders, and probably also as a centre for supervision and consolidation of the newly-won area.

WILLIAM SON OF NORMAN. See Ch. 16 note. DBH (p. 5; see p. 83 note) places his land at *Gedelesford'*, probably Gatsford (GR SO 6126); see 6,1 note below.

6 SHEEP WITH LAMBS. Similar renders of sheep with lambs are to be found on many manors in DB Somerset, being payable mostly to such large royal manors as Curry Rivel, Petherton. See DB Somerset General Notes to 1,4 and 19,17.

1,2   THE KING HOLDS. Repeated at the beginning of 1,2-10.

IN GREYTREE HUNDRED. Either '*Graega*'s tree', or 'grey tree' from OE *grǣg* 'grey' and *trēo* 'tree'.

A SERVANT OF THE KING. *unus serviens regis*. See also in 1,4. *Servientes regis*, the King's Servants or 'serjeants', occur at the end of several DB counties, in a separate chapter, individually named, with, or instead of, the King's Thanes and Almsmen. Unnamed *servientes* are also sometimes listed in villages. Their status is uncertain and they may have nothing but the name in common with later 'serjeantries'. See DB Worcs. 8,11 note.

ONE OUNCE OF GOLD. Written in the left margin of the MS with transposition signs to show its correct position in the entry.

PUT IN THE REVENUE. Or perhaps "put at revenue", i.e., "put out to 'farm' "; see 1,1 note on 'In his revenue'.

REEVELAND. Land that the Sheriff ('shire-reeve') has exclusively for his own use, all customs, payments and services belonging to him. In 1,75 land has been converted into reeveland. DBH records this land in a marginal note as at *Langeford* (p. 5; see p. 83 note) now Longworth (GR SO 5639), the change from 'Longford' being quite recent.

RALPH OF BERNAY. A supporter of Earl William of Hereford (see Introductory Note 2) and Sheriff of Hereford (see 1,70) under him. He was imprisoned by King William and his lands fell to the crown. Bernay is in the département of Eure, France.

1 SMALLHOLDER. As *uñ* generally abbreviates the accusative *unum*, the smallholder is probably also the object of *posuit*; the mill may also have been in Ralph's reeveland.

FOR HIS USE. *ad suum opus*. The meaning of this fairly common DB phrase varies with the context. Here a contrast is implied between the money that goes to the King (the £10 of white pence and the ounce of gold) and what the Sheriff receives for administering the land. See DB Dorset Exon. Notes 11,1 for a correspondence between 'lordship' and 'use' in the Value statement, and DB Somerset General Notes 6,1 for a correspondence between the phrases 'Value for (the holder's) use' and 'Value to (the holder)'. The predominant Latin meaning of *opus*, however, is 'work', and there are occasions in DB where this is the appropriate rendering. It can also mean 'benefit', see DB Devon Exon. Notes 15,67, Worcs. H 2 in DB Worcs. App. V and probably also DB Lincs. Cl. S 19 (col. 375b).

1,3 [?IN STRETFORD HUNDRED]. The heading is a conjecture. In 1316 (FA ii p. 387) Kingstone was in Webtree Hundred which is a later amalgamation of Dinedor Hundred with the southern portion of Stretford. In 1086, Kingstone will have lain near the edge of both Hundreds.

ANOTHER WOULD BE POSSIBLE. *Posset esse*, subjunctive, perhaps with a different nuance from *potest esse* or *possunt esse* (e.g., 1,48) translated 'possible'. The two forms are about equally represented in Herefordshire. The formulae seem to be used as a substitute for the phrase 'land for *x* ploughs' which is common in a number of DB counties. See 1,3 note below.

A REEVE. There are some 38 reeves recorded in DB Herefords. apart from the reeve mentioned in the city of Hereford (C 2;12 — see C 2 note). In most entries they are listed among the villagers with a share in the ploughs and in 2 cases (2,30;49) they are among the subtenants; they also appear to be linked with the beadle (see 1,10a note). Their functions as local officials, in the manor (1,6) and in the village (2,21), were probably varied; see Lennard p. 272 ff.

TREVILLE. *Foresta de Trivel* in RH i p. 186a. The name survives as a parish in an area south of Kingstone that is still heavily wooded. It appears to be this wood that has encroached on Didley and *Stane* (2,2).

HUNTING RIGHTS ... (THE PRODUCE OF) THE HUNT. Latin *venatio*, originally an abstract noun from *venari*, meaning 'an act of hunting', 'a hunt'. Already in CL it can mean game, and here venison, for which a ML word *venisona* exists, may be implied. Ducange defines *venatio* as *ferina, ferae ipsae quae inter venandum capiuntur aut interficiuntur*, 'the flesh of wild animals or the animals themselves caught or killed in hunting'.

THE SHIRE. Latin *scira* from OE *scir* 'shire' equivalent to Latin *comitatus* 'county' as in C 15 above.

ILBERT SON OF THOROLD HOLDS 2 HIDES. DBH (p. 6; see p. 83 note) locates the land at *Hungareston'*, now Hungerstone (GR SO 4435).

CUSOP ... ROGER OF LACY. The identity of the village is uncertain. There is a Cusop near Hay on Wye which would have been a remote outlier of Kingstone on the very edge of the Golden Valley (where it is mapped in this edition), or in Ewias. It should reappear in Roger of Lacy's fief, and may be concealed under another name in the unidentified lands he held in the Golden Valley (10,16–18). There is another Cusop near Bromyard (GR SO 6451), but there are no Lacy lands adjacent.

WAPLEFORD. DBH (p. 6; see p. 83 note) has a marginal entry *Waplefora i hid'* and in a second hand *terra Laur' in Kingest'*, thus locating it as a part of Kingstone.

EARL WILLIAM'S TIME. The phrase, which also occurs in 1,72, replaces the more normal TRE or TRW 'in King Edward's' or 'in King William's time', translated in this series 'before 1066' or 'after 1066'. It refers to the period between 1067 and 1071 when William son of Osbern (William FitzOsbern), brother of Bishop Osbern of Exeter, was palatine Earl of Hereford and, among other powers, allocated lands in the King's place. Because DB concerns itself largely with the tenurial position at two dates, 1066 and 1086, much of the detail of Earl William's grants is obscured. The grants of small parcels and tithes of royal land to the Abbeys of Cormeilles and Lyre, both his foundations, are witness to his administration of the King's estates, as is his drawing into Herefordshire of the revenues of a number of

Worcestershire manors (1,39–47 note). Equally he was responsible for settling a number of Norman families, including the Lacys (Ch. 10), on the Welsh frontier and is mentioned as allocating lands to them at 1,5;61;65. 2,8. 10,41;50;66. 25,9. 29,18. 31,1;7, as well as adjusting manorial boundaries (see 1,4;44. 29,1). On his period as palatine earl see Introductory Note 2. William was joint 'regent' with Odo of Bayeux during King William's absence in 1067 and was responsible for defending the Welsh border. He was married to Adeline, sister of Ralph of Tosny (Ch. 8 note) and died in battle in 1071.

HE COULD GO TO WHICHEVER LORD HE WOULD. He was free to choose any lord as his patron and protector of his lands. Many holdings were 'tied' to a particular manor; see 10,39;54. 15,3. 23,6. 29,19 and 34,1.

LAND FOR 2 PLOUGHS. The estimated number of ploughlands is rarely recorded in DB Herefordshire. They are regularly entered for example in nearby Warwickshire and Staffordshire, but only in a few places in Gloucestershire and Worcestershire. The formula, together with *carucata* derived from it (see 1,48 note), is a convenient way of giving the true arable extent without the complexities associated with the hide (see 1,1 note) and is used where, as in the case of some of the Herefordshire castleries, the land has not been hidated (see for example 8,1). See DB Somerset General Note 1,3 and also J. S. Moore in TRHS 5th ser. xiv (1964) pp. 109-130.

1 HAWK. Hawks were often included in renders to the King; see DB Worcs. C 2 note. Sometimes, as in 25,4 below, such renders took the place of the 'value' statement in an entry.

1,4 [IN THORNLAW HUNDRED]. The Hundred head is supplied from 35,1 (cf. 10,11); see also 2,16 note.

MARDEN. Additional information concerning the royal manor is given in C 3 and 10,11.

2 PLOUGHMEN. *Bouarii*, literally men who look after the oxen (*boves*). Their status was uncertain, some perhaps being servile, while *bouarii liberi* 'free ploughmen' are mentioned at 8,2 and 9,6-7; 9. See Nelson pp. 51-57; Round in VCH (Worcs.) i p. 274 and VCH (Herefords.) i pp. 288-9; Tait in VCH (Shrops.) i pp. 302-4.

4 FREEDMEN. *Coliberti*, former slaves. A continental term, not otherwise found in England, used in DB to render a native term, stated on three occasions to be *(ge)bur* (DB Worcs. 8,10a and Hants. 1,10;23). The *coliberti* are found mainly in the counties in Wessex and western Mercia, particularly in Wiltshire and Somerset. Some of them at least seem to have held land and ploughs and paid various dues, as in 1,6 below, DB Worcs. 8,7 and Glos. 8,1. Only 16 *coliberti* occur in DB Herefords.: here and at 1,5-6; in each case they are entered at the end of the list of population, after the slaves. See Vinogradoff pp. 468-9, and Maitland DBB pp. 36-7, 328-30. On *(ge)bur*, see 2,12 note below and DB Berks. 1,31 note.

25 STICKS OF EELS. A stick contained 25 eels. Renders of eels (as well as money) from mills are common in DB Herefordshire; presumably they were taken from the mill-pond.

FISHERY. *Piscariae* 'fisheries' were not simply places where fishing was done, but 'an apparatus for the catching of fish — perhaps some sort of weir or hatch ... — perhaps almost any kind of contrivance for the purpose' (Lennard p. 248). Cf. 1,39 note on weirs. Usually, though not in this case, a fishery rendered fish or money or, as in the case of the fishery at Portchester in DB Hants. 35,4, it was reserved for the supply of the lord's hall.

SALT-HOUSES IN DROITWICH. See DB Worcs. 1,3a note and Worcs. Appendix III.

9 PACKLOADS OF SALT. *Summae salis*. The size of the packload is unknown, but in the case of salt in Cheshire (S1,4 col. 268b) it contained 15 *bulliones* 'boilings'. It is also used of corn in DB.

WILLIAM SON OF NORMAN HOLDS 3 HIDES, LESS 1 VIRGATE. In 16,3-4 he holds Venns Green and The Vern, 2 hides in all, said to have been attached to the revenue of Marden. The discrepancy in the hidage seems to be accounted for by deducting the land of Norman Pigman and the 1 virgate put outside the manor by Earl William, despite the different holders, but it is possible that one or two entries for 3 virgates in Marden were omitted from William's holding in Ch. 16.

1 VIRGATE OUTSIDE THIS MANOR. Probably the virgate of Stephen (35,1).

NORMAN PIGMAN HOLDS ½ HIDE. DBH p. 6 has a marginal note *Pag' de Burhop' dim' h'* probably implying that the land was at Burghope (GR SO 5050) in Wellington parish; see 10,11 note below.

BOTH OPEN LAND AND MEADOW. *inter planam terram ⁊ pratum*; similar phrases are found elsewhere in DB (e.g., Glos. 1,57 and 10,11; Worcs. 8,6. 9,2 and 10,11; Herts. 10,9).

3 RIDING MEN. *Radchenist(res)* (OE *rād-cniht*, plural -*cnihtas*), similar to *radmen* (OE *rād-mann*, plural *radmen* though regularly written *radmans*, *radmanni* in DB), the latter being translated here as 'riders' to maintain the Latin distinction. Of higher standing than

villagers, they are glossed twice as *liberi homines* in DB Glos. 1,15 and 19,2; in DB Worcs. 8,9b *liberi homines* and in 8,10a *radmans* perform similar services. However, they were apparently not allowed to leave the manor (see this entry and Glos. 3,1). Originally they were men who rode with messages or on escort duty, for the King or for their lord (see DB Worcs. 2,29); they also worked their own lands and those of their lord (see 29,4 below, DB Worcs. 8,10a and Glos. 1,24). From 1,10a below it would seem that they also paid dues. The term *radman* is common in north-west Mercia, up to the river Ribble. In the south-western Welsh marches and in Hampshire *radchenist(res)* predominates. In Herefordshire there appear to be 30 *radmans* and 47 *radchenistres* mainly in the centre and north of the County. In this entry the 3 *radchenist(res)* appear to be the same as the 2 *radmans* and a named sub-tenant in 16,3–4. For discussion, see VCH (Worcs.) i pp. 250–1; Maitland DBB pp. 57, 66, 305–8; Vinogradoff pp. 69–71; Nelson pp. 44–51.

PRODUCE OF THIS MANOR'S LAND. Latin *merces* normally means 'goods', 'sale', 'price'; here probably it means 'profits', 'revenue from produce'.

1,5 [IN HAZELTREE HUNDRED]. The heading is conjectural, but is applied elsewhere in the text to all the members listed below, apart from Hopleys Green which was in Elsdon Hundred in 1086. See 1,64 note.

KINGSLAND. DB *Lene*. DBH (p. 7; see p. 84 note) has a marginal note *Kingeslene*. *Lene* is the Anglicized form of OW *Lien* (< *Lion*, *Lian*), the name of a district on the Arrow and the Lugg. The name is found also in Lene Hundred (1,6), Leominster (Welsh *Llanllieni*), Eardisland, Monkland, Lyonshall and in Leen farm (between Pembridge and Staunton on Arrow GR SO 3859). See DEPN s.n. Leominster.

PASTURE. The only occurrence of pasture (*pastura*) in DB Herefords. apart from in 8,2. This lack of entries for pasture (paralleled in DB Staffs., Shrops. and other midland counties) is unusual, but there are seven references to meadow only for the oxen (see 7,3 note below).

FROM CUSTOMARY DUES ... COME 100s. *exeunt* is used here in the sense of its noun derivative *exitus* 'payment, revenue'.

MERESTONE. in the MS and Farley; the facsimile reproduces *MERESTON*., presumably because the final *E* is partly obscured by a smudge from the ink blot on the facing col. 180a (see 1,8 note). *Merestun* is the form used in 9,1. Ralph of Mortimer built Wigmore Castle there; see 1,19 note. In the place-name *Merestun*, locative *Merestune* (= *Merestone*), the final el. is OE *tūn* 'a farmstead, an estate', but the first el. is ambiguous: either OE *mere* 'a lake, a pool', or OE *(ge)mǣre* 'a boundary', cf. Marston (Stannett) 1,10a note.

HOPLEYS GREEN ... STREET ... LAWTON. Roger's lands are found in his fief at 10,43; 41;40 respectively.

ANOTHER MANOR. In the MS and Farley *M̄* (= *manerium*) as usual; the facsimile does not reproduce the abbreviation line, presumably because of the ink smudge mentioned above, although the line over *aliū* (similarly partly obscured) is reproduced.

WALTER OF LACY. He had been a major landholder in Gloucestershire and Herefordshire and had been settled by Earl William in the castlery of Ewyas Harold (10,1) to strengthen the defence of the border against the Welsh (see Orderic Vitalis ii p. 218 and Introductory Note 2). Walter helped to crush the revolt of Roger, Earl William's son. He was a benefactor of the Churches of St. Peter in both Gloucester and Hereford. On his death in 1085, he was succeeded by his son Roger (Ch. 10 note below).

ALAC. The name recurs at 1,34. If the name refers to one place, then it appears that in 1086 the village was divided between Hazeltree Hundred and the great Manor of Leominster (1,34). J.F. observes that the name-form most likely represents OE *halh* or *halc* 'a nook, a corner of land; a water-meadow (as it were, in the bend of a river); a recess', but it could represent not one but two elements, i.e., an OE place-name *aet lace* or *aet lacum* 'at the stream(s)' from OE *lacu*, perhaps with the OFr preposition *a* 'at' substituted for OE *aet*; or a Normanized name from OE *lacu, La lac* or *Lalac*, with the French fem. definite article *la* (cf. 2,3 note for discussion of *Lacre* 33,1), from which the initial *l* has been lost by dissimilation; or Norman *a l'* (preposition 'at' with definite article) translating an OE place-name *aet thǣre āce* 'at the oak' (from OE *āc*). The appearance of *Ach* in the list of Leominster lands granted to Reading Abbey (see 1,10a note) seems to bear out J.F.'s last suggestion. If this is so, the place is perhaps represented by Cold Oak in Newton (GR SO 4953), more likely, in view of the geographical list of granted lands, than Court of Noke in Pembridge (SO 3759) or Knoakes Court (SO 4555) which are, however, nearer to Kingsland of which a part of *Alac* was a member. Certainty is impossible before a full study of Herefordshire place-names is published.

VALUE. *valebat* or *valuit*, past tenses, *valet*, present; normally means the amount due to lords from their lands (see 1,2 above and 24,13 below). *Reddit* (past *reddidit*), as in 1,3–4 etc., has a similar meaning; see the introduction to the Exon. Notes on p. 310 of the Somerset edition and DB Dorset General Notes 1,7.

IN THE REVENUE AT. See 1,1 note 'in his revenue'.

1,6 LENE HUNDRED. The Hundred is not found elsewhere in DB and if it is not an alternative name for another Hundred it will have been a royal manor with the status of a Hundred: other examples are Wormelow Hundred (1,61 note) and a number of small Hundreds in Somerset (see DB Somerset Appendix I).

EARDISLAND. DB *Lene* (see 1,5 note); DBH has a marginal *Orleslene* (p. 7; see p. 84 note) which appears in the 13th century as *Erleslene*, that is 'Earl's Lene' (OE *eorl*, ME *erle*), referring presumably to Earl Morcar, who held before 1066.

EARL MORCAR. Son of Earl Algar (10,58 note). He stirred the Northumbrians to revolt against Earl Tosti in 1065, and was chosen their Earl, and eventually recognised as such by Harold. He submitted to King William, but rebelled twice and was in custody at the time of the Domesday survey.

2½ SHEEP. Presumably 2 sheep one year and 3 the next; Lennard p. 369 note.

OF THESE TWO MANORS. That is, Kingsland and Eardisland.

HIS LADY. That is, Morcar's wife. There is a similar entry in DB Shropshire 4,1,20 referring to the wife of Earl Edwin, Morcar's brother.

18 *ORA* OF PENCE. An *ora* was literally an ounce; a unit of currency still in use in Scandinavia. It was reckoned at either 16d or 20d. The 16d rate was the normal rate; the 20d rate was primarily a unit of account, found on estates in the King's hands (see 1,39) and was payment 'at face value'. For every 16d due in revenue, 20d was collected, the result being equivalent to a payment in 'blanched' or assayed money (see DB Glos. 1,58). See C 15 note above and S. Harvey in EcHR.

1,7 IN WINSTREE HUNDRED. From OE *Wīgmund*, a personal name, and *trēo* 'tree'; see Introductory Note 7.

(MUCH) MARCLE. In 1,10c the manor is said to have been part of Leominster before 1066.

WHICH PAY TAX ... *geld'*, assumed to be expanded to *geldantes* 'paying tax' (translated 'which pay tax' in this series), rather than to *geldant* 'they pay tax'. *Geldantes* is written out in full in many identical phrases in DB Glos. (e.g., 11,9. 28,4. 31,2). *Geldantes* is interlined above *In Frome sunt x hidę* at 2,21 below; in 2,47 *est geld'* is found which can only be expanded to *est geldans*. However, at 2,49;51 and on a few other occasions, the correct expansion is probably *geldant*; also *7 geld'* which occurs at 1,69. 2,7 etc. is probably *7 gelda(n)t*. Later abstracts of DB often use *geldabiles* 'taxable'.

The rest of the line after *geld'* is left blank in the MS, possibly for some other information on the manor to be inserted later.

VILLAGERS PLOUGH AND SOW WITH THEIR OWN SEED. This service occurs also in 1,10a (see note) and in DB Worcs. 8,5ff. Also see Robertson nos. cix (pp. 204–207, 451–454) and cx (pp. 206–207, 454–456) for the same customs in 11th-century surveys of manors at Tidenham, Glos. (DB Glos. 1,56) and Hurstbourne Priors, Hants. (DB Hants. 3,6); the date of the Hurstbourne text is defined at Robertson p. 454.

BELONG TO WILLIAM SON OF BADERON. In 15,4 he holds ½ hide of the King's manor of (Much) Marcle.

WOODLAND. Timber was used as fuel for salt production in Droitwich; see DB Worcs. 2,15.

60 MEASURES OF SALT. *Mittas salis*; a mitta was commonly reckoned as 8 bushels; see VCH (Worcs.) i p. 270 and VCH (Worcs.) ii p. 257.

4 BURGESSES WHO PAY 18 PLOUGHSHARES. A burgess in Gloucester similarly pays 4 ploughshares (*soccos*); DB Glos. 39,12 and see also Glos. 68,12. Cf. 1,41 below.

TURLESTANE. Unidentified. The iron may well have come from the extensive deposits in the Forest of Dean, the salmon probably from the Wye, perhaps locating the place in the area of Perrystone Court (GR SO 6229).

50 LUMPS OF IRON. *Massas ferri*; the quantity of iron represented by a *massa*, which may not have been a standard measure at all, is unknown. Cf. *blomas ferri* 'blooms of iron'; 17,1 and note.

THE FOREST. See Introductory Note 8.

58 ACRES OF LAND, CLEARED. Above the Latin *projecte*, literally 'thrown out (of the wood)', is written *essarz* from AN *assarter*, OFr *essarter*, 'to clear of wood, convert to arable'. It appears in this form in 10,48–49 and is Latinized as *de exsartis* in 1,10a; Modern English 'assart'. These are the only occurrences of the term in DB.

1,8 CLEEVE. Lying just south of Ross on the eastern bank of the Wye, this composite manor, like Linton in the same Hundred, served to supervise the Welsh district of Archenfield. Two members of the manor, Wilton and Ashe Ingen, were geographically within Archenfield though dependencies of Cleeve and illustrate how Archenfield was being colonised from the

English bank of the Wye before 1066. Kings Caple, another member (see below), though east of the Wye, is said in 1,55 to be in Archenfield.

9 MALE ... SLAVES. In the MS *vii* underlined for deletion with *ix* interlined as a correction. WITH 1 VILLAGER. In the MS the scribe accidentally erased part of the *u* of *uillo* at the same time as erasing a figure under the *.i.*; Farley prints *uillo* complete.

IN KING WILLIAM'S FOREST. DBH (p. 9; see p. 84 note) places the land at *Chingescaple* (Kings Caple GR SO 5628).

WILLIAM BADERON. Probably an error for William son of Baderon, the normal DB designation, although the former occurs in DB Glos. G 4 (col. 162a). The father's name is perhaps on the point of becoming a surname, as Richard Scrope occasionally occurs for Richard son of Scrope. William's land was at Wilton (*Wilton'* in DBH p. 9; see p. 84 note).

GODFREY HOLDS 1 VIRGATE. It was in Kings Caple — *Caple W. de Clinton'* in DBH (p. 9; see p. 84 note).

ASHE (INGEN). DB *Ascis*; DBH (p. 9; see p. 84 note) has a marginal *Hing'*, thus identifying the land. It is given again under Archenfield in 1,57. The DB form is dative plural 'at the ash-trees' of a Latinized form **asca* for OE *aesc* 'an ash tree'.

WHEN HE DIED. At the battle of Hastings, on 14th October 1066.

THIS MANOR PAYS ... . There is an ink blot in the MS which partially obscures *Hoc* $\overline{M}$ and *Rex* in the line below (1,9).

1,9 IN PLEGELGATE HUNDRED. From OE personal name *Pleghelm* and *geat* 'gate or narrow passage'. See Anderson p. 166 and Introductory Note 7.

STANFORD. The manor had belonged to Leominster before 1066, see 1,10c below. The parish is named Stanford Bishop, from a holding of the Bishop of Hereford (FA ii p. 384) not named in DB and either included by it in the total of Bromyard (2,49) or a later acquisition. This DB holding was Kings Stanford or Stanford Regis (Fees pp. 806 and 1482), a lost part of Stanford Bishop parish. In LSR p. 123 it is associated with Grendon Warren and in FA ii p. 384 with Avenbury and Hopton Sollers. The 1 hide of 10,73, known as 'Stanford', may be represented by Hyde Farm (GR SO 6652) and with the 4 hides of this holding will have made a five-hide unit.

QUEEN EDITH. Wife of King Edward the Confessor, daughter of Earl Godwin. She died in 1075.

4 HIDES ... . In the MS there is a gap of about 5 letters' width after *hide* probably left either for a fraction of a hide or for some such word(s) as *geld'* or *non geld'* to be added later. There are a number of such gaps left after the hidage of manors has been given in Herefordshire as also in DB Worcs., Glos. and Shrops. Sometimes as here (and at 2,9. 7,5. 10,23. 16,4. 21,6. 23,3. 25,4 and 26,1) there is a dot after the hidage, sometimes not (as at 2,8;52. 6,3. 10,22. 14,4. 17,1. 19,4–5. 22,8. 24,2. 29,7;13;15). Sometimes (as in 2,52. 14,4(?). 16,4. 22,8. 23,3. 25,4(?). 26,1. 29,7(?)) there are erasures after the hidage; unless, as in 29,16, a line is drawn to cover the erasure, it is not clear whether the scribe intended the space to be left for later filling and so did not write over the erasure, or whether the erasure was done at the correcting stage of the work.

4 SMALLHOLDERS WITH. The gap before *cū* ('with') shown by Farley is due to an erasure in the MS. Farley does not always leave gaps for such erasures (see notes to 1,20;44 etc. below).

1,10a LEOMINSTER. A large composite manor that had been the property of Leominster Abbey, founded *c*.660 by Merewald said to be brother of Wulfhere of Mercia (657–674); see Florence of Worcester i p. 33 and ii p. 252. After its destruction by the Danes, it was restored in 980 by Leofric of Mercia, but was dissolved as a result of Earl Swein's making the Abbess his mistress following his Welsh campaign in 1046 (ASC p. 164). After its dissolution it fell to the crown and had not been fully allotted to other holders at the time of the Domesday survey. The manor appears to have been treated as a large scattered ecclesiastical Hundred, similar to Oswaldslow, 'Pershore' and 'Westminster' Hundreds in Worcestershire DB, Deerhurst and Tewkesbury Hundreds in Gloucestershire, or the Hundred of the Bishop of Wells in Somerset. Of these, 'Westminster' Hundred seems to have been treated as a single manor (see DB Worcs. 8,22 note). DB omits a Hundred heading above the present entry, as above the similar Hundreds of 'Pershore' and 'Westminster' in Worcs. DB.

DB records 80 hides in the manor before 1066 (1,10a): of these, 60 are in lordship in 1086 (1,10a) and another 18½ hides are in the hands of sub-tenants (1,10c); the discrepancy is perhaps accounted for by the land of Leofwin Latimer (1,10c) which is only given a value. Further lands, additional to the 80 hides, are given in 1,11–38 as having belonged to Leominster before 1066 and these, together with Stanford and (Much) Marcle (1,10c), will have given Leominster Abbey a total holding of over 150 hides. These lands appear in Fees,

FA and early feudal lists as parts of the scattered Hundred of Leominster; much later they are in the enlarged Hundred of Wolphy (see Introductory Note 7). Nuns, a remnant of the former community, continued to be supported by some of the lands (see 1,10b), and its former Abbess may be the one mentioned as holding 1,14 Fencote. Leominster with the tithes and churches of many of its former lands was granted to Reading Abbey in 1123, although some of its lands were by then in other hands (see 1,11–38 note below); see B. R. Kemp in EHR lxxxiii (1968). This grant to Reading Abbey by Richard, Bishop of Hereford, is in Mon. Ang. iv p. 56. The list of lands includes the majority of the DB places, listed in geographical order, with some additions. These are in some cases parts of DB villages not mentioned as belonging to Leominster in 1086, such as ?Woonton (2,52 note), Titley, Whyle, Pudleston and Croft, as well as some places altogether unmentioned: 'Lene', Kinnersley (GR SO 3449), Hennor (SO 5358), *Herntun*, Drayton (SO 5366) and Eye (SO 4963).

AYMESTREY. DB *Elmodestreu*; DBH (p. 9) has the same form in its text, with *vel Bedmodestreu* interlined. The spelling *Aylmondestre* found in FA ii p. 377 provides an interesting clue. J.F. observes that DB *Elmodestreu* represents the OE personal name *AEthelmōd* in the genitive singular, and OE *trēow, trēo* 'a tree'; that the interlinear insertion *Bedmodestreu* indicated that the place had another name, from OE *Beadumōdes-trēo* 'Beadumod's tree', at the time of the annotation, whilst the marginal form *Eilmundestro* in DBH p. 11 [whence *Aylmondestre* in FA ii p. 377 noted by Frank Thorn, and the subsequent development noted by Bannister (PNHe), and the modern form (J.McN.D.)] appear to indicate a change of the second theme of the personal name from *-mod* to *-mund*. J.F. points out that if the form *Elmodestreu* had appeared only once in DB it could have been taken to be a form of *Elmondestreu* with *-mod-* in error for *-mōd-* standing for *-mond-* (AN, for OE *-mund-*), but the occurrence of *-mod-* three times seems to reduce this possibility. 'One thus appears to be dealing with three distinct personal names: *AEthelmōd* (DB, DBH), *Beadumōd* (DBH) and *AEthelmund* (DBH and later forms)'. He then observes the possibility that the name of the estate at Aymestrey is here changing along a dynastic succession, in a family with alternating name-themes *AEthel-* and *-mōd*. Cf. F. M. Stenton in *Introduction to the Survey of English Place-Names* (Cambridge 1924) EPNS vol. i pp. 168–169, and J. McN. Dodgson in *Otium et Negotium, Studies ... Presented to Olof von Feilitzen* (Stockholm 1973) pp. 46–48. See *Almundestune*, etc., 29,9–10 note below.

ASHTON. DB *Estune* can represent OE *aesctūn* 'farm where ashes grow' or OE *east-tūn* 'eastern farm'. The modern descendants of these are usually Ashton and Easton or Aston respectively. There is an Aston in Kingsland (GR SO 4662), but the list of Leominster lands in Mon. Ang. iv p. 56 includes *Esscetuna* (*Ayston* in FA ii p. 383; *Asshton'* in LSR p. 130), suggesting that this place is Ashton in Eye, Moreton and Ashton parish.

MARSTON (STANNETT). The order of entries in this list is geographical. 'Marston' appearing between Stoke (Prior) and Upton is likely to be a part of Marston (Stannett), rather than Marston in Pembridge. DB *Mersetone* indicates OE *tūn* 'farmstead, estate' and the element OE *maerse* 'boundary; boundary stream, line, mark' (which has been supposed in the names of the river Mersey in Lancs. and Ches., and Marshfield, Glos.), rather than the more usual *(ge)māere* 'boundary' in genitive singular inflexion as in *Merestone* 1,5.

UPTON. In Brimfield parish. DBH (p. 10) gives the hidage of this member: *Upetona i h*.

(MILES) HOPE. The tentative identification is that of VCH, followed by DG. It is perhaps Hope under Dinmore, see 6,5 note. Mr. Coplestone-Crow points out that if the Miles who named this Hope is Miles *de Mucegros* or Miles Picard, then Miles Hope was probably a part of Laysters (11,2) held by Roger of Mussegros in 1086.

BRIERLEY. J.F. notes: '*Bretlege* DB, *Bradelega* DBH p. 10, *Brereley* 1539 [Bannister] PNHe. The second el. in all three early forms is OE *lēah* "a wood, a glade", the DB form representing the dative singular *lēage*. At first sight the DB and DBH forms appear to contain different els. That in *Bretlege* seems to be OE *bred* "a board, a plank" with AN *-t-* for *-d-* [PNDB| §102(3)]. The meaning of *Bred-lēah* would be "wood where planks were got". The first el. of *Bradelega* seems to be OE *brād* "broad" ... "(at the) broad wood or glade" '. He concludes that the place had alternative names or that its name had changed between the compilation of DB and of the DBH transcripts. 'Possibly the original el. was *bred*, which was replaced by the much more common el. *brād* by analogy with other names. The 1539 form *Brereley* and the modern form Brierley, if they refer to the same place as DB *Bretlege*, show a substitution of a new first el. OE *brēr* "briars". The only way in which *Brereley* might be derived from the same el. as that of *Bretlege* would be to assume that the first el. of both was OE *brerd* "a rim, an edge, a border", probably also "a hill-side" (PNE pt. i s.v., and cf. Bredwardine), see 19,5 note. The first *r* of *Brerd-* could have been lost by dissimilation from the second -r-, giving *Bred-*, and one would then need to assume a loss of the -d- in the consonant-group -rdl- to produce a form *Brereley* by 1524. In view of the phonetic difficulties involved in linking the three extant forms of the name, the identification of the DB form with Brierley ought perhaps to be regarded as tentative.'

IVINGTON. *Iuintune* in the MS; Farley misprints *Lumtune*. The first letter is clearly a capital *I* and the last three minim strokes of the first element divide into *in* rather than *m*.

LEINTHALL. Probably covering the modern parishes of Leinthall Earls and Leinthall Starkes, FARLOW. A remote outlier, geographically within Shropshire in 1086 and later. DB Shrops. 4,28,5 records that "a manor, Farlow, at 1 hide and 3 virgates lies in Leominster, the King's manor in Herefordshire". See E 9 below.

8 BEADLES. DB *bedellus*; an under-bailiff, unpopular, with minor police functions. In DB Herefords. 13 beadles are recorded for 1086 (7 here, and 1 each in 1,39–41;44. 2,39 and 10,9), more than for any other county in DB, though this may be accidental. As the beadle is listed after the reeve in all but the last two of these entries, he may have been his assistant. See Lennard p. 277.

82 SLAVES ... 230 PLOUGHS. From this entry it would seem that slaves had a share in the ploughs in 1066, as also in 1086. See also DB Som. 21,55 and 47,16 and Exon. Notes 45,7.

PASTURE DUES. DB *pasnagium*, 'pannage', payment for pasturing pigs in the wood; the payment was often of one pig for every ten, as below; see notes to DB Middlesex 2,1; Surrey 1,2, Sussex 2,5 and Worcs. 3,3.

6 RIDERS. *Radmans*; see 1,4 note on riding men.

201 PLOUGHS. In the MS an erasure after this extends to the end of the line.

THESE (MEN). 'Villagers' above and in 1,7, but *uillani* there may be being used in the general sense of all the inhabitants of a *uilla* and, as presumably here, all those who shared the ploughs contributed to this duty (see DB Glos. 1,24 and Worcs. 8,10a for examples of riding men/riders ploughing). For the custom of sowing with their own seed, see 1,7 note above.

17s FOR FISH, 8s FOR SALT, 65s FROM HONEY. See fifth note under 1,39.

WOODLAND 6 LEAGUES LONG. DB *leuua, leuga*, a measure of length, usually of woodland, traditionally reckoned at a mile and a half. A subdivision of the league was the furlong, (*quarentina*), reckoned at 220 yards, an eighth of a mile. Both are sometimes used as square measures (e.g. 9,5), but see DB Dorset General Notes 1,1 and 1,2. There is reason to think that the Domesday league was smaller and contained less fulongs; see DB Northants. 1,6 and Worcs. 1,1c notes.

5s ARE GIVEN FOR BUYING TIMBER. Cf.1,7. It would seem that the wood was sold locally to save carting it to Droitwich and 5s of the profits was used to buy more wood in Droitwich to be exchanged for salt. This is a more sophisticated development of the simple exchange of wood for salt, as found in DB Worcs. 1,1a.

FROM CLEARED WOODLAND. See 1,7 note.

1,10b THESE PAYMENTS appear to be based, with two exceptions (Widard's and one Alfward's) on a unit of 20d, probably the *ora*, which is mentioned in the other list of renders to Leominster at 1,38.

BERNARD BEARD. See OEB p. 290. Cf. 15,3 note.

WIDARD. *Vitardus*, also occurring in DB Shrops., Glos., Sussex etc. and in 22,5;8 below as *Widardus*, represents OG *Withard, Witard* (Forssner p. 253 s.n. *Widardus*). OE *Wihtheard* (Searle p. 494) is not convincing.

Against this list of names DBH has a marginal note (p. 11; see p. 84 note) *Nicol de Hedfeld' Dreicote di' h'*, implying the existence of land at 'Draycott', now represented by Draycott Wood in Newton, south of Leominster, (GR SO 5053). DBH does not make clear to which DB holder the note refers.

BESIDES THE SUPPLIES OF THE NUNS. See 1,10a first note.

(PROPERLY) VALUED. *deliberare* has a number of possible meanings: (1) 'to weigh up, assess'; (2) 'to free'; (3) 'to deliver, hand over'. The first has been chosen as a neutral translation; VCH p. 314 has 'if it were freed from other claims', but a translation based on sense (3) 'if it were (fully) transferred (to other holders)' has its attractions, since the manor (1,10a note above) was in the process of being re-allotted to other holders.

1,10c 80 HIDES. See 1,10a first note above.

LEINTHALL. Ralph holds other parts, 9,6–7.

LYE. There are now two villages, Upper and Lower Lye (GR SO 3965 and 4066 respectively). In DB the land is divided among several tenants and was partly in Herefordshire and partly in Shropshire (see ES 9). Soon after DB this border area came under marcher jurisdiction and the Shropshire lands were progressively transferred into Herefordshire. The earliness of this boundary change makes it difficult to determine the 1086 border between the counties. If in 1086 the boundary lay along the river Lugg then it may have turned northwards along the tributary that separates Lower from Upper Lye, keeping Upper Lye in Shropshire, like Lingen which is not far away to the north-west.

EYTON. DB *Ettone*. *Ettone* and *Etone* can both yield modern Eaton or Eyton (see DEPN s.nn.) and it is possible that this holding is at the same place as *Etone*, Eaton, 1,22 below. Lands of William son of Norman later form the Honour of Kilpeck (Ch. 16 note) and *Iatton'* (identified by the indexer as Eyton) appears as held of that Honour in Fees p. 815. The same land appears as *Eatona* in Fees p. 799 and *Eton* in FA ii p. 382.

LEOFWIN LATIMER. The byname is from ML *Latimarus, Latinarius* 'Latin translator' or 'interpreter', see OEB p. 258.

ST. PETER'S. Possibly St. Peter's of Hereford (Ch. 2 note). The dedication of the original church at Leominster (1,10a first note) is unknown. The refounded priory and parish church, granted to Reading Abbey in 1123 by Henry I, is dedicated to St. Peter and St. Paul; RCHM iii p. 111a. See Lennard App. IV pp. 400-401.

STANFORD AND (MUCH) MARCLE. See 1,9;7 above. Much Marcle alone accounts for £30; Stanford for a further 100s.

THEY NOW PAY. *Qui reddunt* in error for *quae reddunt*, as *maneria* is neuter plural; see third note under C 15.

1,11– LAY IN LEOMINSTER (LANDS). The lands were not in lordship before 1066, but let to 38   sub-tenants and here appear to be in the process of transfer to other tenants-in-chief, but although other parts of some villages are found in other Hundreds, these lands appear still to be regarded as part of Leominster 'Hundred' and have not been included in the holders' own fiefs. In 1,12 Osbern son of Richard is claiming that Wapley is in effect part of his fief. The transfers must have been confirmed soon after Domesday, for many of the lands descend to the same later owners (in DBH, and the Feodaries) as lands in individual DB fiefs. For example, Hatfield 1,11 has the same TRE holder as other of Hugh Donkey's Ch. 29 lands. The lands of William of Écouis 1,23–27 have the same later holders as have the lands in his own fief (Ch. 14). Details of these major holders will be found at the heads of their chapters below.

1,11   HATFIELD. See DBH pp. 84–85 note.

OF THESE ... PAID TAX. Probably added slightly later by the scribe; everything after *Ex his* (which appears below *TRE* in the line above) is written into the right margin: this is not clear from Farley.

1,14   THE ABBESS. In the absence of further information, this must be Edith, the Abbess of the dissolved Abbey of Leominster (see 1,10a first note) who probably lived on this land after her House had been dissolved 40 years before.

[VALUE ...]. Probably omitted here in error, as also at 4,1. 23,2–3 etc.

1,15   HAMPTON (WAFRE). The identification is supplied by a marginal note in DBH (p. 12; see p. 85 note) *Hantone*, held by *Rob' Wafre*. The parish name is Hampton (Wafer); the settlement has recently reverted to the earlier spelling.

1,16   HAMPTON. Probably Hampton (Court) in Hope under Dinmore (see DBH p. 86 note), the Hampton *Ricardi* held of the Lacy Honour of Weobley (Ch. 10 note below) in Fees pp. 798, 811. See 1,29 note below.

1,17   SAERIC. Most probably the father of Godmund, see 10,71.

1,19   WIGMORE CASTLE IS SITUATED IN IT. 1,5 and 9,1 contradict this, saying that Wigmore Castle was erected on waste land called *Merestun* held TRE by Gunfrid, apparently a part of the royal manor of Kingsland.

1,20   IN LORDSHIP 1 PLOUGH. In the MS there is an erasure or perhaps a scrubbed patch before *una*; Farley does not show the gap (but see 1,9 note above on 4 smallholders).

1,21   FORD. DB *Forne*; DBH p. 12 has a marginal entry *Forde i hid' et i virg'*. DB *Forne* must be a copyist's error for *Forde*. If a badly written or badly read original used insular *r* and backward-sloping *d* and the ascender of the *d*, horizontal above the *r*, were detached from the bow, *ford* might well resemble *for̄e* or *for̄o*, whence *forne*.

BROADFIELD. DB *Bradefelde*, held of the Honour of Tosny, Fees p. 813.

1,22   EATON. See 1,10c note on Eyton.

1,23   THE VILLAGER PAYS 10d. Or "a villager who pays 10d", separate from the villager above.

1,25   NEWTON. Another part of the village in Thornlaw Hundred, not waste, is held by William as tenant-in-chief in 14,4 (see note). Marginal notes in DBH pp. 13 and 54 record the same later holder, Hugh *de Crofta*, named from Croft (14,5).

BROWNING. *Bruning*. In 14,4 a *Bruns* 'Brown' (the form is Norman French) is given as the TRE holder of ½ hide of waste land in Newton. As other TRE holders of William's lands are the same — or have the same name — in Ch. 1 as in his Ch. 14 (e.g., Edwin 1,23 occurs in 14,2–3 ;5–6 ;8 ;12 and Aelmer 1,26–27 occurs in 14,10) and as Bernard is the sub-tenant in both 1,25 and 14,4, it would seem likely that *Bruning* and *Bruns* are either the same person or closely related. This provides an interesting illustration of the use of the -*ing* suffix in personal-name formation, which might be of interest in connection with the commonplace -*ingtūn* type of place-name (see PNE part i s.v. -*ing*⁴). *Bruning* is an OE name-form, an -*ing* suffix formation upon the base *Brūn* ('Brown; the brown one') and would usually be taken to mean 'person called after *Brūn* ; son of, or member of the family of, *Brūn* ; follower or associate of *Brūn*': i.e., the -*ing* here would be seen as either patronymic or associative, and *Bruning* would be a separate person associated in law or by heredity or inheritance with the said *Brūn*. This is quite possible here, as members of a family or associates could well hold different parts of a village. However, the -*ing* suffix could be taken here as having the adjectival effect of the noun-forming suffix, emphasising the force of the adjective *brūn*: *bruning* would thus mean 'the brown one; that which, or the person who, is characterised by a brown quality'. Compare such OE sets as *lēof*: *Lēof*: *Lēofing* ; *dēor*: *Dēor*: *Dēoring* ; *dunn*: *Dunn*: *Dunning* (see Redin s.nn.).

1,26   DILWYN. Another part of the village was apparently in Elsdon Hundred, also held by William of Écouis, see 14,8 note. The two Ch. 1 holdings have a marginal note *Dilwyn Sorel* in DBH (pp. 13–14), but the relationship between these holdings and the later Dilwyn Sollers and Church Dilwyn has not emerged. See DBH p. 86 note.

1,28   BROADWARD. DB *Bradeford* 'broad ford'. Like Newton (1,25 and 14,4) Broadward seems to have been divided between Leominster manor and Thornlaw Hundred. The substitution of *Bradeford* by Broadward by 1280 is accepted by Bannister PNHe p. 24, DEPN s.n. and the Indexer of the Book of Fees. In Fees p. 101 half of *Bradeford'* is held by the lords of Kilpeck, heirs of William of Écouis (Ch. 14 note) and the other half is held by the monks of *Radinges* (Reading) by gift of Roger, Earl of Hereford. See DBH p. 105 note, VCH i pp. 304–305 and 14,3 note. The later name, Broadward, probably arises from 'broad warth', with OE *waroth, warth* 'land or meadow along a stream or shore; marshy ground near a stream'.

NOW 30[s]. In the MS *sol(idos)* is omitted, probably through lack of space, as happens many times in DB; see 7,5 note below.

1,29   HAMPTON. In DBH (p. 14; see p. 86 note) the marginal note records this hide as held by Adam *de Mapenour'*. Hampton *Mappenore* is found in Fees p. 798 held of the Honour of Clifford (see Ch. 23 note below) and is part of the same village held of the Honour of Weobley (see 1,16 note above). See FA ii pp. 381, 383.

1,30   HAMNISH. Memory of Drogo's land, which passed later to the Honour of Clifford (Ch. 23 note), is preserved in Hamnish Clifford (GR SO 5360).

1,31   DURAND THE SHERIFF. Of Gloucestershire, see 1,61 and Ch. 22 notes.

1,32   DILWYN. See 1,26 note.

1,33   LUNTLEY. See DBH p. 87 note.

1,34   GRUFFYDD BOY. Probably the same as Gruffydd son of Maredudd (Ch. 31 note) since the later holder named in the margin of DBH p. 14, William *de Blez*, also holds some of Gruffydd's Ch. 31 lands. *Puer* 'Boy' probably distinguishes him from King Gruffydd (1,49 note). Cf. Robert Boy in DB Dorset 55, 38-39.

ALAC. See 1,5 note.

1,37   32 HIDES. The total hides listed in 1,11–36 appear to be 34 hides 1 virgate, of which 2 hides 3 virgates at 1,11 and 1 hide at 1,14 did not pay tax, thus giving a total of 30½ hides paying tax.

1,38   FOR THESE PAYMENTS, see 1,10b note.

THEY WORK 2 DAYS A WEEK. *ii dies in ebdomada operantur* which appears to have been added later. It is not clear whether the work is done only by Leofwin, in which case the subject of *opero* is *dies*: '2 days a week are worked'; or, as seems more likely, by all those in the list, in which case they are the subject of the deponent verb *operor*, as translated here. AFTER THIS ENTRY in the MS a space for about 4 lines (larger than Farley shows) has been left, possibly for additional payments.

1,39–   THE LIST OF LANDS contributing to the revenue of Hereford (Ch. 1 note) continues with
47   a series of manors listed under Worcestershire Hundred heads or said by DB to be in that County or in Gloucestershire. Earl William, son of Osbern (1,3 note above), exercising his power as palatine earl on the Welsh frontier, had drawn the revenues of these manors, some of them deep inside Worcestershire, into Herefordshire. When his son Roger forfeited his lands in 1075 after his rebellion, they returned fully to the crown. Martley, Feckenham, Hollow Court and Suckley are cross-referenced in DB Worcs. X 2-3 and 1,1b. Their TRE

holders show that they and the Gloucestershire manors were royal land. The other lands grouped below are portions of church lands accounted for in the text of DB Worcs. under their ecclesiastical holders, but said to be *in manu regis*.

1,39 MARTLEY. In DB Worcs. X 3 (= E 8 below) the hidage is given as 13. The boundaries probably included Areley Kings (GR SO 8070); see VCH (Worcs.) iv p. 288.

2 WEIRS. For trapping fish in a pool; see DB Worcs. E 1 note and 1,4 note above on fisheries.

2,500 EELS AND 5 STICKS. That is, 2,625 eels at 25 to the stick.

A BEADLE. See 1,10a note.

IN PLACE OF FISH AND TIMBER. Purchase of a commodity by a manor is usually represented by *ad*, as in 1,10a *ad pisces...ad sal(em)*. Here *pro* implies that a former render of fish and timber has been commuted, as in 1,49.

OF PENCE AT 20 TO THE *ORA*. See 1,6 note.

GIFTS. Usually to the Queen. OE *gœrsuma, gœrsum(e)* 'treasure, profit of office'; ME *gersum* 'a premium, a fine'. A gift-payment or fine, usually to gain liberty from some other obligation. The word occurs in the same connection in DB Oxfords. 1,12 and Warwicks. B 4 (col. 238a). In Kent 3,18 there is a payment of 100s to the Archbishop of Canterbury *de garsünne*. In Northants. B 36 (col. 219a) in a similar context *donum* 'gift' is used. See Ellis i p. 174, Finn pp. 230–31, 277, Lennard p. 180ff., and OED s.v. *gersum*.

ST. MARY'S OF CORMEILLES. See Mon. Ang. vi pp. 1075–6 which mentions 3 virgates of land. Some land was at *Wigrestun*, now probably Witton (GR SO 7662).

RALPH OF BERNAY. See 1,2 note.

DRUWARD. ME *Druward*, also OFr *Druhard* from an unrecorded OG *Thrūth-, *Drūd-* or *Drut-, -ward* or *-wart*; see Dauzat s.n. *Druard* and O. von Feilitzen CGPN.

1,40 FECKENHAM. The diversion from Worcestershire is recorded in DB Worcs. X 2 (= E 7 below).

FIVE THANES. Capital *Q* for *Quinque* in the MS; Farley misprints *quinque*.

EARL EDWIN. Earl of Mercia *c*.1063–1070; son of Algar who was also Earl of Mercia.

ST. MARY'S CHURCH. The Abbey of Lyre, from later evidence, see Guéry p. 159 and Mon. Ang. vi p. 1092. See also Ch. 4 note.

WALTER OF LACY. See 1,5 note.

HE HAS. *Hic* means 'he', a replacement for *ipse*; not 'here'. Cf. DB Worcs. App. V Worcs. H 2 textual note.

1,41 HOLLOW (COURT). DB *Haloede*; with *Holewei* DB Worcs. X 2 col. 178a, this name has been taken to represent Hollow (Court) and Hollowfields Farm in Hanbury, Worcs., i.e., as 'Holloway'; see EPNS (Worcs.) p. 323, VCH (Worcs.) iii p. 376. The supposition of OE *(se)hola weg* or *(æt thæm) holan wege* 'hollow way; road in a hollow; sunken road' is obviously right for Hollow (Court), *Holewei* DB Worcs. X 2, but not for *Haloede* in the Herefords. folios, which is a different name, etymology not ascertained. Although the names have different origins, both refer to the same place which lay and lies in Worcestershire although its dues had in 1086 been diverted to Herefordshire. The fact that the main description is in the Herefordshire volume is mentioned in DB Worcs. col. 178a (X 2 = E 7 below). The place is called *Holeweya* in Fees p. 1290 (Worcestershire). 1 virgate and the tithe belonged to the Church of Cormeilles, Mon. Ang. vi pp. 1075–6.

A PARK FOR WILD ANIMALS. For hunting. *Parcus* is usually an area of woodland reserved for the chase within the bounds of the manor, contrasting with *foresta* (Introductory Note 8). In this case the park has been taken into the (King's) Forest.

1 *HOCH*. Latinized as *hoccus*, a word of uncertain meaning in connection with salt-making, see DB Worcs. 1,3a note.

1 HOUSE WHICH PAYS 2 PLOUGHSHARES. See 1,7 note.

THESE TWO MANORS. That is, Feckenham and Hollow Court.

1,42–44 BRICTRIC. Brictric son of Algar, a great English thane who held much land in the west. He was the lord of Tewkesbury manor (to which Hanley Castle and Forthampton had belonged); DB Glos. 1,34–35;39. Many of his lands passed to William's queen Matilda (see DB Glos. 1,42 note) and, on her death in 1083, to King William (see DB Worcs. 2,30).

1,42 HANLEY (CASTLE). Geographically it fell well within Worcestershire in 1086, but it is regarded as a part of Gloucestershire both in DB Glos. 1,34 (= E 2 below) and here, Brictric son of Algar having withdrawn it from Worcestershire and attached it to his great manor of Tewkesbury. It is duplicated in Herefordshire because Earl William had withdrawn its revenues there. The Gloucestershire and Herefordshire entries originate from different returns and there are a number of discrepancies:

DB Glos. 1,34 (= E 2 below)	DB Herefords. 1,42
4 hides outside the lordship	4 hides
2 lordship ploughs before 1066	2 lordship ploughs
40 villagers and smallholders	20 villagers, 17 smallholders
–	21½ villagers' ploughs
8 male and female slaves	9 male and female slaves
a mill at 16d	a mill at 2s
woodland containing an enclosure	woodland 5 leagues long and wide, put outside the manor and containing a hawk's eyrie
–	a forester holds ½ virgate
–	a villager of 'Baldenhall' pays 2 *ora* of pence
value before 1066 £15; now £10.	[value given for the group of manors in 1,47 below]

WOODLAND ... IN BOTH LENGTH AND WIDTH. *habet* 'has' may have been omitted after *silua* (cf. 1,43;47), because the genitive *siluae* is normal in this phrase as in 15,8. 24,1. 27,1 etc.
'BALDENHALL'. See EPNS (Worcs.) p. 210. Lost in Great Malvern parish and probably corresponding roughly to the area of the ecclesiastical parish of Guarlford. 1 virgate here was granted to the priory of Great Malvern by Edward the Confessor of the fee of Hanley, suggesting that the village lay within the bounds of Hanley Castle in the 11th century. It was merged with Great Malvern manor in the mid-16th century and in the time of Edward VI was stated to fall between Great Malvern and Guarlford, though it no longer existed; see VCH (Worcs.) iv p. 125. The Church of Hanley belonged to Lyre Abbey, Mon. Ang. vi pp. 1092-3.

1,43   FORTHAMPTON. Lying in the extreme north of Gloucestershire almost entirely surrounded by Worcestershire, Forthampton's revenue had been withdrawn to Hereford by Earl William as the corresponding duplicate entry in DB Glos. 1,35 (= E 3 below) makes clear. There are significant differences of detail in the two accounts of the same land:

DB Glos. 1,35	DB Herefords. 1,43
9 hides	9 hides which pay tax for 4 hides
2 ploughs in lordship	3 ploughs in lordship
20 villagers and smallholders	7 villagers with 5 ploughs
	4 pigmen with 1 plough pay 35 pigs
woodland	woodland 3 leagues in length and width ...
Value before 1066 £10; now £8.	[Value given for the group of manors in 1,47 below.]

[None of the remaining details of the Herefordshire entry is found in the Gloucestershire one].
IN THE ENCLOSURE OF THE KING'S WOODLAND. *In defenso siluae regis*. Similar phrases in DB Oxon. 1,5 (*silua est in defens' regis*), Warwicks. 27,3 (*silua .. sed in defenso regis est*) and Berks. 1,1 (*silua missa est in defensa*) suggest that the woodland has been put into the King's Forest (see Introductory Note 8). Herefordshire entries show the (ablative) forms *defenso, defensu* and *defensione* (2,2;9;24;56).
HAWK'S EYRIE. In the MS *i* is interlined above the *e* of *accepitris* in correction, but the *e* is not underlined or dotted for deletion as one would expect.
ST. MARY'S. Of Lyre, Mon. Ang. vi pp. 1092-3. See Ch. 4 note below.

1,44   BUSHLEY. The land belonged to Worcester Church and is said at DB Worcs. 2,30, which gives additional information, to be *in manu regis*.
LEOFING. Lyfing, Bishop of Worcester 1038-40, then from 1041 to his death in 1046.
3 GOLD MARKS ... A SILVER MARK. The gold mark was worth £6; the silver, 13s 4d.
HE BOUGHT THE WHOLE. The detail of the arrangement in DB Worcs. 2,30 is different.
SERVE ANY MAN FOR IT. The rest of the line in the MS is blank after this, perhaps left for additional information to be inserted later.
A DAIRYMAID. Or 'dairyman', Latin *daia*, either masculine or feminine; see RMLWL s.v. *daya*, the Latinized form of ME *deye*, OE *dæge*, 'a dairymaid' originally 'a baxter'.
IN PULL (COURT). There is an erasure in the MS from the *I* of *IN* to the *L* of *LAPULE*; the *N* of *IN* is very wide to cover the erasure; not shown by Farley. Pull Court is *La Pulle* (again with the French definite article) in Fees p. 139; see VCH (Worcs.) i p. 322 note 3 and EPNS (Worcs.) p. 105. The house that marks the site is now Bredon School. In Fees the place is likewise associated with Bushley to which Earl William had joined it. Bushley, as part

of the lands of Worcester Church, was in Oswaldslow Hundred, but Pull Court had been part of Longdon (DB Worcs. 8,9) a manor of Westminster Church. The 3 virgates of Pull Court probably represent the unnamed 3 virgates of the 5 hides 3 virgates held by Reinbald and Aelfric before 1066 in DB Worcs. 8,9c, the 5 hides being the land at Eldersfield (1,46 below). EARL ODA. Or Odda. He became Earl of Somerset, Devon and Dorset and 'the Wealas' in 1051 on the banishment of Earls Godwin and Harold, but lost the earldom on their return and was compensated with the earldom of the Hwiccas. He was a benefactor of Deerhurst and Pershore Churches; he became a monk at the latter and was buried there on his death in 1056. See VCH (Worcs.) i pp. 257–260 and Robertson pp. 456–458. For the name, see PNDB p. 333.

MONKS OF LYRE ... 1 VIRGATE. Recorded at Bushley in Fees p. 140; Mon. Ang. vi pp. 1092-3.

2 FORESTERS. In the MS *os* is interlined above and after *forestar.*, presumably a mistake for *ios* as *forestarius* is the correct (nominative) form. Farley prints *-ios*, either in correction or because the *-o* of *-os* is not joined at the top and, at a quick glance, could be mistaken for a badly written *io*.

OUTSIDE HIS MANORS. *extra suos* $\overline{M}$, *suos* being an error for *sua* as *manerium* is neuter. See third note under C 15.

TO GUARD THE WOODLANDS. See DB Glos. 37,3. In Fees p. 139 Pull Court is held by Hugh *de Colcumba* 'to look after the hedged enclosure at Bushley' (*per serianteriam custodiendi hayam de Bisseleg*)'. See also RBE p. 568 and 2,23 note.

1,45 QUEENHILL. DB *Chonhelme*; also *Cūhille* in DB Worcs. 2,36; see VCH (Worcs.) i p. 322 note 8 and EPNS (Worcs.) p. 155. The entry here is a duplicate, with different detail, of the Worcs. entry, said to be *in manu regis*. The two place-names are precisely different; *Chonhelme* (Herefords.) represents OE *cūna-helme* "at the cows' shelter or hill-top" (from *cū* and *helm*), and *Cu(n)hille* (Worcs.) represents OE *cuna-hylle* "at the cows' hill" (from *hyll*).

BISHOP BRICTRIC. *Brictrec* here, OE *Beorhtric*; also *Bricsteg* ('Brictheah') in DB Worcs. 2,24, a late 11th century form of OE *Beorhthēah*. He was Bishop of Worcester 1033–1038. See PNDB p. 194.

ST. MARY'S OF LYRE ... ½ VIRGATE. Held by the Prior of Lyre in Fees p. 140.

1,46 ELDERSFIELD. Formed part of the original grant by King Edgar to Pershore Church (BCS 1282 = ECWM no. 120 p. 116 = Sawyer (1) no. 786; see DB Worcs. Ch. 8 note). The land was alienated by Earl William. These 5 hides are probably part of the unnamed 5 hides 3 virgates of Longdon (DB Worcs. 8,9c), the other 3 virgates being at Pull Court, 1,44 above.

REINBALD THE CHANCELLOR. Also called Reinbald the Priest and Reinbald of Cirencester (DB Berks. Ch. 61) of which church he was dean or provost. He was the first chancellor of England and held land in Berks., Dorset, Somerset, Bucks., Worcs., and Glos., etc.; see Round in FE p. 421ff; *Regesta* i pp. xiii, xv; W. H. Stevenson in EHR vol. xi (1896) p. 731 note.

ST. MARY'S ... 1 VIRGATE OF LAND ... In the MS there is no full-stop after *tṝe* and probably an erasure; the scribe may have intended to add more details when available in the space at the end of the line.

ST. MARY'S. Of Lyre. The Prior held 1 virgate in Hardwick in Eldersfield (GR SO 8132) in Fees p. 140. See VCH (Worcs.) i p. 322 note 11; VCH (Worcs.) iv p. 79; Mon. Ang. vi p. 1092, and TE p. 217a.

1,47 SUCKLEY. See DB Worcs. 1,1b and X 3 (= E 4;8 below) for the diversion of its revenue to Hereford.

10 IMPOVERISHED SMALLHOLDERS. That is, without ploughs.

A KEEPER OF 12 BEEHIVES. Literally 'a keeper of the bees of 12 hives'.

ST. MARY'S. Of Cormeilles; VCH (Worcs.) i p. 323 note 1; Mon. Ang. vi pp. 1075-6.

EARL ROGER. Roger of Breteuil, Earl of Hereford from 1071 until his rebellion in 1075 (see Introductory Note 2). He was son of William son of Osbern, his predecessor as Earl of Hereford.

THESE SIX MANORS. That is 1,42–47, the four Worcs. manors of Bushley (with Pull Court), Queenhill, Eldersfield and Suckley together with Hanley Castle and Forthampton, both in Gloucestershire in 1086. This implies that the entry for Pull Court is part of that for Bushley.

1,48 [CASTLE]. The entry concerning Monmouth is not governed by the previous 'Hundred' head at 1,44, nor probably was it in any Hundred, like some other castles; see Introductory Note 3. In such cases [Castle] or [Castlery] is inserted in the translation.

MONMOUTH CASTLE. The castle no doubt played an important rôle in the consolidation of Anglo-Norman rule in Archenfield and in the conquest of Gwent (see Introductory Note 3). The Book of Llan Dâv (pp. 277-8) recalls how the castle was built during King William's reign and how Earl William gave half of it to three of his barons, Humphrey, Osbern and William the Scribe (*scriptor*). After the revolt in 1075 of Earl William's son, Earl Roger, the castle was given to Wihenoc (*gueithenauc*). During his tenancy Bishop Herwald (of Llandaff 1056-1104) consecrated the church of the castle in the presence of King Caradoc (son of Gruffydd ap Rhydderch, King of Gwynllwg and Upper Gwent). Wihenoc founded the priory there some time after 1075 (Mon. Ang. iv p. 596) as a dependency of St. Florent of Saumur (département of Maine-et-Loire, France) and became a monk in it. His tenancy of the Castle passed to Ranulf (*randulf*) of Colville, then to William son of Baderon (*batrun*). For the priory and its dependencies and the lands and tithes bestowed on it by Wihenoc, his brother Baderon and nephew William, see Round in VCH i p. 277 and in CDF p. 395ff. and Marchegay. 2 CARUCATES OF LAND. Here and elsewhere in Herefordshire, Gloucestershire and the south-western counties the *carucata* is not the carucate of former Danish areas (which is equivalent to the hide) but is the same as 'land for *n* ploughs' (see 1,3 note). On many occasions the Exon. Domesday uses the term *carucatae terrae* where Exchequer DB has *terra est ... car*, thus proving that the terms were synonymous. In Herefordshire DB carucates are especially associated with castles and newly occupied lands which had not yet been hidated.

1,49- ARCHENFIELD. The second major division of the *Terra Regis* (see Ch. 1 note above) deals
60 with the district of Archenfield, recently acquired from the Welsh. The introductory section 1,49 is similar to A 1-10 above; the lands listed in 1,50-1,60 are not measured in hides but in carucates (1,48 note), and generally pay 'Welsh' honey and sheep dues. Many lands are held by major landholders but are not listed in their own fiefs. Wormelow 'Hundred' (1,61-63) was a small inroad of English settlement in Archenfield in 1066 and the meetings of the Hundreds were held there (C 3 note). In LSR (1334) Wormelow Hundred is co-extensive with Archenfield and DBH p. 19 has a heading at the place corresponding to DB 1,49 *hic incipy[un]t consetudines de manerium de Wormelowe in Irchynffeld infra comytatum Harfordie* (sic). This is written in a late medieval hand and is not transcribed by the DBH editors.

1,49 20s IN PLACE OF THE SHEEP WHICH THEY USED TO GIVE. A clear example of a payment in kind being commuted to a money rent.
HEARTH TAX. *Fumagium* 'reek-silver' or 'hearth-money', see RMLWL s.v. *fumus*.
MARCH IN THE KING'S ARMY. Compare A 9 above.
IF THEY HAVE BEEN ORDERED. In the MS there is an erasure immediately after the *t* of *fuerit*; the scribe may have written *fuerint* first.
KING GRUFFYDD AND BLEDDYN. Gruffydd ap Llywelyn was ruler of Powys and Gwynedd from *c*.1039. He exerted pressure on Deheubarth and ruled it from 1055 on the death of Gruffydd ap Rhydderch. He conducted a number of raids into England, coming near to Leominster in 1052 (ASC p. 176). In 1055 in alliance with Algar, outlawed son of Earl Leofric, he routed a force under Earl Ralph of Hereford and sacked the town of Hereford, plundering the cathedral (ASC pp. 184,187). It is probably this raid to which DB refers. In 1063 after a further incursion, he was pursued by Harold and Tosti and killed by the Welsh after being driven beyond Gwynedd and Powys. His kingdom was broken up and in Gwynedd he was succeeded by Bleddyn ap Cyfyn (died 1075), probably the man mentioned here. Since *rex* is mentioned only once and refers to Gruffydd, the raid probably took place before 1063 when he succeeded Gruffydd. DB *Blein* corresponds to OW *Bledgint*, MW *Blethyn*, modern Welsh *Bleddyn*; PNDB p. 204.

1,50 GARWAY. DB *Lagademar*, but DBH p. 19 (see p. 87 note) has a marginal *Garwi*. Garway is a shortened *Llan*- name, *Langarewi* etc., "Guoruoe's church", see DEPN s.n. DB *Lagademar* probably represents *Lan-gademar*, that is a *Llan*- name with a different personal name. In this instance, the name of the estate may have changed with a change of church dedication.
BELONGED TO ARCHENFIELD. It lay on the southern edge, far from any other DB place so far identified, and may in 1086 have been regarded as part of Gwent which is surveyed in DB Glos. W 1-19 (cols. 162a,b).
3 OXEN. In 24,7, 3 oxen are also mentioned, apparently in place of a fraction of a plough. There were normally 8 oxen to a plough-team, but perhaps fewer in the south-west; see DB Wilts. 28,10 note and DB Somerset 25,56 where '½ plough' is '3 oxen' in the corresponding Exon. entry. See also DBH pp. xxxi-xxxii for evidence that at least on the King's lordship land in Herefordshire a plough-team of 6 oxen was the norm.

1,51 A MANOR. DBH p. 19 (and p. 87 note) has a marginal entry placing the land at *Baldinga'*, now Ballingham (GR SO 5731) on the west bank of the river Wye.

1,52 WAERSTAN. DB *Werestan*, from OE *Wǣrstān*.
ONE VILLAGE. Harewood, to the east of Llanwarne (GR SO 5226); *Harewuda* in DBH p. 19 (see p. 87 note).

1,53 CADIAND. An OW name, see PNDB p. 213. The man appears in the Book of Llan Dâv (p. 276) as *Catgendu*, holder of the parish.
EXCEPT IN THE ARMY. For this service, see A 8–9 and 1,49 above.

1,56 PONTRILAS. DB *Elwistone*, in Archenfield; identified by VCH as Helvistone Wood in Harewood. This spelling derives from Duncumb and is corrupt; the place is now Elvastone, Elverston on the OS first edition one-inch map (1831 sheet 43, reprint 1969 sheet 59). Earlier spellings cited in Bannister (PNHe p. 69) such as *Evaston* (1443), probably show confusion with Everstone in Peterstow (GR SO 5525), but *Elvareston'* from LSR (1334, p. 126) should certainly be added as a predecessor of the modern name. Such spellings make derivation from DB *Elwistone* improbable. On the other hand, early forms of Pontrilas are *Helyston, Heliston, Elston, Elstones* and the place occurs on early maps as *Elstones* or *Elstones Bridge* (Saxton's map of 1577, Speed's map of 1611, Blohme's of 1670); the earliest occurrence of the modern name Pontrilas cited in Bannister (PNHe) being *c.*1750 (pp. 154–155). *Heliston* or *Elistone* occurs in a number of deeds in the so-called 'Cartulary of Ewyas Harold' (see 19,1 note; Bannister HEH pp. 48–60 and p. 129 note y; Walker *Register* p. 43 nos. 114–116 and p. 50 nos. 147–148). This 'Cartulary' is extracted from Gloucester Cathedral Dean and Chapter MS 'Register A' folios 138r–176v (see Davis MCGB pp. 44,51 (no. 455) and Walker *Register* p. 6). *Elwistone* was held by Alfred of Marlborough and if it is Pontrilas, will have lain adjacent to his castle of Ewyas Harold (19,1), although on the southern bank of the river Dore. *Helistone* was part of Harold son of Earl Ralph's gift of lands to Ewyas Harold Priory (see Walker *Register* p. 8), and it was to this Harold that some of Alfred's lands passed (see Ch. 19 note). Pontrilas is in Kentchurch parish and both this parish and the adjacent Kenderchurch have churches dedicated to Welsh saints. They are the *Ecclesia de Sancta Keyne* (Saint Ceina) and the *Ecclesia Sancti Kenedri* (Saint Cynidr) in TE p. 160b, see IN p. 150b, and they lay in Archenfield both administratively and ecclesiastically, although they were later transferred to the enlarged Webtree Hundred (see Introductory Note 7). The priest at *Elwistone* may well have presided over the church at Kentchurch which was also part of the grant of Harold son of Earl Ralph to Ewyas Harold Priory. *Elstones Bridge* was earlier identified with *Elnodestune* (10,17 note), but that land lay in the Dore or Golden Valley in 1086.

1,57 ASHE (INGEN). Formerly part of the royal manor of Cleeve (1,8 note), where it is assessed at 2 hides less 1 virgate.

1,58 BIRCH. DB *Mainaure*, identified as Mainoaks in Goodrich by Bannister (PNHe p. 127). But DBH (p. 20; see p. 88 note) has a marginal note *Birches* referring to Much or Little Birch.
COSTELIN. A Continental German personal name derived from OG *Costila*, PNDB p. 219.
HE PAYS ... Or perhaps "it pays ...", referring to the manor, as in 1,59 'This land pays ...', although it is the Welshman in the next sentence who pays the money and sesters of honey.

1,59 *PENEBECDOC*. DBH in a marginal entry (p. 20) has *Penebedoc*. In minuscule script, *c* and *r* could be confused, and the DB form could represent *Peneberdoc*, due to metathesis of *r*. The place might be represented by Pendigot in St. Weonards, GR SO 4826.
NOVI. Probably OW *Novgui, Nogui*, PNDB p. 332.

1,60 GODRIC MAPSON ... HOWLE (HILL). For the byname see OEB p. 378. Godric named Goodrich Castle (GR SO 5719), on the western bank of the Wye, with which DBH (p. 20; see p. 88 note) identifies *Hulla* in a marginal annotation *Cast' Godr'*. 'Howle' which simply means 'hill' (see DEPN s.n. and PNE pt. i s.v. *hygel*) is a common word in the area. The most likely Howle is Howle Hill in Walford (GR SO 6020) which suggests that this land lay on both sides of the Wye.
TALDUS. A name of uncertain origin, see PNDB p. 382.

1,61– LAND OF THE KING in various Hundreds (see Ch. 1 note). This third group did not
75 contribute to the revenue of Hereford; 1,61–70 lay on the border of Wales and 1,72–75 close to the Gloucestershire border which had not been finally fixed in 1086 (see Introductory Note 4). Rowden (1,71) in Plegelgate Hundred is exceptional.

1,61 WORMELOW HUNDRED. The 'Hundred' is in fact a small composite manor consisting apparently of only 7 cultivated hides. Such manors, counted as Hundreds for administrative purposes, are found in other counties (see 1,6 note above). For Wormelow, see C 3 and 1,49–60 notes.
'WESTWOOD'. The Gloucester Abbey holding, originating as a grant of Earl William, is *Westwode in Jerchenfeld* in the *History of St. Peter's, Gloucester* i p. 118 and *Westwode in Jerchenffeld in Lawaran* ibidem i p. 123. There are four 'Westwoods' in DB Herefords., the

other three below identified more exactly by DBH: see the article by David Walker (WL). The DB spellings *Westuode* (1,61) and *Westeude* (1,62) could represent different names: 'west wood' (OE *west wudu*) and 'waste, useless wood' (OE *weste wudu*) respectively. Against this entry DBH (p. 20; see p. 88 note) has an unexplained *villa Asmacum*, probably a mistake for *Asmantun* which would represent OE *AEscmantūn* 'farmstead, village, estate called after one *AEscman*'; such a name might have yielded a modern 'Ashminton' or 'Ashenton'.

ONE OF THESE HAS WELSH CUSTOMS. See 2,15;56 for other occurrences of 'Welsh hides'. DURAND ... HIS BROTHER ROGER. Durand was Durand of Pîtres, Sheriff of Gloucester in 1086; Roger his brother was Roger of Pîtres, Constable of Gloucester Castle (*History of St. Peter's, Gloucester* i p. lxxvi) and Sheriff of Gloucester in Earl William's time, but dead by 1086 as this entry shows. See 1,72 and notes to Ch. 22 and 22,8. Pîtres is in the département of Eure, France; OEB p. 106.

ROGER OF LACY HOLDS PART. DBH (p. 20; see p. 88 note) identifies Roger's part as *Wrmenton* in a marginal note. The place occurs as *Wurmetun* as a Weobley Fee (see Ch. 10 note) in Fees (p. 811), and later as 'Wormeton' or 'Wormington' now lost. Like Wormelow, it will have been named from the Worm Brook, see DEPN s.n.

RALPH OF SACEY ALSO HOLDS PART. DBH (p. 21; see p. 88 note) similarly places the land at *Wrmetun* and in Fees (p. 811) Ralph *de Saucey* holds from Walter of Lacy (Weobley Honour) at *Wurmetun*. *Salceit* is either Sacey near Avranches in the département of Manche, France, or Sassy near Falaise in the département of Calvados; OEB p. 112.

1,62 DEWSALL. DB *Westeude* (see 1,61 note); for which DBH has a marginal entry *Dewiswell* (DBH p. 21 and p. 88 note). The prior of Lyre holds it in TE p. 158b.

1,63 9 WASTE MANORS. DBH (p. 21) has a marginal entry *nouem maneria uasta in forestis de xix hid' quas tenet Will' Normanni*. This alteration to the DB entry suggests that the manors were in the area of Archenfield overgrown by the Forest of Dean which then stretched north and east towards Hereford (see Introductory Note 8).

1,64– BURLINGJOBB ... (OLD) RADNOR. All other manors in this area of Hazeltree Hundred
65 which are waste are said in 9,13 and 24,3 to be 'In the Welsh March' (see Introductory Note 1).

1,64 IN HAZELTREE HUNDRED. DB *Hezetre* from OE **hæseltrēo* 'hazel tree'.
SOL. An obscure personal name. PNDB p. 368 offers no explanation, but refers to Redin p. 23f. who discusses and rejects Latin *sol* 'sun' and OE *sol* 'mud'. Bosworth and Toller *Supplement*, and Campbell's *Enlarged Addenda and Corrigenda* thereto, attest the OE adj. *sol* 'dirty' and this would form a good basis for a nickname and personal name *(se) sol*, which would be Latinized *Solus,-a* and which would be comparable with other OE personal names such as *Bigga, Blaca, Brun*, etc. There is a gap of about 2 letters' width in the MS after *Sol*, not shown by Farley.

1,65 HUGH DONKEY ... HIS PREDECESSOR THORKELL. That is, Thorkell White. Norman landholders were often granted all the lands of a particular English man. Thorkell preceded Hugh at 29,2;11;12;16;20 in his fief. Hugh's claim seems to have succeeded as (Old) Radnor is held by William *de Braose*, his successor in other lands in the later survey in DBH p. 78.
WHEN HE GAVE HIM. In the MS there is an erasure after *ded' ei*, extending to the end of the line and perhaps into the right margin. The scribe has drawn in a line to join up the *ded' ei* to the *t'ram* in the next line, in case it was thought he had left a space for other details to be added later. Farley does not print this line nor a similar one in 21,7, though he does in 29,16.

1,66 IN ELSDON HUNDRED. The Hundred-name is represented by a hamlet Elsdon in Lyonshall parish (GR SO 3254).

1,67 *MATEURDIN* ... PART OF THIS LAND. The rest is held by Gruffydd in 31,1 (see note).

1,69 WELSON. *Ulfelmestone* DB, *-tone* DBH p. 22, *Ulfhemeston* DBH (later Survey p. 79). J.F. observes: 'VCH suggests that identification of DB *Ulfelmestone* in Elsdon Hundred with Welson near Eardisley, an identification which is accepted by DG but apparently not by the editors of DBH (*v.* DBH index, p. 145). The DB form represents the OE pers.n. *Wulfhelm* in gen. sg. and OE *tūn* ... Unfortunately, the early forms of the name Welson, which might shed light on the rather drastic reduction of *Wulfhelmes-* to *Wels-*, are lacking. One might, however, have expected a modern form *Wo(o)ls(t)on*, *Wolves(t)on* rather than Welson, since the vowel of the strongly stressed first syllable normally prevails over that of the weakly stressed medial syllable in place-names'.
IN CHICKWARD 1 HIDE. DB *Stiuingeurdin*; DBH (p. 22) has *Stiuichewordin* in the text with *Chicwurdine* interlined and *Chicwordin i hid'* as a marginal entry. The final el. of the place-name is OE *worthign* 'a private curtilage' (probably for a consolidated estate, see PNE

pt. ii s.v.). The first el. of the DB form would represent an OE place-name *Stifinge* (OE *stif* 'stiff, unyielding', perhaps for a heavy soil, see EPNS vol. liv (Cheshire pt. v (i; ii)) p. 353, s.v.); hence 'the manor or estate at *Stifing*'. This name gives way to *Chicwurdine* in which the first el. is probably an OE pers.n. *Cic* ('Chick'?) observed in other place-names (DEPN s.n. Chickney, Essex). Yet another instance of name-change in Herefordshire. Perhaps the *worthign* at *Stifing* belonged to one *Cic*.

IN BOLLINGHAM 1 HIDE. DB *Burardestune*; DBH (p. 22) has *Buracdestone* in the text with *Bollingeshulle* interlined and *Bolingeshulla i hid'* in the margin. J.McN.D. with acknowledgement to J.F. adds that *Buracdestone* is a scribe's error for *Burardestone* through similarity of *c* and short *r* in his script (cf. 1,59 *Penebecdoc*). The first el. is probably the OE personal name *Burgheard*. The new name is based on an OE place-name *Bol(l)ing* to which *hyll* 'a hill', and later *hamm* 'enclosure, hemmed-in place', have been suffixed.

IN RUSHOCK 4 HIDES. The scribe first wrote *.iii.* and then corrected it to *jiii.*, the dot originally written before the *iii* being still visible under the lengthened added minim stroke. The *-or* of *quattuor* was interlined to clarify the correction.

BARTON. DB *Beuretune*, DBH (p. 22) *Beuertona* in the text. VCH i p. 319 note 43 suggests Burton (Burton Court SO 4257), citing FA ii p. 377 *Bourton cum membris in valle de Radenore*; the indexer of FA places *Bourton* in Eardisland, the wrong Hundred for this DB place. Barton near Kington is in the right area, but in view of the DB form the identification is tentative. J.F. notes that the first el. of the DB place-name *Beuretone* appears to be OE *beofor, befer* 'a beaver', and that the development from OE *Befer-tūn* to ModE *Barton* would be regular enough; but Barton near Kington is not sited aptly for the beaver — not on a stream, but on a fairly steep hillside ¼ mile away from, and 100 ft. above, the river Arrow. He suggests an etymology for the DB name, less obvious in form but more fitting the site of Barton, which would see the first el. as a place-name OE *Beofre* (*bē ofre*) '(place) on a hill-slope' (OE *bē* preposition, 'by, near', *ofer* 'a slope, a hill, a ridge', cf. Bure, Hants. (DEPN)) to which the el. OE *tūn* had been suffixed.

1,70 WOONTON. DB The Elsdon Hundred head identifies this place as Woonton in Almeley; see Lord Rennell DM p. 155 and 2,52 and 10,12 notes.
RALPH OF BERNAY. See 1,2 note.
THE REVENUE OF LEOMINSTER. That is, of the great manor with its many members 1,10–38 above.

1,72 'NEWARNE'. In East Dean, EPNS (Glos.) iii pp. 218–219 (which does not cite the DB form); possibly the site of the later Speech House, the judicial centre of the Forest of Dean. The derivation is OE *niwe aern* 'new house'.
CAME TO (HUNDRED) MEETINGS. *Convenire* 'to gather, meet', is correctly used of people, not land (see DB Worcs. 8,25 note). The meaning is explained by the final phrase. In terms of justice and service the land lay in Herefordshire but its payments had been 'diverted' to Gloucestershire. A similar arrangement applied to Kingstone (3,1); both manors lay in an area where the Gloucestershire-Herefordshire boundary had not been finalised, see Introductory Note 4.
ROGER OF PÎTRES. See 1,61 note.

1,73– REDBROOK. DB *Brocote*, see EPNS (Glos.) iii p. 237, which does not cite the DB form,
74 which represents 'cottage(s) at the brook or water-meadows' from OE *brōc* and *cot* (dative singular *cote*, nominative plural *cotu*).
THE KING'S WOOD. The Forest of Dean, see Introductory Note 8 above.

1,74 EARL GODWIN. Earl of the West Saxons, father of Earl (King) Harold and Edith (wife of King Edward the Confessor). He died in 1053; see 19,3 note below.

1,75 AT A REVENUE FROM. In the MS *ad firmā de*; Farley misprints *ad firmā de de*.
HUMPHREY THE CHAMBERLAIN. Brother of Aiulf the Sheriff of Dorset. He was probably of the household of Queen Matilda: he held land in Surrey from her holding (DB Surrey Ch. 31) and she gave him two manors in Glos. (DB Glos. 69,6–7). He was a major landholder in a number of DB counties.
THANELAND. Generally thaneland was part of the lordship land (see DB Somerset 8,16) of either a lay or an ecclesiastical landholder, set aside to maintain a thane, armed and mounted. In return for the land the thane would provide certain services, often military. This land, especially if it was part of the church's land, was usually inalienable: the holder was not free to transfer his allegiance to another lord nor to sell the land (see DB Somerset 8,20). Thaneland was not automatically hereditable, though it could sometimes be granted for a period of 'three lives'. The holder of thaneland was not necessarily a thane, however; see DB Dorset 1,31 where he is a priest. From several entries in DB (e.g., Dorset 1,13) it would seem that thaneland was often simply land once held by a thane. The protest here

seems to mean that the change in the status of the hide in Yatton has deprived the King of revenue.

REEVELAND. See 1,2 note.

COMMISSIONERS. *Legati*; that is, the Commissioners charged with carrying out the DB Survey. Their names are known only in the case of Worcestershire: see DB Worcs. Appendix V (Worcs. H).

Ch. 2   THE CHURCH OF HEREFORD. Like the Church of Shrewsbury (DB Shrops. Ch. 3) this Church comprised several Churches of which St. Aethelbert's (2,13) and St. Peter's (2,58) are separately mentioned. The core of the chapter is 2,4–56, but it opens with a survey of the Bishop's portion of Hereford and a note of alienated lands (2,2–3) and ends with 2,57–58 which are supplementary notes. Cartularies of the Cathedral Church survive in Oxford Bodleian MS Jones 23 (see Rawlinson App. pp. 32–85) and in Bodleian MS Rawlinson B 329 (calendared by A. T. Bannister in TWNFC for 1914–17; see Davis MCGB pp. 54–55 Nos. 480–482). See also notes to Ch. 6 and 10,5.

2,1   THE TOWN OF HEREFORD. OE *port*, 'town' or 'market-town', see DEPN s.n. and notes to C 1 and 2,57.

BISHOP WALTER. Walter of Lorraine, chaplain to Queen Edith and Bishop of Hereford 1061–1079.

THE BISHOP ALSO HAD. *Habebat q; isd' ẽps*; the *q;* (= *que* 'and') is unusually placed: it is normally an enclitic, joining two words or phrases within a sentence. It is possible that the scribe meant to write *qq;* (= *quoque* 'also'); the rest of the entry is neat and with no erasures. Farley misprints ꝙ as occasionally elsewhere with *q;*.

ONE MONEYER. See C 9 above.

BISHOP ROBERT. Robert Losinga, Bishop of Hereford 1079–1095.

40 HIDES. Probably an error for *mansuras*: the 40 dwellings destroyed with the 60 dwellings intact make approximately the 98 that Bishop Walter had before 1066. The city had been devastated by the Welsh in 1055 (see Introductory Note 2).

2,2   DIDLEY ... *STANE*. Didley has been mapped in this edition in the southern part of Stretford Hundred, probably its original Hundred. Having been alienated from the Church, the lands now lay partly in Cutsthorn Hundred (in the castlery of Ewyas Harold, see 10,1. 13,2 and Introductory Note 3), partly in the royal Forest, probably an extension of Treville Wood (1,3 note above). For Enclosure see 1,43 note.

2,3   THESE HIDES PAID TAX. A brief hidage schedule bound up with DBH (p. 77) and based on DB but slightly updated is relevant to this entry. It records Roger of Lacy holding 3 virgates in *Erdeshop'* (Yarsop) *de quibus geldabat cum episcopo* ('on which he paid tax with the Bishop'). Similarly Gilbert son of Thorold pays with the Bishop for 2½ hides in *Salberga* (Sawbury Hill), Charbonnel for 1½ hides and Bernard of Neufmarché (*de Novo Mercato*) on ½ hide. In DB Roger of Lacy holds 1½ hides at Yarsop (10,59); he also holds 2½ virgates in Sawbury Hill (10,65) and 1 hide in Tedstone (10,68). All these amounts are difficult to relate to the DBH list. Charbonnel's land is undoubtedly *Ach* (Noakes 33,1 see below). If DBH is in error in naming Gilbert son of Thorold's estate as Sawbury, it is perhaps the 2 hides of *Chetestor* (probably Tedstone 25,8 note). The 3 virgates of Yarsop could be those of the wife of Ralph the Chaplain (34,1), the implication of the DBH entry being that Roger of Lacy acquired them after 1086. Her other manor Rowden (34,2) adjacent to Sawbury could be the Sawbury of the present DB entry and the ½ hide held by Bernard in DBH. But DBH records her total holding of 1 hide 1 virgate as paying tax directly, not via the Bishop.

TEDSTONE. *Tedesthorne*, DB; on the form see 10,68 note.

NOAKES. *Ach* DB; appears to be the same estate as *Lacre* (33,1), corrected by DBH in the margin to *Lac* (p. 73; see pp. 123–124 note), 1 hide held by Charbonnel. The place appears later as *Hakes*, 1 hide in Broxash Hundred held in 1243 by Thomas *de Lake* (Fees p. 806). The identity of *Ach* and *Lacre* is further suggested by the later survey in DBH (p. 77) where *Carbonellus* 'paid tax with the Bishop for 1½ hides' (see DBH p. 89 note). The two names may be the same: *Ach* represents OE *āc* 'oak' (Noke in Oxfordshire, DB *Ac(h)am*, is similarly derived from *āc*), and *Lac* represents a combination of that name with the French definite article (see DBH p. 124). But they could be different names, perhaps for two manors very closely involved territorially; J.F. observes that *Lac* might represent OE *lacu* 'a stream, a water-course', taken by DEPN as the origin of the place-names Lake, Wilts., Lacon near Wem, Shrops.; the *-re* in *Lacre* is an Anglo-Norman feature, either an excrescent or a representation of a late OE dative plural locative inflexion.

2,4   THESE LANDS ... BELONG TO THE CANONS. The schedule of the lands held by the Church in 1086 now begins. The various holders of the lands — the Bishop, the canons, nuns, some churches — are not always stated. DBH supplies some of the missing information in marginal notes.

POSSIBLE IN LORDSHIP ... The rest of the line after this is blank in the MS; as there is no dot after *dñio*, the scribe may have intended to add something later.

2 CLERKS. Latin *clericus* can refer to a lay job or to an ecclesiastical office, and DB rarely indicates which is intended. The English 'clerk' preserves the ambiguity of the Latin.

VALUE NOW £10. There is no dot after *lib'*, so the scribe may have intended to add to the amount, though there are occasions in DB when the full stop has obviously been omitted in error.

2,5 THEY HAVE 7 VILLAGES WITH 3 PLOUGHS. Following a mistake at the beginning of the line, and the consequent erasure, the scribe wrote *vii uill cu iii car* slightly indented, then added the *Hi hñt* in the left margin and squeezed in *os* after *uill*; this compression is not apparent in Farley.

[VALUE]. *Valet* omitted in error in the MS.

2,6 TYBERTON. The Bishop of Hereford also holds *Childeston* and *Bellimare* (FA ii p. 388) now Chilstone (GR SO 3939) and Bellamore (SO 3940), possibly part of the 6 hides of Tyberton.

2,7 THE CANONS' BARTON. *Bertune* from OE *beretūn*, Latinized as *bertona*, *bartona*, from OE *bere* 'barley, corn' and *tūn* 'farm'. The word refers to a 'corn-farm' and in later times to a 'lordship farm' or 'outlying grange'. See PNE pt. i s.v. It is frequently associated with church or monastic lands and is a common place-name, see 2,11 below.

2,8 5 HIDES ... See 1,9 note.

2 FURLONGS. See 1,10a note on woodland.

MARKET. Presumably in Hereford; see DGM pp. 104,107; VCH i p. 272.

LYDNEY. In Gloucestershire (GR SO 6302). DB Glos. 1,55 records 'In Lydney Earl William made a manor from 4 lands which he received from their lords. From the Bishop of Hereford's lordship 3 hides ...'.

2,9 3 HIDES ... See 1,9 note.

2,10 VALUE OF THE WHOLE MANOR. The two parts of the Bishop's barton (2,9-10) seem to be treated as a single manor, the value clause referring to both.

2,11 'BARTON'. DB *Bertune*, on which see 2,7 note above. The land was in Dinedor Hundred, and VCH and Bannister PNHe identify a 'Burton' in Holme Lacy which has not been traced. Outside the medieval city of Hereford lay both a Canons' Barton and a Barton Episcopi. John Taylor's map of 1757 records a Barton Field, Orchard and Farm west of the city at GR SO 4939 in the area to which Barton Road now leads; Barton is likewise marked there on Bryant's map of 1835. To the east of the city still lies a Bartonsham (GR SO 5139). If DB's *Bertune* was one of these, a part of Dinedor Hundred will in 1086 have lain north of the river Wye (see Baddeley HePN p. 108). The 10 hides will have covered a large area, perhaps north and south of the river.

2,12 HOLME (LACY). Held by Roger of Lacy under the Bishop; see FA ii p. 387, Fees p. 812, Wightman LF pp. 128-129 and the article by Colvin, also V. H. Galbraith *An Episcopal Land Grant* in EHR xliv (1929).

4 BOORS. Latin *buri* from OE *(ge)bur*; the plural is also found as *burs* in DB (e.g., Berks. 1,31. Hants. 1,10). *Buri* are found in several counties in DB, including Worcs., Oxfords., Devon, Bucks. and Berks., though not in any great number except on individual estates (e.g., 17 *buri* in Bampton, Oxfords. 1,6). In Herefordshire they occur only on land of the Church of Hereford (here, and at 2,25-26;29-30;57), on each occasion having a share in some ploughs. They were not exactly the same as the *geburs* of pre-Conquest documents who were of higher standing, but are equated on three occasions in DB with *coliberti*; see 1,4 note above. For the rights and dues of the Anglo-Saxon *(ge)bur*, see *Rectitudines* p. 446. See also DB Oxon. 1,6 note and Maitland DBB pp. 36-7;328-30.

LLANWARNE. DB *Ladguern*, an outlying dependency lying within the bounds of Archenfield.

EARL HAROLD ... WRONGFULLY. He had appropriated land in some 8 manors from the Church of Hereford (see also 2,26;31-33;37;50); King William had restored them. In DB Worcs. 3,3 he had also taken Inkberrow from this church and it had been restored. See also Pembridge, 19,8 below, which was still lost to St. Guthlac's.

FOR THE CANONS' SUPPLIES. Its revenues were devoted to supplying the needs of the canons. Cf. 1,10b.

2,13 IN GREYTREE HUNDRED. DB *Tragetreu*. This form of the heading only appears here in DB. All three places lie at the southern end of Greytree Hundred and it is probable that the Hundred head is a mistake for *tra gretreu* 'the land (of, called) *Gretreu*' i.e., the Hundred name in singular inflexion. The places have been mapped in Greytree Hundred in this edition; see Anderson pp. 167-8.

WOOLHOPE. DB *Hope*. Fees (p. 801) records 15 hides held at *Wulveve Hope* by the Canons of St. Ethelbert's (Albert's), by gift of Wulfeva (*Wulveve*, OE *Wulfgifu*, fem.) and Godiva (*Godheva*, OE *Godgifu*, fem.); see FA ii p. 383.

THE CANONS OF ST. ALBERT'S. The Church of St. Ethelbert, the predecessor of the modern Cathedral of St. Mary and St. Ethelbert. It was dedicated to King Ethelbert of East Anglia, murdered in 794 by Offa of Mercia and said to have been buried at Hereford. This church was begun by Bishop Aethelstan II (1012–1056) and was the one seriously damaged by the Welsh raid of 1055 (ASC p. 187) although Florence of Worcester (i pp. 212-3) in describing the 1055 raid refers to the sack of a monastery established by Aethelstan and containing the relics of Ethelbert. The existing cathedral was begun by Bishop Reinhelm (1107–1115); see RCHM (*Herefords.*) i (1931) p. 90. The Dean and Chapter of St. Ethelbert's later held Canon Pyon (2,39; see FA ii p. 385).

2,15 BROCKHAMPTON. DB *Caplefore* probably for *Capleford*; DBH (p. 26) has a marginal entry *Brochamtona*. Bannister PNHe p. 40 note 1 thinks this adjacent to How Caple (2,14 above) and cites a spelling *Capulfford* 1420 in an Inquisition Post Mortem relating to Foy; on this construction we have a place or two places *Capele* ('chapel', either OFr or Welsh) whose manorial parts or separate identities are distinguished by the affixed personal name *Hugh* and the place-name element *ford*. The Greytree Hundred head at 2,15 leaves little doubt that the place is Brockhampton parish rather than Brockington in Norton near Bromyard (Bannister PNHe p. 30); the three Welsh hides point to the same conclusion. If the 'ford' was in the river Wye then the land may have been a Welsh intrusion onto the English bank or an English extension into Archenfield.

2,16 IN THORNLAW HUNDRED. The name is lost, the Hundred having contributed at an early date to the formation of Broxash Hundred, see Introductory Note 7. It is derived from OE *thorn* and *hlāw* 'thorn hill'.

PRESTON (WYNNE). Preston *Inferior* and *Superior* in FA ii p. 390; see LSR p. 124.

2,17 WITHINGTON. DBH p. 26 in a marginal note *Canonicorum* attributes the 8 hides to the Canons.

1 MALE AND 2 FEMALE SLAVES. In the accusative case following *habent*, like the villagers, smallholders and meadow; likewise the villagers and meadow in the following subtenancy of Withington.

NUNS. Mr. Coplestone-Crow points out that their land was probably at Nunnington (GR SO 5543).

2,18 ULLINGSWICK. The Bishop of Hereford holds *Brige* ('Bridge') and *Ulingwike* in RBE p. 496.

2,20 IN RADLOW HUNDRED. DB *Radenelau, Radelau*, from OE *rēad* 'red' and *hlāw* 'hill'. The name survived to be marked on early 6-in. OS maps as Radlow Wood just north of the former Stoke Edith railway station (GR SO 611416). Bryant's map of 1835 marks a Radlow field to the south at approximately SO 611410; see Duncumb iv p. 5 and Anderson p. 167.

2,21 (BISHOPS) FROME. Its position athwart the border between Plegelgate and Radlow Hundreds identifies this *Frome* as Bishops Frome. A further hide lies in Plegelgate Hundred 10,67.

6 PLOUGHS. In the MS *vi* has been corrected from *iii*.

2,22 'WHIPPINGTON'. A lost place, the name surviving in the Whippington Brook which separates the parishes of Staunton and English Bicknor; see EPNS (Glos.) iii p. 213, although the earliest form there cited is *Wybaltunesbroke* 1282.

2,23 3 HEDGED ENCLOSURES. Frequent in the west midland shires. From OE *(ge)haeg* Latinized as *haia* 'hedge' (cf. Mod.Fr *haie*); a 'hay' or hedged enclosure into which game were driven for capture; see DB Worcs. 18,4 *i haia in qua capiebantur ferae*. In Shropshire (4,8,10 and 6,15) 'hays' are 'for capturing roe-deer' *capreolis capiendis*. See Ellis i p. 114; Ducange s.v. *haga*; PNE pt. i s.vv. *(ge)haeg, haga*. In Herefordshire, as well as in this example and in Upton Bishop in Bromsash Hundred (2,25) 'hays' are also found on the borders of Malvern Chase at Eastnor (2,27), Cradley (2,30) and Colwall (2,31). There is also a group in Elsdon and Hazeltree Hundreds at Downton on the Rock (9,2), Rushock (14,7), Titley (24,6), 'Bernaldeston' (29,16) and *Mateurdin* (31,1).

2,26 1 BOOR. In the MS *uñ burũ*; Farley misprints *unũ burũ*. *Uñ* is a regular abbreviation in DB for the accusative *unum* (see 1,2 note under '1 smallholder'), but it is not clear why the accusative should be used here, as there is no verb (such as *habet*) requiring it. The accusative also occurs without reason at 2,29.

2,28 'BAGBURROW'. DB *Bageberge*. It is unlikely to be Backbury identified by VCH and DG, since the latter is in Greytree Hundred, whereas *Bageberge* is listed in DB in a group of Winstree Hundred places. Just south-east of Mathon Court, Bagburrow Wood (*grava de Baggebarwe* 1275, EPNS (Worcs.) p. 66, ex inf. J.F.) is found on modern 6-in. maps and on the 1st edition OS map (sheet 55 of 1832, 1970 reprint sheet 50). This is likely to be the modern representative of *Bageberge* ('Bacga's barrow' or 'badger's hill or barrow' from the OE personal name *Bacga* or from OE *bagga* 'a badger', and *beorg*, J.F.). For the implications for the boundary of Mathon, see 10,39 note below.

2,29 A PRIEST ... HAS 1 PLOUGH. There is an erasure of about 9 letters' width after *car'*. The resulting space was probably not intended to be filled later, but is the space very commonly left before the value of a manor is given.

2,30 6 BOORS. In the MS *vi* corrected from *v*.
28 PLOUGHS. In the MS *xxviii:*; Farley does not print the larger dot above the usual dot after a number.

2,31 THORMOD. ON *thormōthr*, ODan *Thormoth*, ME *Thormod*. See PNDB p. 395; Fellows-Jensen s.n. *thormōthr* and Reaney p. 348 s.n. *Thurman*.

2,33 6 VILLAGERS AND 5 SMALLHOLDERS. In the MS *vi uilli* has been corrected either from *iv* or *v;v bord'* has also been corrected, perhaps from *ii*.

2,34– TUPSLEY ... WARHAM. DBH (p. 27) after the marginal place-name and hides adds *Epc'*,
38 '(belonging to) the Bishop', in each case.

2,37 SUGWAS. Now combined with the Domesday village of Stretton (10,24. 29,13) into the parish of Stretton Sugwas. The 1 hide was perhaps at Breinton, FA ii p. 386.

2,39 (CANON) PYON. DBH (p. 27) has a marginal note *In Piona xii hid' Cañ*, identifying Canon Pyon. See 2,13 third note.

2,42 FROM THE BISHOP. In the MS and Farley *de epo*; the facsimile does not reproduce the line over *epo*.

2,43 PIPE. Now combined with Lyde (next entry and 10,25–26. 24,11) into the parish of Pipe and Lyde.
1 PLOUGH THERE. The 'villagers' to work the plough appear to have been omitted (as also in 10,12), unless members of another village worked it (see 6,8).

2,44 LYDE. A number of holdings in the village have distinctive epithets in the Feodaries; see 10,25–26 note.

2,45 NORTON (CANON). DBH (p. 28) has a marginal entry *In Nortona vi hid' Can' H'*, that is, belonging to the Canons of Hereford.

2,46 BISHOPSTONE. DB *Malveshille* from OE **malu*, genitive *malwes*, related to ON *mǫl* 'gravelly soil', giving *Malwes-hyll* 'gravel or sand hill', see DEPN s.n. It is an area name covering three holdings in DB, a total of 18 hides: Mansell (Gamage) 10,56; Mansell (Lacy) 31,4–5 and the Bishop of Hereford's 'Mansell' said by a marginal entry in DBH (p. 28; see p. 90 note) to be *Bissopestona*, modern Bishopstone lying between and slightly to the south of Mansell Lacy and Mansell Gamage. In FA ii p. 376 (1303) *Bysshoppeston* is held by the Bishop of Hereford in Grimsworth Hundred into which DB Staple Hundred was incorporated.
1 PLOUGH; ANOTHER IDLE. Compare 2,5 'the villagers have more ploughs than ploughable land'. For other examples of actual ploughs on the land exceeding the estimate, see DB Cambridgeshire 26,18 and note, and Dorset 56,20.

2,47 ½ HIDE WHICH PAYS TAX. *est geldans*, see 1,7 note.
VALUE ... 4s. In the MS the *sol'* is written badly, over an erasure, and there is no dot after it, as though the scribe intended to add something later.

2,48 BRIDGE (SOLLERS). DBH (p. 29; see p. 91 note) has a marginal entry *In Bruge v. hid' H. de Solers*; see FA ii p. 376.

2,49 BROMYARD. DBH p. 29 has a marginal entry *In Bromiarde xxx hid' Epc*, denoting a holding of the Bishop. The 30 hides probably contained Upper Sapey (FA ii p. 378) GR SO 6863, and Whitbourne (FA ii p. 384) GR SO 7256, as well as Stanford Bishop (FA ii. p. 384, see 1,9 note above) and possibly Grendon Bishop (FA ii p. 384, see 10,72 note below).

2,50 THAT MENTIONED ABOVE. Bridge Sollers was noted at 2,48.

2,51 IN WOLPHY HUNDRED. DB *Wlfagie* also *Vlfei*; *Wolfeye* in FA ii p. 377 (1303) and *Wolfheye* in FA ii p. 413 (1428). It is probably from OE **wulf-(ge)haeg* 'hay in which wolves are caught'. The Hundred name survived until recent times, see Introductory Note 7; the meeting-place may have been at 'The Hundred' (GR SO 5263) where the parishes of Kimbolton and Middleton meet that of Eye, Moreton and Ashton. Farley omits the abbreviation line over the *D* of *HD* (= *Hundredum*) in error; it is in the MS.
LITTLE HEREFORD. A rare example of a distinguishing adjective with a DB place-name. The Bishop of Hereford holds *parva Herefordia* in RBE p. 496.

2,52 *WINETUNE*. The form given by DBH (p. 30) is *Winestone*. This place is identified by VCH and by Bannister (PNHe p. 208) as Winnington, a place not included on the VCH map and not so far found in the County by the present editors; this identification, although accepted without comment by DBH, may well be an extrapolation by Duncumb (vol. i p. 64) of the

DB form. DG leaves the place unidentified. It appears to be in Wolphy Hundred (heading at 2,51) and should be derived from the OE personal name *Wine* (gen. sing *Wines*), which is a different name from OE *Wynna* (gen. sing *Wynnan*), the first element of Woonton in Almeley (DB *Wennetune* 1,70 and 10,45 in Elsdon Hundred) and of Woonton in Laysters in Wolphy Hundred (DB *Wenetune* 10,12; *Woneton* FA ii p. 385 (1316); *Wynetun'* LSR p. 130 (1334)); see DEPN s.n. Despite this formal difference, it is tempting to take *Winetune*, an otherwise unidentified place in Wolphy Hundred, as standing for Woonton in the same Hundred. PNDB p. 428 s.n. *Wyn(n)-* alleges DB spellings *Win-*, *Wine-*, *Wen-*, *Wene-*; moreover, in the charter of Richard, Bishop of Hereford, enumerating the lands of Leominster Church possessed by Reading Abbey (Mon. Ang. iv p. 56; see 1,10a first note) are *Lunthelega*, *Chinardeslega*, *Winnetone*, two places called *Sernesfelda* and one called *Titellega*. These places are Luntley, Kinnersley, Sarnesfield and Titley lying in a geographically compact group west of Leominster, and it is difficult to avoid concluding that *Winnetone* represents Woonton in Almeley. It is possible that the same spelling was sometimes applied to Woonton in Laysters. The problem requires further investigation.
½ HIDE ... See 1,9 note.

2,54 IN STRADDLE HUNDRED. DB *Stradel*. The land is only described here as a 'Hundred'. Elsewhere DB uses 'in the Straddle Valley', that is in the Dore (or Golden) Valley. The name is OE *Straddael*, a conflation of Welsh *Stratdour* 'valley of the Dore', the first element being Welsh *ystrad* 'valley', with OE *dael* 'valley'. It survives in Stradel Bridge and Monnington Stradel in the Valley; see DEPN s.n. Straddle, and Anderson p. 167. Dore is from OW *Dovr*, derived from a British *dubra* (whence also Dover, Kent). 'Golden' is the result of false etymology as if Dore were from French *d'or* or *doré* 'of gold, golden, gilded', or from OW *our*, Mod.W *aur* 'gold'; both the Welsh and the French words are ultimately from Latin *aurum* 'gold'.
    The term 'Hundred' is not strictly appropriate as the valley contained only 56 hides (25,7 note) many of them waste. The scribe seems to have been uncertain of the correct designation of the area; at 10,16 and 14,6 (see notes) the heading 'In the Straddle Valley' is incorporated in the text.

2,57 AROUND THE TOWN OF HEREFORD. *portam* is more likely a Latinization of OE *port* (see C 1 and 2,1 notes) than from Latin *porta* 'a gate'.
A MAN-AT-ARMS (HOLDS) 1 HIDE. This is written over an erasure, perhaps later, hence the cramped style, which is not visible from Farley.
300 HIDES. The hides accounted for in the Chapter amount to 297½. Allowing for the fact that a few entries may need correction, this is close to the total of 300 hides. The 33 hides for which no account has been given are therefore additional. The lands mentioned in 2,57 must have been of some considerable extent in view of the other details. Worcester Church holds a round 300 hides in its Hundred of Oswaldslow in DB Worcs. Ch. 2. The original grant to Pershore Church was of the same extent.

2,58 ST. PETER'S OF HEREFORD. A pre-conquest college of prebendaries in Hereford (see Ch. 6 note). Walter of Lacy (1,5 note above) was its great benefactor. Other of his gifts to St. Peter's are in 10,5;37;48;75.
(PRIORS) FROME. In Fees p. 801 1 hide is held by the Prior of Hereford in Greytree Hundred, though it is said to have been given to the church by *Wige*.
EDWY YOUNG. The man also occurs as plain Edwy in Herefords. DB: Alwin is said to be son of Edwy at 10,15 and of Edwy Young in 10,70. *Cilt* is from OE *cild*, 'childe', 'born to an inheritance', 'well-born', 'a young nobleman'; see OEB p. 244.
In the MS *Eduuj* is cramped and runs into *cilt*, as it is written over an erasure of a smaller word(s).

Chs. THESE CHAPTERS are compressed and were no doubt added later, the space initially left
3-4 for them proving insufficient.

Ch. 3 THE CHURCH OF CORMEILLES. This Benedictine Abbey, near Pont L'Evêque in the département of Eure, France, was founded *c*.1060 by Earl William (1,3 note) who was buried there in 1071. He is stated in 1,39-40 to have granted land, churches and tithes to Cormeilles from the royal land over which he had presided as palatine earl; he was probably also responsible for similar holdings of the Abbey mentioned in 1,1-3;6-9;47 and 10,50. See Mon. Ang. vi pp. 1075-6.

3,1 KINGSTONE. See 1,1 note. DB Glos. 1,11 (= E 1 below) records that this land was withdrawn from the manor of Westbury (on Severn) in Gloucestershire. For the Church's holding, see Mon. Ang. vi pp. 1075-6.
WHO LIVE THERE. The phrase *q̊ ibi manent* was squeezed in as an afterthought, to give a human subject to *conueniunt*, the subject having previously been the 2 hides in the line above; see 1,72 note.

COME TO PLEAS. That is, attend the Hundred court, see 1,72 note.

Ch. 4 [LAND]OF THE CHURCH OF LYRE. *Terra* is omitted from the heading through lack of space (see Chs. 3-4 note above). The Abbey at La Vieille-Lyre in the département of Eure, France, was founded in 1046 by Earl William (see 1,3 note). The Church also held the tithe, a villager and ½ virgate of land in Queenhill (1,45) and the church and priest as well as land for 1 plough in 'Westwood' (1,62), both probably grants of Earl William.

4,1 (MUCH) MARCLE. Much Marcle and Little Marcle are in different DB Hundreds, so the Hundred head can only be supplied when the place is identified. The Priory of Lyre holds the church of *Magna Marcle* in TE p. 161a.
[VALUE ...] Details of the manor and its value are omitted. The entry should perhaps have been included in 1,7 in the same way that grants of land to the Church of Cormeilles from royal manors are included under these manors (see Ch. 3 note).

Ch. 5 ST. PETER'S OF GLOUCESTER. Gloucester Abbey.

5,1 BRAMPTON (ABBOTS). In Fees (p. 801) 1 hide is held by Gloucester Abbey at *Bromtun'* in the later Greytree Hundred that absorbed Bromsash; see also FA ii p. 383.

5,2 THIS ENTRY has been added later by the scribe and is compressed.
LEA BY GIFT OF WALTER OF LACY. Walter of Lacy was buried at St. Peter's, Gloucester, of which his son Walter was to become Abbot in 1130.

Ch. 6 ST. GUTHLAC'S. A pre-Conquest foundation lying at first in the Castle at Hereford. Some time in the 12th century, certainly by 1139-1148, but possibly earlier, it was united with the Church of St. Peter (founded under William I by Walter of Lacy, see 1,5 note) which lay in the market-place at Hereford, and a new joint church called after SS. Peter, Paul and Guthlac was built outside the City. St. Peter's had become a dependency of Gloucester Abbey in *c*.1100 (see 10,5 note) and St. Guthlac's had the same status after the merger. See Bannister MOH pp. 118-119; VCH (Glos.) ii p. 54 and D. Knowles and R. N. Hadcock *Medieval Religious Houses, England and Wales* (London 1953) p. 68. In the *History of St. Peter's, Gloucester* ii p. 65 the joint name of the Church appears to be in use by 1109-1114. The Church appeared to be having difficulty in retaining its lands at the time of the DB survey. As in Worcestershire lands had been lost to Nigel the Doctor (7,1;5;7 below); Maund (14,2) was in the hands of William of Écouis; and Pembridge (19,8) was held by Alfred of Marlborough. Dormington (6,2), although listed in its fief, seems to have been alienated. A cartulary of the Church is found in Balliol College MS 271 and is described by R. A. B. Mynors *Catalogue of Manuscripts of Balliol College, Oxford*, Oxford 1963 pp. 286-288. See also Davis MCGB p. 55 no. 484.

6,1 BRAMPTON (ABBOTS). DBH (p. 31; see p. 91 note) has a marginal entry, *Gadelesford'*, in a later hand, the name being found in the later survey bound up with DBH as *Gedesford* (p. 79). This suggests that part or all of the 1 hide was at Gatsford (GR SO 6126), see 1,1 note under William son of Norman.
WASTE. HOWEVER IT PAYS. Waste land has a value on several occasions in DB Herefs. (see also 6,10. 8,3. 20,2. 29,10. 34,2. E 5 and cf. 2,23 and 29,2). Apparently not all of the holding was waste, some population and resources being mentioned. There are also several examples in Worcs. of waste land with a value; see DB Worcs. 8,8 note.

6,2 THE CHURCH ITSELF HELD. *Tenuit* if not an error for *tenet* 'holds' suggests that the Church has lost the land to the current holder, Walter. The usual formula for a normal tenancy is seen in 6,8 "The Church holds Almeley. Roger of Lacy holds from it".
ESTAN. *Aestanus*; see PNDB p. 182.

6,3 THE CHURCH ITSELF HOLDS. Repeated at the beginning of 6,3-10.
HINTON. Identified by VCH and DG as Hinton in Vowchurch in the Golden Valley. But in TE p. 170a *Hyniton* is coupled with *Felton* (Felton 6,6) which is in Thornlaw Hundred. The Thornlaw Hundred head has thus been placed in error at the end of this entry rather than at the beginning, as happens elsewhere in DB.
1 HIDE WHICH PAYS TAX ... See 1,9 note.
4 COTTAGERS. *Cot'* for *cotarii* apparently similar to *cotmanni, cotmani* (translated "cottage-men") who appear in other counties. For an allied group *coscet* (singular), *coscez* and *cozets* (plural) in the south-western counties, see DB Somerset 8,30 and Wilts. M 3 notes. *Cotarii* often occur in DB Wilts. in the same entry as *coscez* suggesting a distinction; likewise *cotarii* are distinguished from *cotmanni* in other documents, though in each case the distinction is obscure. See Maitland DBB pp. 39-40. Cottagers (*cotarii*) are rare in Herefordshire; see also 8,8.

6,5 THIS ENTRY is written below the bottom marginal ruling, some 4 letters into the central margin. The transposition signs level with the first lines of 6,6 and 6,5 are as printed in the translation, not quite as Farley prints them. The Thornlaw Hundred heading before 6,4 governs this displaced entry as well as 6,6.

HOPE (UNDER DINMORE). The identification is tentative. There is a Lower Hope in Ullingswick parish in Thornlaw Hundred (GR SO 5850).

DOES NOT ... SLAVES. In the MS an ink blot, or perhaps a smudge from the blot mentioned in 6,10 note below, partially covers *non* and *serui*.

6,7 MOCCAS. From OW *Mochros* 'moor for swine'. For another part, formerly held by St. Guthlac's, see 7,7.

6,8 ANOTHER VILLAGE. A marginal note in DBH (p. 32; see p. 92 note) identifies this as *Upcote i h'*. The additional hide would make a 5-hide unit here. *Upcote* is now Upcott (GR SO 3250) to the south-west of Almeley.

THE VALUE of this holding may have been omitted, as on a number of other occasions (see 1,14 note), or the payment by the villagers from outside may take the place of the value statement (as probably in 1,57. 10,46 and 25,4; see DB Dorset 47,7 General Notes), but see 1,23;26. 2,24-25 etc.

6,9 'MIDDLEWOOD'. DB *Mideurde* (from OE *midel-worth*, 'middle estate or manor'); DBH (p. 32; see p. 92 note) has *Midewrde* in the text and *Midelwud'* ('middle wood', OE *wudu*) in the margin. Perhaps this indicates a degeneration of the estate. Lord Rennell (DM p. 153; VM p. 82) suggests Winforton Wood and it is so placed by DG (GR SO 2848); but the name survives on the 6-in. OS map as Middlewood Covert in Winforton, south of Court Barn, just across the Wye from the Middlewood in Clifford (25,5) with which it may in some way be connected.

6,10 THEY PAY 6s. In the MS a large ink blot covers *solid'*, but the word is visible underneath it.

6,11 THIS ENTRY is written below the bottom marginal ruling, some 4 letters into the central margin and at the same time as 6,5 above it. As it is in another Hundred it would appear to be an addition to the end of St. Guthlac's holding; it may be that the scribe intended to put transposition signs beside it and 6,10.

WESTELET. The place occurs as *Westeleg'* in the later survey in DBH (p. 79), but has not been identified. The name looks like OE *weste-lēah*, the first element OE *weste*, adj., 'waste, desolate'.

Ch. 7 NIGEL THE DOCTOR. One of King William's doctors, and possibly also doctor to Earl Roger of Shrewsbury (Mon. Ang. vi p. 750, but see VCH Shrops. i p. 290). He also held land once belonging to St. Guthlac's in DB Worcs. 12,1-2.

7,1 MEADOW THERE ... The extent is not given, the gap of about 9 letters' width left after it suggesting that the scribe intended to add the dimensions later, if available.

AN OUTLIER. The berewick is named in the margin in DBH (p. 32; see p. 92 note) as *Dormintona*, now Dormington (GR SO 5840).

7,2 NIGEL ALSO HOLDS. Repeated at the beginning of 7,2-9.

7,3-4 SUTTON. Now two parishes Sutton St. Nicholas and Sutton St. Michael south of Marden; in Marden parish lies a Sutton Frene and in Sutton St. Michael a Freen Court. These are named from *del Fresne* the family name of Walter of Moccas who later held some of Nigel's manors (see DBH p. 92 note). The holdings thus probably extended beyond the two modern parishes. In Fees p. 807 Hugh *de Fraxino* (OFr *Fresne*) holds 2 hides in *Suttune* and *Magene* (Sutton and Maund, see 7,5) from the Honour of Kington.

7,3 MEADOW FOR THE OXEN. Meadow for the plough-oxen (see 1,50 note), for pasture as well as to provide hay. Other similar entries are 7,4. 8,5. 10,9;27 and 14,2-3. In the MS *bob'* is written partially over an erasure and is compressed: the 7 after it has been squeezed in later.

A MILL WHICH HUGH DONKEY HOLDS. Hugh holds another part of Sutton in 29,5.

HUGH HELD THIS MANOR. Hugh Donkey was apparently the successor of Leofled (OE fem. pers. name *Lēofflǣd*) here as in 1,11. 29,3-8 and 10,15, but Nigel the Doctor seems to have taken this manor from him (Nigel also succeeded to some of Leofled's lands). The gap after *tempore Willelmi* (see next note) may have been left for the later inclusion of details of a dispute (if there was one) about the tenancy of Sutton.

IN WILLIAM'S TIME ... In the MS the rest of the line is blank after *t̄pr Wiłłi* which has no dot after it. It would seem that the scribe was unsure whether *regis* (= 'in the time of King William', i.e., 'after 1066') or *comitis* (= 'in the time of Earl William', i.e., 1067-1071) should be written after *Wiłłi*. Though *t̄pr Wiłłi regis* (often abbreviated *TRW*) is a common phrase in DB, *t̄pr W. comitis* occurs in 1,3;72 above and fits the context better (see previous note). On Earl William's extra powers in Herefords., see 1,3 note.

7,4 SPIRTES THE PRIEST. A wealthy churchman who had held a total of nearly 80 hides in Somerset, Hampshire, Wiltshire, Shropshire and Herefordshire. According to Hemming (Hearne p. 254; DB Worcs. App. V: Worcs. G 8) he was a favourite of King Cnut's sons Harold and Harthacnut but he was banished by King Edward (DB Shrops. 3d,6). He is described as one of twelve canons of St. Mary's, Shrewsbury, who alone held in 1066 10 out of the 20 hides in Bromfield (Shrops. 3d,6). He was Nigel's predecessor in several of the latter's holdings.

THEY ARE IN LORDSHIP. The 2 ploughs; this is the only occurrence of this formula in DB Herefords., although it occurs regularly elsewhere, e.g., in Somerset 21,8. 45,1. 46,9 etc.

7,5   MAUND. Originally a region name, from OW *maen* 'stone', perhaps in an archaic sense 'plain' here. The inhabitants are called *Magesaete* in 1016 (ASC) and the area *Magonsetum* and *Magesaetna* in Saxon Charters, the termination being OE *sǣte* 'inhabitants' (cf. the county names Somerset and Dorset). This interesting name is discussed in M. Gelling *Signposts to the Past*, London 1978, pp. 101–105; see also DEPN s.n. Maund. Maund Bryan, Whitechurch Maund and Rosemaund survive on modern maps and other divisions are found in the Feodaries: see 10,6 and 14,2 notes. It has not proved possible to identify this holding more precisely.

2 HIDES WHICH PAY TAX ... See 1,9 note.

NOW 30[s]. In the MS *solid'* omitted in error (as also at 14,10), not through lack of space; see 1,28 note above.

7,7   MOCCAS. The Dinedor Hundred head is probably an error. At 6,7 Moccas is said to be in Stretford Hundred. It is close to the boundary with Staple Hundred, but not with Dinedor, unless a detached portion is implied.

7,8   (LITTLE) COWARNE. DB *Colgre*. In Plegelgate Hundred in 1086, whereas (Great) Cowarne was in Radlow (19,10 note). A marginal note in DBH (p. 34 and p. 93 note) reads *Parva Cour'*, and Fees p. 807 also places these 3 hides at Little Cowarne. Land in Cowarne (*Cogre*) had formerly belonged to Worcester Church, see 10,5 note below. J.McN.D. observes that DB *Colgre* cannot represent the place-name *Cowarne* (see 19,10 note) even if there is other evidence for the identification of the place with Little Cowarne; and that, without further spellings it is hard to explain *Colgre* — the first element could be OE *col* 'charcoal', *cōl* 'cool', *cole* 'a hollow' or *cū* 'a cow' (cf. Cowarne above), and the second element OE *grēd* 'pasture' or *grēne* 'a green, a piece of grassland'.

col.   IN THE BOTTOM LEFT-HAND corner of this folio, below the last marginal ruling, is
183a   written *STE PLESHET*, the *STE* being above and slightly to the left of *PLESHET*, in a contemporary hand and in a mixture of capital and large lower-case letters. Farley does not reproduce it. It would appear to be *Stepleshet* 'Staple (Hundred)' and may have been a note by the scribe to remind himself to insert holdings of Nigel in that Hundred (if they existed) in the space he had left at the end of Ch. 7.

Ch. 8   RALPH OF TOSNY. Ralph III, also called Ralph of Conches, was brother-in-law of Earl William son of Osbern. He was lord of Clifford Castle, his chief seat being at Flamstead in Hertfordshire. He died some time before March 1102. See Douglas WC pp. 85–6. His father was Roger of Conches, founder of the Abbey of St. Peter of Castellion to which Ralph granted Monkland (8,2; see note). Ralph also bestowed land on St. Évroul. His lands later form the Honour of Clifford. Tosny and Conches-en-Ouche are in the département of Eure, France. Tosny occurs in the forms of *Todeni, Thoney, Toney* in later documents.

8,1   CASTLE ... CASTLERY. See Introductory Note 3.

EARL WILLIAM. See 1,3 note and Introductory Note 2.

WASTE LAND. Presumably it had been a part of the Golden Valley 'Hundred' before the castle was built.

LAND THERE FOR 3 PLOUGHS. 3 carucates; see notes to 1,3;48.

AND THE PLOUGH ... Possibly that mentioned above, but *car'* can abbreviate both *carruca* and *carucata*. The entry appears to be unfinished since in the MS there is a gap of about 3 letters' width after *car'*, which does not have a dot after it, and before the side marginal ruling. Since a plough would not usually be 'farmed' (see 1,1 note on revenue), but a ploughland would be, it is possible that *carucata terrae* is meant here, although the *terrae* has been omitted.

ROGER HOLDS LAND FOR 4 PLOUGHS. Probably Roger of Lacy who holds 4 carucates here in 10,3, although these carucates were and are waste.

DROGO. Drogo son of Poyntz; VCH i p. 278.

6 MALE ... SLAVES. In the MS the *vi* has probably been corrected from *iiii*.

3 MEASURES OF CORN. The *modius* was a liquid and dry measure of uncertain size, possibly a bushel, of which the sester (A 6 note above) was a fraction.

8,2   RALPH ALSO HOLDS. Repeated at the beginning of 8,2–10.

MONKLAND. DB *Leine*, originally a district name, see 1,5 note above. DBH (p. 34; see p. 94 note) has a marginal entry *Monecheslene v h' d' Castellion*. In Fees (p. 804) *Munekelane*, 4 hides, is held by the Abbey of Conches from *Thoney*; see FA ii p. 387. For the grant

(1174–1186) of Monkland to St. Peter's of Castellion (see Ch. 8 note), see Round CDF pp. 138–139 no. 416, which includes the tithes of the demesne of *Chabbenour'* (Chadnor 8,5 below), the tithe of *Hide* (Westhide 8,8) and two-thirds of the tithe of *Edithestoc'* (Stoke Edith 8,10), as well as tithes in Gloucester (Bromsberrow) and Worcester (Worsley, Lindon) also held by Ralph.

VALUE BEFORE 1066. In the MS *TRR* in error for TRE; also occurs elsewhere in DB.

8,5   A FURTHER. In the MS *adhuic* in error for *adhuc*, the usual word in this phrase, which Farley prints.

THE THIRD PART OF 1 HIDE. See 10,52 note.

8,6   MONNINGTON (ON WYE). Distinct from Monnington (Stradel) in the Golden Valley. In Fees (p. 802) it is held in Grimsworth Hundred (a later amalgamation of Cutsthorn and Staple) of the Honour of *Thony*.

ROGER. Roger of Mussegros; a descendant of his, Walter, held Monnington and Winforton from Roger *de Tony* by service of one knight's fee; Cal Inq PM 49 Henry III (no. 606, p. 193).

8,7   IN THE RIVER. *In aqua* literally 'in the water'. The river Wye flows just to the east of the modern village.

8,8   WESTHIDE. In the MS *STOCHES* is underlined for deletion and *HIDE* interlined above it. As rubrication normally takes place after a county is complete, and *STOCHES* but not *HIDE* is rubricated, it would seem that the correction by the scribe was a late one, or possibly that the rubricator failed to see the correction. DBH p. 36 (see p. 94 note) has a marginal note *Hida ... Walteri* which enables other parts of Westhide (29,4 unnamed and 29,15 *Lincumbe*, as well as 10,35) to be identified. Part of the DB land was in Radlow Hundred, part in Thornlaw. The tithes of this land were granted to the Abbey of Conches by Ralph of Tosny (see Ch. 8 note above). In Fees (p. 809) 2 hides are held at Westhide from the Honour of *Thony*.

4 COTTAGERS. See 6,3 note.

8,9   IN RADLOW HUNDRED. The Hundred head has, unusually, been incorporated in the entry. It is rubricated like the other Hundred heads.

IT IS CALLED ASHPERTON. Probably added later, though neatly, the last letters of the name and the interlineation being written in the central margin.

8,10   STOKE (EDITH). DB *Stoches*; the modern name derives from the TRE holder. DBH (p. 36) has a marginal *Edithe Stoka*. In Fees (p. 809) 2 hides are held here of the Honour of *Thony*.

Ch. 9   RALPH OF MORTIMER. Son of Roger of Mortimer (Mortemer in the département of Seine-Maritime in France; see OEB pp. 101–2). Ralph received a number of estates forfeited by Roger son of Earl William on his rebellion in 1074, including Wigmore Castle (9,1) which became his seat. His lands form the later Honour of Wigmore.

9,1   WIGMORE CASTLE. See Introductory Note 3.

MERESTUN. See 1,19 note.

GUNFRID. DB *Gunuert*. From OScand *Gunfrøthr* see PNDB p. 277 and Fellows-Jensen p. 114.

9,2   RALPH ALSO HOLDS. Repeated at the beginning of 9,2-19.

ODILARD. For the name, see Forssner p. 195.

THURSTAN OF FLANDERS. Also known as Thurstan of Wigmore (19,10); see 19,6 note.

9,3   EDRIC THE WILD. *Saluage* interlined (Farley misprints *Salvage*), from OFr *salvage*, Mod.Fr *sauvage* 'wild, untamed' from L.Lat *salvaticus*, CL *silvaticus* from *silva* 'wood': his byname appears as *siluaticus* in Orderic Vitalis, Florence of Worcester etc. He was nephew of Edric Streona (Ealdorman of the Mercians, died 1017); Orderic Vitalis ii p. 166. He held lands in Herefordshire and Shropshire under Edward the Confessor. Though he acknowledged William as King in 1066, he joined Kings Bleddyn and Rhiwallon of Gwynedd and Powys in devastating Herefordshire in 1067; he also burnt Shrewsbury in 1069 (see Introductory Note 2). He submitted to King William in 1070; Florence of Worcester ii p. 7.

9,4   ASTON. DB *Hesintune*. DBH has *Hesintone* with an explanation *id est Asciston* (p. 37; see p. 95 note) in the margin. J.McN.D. observes: DB and DBH represent OE **Escingtun* 'estate called after the ash-tree(s)', from OE Mercian *esc*; the gloss with *Ascis-* (genitive singular of standard OE *æsc*) bears evidence of interchange between the characteristic *-ing-* and genitival compositions of place-names.

9,5   WOODLAND, 2 FURLONGS. Used here as a square measure, a furlong by a furlong; see 1,10a note.

9,6-7   LEINTHALL. See 1,10c note.

9,7   MILL AT 30s. In the MS *xxx* has been altered from *xx*, with *ta* for *triginta* interlined to clarify the correction.

9,8   LYE. The land appears to have been at Lower Lye, since *Netherlege* is held of the Honour of Wigmore in FA ii p. 377; see DBH p. 38 and p. 95 note and 1,10c note above. Another part of Lye, also held by Ralph, was in Shropshire in 1086, see ES 9 below.

9,10   EDITH HELD IT ... There is a neat erasure in the MS after *tenuit*, extending almost to the end of the line; either the erasure was done after the next line was written or the scribe intended to add something here later, as erasures are generally written over.
       WOODLAND. *Siluae*, genitive; in the MS the squiggle denoting an *e* was added to the *a* of *siluae* later in slightly paler ink; see also in a similar phrase in 27,1.

9,11   STAUNTON (ON ARROW). 2 hides are held from the Honour of Wigmore in Fees (p. 803) in the later Stretford Hundred which included a number of places counted by DB in Hazeltree Hundred.

9,12   3 [MEN?]. Some such noun as *homines* 'men' or *uillani* 'villagers' is omitted before *habentes*.

9,13   HARPTON. This place has been identified with two DB entries. Here, *Ortune* DB; *Hortona* DBH p. 38 marginal; a straightforward representation of the common place-name *Horton*, OE *Hor(e)tun* from *horh, horu* 'filth, shit, slime' and *tūn* 'farmstead, village, estate'. At 24,3, *Hertune* DB; *Hortona* DBH p. 65 marginal; perhaps a DB scribal error for *Hortune*, but more likely a name-change from DB *Hertune* (OE *hearra, hierra, herra* 'higher' – perhaps 'Higher Harpton') to *Hortune*. DEPN notes Harpton as *Herton* 1308 Cal Inq PM, so the original *Her-* form persisted alongside the *Hor-* form for some time before 'Horton' prevailed over 'Herton'; but there is, as yet, no evidence of the epoch at which 'Horton' in its turn was overtaken by 'Harpton', see 24,3 note on Lower Harpton. Harpton is now in Wales, Lower Harpton remains in Herefordshire.
       MIDDLETON ... WESTON. DB *Mildetune* is identified by DG with Milton in Pembridge and DB *Westune* as Weston in Pembridge. Milton in Pembridge is included in DB at 24,1, but both the places mentioned here are specifically said to be 'In the Welsh March'. They are likely to be on or beyond the boundary of modern Herefordshire and adjacent to those Welsh March places (see Introductory Note 1) that have been positively identified. Weston is here tentatively identified with Lower and Upper Weston to the west of Pilleth. A Vron Weston is found here on the 1st Edition OS map of 1833 (sheet no. 56 reprinted in 1970 as sheet no. 49). Weston was formerly an important settlement, Weston Hall featuring on Saxton's map (1578) of Radnorshire. *Mildetune* is probably now represented by Middleton Barn south of Lower Harpton; metathesis of *dl* in *midle-* occurs in other place-names.
       IN THE WELSH MARCH. Here and at 24,3 the manors lying on the Welsh border are apparently a part of Hazeltree Hundred (see Introductory Note 1). Latin *marcha* represents OE *mearc* 'boundary, border'.

9,14   GRUFFYDD'S MANOR OF LYE. See 31,7.

9,15   RALPH ALSO HOLDS. Repeated at the beginning of 9,15-19.
       KINNERSLEY. DB *Elburgelega* which DBH (p. 39; see p. 95 note) changes to *Edburgelega* by a marginal entry in red. This latter is annotated in black *Kinardesleg'* thus identifying the place. In both place-names the common element is OE *lēah* 'open woodland; settlement in a woodland setting'; the first element personal name changes from OE fem. *Ethelburg* (DB) to OE fem. *Eadburg* to OE masc. *Cyneheard*. The ladies' names may be kin-related, by alliteration and common element *-burg*. In Fees p. 803, 1 hide is held in *Kynardesle* from the Honour of Wigmore; see also FA ii p. 377.

9,16   RUILLIC. Probably an old Welsh name, PNDB p. 350.

9,18   WOLFERLOW. DBH (p. 39; see p. 95 note) in a marginal entry specifies *Underlide*, now Upper and Lower Underley (GR SO 6562, 6561); see 10,66 note below. In Fees (p. 806) *Hunderlithe Walteri* is held from the Abbot of Wigmore.

9,19   ORLETON. See 12,2 note. In Fees (p. 810) 4 hides at *Alretun'* are held from the Honour of Wigmore.

Ch. 10   ROGER OF LACY. Son of Walter of Lacy (Lacy, now Lassy in the département of Calvados, France; he died in 1085, see 1,5 note) and Ermelina (Emma). His extensive fief with land at Ewias Lacy (now Longtown 10,2) and its *caput* at Weobley (10,48), where Roger had his park, made him an important defender of the English frontier against the Welsh. He rebelled against William Rufus in 1088 and 1094, was banished and his lands, which later form the Honour of Weobley, were given to his brother Hugh. Roger died some time after 1106 in Normandy where he had attained high office under Duke Robert. In DB Worcs. 18,6 (= E 6 below) land in Droitwich is said to belong to his manor of Hereford. Although Roger holds some houses in the Borough, his principal Herefordshire manor, Weobley, is probably meant. For Walter, Roger and the Honour of Weobley, see Wightman LF, especially pp. 117-166.

10,1   IN CUTSTHORN HUNDRED. The rest of Cutsthorn Hundred lay in the centre of Hereford-shire and was not adjacent to Ewyas Harold. Didley and *Stane* (2,2) had been drawn into the Ewyas Harold Castlery, suggesting that the land lay close to the castle (see Introductory Note 3).

CASTLERY. See Introductory Note 3.

4 CARUCATES. On 'carucate' see 1,48 note.

WALTER OF LACY. See 1,5 note.

THEY HAVE 1 PLOUGH. The Welshmen have the plough. William and Osbern have the slaves in the next statement, and probably also the smallholders, though, as is often the case with *bord'*, the accusative is not indicated.

10,2 LONGTOWN. Formerly Ewias Lacy. Longtown is dominated by the castle (GR SO 321291), erected at the confluence of the valleys of the Monnow, the Olchon and the Escley Brook in the late 12th century. No castle of Roger is mentioned in DB, but he may well have built one, possibly at Oldcastle (GR SO 3224). His immediate successors built at Pont Hendre (GR SO 326282).

WITHIN THE BOUNDARY OF EWIAS. That is, the Welsh Commote of Ewias, not the castlery of Ewyas Harold; compare 1,53 *In fine Arcenefelde*.

DOES NOT BELONG TO THE CASTLERY NOR TO THE HUNDRED. It probably lay within the Welsh commote of Ewias, then about to be conquered.

(ADMINISTERS) JUSTICE. *habet . . . placita*, literally 'has pleas over them'. His court replaces that of a Hundred, to which this land does not belong.

10,3 IN THE CASTLERY OF CLIFFORD. Clifford Castle (8,1) is not in a Hundred; the castlery may similarly have been extra-hundredal.

4 CARUCATES. These may be the 'land for 4 ploughs' held by Roger in 8,1 (see note).

10,4 PUTLEY. DB *Poteslepe*. In the margin of DBH (p. 40; see p. 96 note) *Poteslepa* has been glossed *Puttelee*. J.F. observes that the ME and ModE spellings of the place-name represent the *Puttelee* form; and that there may be two names for Putley. *'Poteslepe* is also the DB form of Postlip, Gloucs., but there the later forms clearly derive from the DB form. Ekwall (DEPN s.n.) takes the second el. of Postlip to be OE *slǣp* ... "slippery or miry place", but perhaps also having a secondary sense "portage, place where boats or other objects are dragged". The first el. may be OE *pott* "a pot; a pool, a hollow, a hole".' He notes that Ekwall (who omits the DB *Poteslepe* form in both DEPN and *Studies*, perhaps as a scribal error) discusses the later forms of Putley in *Studies* pp. 91–92, finding a place-name in OE *lēah* with first el. the OE pers.n. *Putta* or the noun **putta* 'a kite, a bird of prey'. J.F. concludes 'If ... one accepts DB and DBH *Poteslepe* as a genuine form, a solution might be to take *Poteslepe* to represent not *pottes-slǣp* but *Puttan-slǣp* "Putta's *slǣp*", which, with reduction of the weak genitive *-an-* to *-e-* and with AN *-o-* for *-u-* (PNDB §17) and AN simplification of *-tt-* to *-t-* (PNDB §147), would result in a DB form *Poteslep(e)*. *Puttelee* might then represent an alternative name of the place, *Puttan-lēah* "Putta's wood or glade", containing the same pers.n. as *Poteslepe'*.

TOSTI. *Thostin* from ON *Tosti*; see PNDB p. 387 and §148.

10,5 OCLE (PYCHARD). The portion given to St. Peter's of Hereford (on which see 2,58 note) is called *Acla monachorum* (Monkton, GR SO 5745) in the margin of DBH p. 40. In Fees (p. 807) 4 hides are held by Roger *Pichard* of the Honour of Weobley. Hemming, in his list of former possessions of Worcester Church (folio 127v (= new 128v), Hearne p. 274), records how Edmund Ironside, after dividing England with Cnut (in 1016), awarded Herefordshire to Earl Ranig. He and his soldiers seized from the Church *Pencofan* (unidentified in ECWM p. 140 no. 412, possibly Pencombe, 19,6 note), *Cogre* (Little Cowarne 7,8 and note), *Upledene* (Upleadon 18,1, 9 hides), *Aclea* (Ocle 10,5 and 29,3 note) and *Ræccesford* (Rochford 22,5 and 23,1). DB does not record the Worcester interest in these villages and it is not possible to decide which parts of divided villages it had held. For a discussion of Hemming's Cartulary, see DB Worcs. Appendix V. Finberg in ECWM pp. 225–7 and EPNS (Glos.) iv p. 32 note I identify the Upleadon in Gloucestershire with *Upledene*, and hence use it as additional proof that this part of Glos. was at first in Herefordshire; see Introductory Note 4.

WALTER OF LACY ... ST. PETER'S OF HEREFORD. Walter (see 1,5 note) had founded the monastery. His second son Hugh gave the monastery and all its lands to St. Peter's of Gloucester either in 1100 (*History of St. Peter's, Gloucester* i p. 326) or in 1101 (*ibidem* i pp. 84–85) or in 1096 (*Regesta* ii p. 410). See also Ch. 6 note.

10,6 THIS ENTRY, added later, is squeezed in at the foot of the column, the last line being written below the bottom marginal ruling, with *h'* for *hic* in the left margin corresponding to a marginal *h'* level with the last line of 10,5 above.

MAUND. For the name, see 7,5 note. These 2 hides appear to be *Magene Albini*, a lost place listed in Fees p. 805; see DBH p. 105 note.

10,7 A FISHERY ON THE (RIVER) WYE. It cannot have been in Thornlaw Hundred (heading at 10,5), which does not touch the Wye. In DBH (p. 41) a marginal note reads *piscaria de Hodenac*. The place has not been located, but the name might be a metathesis of *Hadenoc* now Hadnock Farm on the Wye just north of Monmouth (GR SO 5314), for which see TE p. 170b, and Round CDF pp. 412–413 no. 1148.

10,8 ROGER ALSO HOLDS. Repeated at the beginning of 10,8–15;19–75.
MAUND. Rose Maund which passed from the Lacys to the lords of Richards Castle, *Magene Mauricii* in Fees p. 807.
WONNI. Perhaps from OE *Wunning*, see PNDB pp. 416–7.

10,9 A BEADLE. See 1,10a note.
MEADOW ONLY FOR THE OXEN. See 7,3 note.

10,11 ONE HIDE. DBH (p. 41; see p. 96 note) has a marginal annotation *P.de Burh'*, which suggests that the land was at Burghope (GR SO 5050) in Wellington parish; see 1,4 note.
MARDEN, THE KING'S MANOR. See 1,4.

10,12 WOONTON. In Laysters, identified by the Wolphy Hundred head; see 1,70 and 2,52 notes.
1 PLOUGH THERE. See 2,43 note.

10,13 HEATH. DB *Hed*; DBH p. 41 in the margin has *Heth*. The place is now represented by Great Heath farm and Little Heath farm, the latter on the 6-in. map.

10,14 PUDLESTON. DB *Pillesdune*; DBH p. 41 has a marginal *Putlesdona*. The first el. of the place-name is OE *pidel, pydel* 'a stream'; the second el. OE *dūn* 'upland tract, upland pasture'.

10,15 ONE MANOR OF 1½ HIDES. The land was possibly at Whyle in Wolphy Hundred. In Fees (p. 810) 2 hides in Whyle are split between the Honour of Richards Castle (24,10) and the Honour of Weobley.
ALWIN ... HIS FATHER EDWY. Probably Edwy Young who had a son called Alwin; see 10,70 below.

10,16 GOLDEN VALLEY. In the MS *STRADELEI* is in capitals and rubricated as if it were the
-18 manor's name, whereas *Bachetune* and *Wadetune* are in lower-case letters, the same as the rest of the entry, though also rubricated; see 2,54 note. Some of Roger's holdings in the Valley are unidentified: one may have been at *Cheyneston* (now Chanstone GR SO 3635) held from the Honour of Weobley in Fees p. 817, FA ii p. 380. This may be the Domesday *Elnodestune* (10,17) against which *W.Ebrois* is entered as holder in the margin of DBH p. 42. He may have been ancestor to the *Devereux* who held Chanstone in Fees. Another holding may have been at Howton in Kenderchurch (GR SO 4129), held in Fees p. 812 by Walter *de Scotot* from the Honour of Weobley. Mr. Warren Skidmore identifies this with *Wadetune* on the ground that the 1086 holder Gilbert (probably Gilbert of Bacton, see DBH pp. 85;96;100) was Gilbert of *Esketot*, ancestor of Walter *de Scotot*. A third Lacy holding was at Walterstone (GR SO 3425), in Fees p. 1479. The place-name could derive from the tenant of the unidentified *Edwardestune* (10,18), or from the early 13th century Walter of Lacy, or from some other Walter. The position of Walterstone, south-west of Ewyas Harold, close to Ewias Lacy (Longtown), suggests, however, that it was acquired as part of the Conqueror's thrust into Ewias at the end of his reign: it is therefore unlikely to have been hidated or in the Golden Valley in 1086.

10,17 *ELNODESTUNE*. 'Elnoth's farm or estate', from the OE personal name *Elnoth, Alnoth*, PNDB p. 149. Identified by Round in VCH as 'Elstones Bridge' at the southern end of the Golden Valley. 'Elstones Bridge' is, however, to be identified with Pontrilas and is probably DB *Elwistone* (1,56 note), which lay in Archenfield in 1086. See previous note.

10,18 *EDWARDESTUNE*. A marginal entry in DBH p. 42 has *In Edwardeston' Uilla Huardi*. *Huardus* also holds Poston (DBH p. 54 = DB 14,6) which may have been close to this unidentified holding.

10,19 ROGER ALSO HOLDS. See 10,8 note.
BULLINGHOPE. DB *Boniniope*. DBH has a marginal *Bulinghop'* (p. 42; see p. 96 note). In the Middle Ages there were two villages *Bollynghop' Superior* and *Inferior*; see FA ii p. 388 and LSR p. 127. The first edition OS map distinguishes them as Bullingham and Lower Bullingham respectively. On recent maps (Upper) Bullingham has become Bullinghope once more, Lower Bullingham (GR SO 5238) remaining in that form.
THE THIRD PART OF 2 MILLS. The remaining parts, with the same value, are at 21,6 and 25,2 (but see note to latter).

10,20 COBHALL. DBH (p. 42) has a marginal note *Archetestoñ i h'*, 'the estate of Arketel' (*Arnketill*, an OScand personal name), indicating that the land was at Arkstone (GR SO 4336) close to Cobhall.
4 SMALLHOLDERS WITH 1 HIDE. In some DB counties it is normal for the hidage of the villagers' land to be mentioned. This is not so in Herefordshire. There is clearly an error here

since the total holding is only 1 hide. DBH p. 42 corrects to '4 smallholders with 1 plough' (*una caruca*).

10,22 ½ HIDE ... See 1,9 note.

10,23 WEBTON. Lined through in red in the MS as usual; the facsimile does not have the rubrication. Part of the land was at Meer Court (GR SO 4336): in Fees p. 811 *Webbetun'*, *Cobbewell'* (10,20) and *La Mare* are held from the Honour of Weobley. 2½ HIDES ... See 1,9 note.

10,24 STRETTON. See 2,37 note.

10,25 LYDE. Two manors are distinguished in the margin of DBH (p. 43; see p. 97 note) as
-26 *Luda ... Salcei* and *Luda ... Monesl'*. Land is held of the Weobley Fee in Lyde *Mucegros* (also Lyde *Beaumyes*) and Lyde *Godfrey* (also Lyde *Arundel*); see Fees p. 803 and FA ii pp. 376;386;392. See 2,44 note above. Roger holds another part of Lyde under Osbern son of Richard in 24,11. Lyde *Arundel* is now Arundel Farm (GR SO 4943).

10,27 WESTON (BEGGARD). 1 hide is held in the Weston in Radlow Hundred from the Honour of Weobley in Fees (p. 809).
GUNFRID. *Gunuer*; see 9,1 note.

10,28 YARKHILL. DB *Archel*. It is coincidental that the TRE holder was named Arkell, the place-name being derived not from him but from OE *geard* 'yard', 'enclosure' and *cylen* 'kiln', see DEPN s.n.
ARKELL. *Archil*; see PNDB p. 163 s.n. *Arnkell*.
A THANE. In the MS *tan'*, probably a mistake for *tain'* (cf. DB Shrops. 4,1, 35 *ta͡ini*) which, with *teinus* and *tegnus*, is the usual DB form for 'thane'; *tanus*, however, is evidenced as a form in 1160 (RMLWL s.v. *thanus*), and *tannus* is the form used sometimes in Exon.

10,29 (HALMONDS) FROME. DB *Nerefrum* represents OE *nearra-*, ME *nerre-*, 'the nearer Frome', perhaps nearer to the river than the land of the next entry, Castle Frome, which occupies the hill above it. VCH reverses the identifications of the two Fromes, but DBH (p. 44; see p. 98 note) makes the identifications clear. This Frome in a marginal note is *Nederefroma ... Hamonis*, which contains OE *neothera*, ME *nethere* 'lower'.

10,30 (CASTLE) FROME. DB *Brismerfrum* named after the TRE holder (OE *Brihtmer*, see *Beorhtmǣr* PNDB p. 195). DBH (p. 44; see p. 98 note) has *Brichtmer(es) froma ... Castelli* in the margin.

10,32 (LITTLE) MARCLE. In Radlow Hundred, Much Marcle being in Winstree. DBH (p. 44; see p. 99 note) records the later holder as *O. Tirel* and in Fees (p. 807) Little Marcle is held by Roger *Tirel* from the Honour of Weobley in Radlow Hundred; see FA ii p. 379.
ODO NOW HOLDS IT WITH. In the MS and Farley *cū*; the facsimile reproduces it as *cō*.
THE OTHER LAND. Although *alius* normally means 'another' it seems here to refer to the rest of the 5 hides. There were two holdings before 1066, held by Thorkell and by Alric; they were later combined and held in 1086 by Odo.

10,33 (CANON) FROME. DBH (p. 45; see p. 99 note) has a marginal addition *Canonicorum*. In Fees (p. 808) it is held by the Canons of Llanthony from the Weobley Honour.

10,35 MONKHIDE. DB *Hide*, part of Westhide (see 8,8 and 29,4 notes). In Fees p. 808 1 hide is held at Monkhide by the Church of Gloucester by gift of Walter of Lacy, from the Honour of Weobley. DBH (p. 99 note) is inclined to identify the *villa Ricardi* of Fees p. 809. There was also a *parva Hida*, held by Gloucester Abbey in FA ii p. 389, but Monkhide and *Parva Hida* appear as separate lands in LSR p. 128.

10,36 TARRINGTON. Possibly Little Tarrington, see DBH p. 100 note and VCH i p. 331 note 75. Ansfrid is Ansfrid of Cormeilles who holds another part of Tarrington in chief (21,1); he was Roger's cousin by marriage (DB Glos. 68,13).

10,37 IN THE LEFT MARGIN of the MS, level with the first line of this entry is written a + sign. It is contemporary with DB and draws attention to the fact that the manor is held by a church. These crosses occur in several DB counties; see DB Somerset General Note to 5,43. Farley does not reproduce this cross here, though he does in several counties (e.g., Glos. 1,27ff.). Not all land held by the church from lay tenants is so distinguished in DB.

10,37 LEADON. DB *Lede* (for *Leden*); DBH (p. 45) has a marginal *Ledena*. In Fees p. 808 ½ hide
-38 is held here by St. Guthlac's of Hereford from Walter of Lacy of the Honour of Weobley; see FA ii p. 389. St. Peter's of Hereford and St. Guthlac's later merged, see Ch. 6 note. St. Peter's of Gloucester, which became their mother church, also held land at Upleadon in Gloucestershire (DB Glos. 10,10); see *History of St. Peter's, Gloucester* i pp. 374-5.

10,39 THIS ENTRY is written below the bottom marginal rulings of col. 184c and some 10 letters into the left margin. The transposition signs are as printed in this translation, not the crosses of Farley.
MATHON. The parish was formerly partly in Herefordshire and partly in Worcestershire, it being fully transferred to Herefordshire in 1897. The division is found in Domesday.

Worcestershire 9,6a (= E 5 below) records the Church of Pershore as having held 5 hides at Mathon, of which 4 are in Worcestershire and 1 is in Herefordshire in Radlow Hundred. DB Herefordshire here and in 23,6 records two half-hides both held before 1066 by thanes of Earl Oda. Round in VCH i p. 331 note 76 regarded the 1 Herefordshire hide (held by two riders in 1086) mentioned in Worcs. 9,6a as the same as that given in Herefords. 10,39 and 23,6. If so, the two half-hides will have been alienated Church land, of which fact no mention is made in Herefordshire; Earl Oda (see 1,44 note) was buried in 1056 in Pershore Church and may have been holding these lands from that church. The uncertain status of these half-hides is perhaps shown by the fact that 10,39 certainly (see previous note), and 23,6 possibly, are later additions to the schedule. The village of Mathon has been mapped in Worcestershire in this volume. For centuries Mathon was a westward projection of Worcestershire; but if 'Bagbarrow' (2,28 above) is correctly identified, Mathon will in 1086 have been divided from Worcestershire by a part of the Herefordshire Hundred of Winstree, thus forming a detached portion of the former county.

HE COULD NOT WITHDRAW. See 1,3 note.

10,40 LAWTON ... STREET. Both lands had been part of Kingsland before 1066, see 1,5.
-41

10,42 AELFLED. DB *Elflet*, see PNDB p. 144.

10,43 HOPLEYS (GREEN). It had been part of Kingsland before 1066; see 1,5. For the identification see Lord Rennell DM p. 154. Mr. Coplestone-Crow points to an alternative identification in the existence of a 'Hope' in Lyonshall (10,44) marked on the first edition OS map of 1833 (sheet 56, reprint sheet 49 (1970)) at GR SO 337568.
RIGHT TO SETTLE. Colonists invited by the lord to settle on his land in order to cultivate it. Such an influx of people would be useful in bringing new or waste lands under the plough on the Welsh Marches. Other examples of *hospites* are 10,47 (cf. 10,44), DB Cheshire 2,9 and Shropshire 4,23,17. 4,25,3. 4,27,27. See Nelson pp. 57–61.

10,45 WOONTON. See 1,70 note.
NOW 64d. In the MS and Farley *lxiiii*; the facsimile reproduces the figure as *lxiii·.*, the photozincographic process not 'picking up' most of the final *i*.

10,46 ROBERT. Robert of Baskerville; Eardisley was *caput* of the later Baskerville fief; see Wightman LF p. 154; DBH p. 100 note.
NOR LIES IN ANY HUNDRED. The land containing a small-scale castle is treated like a castlery; see 8,1 and 10,2 and Introductory Note 3.
A FORTIFIED HOUSE. Probably with a moat and wall. The building was perhaps the germ of the later Eardisley Castle (see Nelson p. 71 and RCHM iii (1934) pp. lxiii and 52b). Another *domus defensabilis* in the same area is mentioned at 25,9.
1 WELSHMAN WHO PAYS 3s. See 6,8 note.

10,47 LETTON. In Fees (p. 803) Letton is held, in the later enlarged Stretford Hundred, from the Honour of Weobley.
EDWY YOUNG. The facsimile fails to reproduce all of the interlined *cilt*, probably because the *i* and *t* are rather faint in the MS.
7 SETTLERS. See 10,43 note.

10,48 WEOBLEY. *Caput* of the Lacy barony.
3½ HIDES WHICH PAY TAX. *Ibi iii hidę 7 dimid' geldant'* were interlined later, though by the same scribe as the rest of DB, and are squeezed in with a gap between *iii* and *hidę*, and *dimid'* and *geldant'* to accommodate respectively the *g* of *Roǥ* in the line above and the abbreviation sign of *caꝛ* and *7* in the line below; Farley does not show these gaps.
A PARK. For hunting wild animals within the boundaries of the manor. See 1,41 note.
ST. PETER'S. Of Hereford. See 10,5 note.
ONE OF THESE VILLAGERS. *Unā de istis uiłł*, which could be translated as 'one of these villages' (*uiłł* abbreviating *uillis*), implying Weobley or one of the preceding villages. However, it is much more likely that *unā* is a scribal error for *unū* (= *unum*) and that the meaning is that St. Peter's had (the services of) one of the 10 villagers mentioned above. See the *History of St. Peter's, Gloucester* i p. 85 where a villager in *Webbeleya in Herfordscire* is mentioned as part of a grant by Walter of Lacy to St. Peter's of Hereford (which later became a dependency of St. Peter's, Gloucester; see Ch. 6 note).

10,49 FERNHILL. Bannister PNHe and DBH (p. 101 note) identify 'Fernhale' a place now lost in Staunton on Wye. A Fernhill occurs on the modern 6-in. OS map south-west of Weobley and is the likely identification in Stretford Hundred, whereas Staunton on Wye lay in 1086 in Staple Hundred.
1 RIDING MAN. In the accusative (*unū* = *unum*) in error, as there is no verb such as *habet* requiring an object.

HOLD. Or perhaps "who holds" referring only to the riding man, as *teñ* can abbreviate both *tenent* and *tenens*.

10,50 (KINGS) PYON. In DBH p. 48 there is a marginal *Regis* to distinguish this land from Canon Pyon (2,39). *Pyonia Regis* is a member of Weobley in FA ii p. 377.
GRUFFYDD. Probably son of King Maredudd who has a separate fief in DB (Ch. 31). In DBH p. 48 the later holder is *W. de Braosa* who holds a number of Gruffydd's Ch. 31 lands.
GRUFFYDD ... LAND. The fact that the rest of the line is left blank after this in the MS and that there is a *7* at the beginning of the next statement (and no verb there) suggests that the scribe intended to add details of another sub-tenancy later when available.

10,52 ALTON ... TWO PARTS OF 1 HIDE. DB *Pletune* has defied identification, but at Chadnor (8,5), also in this Hundred, DB records the third part of 1 hide, an unusual fraction, that appears to belong with the two parts of 1 hide at *Pletune*. Moreover, *Alleton* and *Falle* (Alton Court and ?Fields Place, GR SO 4153) are members of Weobley Honour in FA ii pp. 377 and 392. It is likely that *Pletune* is a scribal error for *Aletune*.

10,55 STAUNTON (ON WYE). Both the Lacy holdings (see 10,57) reappear in Fees (p. 802) as respectively 2 hides and 4 hides held at *Standun* of the Honour of Weobley in Grimsworth Hundred which was a later merging of Cutsthorn and Staple Hundreds. The 10,55 entry is *Standon Leurici* in the margin of DBH (p. 48; see p. 101 note). Part of the larger Lacy holding, held by Miles *Pichard* in Fees p. 802 was at Letton (GR SO 3346); see FA ii p. 376.

10,56 MANSELL (GAMAGE). 'Mansell' is represented by two other DB entries (2,46 now Bishopstone and 31,4–5). Mansell Lacy, despite the distinguishing name, does not refer to this land which DBH (p. 49 and p. 101 note) qualifies in the margin as *Melueshull' ... G. de Gamag*. 'Gamage' is derived from Gamaches in Les Andelys in Normandy. DBH also has a marginal *Stand' Mah' iii h.*, suggesting that 3 of the 8 hides were a part of Staunton on Wye. These are probably the 3 hides at *Staunton* in Grimsworth Hundred held by Matthew *de Mauns* from Walter of Clifford in Fees p. 802. Mansell Gamage is similarly held from the Weobley Honour in Fees (p. 802) and FA ii p. 376.

10,57 STAUNTON ON WYE. See 10,55 note.
IN LORDSHIP. *In dñio* in the MS and Farley; the facsimile does not reproduce the rather faint line over *dñio*.

10,58 LUDRIC. *Ludri*; see PNDB p. 321.
EARL ALGAR. Earl of East Anglia 1051–1052 and 1053–1057, then Earl of Mercia 1057–1062. He was outlawed in 1055 and again in 1058, but won back his position on each occasion with the help of Gruffydd ap Llywelyn, King of Gwynedd and Powys (see 1,49 note). Algar was the son of Earl Leofric and the Lady (Countess) Godiva; father of Earls Edwin and Morcar. He died *c*.1062.

10,59 SAEMER. In the MS *Semar* has been badly written over an erasure, probably of an ink blot, parts of which still remain.

10,60 4 MORE PLOUGHS. In the MS *ii* with *ii* interlined, making the figure *iiii*.

10,62 HADWIC. For the name, DB *Haduic*, see 15,2 and PNDB p. 282 note 4.

10,63 STOKE (LACY). Not Stoke Prior (VCH). Stoke Lacy is held from the Honour of Weobley in 1243 (Fees p. 807); see DBH p. 103 note. The land included *Muntrich* (now Mintridge Farm GR SO 6352) in Fees p. 806.

10,66 IN WOLFERLOW, 6 HIDES. DBH (p. 50) has a marginal '6½ hides', the *7 di'* ('½') being added later and at the same time as another marginal note '½ hide at *Underlide*' (Underley Upper and Lower, GR SO 6562, 6561); see 9,18 note above.
ALWIN THE SHERIFF. A former Sheriff of Gloucestershire.

10,67 (BISHOPS) FROME. See 2,21 note.
LEOFSI. DB *Lepsi* here and at 10,69;74. See PNDB §90.

10,68 TEDSTONE. Tedstone (Wafer). DB *Tetistorp*; DBH has a marginal entry *Tedestorna ... R. Walfr'* (p. 51 and p. 104 note; see Fees p. 806). J.McN.D. points out that this and *Tedesthorne* (2,3 above), both identified with Tedstone, are different names. The first el. in both appears to be the same OE personal name; the final el. of the one is OE *thorn* and *thyrne* 'thorn-bush; thorn-brake', and of the other OE *thorp, throp* 'dependent or outlying settlement' (cf. Urs Wagner *Studies on English Place-Names in Thorp*, Basel 1976, pp. c, ci).

10,69 BREDENBURY ... 1 HIDE. DBH p. 51 has a marginal entry *In Bridenebiria ii h'*.

10,70 BUTTERLEY. Mr. Coplestone-Crow points out that the Lacy land included *Wakintun'* (Wacton, GR SO 6157), where 2 hides are held in Fees p. 806.

10,71 MARSTON (STANNETT). The Plegelgate Hundred head identifies the place, see notes to 14,12. 27,1 and 32,1. In Fees p. 805 1 hide is held in Marston in Broxash Hundred (which included the Domesday Plegelgate) from the Honour of Weobley. To the ½ hide mentioned here may have been added the ½ hide of 32,1.

10,72 GRENDON. There are now two adjacent parishes, Grendon Bishop and Pencombe with Grendon Warren. Grendon Bishop was a holding of the Church of Hereford (FA ii p. 384) perhaps included under the 30 hides of Bromyard (2,49) in DB. Grendon Warren appears to have been the Lacy holding (DBH p. 104 note; see Fees p. 806 and FA ii p. 379).
EDWY HELD IT, AND ORDRIC. *Tenuit* is singular; the scribe presumably wrote *Eduui tenuit* and put a full-stop after it before he realised there were two TRE holders; see 22,8 note below for a similar omission.

10,73 STANFORD. 'Stanford Regis'. In Stanford Bishop parish. Fees (p. 806) records 1 hide held in *Stanford'* in the later Broxash Hundred from the Weobley Honour. See 1,9 note.

10,74 'CUPLE'. DB *Chipelai*, DBH (p. 52 margin) *Cupleai*. This 1 hide, held of the fee of Walter of Lacy, was subsequently granted as 'Cuple' by Earl Roger of Hereford to St. Guthlac's; see Walker CEH p. 39 note 2; HEH p. 186. The modern representative of the place, which was not certainly in Plegelgate Hundred (see next note), has not been found. J.McN.D. adds: "the place-name forms indicate second element OE *lēah* 'open woodland; settlement in a woodland setting', and suggest first element OE *cȳpe* 'a kipe, an osier basket for catching fish'; but we must await confirmation by further research".

10,75 HANLEY. Both the final entries in this chapter are left unidentified by VCH. Since the last items in any chapter can be late additions out of Hundred order, *Chipelai* and *Hanlei* are not necessarily in Plegelgate Hundred, in which 10,63-73 places all seem to have lain. If no other Hundred head has been omitted, this *Hanlei* can hardly be the same place as that at 23,5 which is said to be in Winstree Hundred. The most likely identification is with Hanley William and Hanley Child just over the Worcestershire border (DB Worcs. 20,3-4). This holding is so identified by Wightman LF (map pp. 118-9). The ½ hide of this entry added to the 4½ hides of the Worcestershire schedule would make a 5-hide village. The division between counties would then be similar to that of Mathon (10,39 note).
ST. PETER'S. Probably St. Peter's of Hereford, see 10,5 note.

Ch.11 ROGER OF MUSSEGROS. Mussegros, dép. Eure, France, close to Les Andelys; OEB p. 102. The surnames Musgrove and Mucegros are derived from the French place.

11,1 ARKETEL. DB *Archetel*, see PNDB p. 163 s.n. *Arnkell* and Fellows-Jensen p. 14 and
-2 addenda.
ARNGRIM. DB *Ergrim*, from ON *Arngrimr*, ODan *Arngrim*; PNDB p. 162. The holdings of an Arketel and an Arngrim were also combined in DB Shrops. 4,5,3.

11,2 LAYSTERS. DB *Last*. A marginal entry in DBH p. 52 has *Lastes*. See 1,10a note on Miles Hope.

Ch.12 ROBERT GERNON. From OFr *grenon, gernon, guernon* 'moustache'; OEB pp. 314-5.

12,1 YARPOLE. *IARPOL* in the MS; Farley misprints *LARPOL*.
RICHARD SCROPE. A Norman who settled in Herefordshire at the time of the Confessor, continued to hold land after the Conquest and was succeeded by his son Osbern (Ch. 24 note), although here his lands passed to Robert Gernon. For Scrope, see OEB p. 224, DEPN s.n. Shrewsbury, PNDB p. 349 note 1. The surname, despite OEB's hesitations and DEPN's accidental complication (this family's surname is not the origin of *Shrewsbury*), is obviously an Anglo-Scandinavian nickname, the ON byname *Skrópi*, presumably anglicized *Scrōp(e)* which would produce AN *Scrupe, Escrob, Scrob*: see E. Björkman, *Zur Englischen Namenkunde* (Halle 1912) p. 76 and E. H. Lind, *Norsk-Isländska Personbinamn från Medeltiden* (Uppsala 1920-21) p. 333. It looks as if a pre-Conquest Norman settler has been given an Anglo-Scandinavian surname.

12,2 (RICHARDS) CASTLE. DB *Auretone* (representing OE *Alretune*). Now represented by Orleton (GR SO 4967), see 9,19 above and DEPN s.n. In a marginal note, DBH (p. 52) has *Castellum Ricardi*, the name deriving from Richard Scrope. The castle may have been erected under the Confessor like the first construction of Ewyas Harold (19,1), see Introductory Note 3.
Part of Richards Castle parish was later transferred to Shropshire, a part, including the Church and the Castle, remaining in Herefordshire (see Introductory Note 4).
4 MEASURES OF CORN. See 8,1 note.

Ch.13 HENRY OF FERRERS. Ferrières-Saint-Hilaire in the département of Eure, France; OEB p. 88. He was one of the Domesday Commissioners named in Worcs. F in Hemming's Cartulary (see DB Worcs. App. V) and was lord of Tutbury Castle in Staffordshire (DB Staffs. 10,1), holding much land in Derbyshire (see Lennard pp. 32-33). His heirs were the Earls of Derby and Nottingham.

13,1 (PRIORS) FROME. In Mordiford parish. In Fees p. 801, 1 hide in Mordiford is held in socage by Ralph *de Beaufey* of the Honour of the Earl of Ferrers. See DBH p. 104 note.
BISHOP AETHELSTAN. *Estan*; see PNDB p. 188. According to HBC p. 229 Aethelstan was

consecrated in 1012 and was Bishop of Hereford from some time between then and 1052 until his death in 1056.

2 HIDES. Part of this is written over an erasure in the MS; *ii* is a correction from *i* with the *e* (= *duae*) added to clarify the correction, and *hida* has been made plural by the addition of the diphthong squiggle on the top of the *a*.

13,2   CASTLERY. See Introductory Note 3.

ROGER. Roger of Lacy. This property descended to his grandson, Hugh II; see DBH p. 53 and Wightman LF p. 132. The three churches may well have been at Walterstone (GR SO 3424), Llancillo (SO 3625) and Rowlstone (SO 3727) which were numbered among the possessions of Llanthony Priory, a foundation of Hugh (I) of Lacy, Roger's brother.

2 DWELLINGS. *Masuras* (for *mansuras*); see C 3 note above. Their existence here implies the beginning of a *burgus* as at the castles of Clifford (8,1) and Wigmore (9,1).

Ch.14   WILLIAM OF ÉCOUIS. DB *Scohies*; Écouis in the département of Eure, France (see OEB p. 114). In later Feodaries his lands are held of the Honour of Dilwyn.

14,1   CASTLERY OF CAERLEON. Caerleon is a strategic site, commanding the Usk, just north of the modern Newport (Casnewydd). The castle, whose existence is deduced from the mention of a castlery, will have been erected as part of the Norman advance into South Wales from Gloucestershire and represents a forward fortified position beyond Chepstow (Casgwent). Brief details of these newly conquered lands 'between the Wye and the Usk' and 'beyond the Usk' are given in DB Glos. W 1–19 (cols. 162a–c) under the heading 'In Wales'. In Glos. S 2 (col. 162a) it is stated that '£7 10s comes from the payments of Caerleon, from 1 plough which is there, and from 7 fisheries in the Wye and the Usk'. The details of Caerleon rightly belong in DB Glos. and may have been included in Herefordshire in error since William has no fief in Gloucestershire. It is also possible that the land in the castlery was remote from the castle, within Herefordshire proper; see 1,48 note and Introductory Note 3. The mention that the land was waste TRE is puzzling, for if the castlery was at Caerleon, it is unlikely that King Edward formally held it as part of his kingdom of England before 1066, although he had begun to establish client kingdoms in the area (see Introductory Note 2). The erection of Monmouth and Chepstow Castles are due to Earl William (1067–1071) and it is unlikely that Caerleon Castle, occupying a forward position, was of an earlier date. The land here was possibly devastated, like Archenfield, by Gruffydd and Bleddyn (1,49 note) or by Caradoc ap Gruffydd ap Rhydderch in his raid on Portskewett in 1065 (see DB Glos. W 2 (col. 162a) and note).

THURSTAN. Probably Thurstan son of Rolf who held other land in the Caerleon area; DB Glos. W 18 (col. 162b): 'Thurstan son of Rolf ... has 6 carucates of land beyond the Usk'.

2 MALE SLAVES, 1 FEMALE. There is no full-stop after *ancilla*, although Farley prints one, and the rest of the line has been left blank in the MS, perhaps for details of 'resources' to be added if and when available.

WASTE. In the MS *Wasta*; Farley prints *wasta*. The scribe frequently, especially in Shropshire, uses a large *W* in *Wasta, Wastata* etc., even in the middle of a phrase, where Farley prints a small *w*. It is not always possible to tell whether the scribe intended a capital, as he writes many sizes of *w*; attention is therefore not drawn elsewhere in these notes to apparent discrepancies between Farley and the MS on this point.

14,2   WILLIAM ALSO HOLDS. Repeated at the beginning of 14,2–12.

MAUND. Maund (Bryan). DBH has a marginal *Maga ... Nicol'*, found as *Magene Nicholae* in 1195. The same holding is 1 hide at *Magene Brian'* in 1243, Fees p. 805; see DBH p. 53 and p. 105 note. On 'Maund' see 7,5 note.

3 SMALLHOLDERS. In the MS *ii/* has been corrected from *ii*, the original final dot being still visible under the last *i* of *ii/*.

MEADOW FOR THE OXEN. See 7,3 note.

THE CLERKS OF ST. GUTHLAC'S CLAIM. Their holdings at Hinton and Felton (6,3;6) are close by.

14,3   BROADWARD. If correctly identified (see 1,28 note) Broadward (like Newton 14,4) was divided between the great manor of Leominster and the Hundred of Thornlaw. Although Broadward seems separated from Thornlaw Hundred by Leominster members, and Newton nearly so, such intrusions of ecclesiastical manors into 'secular' Hundreds are not unusual in Herefordshire, Worcestershire and Gloucestershire (see Introductory Note 7).

14,4   NEWTON. In Hope under Dinmore parish. Another part of the same village was held by William from the King in 1,25, having formerly been a part of the great manor of Leominster. In DBH p. 54 the marginal annotator has entered *H. de Crofta* as the holder of this land as of the Leominster share. The same man holds *Wafreton* and *Newton* from the Honour of Dilwyn in FA ii p. 381 and in Fees p. 798). *Wafreton* is Wharton (*Wavertune*, DB 1,24). WHICH PAYS TAX ... See 1,9 note.

BROWN. DB *Bruns*, probably from OE *Brun*, PNDB p. 210. DBH p. 54 has *Brunus*. See 1,25 note.

14,6 POSTON. DB *Poscetenetune*, DBH (p. 54, margin) *Pocintona*. Poston House has been mapped and indexed in this volume. There is a Poston Court Farm on the western side of the river, GR SO 3537. See 10,18 and 23,3 notes.

IN THE GOLDEN VALLEY. It would seem that the scribe failed to leave room on the first line of the entry for the heading *In Valle de Stratelei'* and so had to incorporate it in the entry rather belatedly. The rest of the entry is neat, however. The rubricator seems to have been unsure as to the scribe's intention for the 'heading' because the *I* of *In* and the *V* of *Valle* are outlined in red, rather than a red line being drawn through the words as with normal hundred headings and place-names. See 2,54 note.

14,8 DILWYN. Like Broadward and Newton (14,3-4 above) Dilwyn was divided between
-9 Leominster and an ordinary territorial Hundred. Though later in Stretford Hundred, there is no reason to doubt the Elsdon Hundred head at 14,7. Dilwyn will have been separated from its Hundred by the intrusion of Luntley, another member of Leominster manor. See 1,26 note.

14,10 LATER 15[s]. See 7,5 note.

14,12 MARSTON (STANNETT). The identification is uncertain. VCH identifies 'Marston' without specifying; DG chooses Marston in Pembridge (27,1 note). The descent of some of William's manors is obscure, but there is no Marston in Staple Hundred (14,10 Hundred head). In Fees p. 1482 *Hugo de Croft*, who holds other Ch. 14 lands (see 14,4 note) holds Marston in Broxash Hundred, that is, Marston Stannett in the 1086 Hundred of Plegelgate. *Hugo* is said to hold from the Honour of Weobley and it may be that the Lacy family, who held another part of Marston Stannett (10,71 note), had acquired William of Écouis' portion without disturbing the sub-tenancy. Although the text of DB lacks a Plegelgate Hundred at this point, Plegelgate places tend to be entered at this point in individual fiefs (see Introductory note 7).

Ch.15 WILLIAM SON OF BADERON. The *caput* of his lands was Monmouth Castle of which he was keeper. See 1,48 and note.

15,1 HOPE (MANSELL). A marginal note in DBH has *H. Maloisel* as the later tenant, DBH p. 55 and p. 106 note. The land was granted by King William to Wihenoc of Monmouth, see Round CDF pp. 403-11.

ST. PETER'S CHURCH OF GLOUCESTER. The Abbey seems to have recovered its land, since it is found holding here in Fees p. 800 and FA ii p. 383.

15,2 WILLIAM ALSO HOLDS. Repeated at the beginning of 15,2-10.

RUARDEAN. This village was in Herefordshire in 1086 but had been transferred to Gloucestershire by 1316 (*Nomina villarum* in FA ii p. 275), probably at the time of the extensive forest clearings that took place under Edward I. The whole area between the Severn and the Wye appears originally to have been in Herefordshire, see Introductory Note 4.

HADWIC. DB *Hadeuui*; see 10,62 and PNDB p. 282.

15,3 LINTON, THE KING'S MANOR. See 1,1 note.

LEVEL WITH THE LAST LINE of this entry, which is written on the bottom marginal ruling, and in the left margin on the extreme edge of the parchment are written the words *... ƚm'cū barba*, the rest of the word/words being lost due to bleeding of the MS; *ƚm'* probably is the end of *Wiƚƚm'* making the reading "William with a beard". They seem to have been written by the same scribe as the rest and were probably a note to add something. See DBH p. 107 note on Linton; cf. Bardsley pp. 88,821. In DB Cambs. 20,1 Gilbert, a sub-tenant of Robert of Tosny, is described as *cum barba* in the *Inquisitio Comitatus Cantabrigiensis* (ed. N. E. S. A. Hamilton, 1876) p. 42.

15,4 (MUCH) MARCLE, THE KING'S MANOR. See 1,7 note.

15,5 VALUE. In the MS the scribe wrote 3 strokes of a *W* for the first letter of *Valet*, presumably influenced by the two *W*'s above; Farley corrects to a *V*.

15,6 STRETTON (GRANDISON). In FA ii p. 379 William *de Grande Sono* holds Ashperton (see 15,8) and Stretton from the Barony of Monmouth.

15,8 ASHPERTON ... 5½ HIDES. The land recurs in Fees (p. 808) as 5 hides in *Asperton* and *Strattun'*, held of the Monmouth fee, probably implying that some of the land was in Stretton Grandison. But see 15,6 note.

15,10 MUNSLEY. Part of the land was at *Maynestun'* or *Maineston*, Mainstone in Munsley (GR SO 6539), held in Fees from the Honour of Monmouth (p. 808), see VCH i p. 336 note 91. DBH (p. 56 and p. 108 note) has a marginal entry *item in Hundeslawa di' h'*, referring to an unidentified place.

1½ HIDES; THEY PAY TAX. *Ibi i hida 7 dimid' geld' 7* in the MS; Farley does not print the final *7*, which was probably inserted at the same time as the *geld'* was interlined.

Ch.16 WILLIAM SON OF NORMAN. He held land in Archenfield 1,53–55 with his *caput* at Kilpeck. He seems to have had some responsibility for supervising the Forest of Dean (1,63; cf. DB Glos. 37,3). His descendants hold land in Little Taynton "for keeping the hay [see 2,23 note] of Hereford" and his son Hugh is described as 'son of William the forester of Herefordshire'; see VCH i pp. 276-77.

16,1 MUNSLEY. The land was at Court y Park in Munsley (GR SO 6439). In Fees (p. 808) Eleanor *de Parco* holds 1 hide *in villa de Parco* of Hugh of Kilpeck. See VCH i p. 336 note 92 and DBH p. 108 note.

16,2 HOPTON (SOLLERS). The land will have included both Hopton Sollers and Lower Hopton; see DBH p. 108 note.

16,3 7 SMALLHOLDERS WITH 3 PLOUGHS. In the MS *vii* has been corrected from *iii; iii* has been corrected from *ii* (the interlined *b,* for *-bus* for *duabus/tribus*).

16,4 ½ HIDE ... See 1,9 note.

MARDEN, THE KING'S MANOR. See 1,4 note.

Ch.17 THURSTAN SON OF ROLF. Perhaps the standard-bearer at the battle of Hastings (Ellis DTG pp. 186–7) who was rewarded with land in Gloucestershire, Somerset, Dorset, Herefordshire and other counties.

17,1 ALVINGTON. On the western shore of the river Severn, now in Gloucestershire. The land remained for a time in Herefordshire after the area between the Severn and the Wye had been mostly transferred to Gloucestershire before 1086, see Introductory Note 4. Since Alvington was held by Brictric TRE and therefore probably from Earl Harold, William son of Osbern may well have administered the land as palatine Earl, keeping it in Herefordshire as he had transferred other lands (see 1,39–47 and Introductory Note 2; DBH p. 57 and p. 109 note). EPNS (Glos.) iii p. 249 does not cite the DB reference.

6 HIDES ... See 1,9 note.

20 BLOOMS OF IRON. DB *Bloma*, also *plumba* (as in DB Somerset 17,3). A dish used as a measure for ore; afterwards the due payable on the measure. See 1,7 note on 'lumps of iron' (*massas ferri*).

17,2 (LITTLE) MARCLE. A marginal note in DBH reads *In Eilinetona*, that is, Aylton (GR SO 6537) a mile to the north-west of Little Marcle; DBH p. 57 and p. 110 note. Much Marcle (1,7 etc.) was in Winstree Hundred.

ANOTHER THURSTAN. *Alter* should strictly mean 'the other', but see 19,2 where *alter quidam* means 'another man', a sense strictly covered by *alius*. Further examples of *alter* meaning 'another' are to be found at 2,48. 6,8 and 31,5.

Ch.18 ALBERT OF LORRAINE. Also known as Albert the Clerk, see DB Rutland R21 note.

18,1 UPLEADON. DB *Ledene; Upledena* in the margin of DBH p. 57 (see p. 110 note). Part or all of the village had probably belonged to the Church of Worcester (see 10,5 note). Part of the land was at *Kantel* (Catley GR SO 6844) held with *Hupledene* in Fees p. 808.

Ch.[19]. THE CHAPTER NUMBER is mistakenly given as *ix* in the MS. There is no question of the first *x* being cut off, as this is the fold of two pages of parchment.

ALFRED OF MARLBOROUGH. A Norman whose family settled in Herefordshire under the Confessor. Nephew of the Norman Osbern "Pentecost" (19,3 below) and father-in-law of Thurstan of Wigmore (19,10 below). Ewyas Harold Castle was the head of his Honour. Apart from Pencombe (19,6) which he held himself before 1066, Alfred's lands had been held by Earl (later King) Harold. They were no doubt conferred on him by William son of Osbern and with them he acquired Harold's responsibility for the frontier with Wales. His fief is variously divided at his death, some lands falling to Harold son of Earl Ralph.

19,1 EWYAS (HAROLD) ... REFORTIFIED. DBH has a marginal entry *Ewias Haroldi* (p. 58 and p. 110 note); the distinctive name probably being derived from Harold, son of the Earl Ralph who was nephew of Edward the Confessor and first Earl of Hereford. The Castle may have been the one mentioned in 1052 in ASC (D version) p. 176 at the time of Gruffydd's invasion of Herefordshire. It was probably Osbern Pentecost's castle (ASC (E version) p. 181, see Round FE pp. 323–324), a Norman castle built in the days of Edward the Confessor by Osbern the uncle of Alfred of Marlborough (19,3). The refortification mentioned here was probably a result of Gruffydd's attack (see Introductory Notes 2 and 3). Harold son of Earl Ralph founded the priory of Ewyas Harold *c*. 1100 as a cell of St. Peter's, Gloucester; see 1,56 note and Walker *Register* p. 6ff.

5 CARUCATES OF LAND. In the MS *car* (the abbreviation for both *carucata* and *carruca*) was originally written and then extended to *carucatas*, but the abbreviation mark was not erased.

5 OTHER CARUCATES AT MONNINGTON. 5 hides are mentioned at Monnington in 19,4, possibly a confusion about the same piece of land (see Introductory Note 3).
RALPH OF BERNAY. See 1,2 note.
12 SMALLHOLDERS WHO WORK 1 DAY A WEEK. The only reference to week-work in DB, though later evidence suggests that it was common; Lennard p. 370 note 1.
FISHERIES; MEADOW, 22 ACRES. Both the object of *habent*, as smallholders were probably also.

19,2 ALFRED ALSO HOLDS. Repeated at the beginning of 19,2-10.
BURGHILL. Mr. Coplestone-Crow points out that six of the eight hides are accounted for in Fees pp. 802-3 by two at *Tulintun'*, two in *Burchull'* and two in *Burwelton'*, that is, at Tillington (GR SO 4645), Burghill and Burlton (GR SO 4844).
ANOTHER MAN. See 17,2 note.
THIRD PENNY. A third of the revenue from the pleas, to which the Earl (Harold) had been entitled as holder of this manor; see Round GM p. 291. See also C 12 note above.
TWO HUNDREDS. Burghill is in Cutsthorn Hundred; Stretford Hundred, divided into two parts, was contiguous on the western side. For a similar entry, see 19,10 below. In DB Somerset 1,13 the third penny of the 'borough-right' of 4 Hundreds was attached to the manor of Old Cleeve.

19,3 BRINSOP. DB *Hope*. DBH (p. 58 and p. 112 note) has a marginal *Bruneshop'*.
15 SMALLHOLDERS. Or possibly '16'; the usual dot after a figure is large here and written level with the top of the *xv*, probably in error. A similar large dot occurs in 24,6 (see note to it below); cf. 2,30 note.
OSBERN. Osbern "Pentecost"; see Ch. 19 note.
AFTER GODWIN AND HAROLD HAD BEEN EXILED. Earl Godwin and all his sons (Swein, Tosti, Gyrth, Harold and Leofwin) were banished in 1050 (ASC (C version) p. 172). They were restored to power in 1052. Earl Godwin died the next year (see 1,74 note).

19,4 5 HIDES ... See notes to 19,1 and 1,9.
19,5 BREDWARDINE. DB *Brocheurdie*. DBH has *Brodewordin* in the margin of p. 59 (see p. 113 note). J.F. (starting from Ekwall's discussion of the name Bredwardine in *Studies* pp. 133-135, and comparing Brobury 10,54, *Brocheberie* DB) subjected these spellings to careful analysis, and concluded ". . if *Brocheurdie* is Bredwardine, the place probably bore alternative names in the 12th century, one with the OE el. *brōc* ['a marsh, water-meadow, stream'] or the pers.n. *Broca*, and the other with the el. *bre(o)rd* (<*bre(o)d*) [OE, 'brim, margin, rim; shore, bank, brink'; cf. Brierley 1,10a note]. The second el. of the forms from DBH onwards is OE *worthign* 'an enclosure, a curtilage', an el. common in the West Midland counties, particularly Herefordshire and Shropshire. The DB form in *-urdie*, on the other hand, seems to suggest OE *worthig, wurthig* 'an enclosure', apparently in dative singular. This might support the argument that the DB form represents a different name, i.e., *Broc-wurthig* or *Brocan-wurthig*, as against DBH and subsequent *Breordworthign*".
5 HIDES ... See 1,9 note.

19,6 THESE ENTRIES are written in a compressed way in the MS.
-8

19,6 THE UNNAMED MANOR is given as *Pencumba*, that is, Pencombe (GR SO 5952), in a marginal entry in DBH p. 59 (see p. 113 note). 15 hides in Pencombe are held of the Honour of Ewyas in Fees p. 806. Land here may formerly have belonged to Worcester Church, see 10,5 note.
HIS DAUGHTER. Agnes, wife of Thurstan of Wigmore, who also held (Much) Cowarne from her father (19,10). See the *History of St. Peter's, Gloucester* i pp. 107;115 for a grant to that monastery by her and her son Eustace of 1 hide in Pencombe. Eustace is called *filius Thurstini Flandrensis* there, thus proving that Thurstan of Wigmore and Thurstan of Flanders were one and the same.
21 VILLAGERS. *xxi uill(anu)s*; the singular occurs regularly in DB with the figures 21,31 etc.

19,7 (HILL OF) EATON. In Foy. *Edtune* DB, *Eatona* DBH p. 59 (margin), *Ettone* DBH p. 59 (text). Formerly *Eton Tregos* (FA ii p. 383). In Fees (p. 801) 2½ hides are held from the Honour of Ewyas in Greytree Hundred which later absorbed Bromsash Hundred. J.F. observes, "The name [Eaton] is composed of the OE els. *ēa* 'a river, a stream' and *tūn* 'a farmstead', an appropriate enough description of this place near the Wye. The DB form *EDTUNE* is probably due to scribal misreading of a form *EATUNE*, since the two letters D, A, are quite similar in the majuscule script used for the names of manors in DB. The DBH form *Ettone* may be an unsuccessful attempt to correct the DB form, or it may show that the scribe was copying from dictation, hearing *Edtune* as *Ettune*". See 29,20 note.
6 SMALLHOLDERS. In the MS *vi* has been corrected from *iii*.

19,8 PEMBRIDGE. DBH p. 59 has a marginal note *Item in Morcote*, referring to Moorcot
(GR SO 3555), a couple of miles south-west of Pembridge. This rules out identification
with Pembridge in Bromsash Hundred (VCH i p. 338 note 94a; Lord Rennell VM p. 39) and
makes it necessary to restore a Hundred head to the text. Neither Marston (27,1) nor
Pembridge is entered under a Hundred head; both were later in Stretford Hundred which
contained places from both Elsdon and Hazeltree Hundreds. The 1086 boundary between
these latter Hundreds was probably the river Arrow and on this assumption both Marston
and Pembridge have been mapped and indexed in Elsdon Hundred. Pembridge is, however,
associated with Staunton on Arrow on the other bank of the river in LSR and if the older
identification of Weston (9,13) as Weston in Pembridge is maintained, both Pembridge and
Marston will have been in Hazeltree Hundred in 1086.
IF IT HAD PRODUCED (MAST). *si fructificasset*, literally 'if it had borne fruit', the
particular fruit being that of the oak, beech, chestnut and other forest trees on which the
swine fed. VCH i p. 295 paraphrases "in a good season".
CANONS OF ST. GUTHLAC'S CLAIM ... See 2,12 note on Earl Harold's appropriation
of church land.
VALUE NOW £10 10s. In the MS the *x* in *x sot* has probably been altered from another
figure and the *sot* is written in the right margin.
19,9 WOODLAND. No extent is given. Compare 29,16 below where an explanation is added
silva, sed quantitas non fuit dicta.
19,10 (MUCH) COWARNE. DB *Cuure* for OE *Cuuren (cū, aern)* 'cow-house'. The two later
Cowarnes seem to be distinguished in DB by their being placed in different Hundreds.
DBH (p. 114 note) is inclined to think that this entry covers both. Certainly *Colgre* is a
different name from *Cowarne* (see 7,8 note).
THURSTAN OF WIGMORE. See 9,2 note.
THREE HUNDREDS. Compare 19,2 where the Hundreds are named. (Much) Cowarne is
close to the junction of Radlow, Plegelgate and Thornlaw Hundreds.
HAS BEEN REMOVED. In the MS *abblaī est* in error for *ablaī est*.
Ch.20 ALFRED OF 'SPAIN'. *Hispan(iensis)*, also *de Hispania* in 20,1. He came from Épaignes in
the département of Eure, France; OEB pp. 92,134. The Latin *Hispaniensis* is a kind of word-
play. He held land also in Dorset, Devon, Somerset, Wiltshire and Gloucestershire.
20,2 ALFRED ALSO HOLDS 1 HIDE. In Netherwood, Duncumb ii p. 203.
Ch.21 ANSFRID OF CORMEILLES. Cormeilles in the département of Eure, France. He owes his
holding in Herefordshire to Earl William, see Introductory Note 2.
21,1 TARRINGTON. See 10,36 note.
21,2 ANSFRID ALSO HOLDS. Repeated at the beginning of 21,2–7.
VALUE ... 8s. In the MS *viii* has been corrected from another figure: there are two minims
visible under the *v*.
21,3 ASTON (INGHAM) ... 2 HIDES. DBH (p. 61; see p. 116 note) has a marginal *Estona ... Hing'*.
In Fees p. 100 *Eston'* is held by Richard *Ingan* and in Fees p. 800 *Estun' Ingan* is held by
Roger *de Estun'* from the Honour of Cormeilles. The 2 hides may be a duplicate of those
mentioned at 1,1. Although the details of villagers and ploughs differ, King Edward held
both before 1066.
21,4 (SOLLERS) HOPE. A marginal entry in DBH (p. 61; see p. 116 note) has *Hop' ... Solers*. In
Fees (p. 801) it is *Hope Solers* held from the fee of Cormeilles.
HAGEN. OScand *Hagni, Hogni*, see Fellows-Jensen p. 122. OG *Hagona, Hagana, Hagena*, see
Forssner p. 138.
21,6 REVER HELD IT ... *Reuer* is probably a British name, the first element being Welsh *rhew*
'cold', PNDB p. 348. There is no dot in the MS after *tenuit*, but an erasure which extends
almost to the end of the line; the space may have been left intentionally.
2 HIDES ... See 1,9 note.
THE THIRD PART OF 2 MILLS. See 10,19 note. The *redd'* is more likely to abbreviate
reddens than *reddentium* (to agree with the 2 mills) in view of the values given in 10,19
and 25,2. See DB Dorset General Notes 55,13.
WHICH PAYS 14s 8d. In the MS there is an erasure before *xiii sot*; the *redd'* was interlined
because the space left was not sufficient. Below the *r* is a hair-line (rather wavy because of
being written over the erasure) to indicate the correct position in the text of *redd'*; Farley
does not print it, though it is frequently his policy to show hair-lines (as, for example, with
the interlined *non* in 29,3 below).
21,7 CLEHONGER. DB *Cleunge*; DBH gives a more recognisable form in the margin (p. 62; see
p. 117 note) *Clahungra* ('Clayhanger'). The village seems to have been divided between
Stretford Hundred and Dinedor in 1086 (see 26,2). It has been mapped in the former which
contains 5 of its 6 hides.

IN LORDSHIP 2 PLOUGHS. There is an erasure in the MS between *car'* and 7 *iii uilli* and the scribe has drawn in a line, not shown by Farley (as also at 1,65, though he prints a similar one in 29,16) to join up the two phrases. It is possible that the whole line was written over an erasure.

Ch.22 DURAND OF GLOUCESTER. Durand of Pîtres, constable of Gloucester Castle (*History of St. Peter's, Gloucester* i p. lxxvi) and Sheriff of Gloucestershire in 1086 (called Durand the Sheriff in DB Glos. G 4). He succeeded his brother Roger as Sheriff, see 22,8 and 1,61 note. He seems to have been dead by 1095 as his nephew Walter was holding most of his lands by that date; see D. Walker HEH pp. 174, 179 and D. Walker CEH pp. 37-8.

22,4 COLDBOROUGH. DB *Calcheberge*. Later evidence suggests the identification of this place, which must be in Bromsash Hundred; see DBH p. 117 note. J.McN.D. observes, "The divergence in modern and 11th century spelling may be more apparent than real; *calche-* could be a misreading of *calde-* from an original return; hence OE *(aet) calde beorge* or *(aet thaem) caldan beorge* '(place at) cold barrow or hill'. Otherwise, *Calche-* [*kælkϸ*] looks like OE (Anglian) *calc* 'chalk, limestone', perhaps in a derivative suffixed form *calcen* 'made of limestone'; this raises questions of geology or archaeology".
GUNNAR. *Gunuer*; the second *u* is obviously a scribal error for *n* (making *Gunner*), as the *Isdem* indicates he is the same person as the *Gunner* of 22,2-3; see PNDB p. 277 s.n. *Gunnarr*.

22,5 ROCHFORD. Part or all of the village had formerly belonged to Worcester Church; see 10,5 note. Rochford was transferred to Worcestershire in 1837; see Introductory Note 4.
AND HIS NEPHEW WALTER TOO. Walter of Pîtres, Sheriff of Gloucestershire after Durand, though perhaps not immediately; see Round FE p. 313. He was also known later as Walter the Constable and was constable of Gloucester Castle like his uncle (*History of St. Peter's, Gloucester* i p. lxxvi). See G. H. White 'The Household of the Norman Kings' in TRHS 4th ser. vol. xxx (1948) pp. 149-151. His son Miles became Earl of Hereford in 1141. The scribe appears initially to have omitted Walter as co-holder with his uncle, hence the word order.

22,6 BERNARD FROM HIM. The Latin should read *de eis* 'from them', as in 22,5.

22,7 THRUXTON. DB *Torchestone*; DBH has *Turchelestune* in the text and *Turkelestona* in the margin (see p. 63 and p. 118 note). The place-name contains the OScand personal name *Thorkell* in an anglicized form.

22,8 REVER HELD IT, AND ALWIN. In the MS 7 *Aluuin* appears to have been added (a dot is visible under the 7), hence the singular *tenuit*; see 10,72 note.
1 HIDE ... See 1,9 note.
ROGER OF PÎTRES. Durand's brother; see notes to Ch. 22 and 1,61.

Ch.23 DROGO SON OF POYNTZ. Founder of the House of Clifford, see VCH i p. 278.

23,1 ROCHFORD. See 22,5 note.

23,2 DROGO ALSO HOLDS. Repeated at the beginning of 23,2-6.
[IN THE GOLDEN VALLEY]. A Hundred head has been omitted above 23,2 which is certainly identifiable and 23,3-4 are probably also in the same Hundred. The erasure noted in 23,4 could be a misplaced Hundred name, later erased but not replaced.
DORSTONE. DB *Dodintune*; DBH p. 64 has *Dodintone* in the text and an explanatory *id est Dorsinton'* in the margin, which confirms the identification and is evidence of a name-change, from *Dod(d)ing-* 'called after *Dodda*' or 'after a *dod* (hill)', to *Dorsing-* 'called after *Dēorsige*'. *Dorsynton* in Webtree Hundred is held from the Barony of Clifford in FA ii p. 380.

23,3 *BURCSTANESTUNE*. From the OE masculine personal name *Burgstān* and *tūn*. DBH (p. 64) has a marginal *Burstanestona*; but the place remains unidentified. It is possible that this was part of Poston, held as *Puteston'* by Walter *de Scudemor* from the Honour of *Toenei* and Clifford in Fees p. 813; see 14,6 note. A holding of Drogo at Poston is not otherwise accounted for in DB.
ALFHILD. DB *Elfild*, see PNDB p. 175.
3 HIDES ... See 1,9 note.

23,4 MYNYDDBRYDD. In the MS there is an erasure after this place-name, extending almost to the end of the line, with some ink spilt there as well. *Ruuenore* DB; *Ruuenoure* DBH p. 64 where also there is a marginal gloss *Rugenoura* with a later addition *Fagemeneda* written above. The later survey (DBH p. 78) has *Rogenoura*. J.F. observes that *Ruuenore*, listed as the fourth manor in Drew fitz Pons's fief under the heading for Wolphy Hundred, cannot actually have been in that Hundred, for DBH p. 119 indicates that only the first of those manors could have been therein and that the erasure noted by the County editors may have contained another Hundred name [see 23,2 note]. He identifies *Ruuenore*: '*Ruuenore* probably represents OE *rūwan-ofre* .. "at the rough slope" (v. PNE s.vv. *rūh*, *ofer²*). In DBH the word *Fagemeneda* .... written above the marginal form *Rugenoura* .... apparently represents an alternative name of the place ... to be connected with *Fowemenede* 1327,

Fowmynd 1577, *Vowmynd* 1786 (Bannister PNHe p. 141). B. G. Charles (A&B p. 94) states that this is still a locally current name for the place now ... on maps as Mynydd Brith (SO 2740) near Dorstone 23,2 above. *Fowemenede* and DBH *Fagemenede* represent the OE adj. *fāg* "variegated, multi-coloured, coloured" and Welsh *mynydd* .... "a mountain, a hill", ... modern Welsh *Mynydd Brith* "speckled hill" is an almost direct translation of this. DB *Ruuenore* is thus to be regarded as a lost place-name in, or supplanted by, Vowmynd or Mynydd Brith'. The modern settlement Mynyddbrydd lies on the north-east slope of the hill (GR SO 2841). The locality is marked as 'The Township of Vowmine' on Bryant's map of 1835.

1 HIDE. *Ibi ē i hida* is written over an erasure; a ⁷ abbreviation sign (not printed by Farley) remains above the *a* of *hida*.

23,5 'HANLEYS (END)'. This Winstree Hundred holding reappears in Fees p. 808 as 1 hide held in Radlow Hundred from the Honour of Clifford and appears to be distinct from the Hanley in Plegelgate Hundred (10,75 note). In addition to 'Hanleys End', a place now lost, but found on the first edition one-inch OS map of 1832 (sheet 55, 1970 reprint sheet 50) in Cradley parish, there was a 'Hanley' at GR SO 6643 in Canon Frome (OS first edition map of 1831, sheet 43; 1969 reprint sheet 59).

1 BURGESS. The burgess may well have been in Hereford.

23,6 MATHON. See 10,39 note. This entry may have been added slightly later: study of the MS shows that it has been squeezed in above the last ruled line and the whole entry (like 25,2 the final one in the adjacent column) looks different from the others in the column, although this is due to the parchment's being shiny here rather than rough.

Ch.24 OSBERN SON OF RICHARD. Son of Richard Scrope (12,1 note) and Lord of Richards Castle. In later Feodaries, many of his lands are held of the Honour of Richards Castle (*Castrum Richardi*) which assists the identification of some places.

24,1 MILTON. In Pembridge, 2 hides being held there in Fees p. 804 in the later Stretford Hundred, from the Honour of Richards Castle.

24,2 2 HIDES ... See 1,9 note.

1 WATER-MEADOW. *Ibi est una broce*; *broce* is probably a scribal mistake for the nom. sing. *broca*, although it is possible that *broce* is gen. sing. and a word such as *acra* has been omitted in error after *una*, or that it is nom. pl. representing a clumsy transposition of a reported item *broce*: *ibi est una*. In all these cases and in DB Glos. 19,2, Dorset 31,1. 34,5 and Leics. 13,18 *broca* is a first declension Latinization of OE *broc*. In DB Derbys. 1,26 (and perhaps 2,1) the form is *broces* which is the gen. sing. of the OE masc. *a*-stem noun *broc*. *Broc* came to mean "a brook", but originally the word (like its cognates MDu, Du *brock*, LG *brok*, OHG and Mod.G *bruch*) meant "marsh, bog" etc., a sense retained by *brook* "water-meadow" in the Mod.E dialects of Kent, Sussex and Surrey and in medieval field names in Cambridgeshire and Essex and in some place-names; see DEPN s.v. *broc*. The river Lugg runs north and west of Byton and there is marsh to the south at Combe Moor.

24,3 BRADLEY. Now represented only by Bradley's Cottage on the 6-in. OS map: see Lord Rennell VM pp. 58-63.

TITLEY. Another part of the village is 24,6 in Elsdon Hundred; see Lord Rennell DM p. 134; VM pp. 63-66.

(LITTLE) BRAMPTON. So called to distinguish the place from Brampton Bryan which was in Shropshire in 1086.

(LOWER) HARPTON. *Hercope* DB; *Herecopton* in later records (Lord Rennell DM p. 145; VM pp. 70-71) associated with Knill manor and eventually merged with it. The place-name probably represents an OE place-name in *hop* 'a valley' with, say, the OE personal name *Hēahrīc* or *Hearca*, to which ME *ton* (OE *tūn*) is added. ME *Herecopton*, reduced to *Harpton*, seems to be the origin of the name which, at some juncture as yet unascertained, has replaced *Ortune*/'Horton' (9,13 note s.v. Harpton) and *Hertune*/'Horton' (see next note). HARPTON. *Hertune* DB; *Hortona* DBH p. 65 margin. See 9,13 note and preceding note on Lower Harpton. Harpton is now in Wales, Lower Harpton remains in Herefordshire.

CLATTERBRUNE. Thus DG. *Clatretune* DB represents OE *tūn* with an early instance of the el. *clater* 'loose stones; a clatter; a noisy stream' (see PNE pt. i s.v.), named from the Clatterbrook, the river which flows immediately to the south of Presteigne. The name now survives as a house-name Clatterbrune House (age of name not yet known, etymology not yet ascertained).

QUERENTUNE. Probably representing OE *cweorn-tūn* 'mill-stone farm' — a mill-site or a place noted for having or quarrying millstones; but a different commodity may be on hand. If the form were a mistake for *Quenen-*, the first el. could be OE *cwene*, genitive singular *cwenan*, 'a woman, a quean'. The site is quite unknown. Lord Rennell in VM p. 73 and DM p. 146 speculates on the possible 'itinerary' of the DB Commissioners.

CASCOB. ½ hide is listed here in DB Shropshire 5,6 held by Osbern in Leintwardine Hundred. It is not certain that the entries duplicate each other.

THE WELSH MARCH. See 9,13 note and Introductory Note 1.

24,4 LYE. See 1,10c note.

24,5 WASTE LANDS. The lands have been waste long enough for a wood suitable for hunting to grow. The devastation in this area was probably caused during the invasion of Gruffydd ap Llywelyn recorded by the Anglo-Saxon Chronicle for 1052 (see Introductory Note 2).
HAS FROM IT WHAT HE CAN CATCH. See 29,16 below for a similar right; cf. DB Worcs. 2,15;22.

24,6 TITLEY. See 24,3 note.
LAND FOR 6 PLOUGHS. Or possibly '7 ploughs': there is a large dot after *vi* in the MS, written level with the top of the *vi* instead of in its usual position level with the bottom. See 19,3 note.

24,7 NEWTON. The place is said to be near Bredwardine in VCH and near Clifford in DG. The DB village is in Stretford Hundred and this identifies Newton in Dilwyn, held as ½ hide in Fees p. 804 from the Honour of Richards Castle.
RICHARD SCROPE. See 12,1 note.
3 OXEN. See 1,50 note.

24,8 STAUNTON (ON ARROW). The Staple Hundred head points to Staunton on Wye (see 10,55;57), but the marginal entry in DBH p. 65 *Vure Stanton ' et Maldelega* points to Staunton on Arrow, in Hazeltree Hundred (see 9,11). *Vure* is 'Upper' (OE *uferra* adjective 'higher, over'), perhaps a temporary distinction from the other Staunton, perhaps indicating that this holding was on the hill above the river. *Maldelega* must be Mowley (GR SO 3360) in Staunton parish. Mr. Coplestone-Crow cites an *Inquisitio post mortem* of 1287 (ii no. 640), where this holding appears as Staunton and *Moldelege*.
SEISYLL. DB *Saissil, Saisi*, probably from OW *Seisill*; PNDB p. 351.

24,10 WHYLE. See 10,15 note.

24,11 LYDE. See 2,44 note. The holding was *Lyde Prior*, the monks of Hereford annotated in the margin of DBH (p. 66) being of St. Peter's, Hereford.
ROGER (OF) LACY. In the interlineation *de* has been omitted in error before *Laci*.
SEISYLL. See 24,8 note.

24,12 LUDFORD. A Wolphy Hundred head has apparently been omitted, since in Fees (p. 809) land is held in *Ludeford* of the Honour of Richards Castle; see VCH i p. 341 note 102. The area was later transferred to Shropshire, see Introductory Note 4.

24,13 (RICHARDS) CASTLE. For *Auretone*, see 12,2 note. For the castle see Introductory Note 3.

Ch.25 GILBERT SON OF THOROLD. Probably the same man as Gilbert of Bouillé (see DB Warwicks. B 2 note). He was a fairly important follower of Earl William, holding land in Worcestershire, Gloucestershire and Somerset, as well as the odd manor in Warwickshire, Cambridgeshire and Essex. In DB Worcs. 11,2 (Sheriffs Lench) he is said to have collected the gold for the King's use (*qui aurum recepit ad opus regis*).

25,2 GILBERT ALSO HOLDS. Repeated at the beginning of 25,2-6. See 23,6 note on the appearance of this entry.
THE THIRD PART OF A MILL. Almost certainly an error for 2 mills, the remaining two-thirds being given at 10,19 and 21,6 with the same revenue, 14s 8d.
WHICH PAYS. *redd(en)tis*, referring to the mill, but in fact it is the third part which is worth 14s 8d (see 10,19), the whole mill paying 44s.

25,4 (THE) BAGE. The principal medieval manor of Bach, formerly Bach or the Bach; the new (phonetic) spelling first appears on post-war 7th edition 1-in. OS maps. The name is common in the Golden Valley area. See Bannister PNHe p. 11; PNE pt. i s.v. *bece*.
3 HIDES ... See 1,9 note.
1 HAWK AND 2 DOGS. This render appears to take the place of the normal 'value' statement; see last note under 1,3 and 6,8 note.

25,5 MIDDLEWOOD. DB *Midewde*; DBH p. 67 has *Midelwude* in the margin; see 6,9 note.

25,6 TURNED BACK INTO WOODLAND. *in siluam est ... redacta*; or perhaps 'reverted to woodland', implying a natural process; cf. the woods grown on waste lands in 24,5 above.

25,7 112 PLOUGHS. This figure of 112 ploughs (a doubling of the hidage figure, as in other entries in the County) seems to be the ideal number if all the land were under cultivation. Much was waste in 1086 and less than 40 ploughs are mentioned in the entries relating to the Golden Valley (see next note).
56 HIDES. *lvi hidis*, ablative, interlined and in apposition to *In Valle Stradelie*. The total of hides for those places that seem to have been in the Golden Valley is 59 hides 2 virgates, represented by the entries at 2,54-56. 10,16-18. 14,6. 19,4-5. 23,2-4. 25,4-6. 29,6-10. Of these, 4 hides at 25,6 pay nothing. Such figure discrepancies in DB are not uncommon.

PAID TAX. Or perhaps 'pay tax', as *geld'* can abbreviate both the present and the past tenses. The subject is taken to be the 56 hides. *7 geld'* appears to have been added later (perhaps when the '56 hides' was interlined), as there is a full-stop after *carucẹ* and *geld'* is mostly written in the central margin and rather compressed; the addition must have been fairly early as *7 geld'* is lined through in red like the rest of the entry.

25,7 A WHOLE LINE between 25,7 and the Hundred head for 25,8 seems to have been erased,
-8 though the parchment is very rough all round here; Farley does not print the gap above the Hundred head.

25,8 *CHETESTOR*. Possibly a corruption of *Testestorp* (see 10,68 note), that is, Tedstone Delamere where 2 hides are held by William *de la Mare* from the Earl of Hereford in Fees p. 806. If this is so, part or all of the land may have belonged to the Church of Hereford, which had held 2½ hides at Tedstone (2,3 note).

25,9 2 HIDES ... EARL WILLIAM GAVE THESE. In the MS *hidẹ* is written over an erasure and is black and smeared; the *Has* has been added and is squeezed in before the *Com̄*.
A FORTIFIED HOUSE. See 10,46 note. The earthwork called Lemore Mount (GR SO 3151) in Eardisley may be the site in question, see Nelson p. 71 and VCH i pp. 226-227.

Ch.26 IN THE MS THIS CHAPTER NUMBER is written correctly as *xxvi*, but the red *i* is written on top of the large dark brown *I* of *Ilbertus* (the rubricator having begun the number too close to the text), which is probably why Farley missed it; it is not very clear in the facsimile either.

26,1 WULFWARD HELD IT ... In the MS there is a space for 3 or so letters after *tenuit*, perhaps left intentionally as there is no dot after *tenuit*.
1½ HIDES ... See 1,9 note.
6 SMALLHOLDERS. In the MS the *vi* has been corrected from some word or perhaps figure and is partially written in the right margin.

26,2 CLEHONGER. See 21,7 note. The land in Dinedor Hundred was probably at *Hunegarestun'* (Hungerstone GR SO 4435), held in Fees p. 812 by Robert *le Rus*, the margin of DBH giving *R. Rus* as holder of the manor (see DBH pp. 68,79).

Ch.27 HERMAN OF DREUX. Dreux is in the département of Eure-et-Loir, France.

27,1 MARSTON. Left unidentified by DG. The absence of a Hundred head makes it unclear whether the place was Marston in Pembridge (probably Elsdon Hundred in 1086, see 19,8 note) or Marston Stannett in Plegelgate Hundred (see 10,71. 14,12 and 32,1 notes). In Fees pp. 803,816, 2 hides in Marston are held in Stretford Hundred, a later amalgamation of Elsdon and Hazeltree Hundreds (see Introductory Note 7), from the Honour of Weobley by William Pichard. Although the Lacy family, whose lands later form the Honour of Weobley, hold Marston Stannett (10,71) only the present entry has sufficient hides to be represented in the Fees entry.

Ch.28 HUMPHREY OF BOUVILLE. DB *Buiuile* probably Bouville near Rouen in the département of Seine-Maritime, France, rather than one of the two Beuvilles in Calvados; see OEB p. 78.

Ch.29 HUGH DONKEY. *Lasne*, 'The Donkey', from OFr *asne* (which form occurs in 1,65 above; cf. Mod.Fr *âne*) and the French definite article; the Latin form *asinus* also occurs in DB, e.g., Worcs. Ch. 27. Hugh probably came to England with William son of Osbern and served under him defending the English border against the Welsh. His heirs are the Chandos family and his lands formed the later Honour of Snodhill named from the place in the Golden Valley (GR SO 3240) where a castle was built to guard the northern entrance to the valley. (See DBH pp. 84-85 note.) Snodhill was an exchange for Hatfield (1,11) with Malvern Priory (Mon. Ang. iii p. 448). Fees p. 814 gives a list of the Fees held of the Honour of Snodhill. Among them were a number of DB places together with *Turneston'* (Turnastone); *Wirkebrok* (Welbrook in Peterchurch), *Thurlokeshop'* (a lost place in Peterchurch) and *Haya Wiri* (Urishay), these latter probably corresponding to some of the places so far not identified in Hugh's DB holding.

29,1 FROM THE SAID WULFWY: *de Vluuino supradicto*: not 'Wulfwin' (OE *Wulfwine*) but OE *Wulfwig*; cf. DB Hunts. 2,7 *Vluuine episcopo* 'to Bishop Wulfwy (of Dorchester)'. See PNDB pp. 426-7.
LEASED 1 HIDE. The land is probably at Bunshill 31,3 although the details differ.
KING MAREDUDD. HIS SON GRUFFYDD. See Ch. 31 note.

29,2 HUGH ALSO HOLDS. Repeated at the beginning of 29,2-13;15-20.
FOWNHOPE. The land was granted by Hugh Donkey to the Church of Lyre, VCH i p. 276 note 80; Mon. Ang. vi p. 1093. 5½ hides are held at *Fauue Hope* in Fees (p. 801) of the Honour of Snodhill, possibly the 'member' here mentioned.
BETWEEN THEM ... 25 PLOUGHS. The Latin does not make it clear whether the ploughs are shared by just the reeve, smith and carpenter or by the villagers, smallholders and priests as well.

3 FISHERIES. *piscarias* (accusative) in error for *piscariae* (nominative).

29,3 ONE MANOR. DBH p. 69 (see p. 120 note) identifies this in a marginal note as *Acla monacorum de Lira*, Ocle Lyre now Livers Ocle (GR SO 5746). The confirmation grant by Henry I in 1100 is in Round CDF p. 135 no. 402. *Acle Lyre* is held in Fees (p. 807) from the Honour of Snodhill. Part or all of 'Ocle' had once belonged to Worcester Church, see 10,5 note.

4 SLAVES. *servos* (accusative) in error for *servi* (nominative).

29,4 ONE MANOR. A marginal note in DBH p. 69 (see p. 121 note) reads *In hida Willelmi*. The same phrase is applied to Westhide (8,8) and to *Lincumbe* (29,15) in DBH marginal notes, thus identifying this manor as a part of Westhide, where land is held in Fees (p. 809) of the Honour of Snodhill. Most of Westhide is in Radlow Hundred, but on the Thornlaw Hundred boundary and this portion appears to have been in the latter Hundred.

29,5 SUTTON. Part of Sutton St. Nicholas or Sutton St. Michael; see 7,3–4 note.

29,6 *BELTROU*. DBH p. 70 (see p. 121 note) has *Bestrov* in the text and *Benitrou* in the marginal addition. The place has not been identified but there is said to be a wood of similar name on the ridge above Wilmastone at Godway (GR SO 352410); see the article by Marshall. On the relationship of the three forms, J.F. observes a series of phonological and orthographical evolutions which would explain the variants and confirm their identity, but would leave the etymology in a 'highly speculative' state — between OFr *bel trove* 'beautiful find' (cf. the place-name Butterby in County Durham, DEPN) and OE **Bening-troh* or **Bening-treow* 'valley (lit. trough), or tree, at or called *Bening*', *Bening* being 'thing or place called after one *Benna*'. Gilbert of Bacton gave *Bautre* of the holding of Robert *de Chandos* to Dore Abbey (Mon. Ang. v p. 555) in whose possession DBH (p. 70) shows it.

29,7 *WLUETONE*. DBH has a marginal note (p. 70; see p. 121 note) *In Wuluetona ... Lenhal'* identifying the place with a part of Lyonshall in Peterchurch (GR SO 3539).
2 HIDES ... See 1,9 note. The gap is larger than appears in Farley, as *hidǫ* is written below *dimid'* in the line above.

29,8 WILMASTONE. Probably included *Thurlokeshop'* (OE *hop* 'valley' with an Anglo-Scandinavian personal name *Thurlāc*), a lost place in Peterchurch, mentioned with it in Fees p. 814 as held from the Honour of Snodhill (see Ch. 29 note).
2 SMALLHOLDERS ... 2 SMALLHOLDERS. Probably one of these is in error; the entry is not a neat one in the MS with *In dñio sunt ii* written over an erasure.
VALUE NOW. In the MS *Modo*; Farley misprints *modo*.

29,9 ALFWARD HELD IT. There is no gap in the MS between *tenuit* and the side marginal ruling, though because the place-name in Farley occupies less space than in the MS there appears to be a gap; *tenuit* has no full-stop after it, however.

29,9 *ALMUNDESTUNE, ALCAMESTUNE*. J.F. observes that both these unidentified places
-10 were somewhere in the Golden Valley; that *Almundestune* represents OE *Alhmundes tūne* 'at Alhmund's village or estate'; that *Alcamestune* is more likely to represent OE *Alhhelmes tūne* 'at Alhhelm's estate, etc.' than OE *Alhmundes tūne* (as in *Almundestune*). Although the latter relationship is possible — there is ample evidence in DB for reduction of *-mund-* to *-men-* and a feasible model can connect *-men-* to *-ame-* — it is not necessary unless we are required to suppose the different name-forms represent the same place-name. More interesting is the likelihood that here we may have evidence of neighbouring estates named after men with personal-names *Alhmund, Alhhelm*, whose common theme suggests a family relationship. See Aymestrey 1,10a. *Almundestune* with a priest and a church was perhaps Peterchurch, and certainly belonged to it since a marginal note in DBH (p. 70) says *Sancti Petri* 'of Saint Peter' referring to the 3 hides.

29,11 WELLINGTON. Part of this holding or that at 29,14 was in Wootton (GR SO 4848), held as *Wudetun'* ('farmstead or estate in or of woodland', OE *wudu tūn*) from the Honour of Snodhill in Fees (p. 803).
17 MEASURES OF SALT. See 1,7 note.

29,12 THORKELL. Almost certainly Thorkell White, Hugh's predecessor, as also at 29,16; see 1,65 note.

29,13 STRETTON. See 2,37 note.
½ HIDE ... See 1,9 note.

29,14 HUGH ALSO [HOLDS]. *tenet* is omitted in error.

29,15 HUGH ALSO HOLDS. See 29,2 note.
LINCUMBE. An unidentified place although it is mapped by DG. In DBH p. 71 a marginal *in hida W.* is added, thus indicating a part of Westhide — see 29,4 note — this time in Radlow Hundred. The final element of the place-name is OE *cumb* 'a valley'.
3 VIRGATES ... See 1,9 note.

29,16 'BERNALDESTON'. The place, now lost, is found in this form in FA pp. 377,392,412. See
DBH p. 71 and p. 122 note. DB *Bernoldune* represents OE *Beornwald-dune* 'upland tract
called after one *Beornwald*'; the later form 'Beornwald's village or estate', from *tūn*.
Identified as Barland (GR SO 2862) by B. G. Charles *Non-Celtic Place-Names in Wales*,
London 1938 p. 172.
THORKELL. See 29,12 note.
2 HIDES. There is an erasure in the MS after *hidę* and the scribe has drawn a line to join
the *hide* to the *silua* to indicate that he did not intend to add anything in the space. Farley
does not always print these link lines; see 1,65 and 21,7 notes.
MAY KEEP WHAT HE CAN CATCH. Cf. 24,5 and note to it.

29,18 1 HIDE AND 1 VIRGATE OF LAND. *i hid' 7 i v⁴* is written over an erasure in the MS; *trę*
is interlined because of lack of space.

29,19 *LEGE*. A lost 'Lea' or 'Ley' in Elsdon Hundred where there are a number of modern places
with this termination, e.g., Hurstley, Kinley, Red Ley. See DBH pp. xxii and 122.
½ HIDE WHICH PAYS TAX. In the MS there is a small erasure between *hida* and *geld'*;
Farley does not show the gap caused by it.

29,20 THIS ENTRY may have been added later as it is written below the bottom marginal ruling
and slightly into the central margin.
IN SELLACK HUNDRED ... STRANGFORD. DB has *Sulcet* for the Hundred name and
Etone for the place; above the place-name DBH (p. 71; see p. 122 note) has *St(ra)ngef'*. The
Hundred head occurs only here in Herefordshire DB and has been thought to represent an
alternative name for another Hundred. Anderson (p. 163) regards a corruption of **Wulfei*
(Wolphy) as possible, but the honey renders suggest a place in the Welsh area. There is an
Eaton Hill in Vowchurch (GR SO 3735). J.F. notes: 'The meaning of the place-name is the
same as that of Eaton in Foy [19,7 note], i.e., OE *ēa-tūn* "farmstead by or near a river" ....
The supposition that the place is in a Welsh area would make Anderson's suggestion that
Sulcet is a corruption of **Wulfei* (Wolphy) Hundred unlikely, since the latter is in the NE
part of Herefordshire ... The word *St(ra)ngef'* .... the editors of DBH take to be the name of
a later unidentified tenant (DBH p. 122). It is possible, however, that this represents a place-
name .... by which the DB manor *Etone* was known at the time of the later annotation. Not
far from Foy there is a place Strangford (SO 5828). No early forms ... have been published,
and it is possible that this is the place called *Etone* in DB and annotated as *St(ra)ngef'* in
DBH. Furthermore, it is now in the parish of Sellack, which is *Lann Suluc c*.1130 in the
Book of Llan Dâv (*sic*, not *Sulac* as given in [Bannister]PNHe p. 169). This is a Welsh name
meaning "*Suluc*'s church", *Suluc* being a hypocoristic form of *Suliau* or *Tysilio*, to whom
the church is dedicated (DEPN s.n.). It is possible that the *Sulcet* Hundred in which *Etone*
is placed .... is to be associated with this early form of Sellack. *Sulcet* may be a misreading
of *Suluc* itself, or it may contain a Welsh suffix or terminal el., or *Suluc* may have been
gallicized by the addition of the OFr suffix *-et* (v. PNE pt. i s.v.). If the above suggestions
are valid, it would be possible to regard DB *Edtune* [see 19,7 note, s.n. (Hill of) Eaton] as
the same name as DB *Etone*, but to accept that they represented two distinct manors in
DB, one of which, *Etone*, was later renamed Strangford. It is clear that to verify this, the
manorial history of Strangford will have to be examined in detail'.
     If this suggestion proves to be correct, Sellack 'Hundred' will have been, like Wormelow
'Hundred' (1,61 note), an English manorial intrusion into Archenfield. Hill of Eaton lies
east of the river Wye, in Foy parish which spans the river. The village of Foy itself, like
Sellack and Strangford, lies to the west of the river. Although Foy was later in the English
Hundred of Greytree, it was formerly counted as a part of Archenfield, see FA ii p. 404,
and the Welsh form of the name given in the Book of Llan Dâv (*Lannimoi, Lanntivoi*)
suggests an original dedication of its church to a Welsh saint St. Moi or St. Mwy (see DEPN
s.n. Foy). If the Hundred name *Sulcet* represents Sellack, Sellack and Strangford will have
been separated parts of this small 'Hundred', divided from each other by Baysham (1,54)
which is surveyed by DB as part of Archenfield.

Ch.30 URSO OF ABETOT. Abetot in the département of Seine-Maritime, France. Urso was the
brother of Robert the Bursar, and Sheriff of Worcestershire, being called Urso of Worcester
in DB Glos. 65,1. He was probably also Constable; see Round GM pp. 313–315. He helped
to crush the revolt of Earl Roger of Hereford in 1075. See DB Worcs. Ch. 26 note.

30,1 WICTON. Identified by VCH and DG as Wickton in Stoke Prior parish near Hope under
Dinmore (GR SO 5254). But this Wickton is some distance from the western edge of
Plegelgate Hundred. Wicton in Bredenbury is a more likely identification. J.F. observes,
'DB *Wigetune* probably represents the OE pers. name *Wi(c)ga, Wigga* .... with OE *tūn*.
Formally, the first el. could be OE *wigga* "a beetle", but this can be discounted on semantic

grounds in a composition with the habitative el. *tūn*. Wickton in Stoke Prior, though spelled *Wickton* in the first ed. of the 1-in. OS map, is given as *Wigton* in [Bannister]PNHe and [Baddeley]HePN, and if this represents a local pronunciation or traditional spelling the identification with DB *Wigetune* would present no difficulties. There is also a Wig Wood near Wickton on modern OS maps, and this may go back to OE *Wicgan-wudu* "Wicga's wood". A pronunciation *Wick-*, on the other hand, would imply the unvoicing of [g] to [k], possibly under the influence of the following unvoiced [t]of the second el. In order to confirm an identification of DB *Wigetune* with Wicton in Bredenbury one would need some early forms in *Wig-*, since the name might otherwise go back to OE *wĭc-tūn* "farmstead with a *wĭc*" (*v.* PNE pt. ii s.vv. *wĭc-tūn, wĭc*)'.

BY EXCHANGE. The exchanged land does not seem to be mentioned elsewhere in DB Herefordshire.

Ch.31 GRUFFYDD SON OF MAREDUDD. Maredudd ab Owain ab Edwin of the house of Hywel ab Edwin was King of Deheubarth *c*.1063 having succeeded Gruffydd ap Llywelyn (1,49 note). He seems to have allied himself with Earl William and was rewarded with estates in England. He was killed in 1071 on the banks of the river Rhymney by Caradoc ap Gruffydd ap Rhydderch with Norman help. He was succeeded by his brother Rhys ab Owain then by Rhys ap Tewdwr (A 10 note). Maredudd's son Gruffydd lived as an exile on his father's English estates and was killed in 1091 by Rhys ap Tewdwr while trying to recover his Welsh kingdom; see Introductory Note 2. Apart from the lands he held in chief, he held *Alac* 1,34–35 from the King and part of Kings Pyon from Roger of Lacy (10,50). In both the latter cases DBH enters in the margin the same later holders as for Gruffydd's Ch. 31 holdings.

31,1 *MATEURDIN*. The same form occurs at 1,67. DBH p. 72 assimilates this name to Marden (DB *Maurdine* C 3. 1,4. 10,11. 16,4. 35,1; and see DEPN) by giving *Mauuerdin* in the text and in the margin (see p. 122 note). The correct form seems to have been *Mathewurda'* (DBH p. 21 = DB 1,67) or *Mathewordin* in the later survey (p. 79) of the lands of Ch. 1,66–71. Perhaps the *Mauuerdin* form is by mistake, reading ꝥ (th) as ꝥ (*w,uu,u*); but *Mau-uerdin* could represent *Mav-w-* with [v] for [ð], from a form **Math-worþign* with voiced *th*. *Math(e)-* still eludes identification. The final el. exhibits the alternation of OE *worth* (*-wurda*) and *worthign* (*-urdin, -uerdin, -worden*), see PNE pt. ii s.vv.

THE THIRD PART OF 2 HIDES. The rest of the land is described in 1,67 (DBH p. 21).

31,2 GRUFFYDD ALSO HOLDS. Repeated at the beginning of 31,2–7.
CURDESLEGE. Identified by VCH tentatively as Kinnersley, but there are grounds for thinking that the latter is DB *Elburgelega*, 9,15 note. The DB form probably represents OE *Cuthredes-leage* 'at Cuthred's *lēah'*.

31,3 BUNSHILL. See 29,1 note.

31,4 MANSELL (LACY). For the identification, see DBH p. 123 note, and 10,56 note above.
-5

31,6 STOKE (BLISS). DBH (p. 72 and p. 123 note) adds the later holder as *G. de Blez* in the margin.

31,7 LYE. The *Blez* family, who held other lands of Gruffydd later, had a connection with Upper Lye, but see DBH p. 123 note and 1,10c note above. DBH p. 73 has an unexplained name *Putangle* in the margin.
OWEN. From OW *Oue(i)n*; see PNDB p. 342.
THEY WERE WASTE. *Wasti erant* is a mistake for *wasta erant*, correctly referring to *maneria*.
RALPH OF MORTIMER. His holding is cross-referenced at 9,14.

Ch.32 [LAND]OF RAYNER. The rubricator omitted *Terra* probably through lack of space caused by the interlineation *carpent'* above *Rayner'*.

32,1 MARSTON (STANNETT). In Plegelgate Hundred, see 10,71 note.
LUDI. For the name, see PNDB p. 321.

Chs.33 THESE FOUR CHAPTERS are numbered and headed in the list of landholders, col. 179b; -36 they are numbered here, but the scribe did not leave the rubricator room to insert the headings.

Ch.33 CHARBONNEL. A French surname, see Reaney p. 64; Dauzat p. 111 s.n. *Carbonnell*.

33,1 NOAKES. DB *Lacre*; see 2,3 note.

34,1 WULFNOTH. *Oruenot*; see PNDB §60.
4 CATTLE. *Animalia*, commonly called *animalia otiosa* 'idle animals' elsewhere, that is, beef or dairy cattle in contrast to ploughing oxen, though occasionally they seem to be oxen (see DB Som. Exon. Notes 25,41; Cornwall Exon. Notes 4,23; and perhaps in Worcs. 19,9 and here they take the place of the plough-team statement). Cattle and other animals were counted in the surviving circuit returns (the Exon. and Little Domesdays), but were normally omitted from the Exchequer version, except to make a particular point, as probably in

Herts. 31,8 where a catalogue of livestock etc. is given for land appropriated wrongfully by Bishop Odo.

34,2   AELFEVA. *Aueue*, probably a mistake for *Auueue*; other DB forms include *Aelueua, Elueua, Elfgiua*, from OE *Aelfgifu*; see PNDB §64 and p. 173.
VALUE WAS 3s. In the MS *iii solid'*; Farley misprints *iiii solid'*.

35,1   1 VIRGATE ... IN MARDEN. See 1,4 note.

Ch.36   MADOG. *Madoch* in the list of landholders, col. 179b; *Madoc* here. From OW *Matoc*, Welsh *Madog*; see PNDB p. 325.

36,1   ASHPERTON. The land was at Little Ashperton, see Fees p. 809; DBH p. 73 and p. 124 note.

PLACES ELSEWHERE. A distinction is here made between places that were in the County in 1086, but entered in the folios of adjacent counties (prefixed E), and those in adjacent counties in 1086, but later transferred to Herefordshire (ES for Shropshire places, EW for Worcestershire places).

E 1   WESTBURY (ON SEVERN) and Newent were in Gloucestershire in 1086 and Kyre, Clifton (on Teme) and Edvin (Loach) were in Worcestershire. Edvin (Loach) was transferred to Herefordshire in 1893 (see EW 2). Kingstone was in Herefordshire in 1086, see 3,1 note.
6 HIDES IN KYRE. These were held by the Bishop of Hereford (2 hides in DB Worcs. 3,2) and Osbern son of Richard (4 hides in Worcs. 19,4;7).
IN CLIFTON (ON TEME) 10 HIDES. Osbern son of Richard held 3 hides in Clifton on Teme, 1½ hides in Stanford on Teme, 1 hide in Shelsley, 1 hide in Homme Castle and 3 hides in Lower Sapey, recorded in DB Worcs. 19,3;5–6;8–9 respectively. The remaining ½ hide of the 10 was held by the Abbey of Cormeilles at Tenbury Wells (DB Worcs. 6,1).
IN NEWENT AND KINGSTONE 8 HIDES. The Abbey of Cormeilles' 6 hides at Newent are recorded in detail in DB Glos. 16,1, and its 2 hides at Kingstone in 3,1 above.
IN EDVIN (LOACH) 1 HIDE. Osbern son of Richard's hide here is recorded in DB Worcs. 19,11.
ABBOT OF CORMEILLES. Or 'Abbey', as *abb'* can abbreviate both *abbas* 'Abbot' and *abbatia* 'Abbey' (as well as, occasionally, *abbatissa* 'Abbess').
SONS. *f.* with no abbreviation sign, perhaps singular *filius*, referring to William, though more likely plural *filii* as Osbern was also son of Richard (Scrope); see Ch. 24 note. William son of Richard does not recur in DB Worcestershire or Herefordshire as holding any of these lands taken from Westbury on Severn manor.
FIR-WOOD. Perhaps the Forest of Dean. *Sapina*, however, might result from an earlier mistranscription of *Sapian* (Lower Sapey, Worcs.); see BCS 240 and EPNS (Worcs.) p. 75.

E 2–3   HANLEY (CASTLE), FORTHAMPTON. See 1,42–43 notes.

E 2   40 VILLAGERS AND SMALLHOLDERS. The total of both classes is 40. Similarly in E 3.

E 3   THESE TWO LANDS. Hanley Castle and Forthampton.

E 4   SUCKLEY. The information is repeated in DB Worcs. X 3 (= E 8 below). See 1,47.
BELONGED TO THIS MANOR. The manor of Bromsgrove (DB Worcs. 1,1a).
IN TOTAL. Referring to the whole manor of Bromsgrove.
SO LONG AS HE HAD THE WOODLAND. For supplying the salt-houses at Droitwich with fuel; see 1,7 note.

E 5   MATHON. 1 hide of Mathon, possibly additional to these 5, is accounted for in the Herefordshire folios; see 10,39 note. The rest of Mathon was transferred to Herefordshire in 1897.
WALTER PONTHER. *Ponther* here, also *Pontherius* in DB Worcs. and Glos.; perhaps from ML *pontarius* 'bridge-builder' or *puntarius* 'sword-fighter'; OEB p. 265. The same man apparently occurs with the surname *Puchier* (occasionally miswritten *Pubier*) in Worcs. B (folios 136v (= 137v) and 137v (= 138v), Hearne pp. 299,305; see DB Worcs. App. V): *Wallterius Pubier* and *Walterus Puchier* there = Walter Ponther of DB Worcs. 2,5;58. This man obviously bore two surnames: he was Walter *Ponther*, but presumably he or his family came from Picardy (whence *Le Poher, Puhier*), see Reaney p. 278 s.vv. *Ponter* and *Poor*.

E 6   THIS ENTRY was added at the foot of col. 176c; see DB Worcs. 18,6 for fuller details.
AELFRIC MAPSON. *Mapesone* in the MS; Farley misprints *Mapes ne*; for the byname see OEB p. 160.
THEY PAY. *Redd(un)t*, referring to the burgesses and the salt-houses, as the figure 1½ in Latin is normally followed by a singular verb. The formula also occurs in DB Worcs. 22,1. The measures are presumably of salt.
HIS MANOR OF HEREFORD. See Ch. 10 note.

E 7   FECKENHAM, HOLLOW (COURT). See 1,40–41 notes.

RETURN. *Breve*, usually in DB meaning a 'writ': *breve regis*, the King's writ, putting a man in possession of land. But here and in E 8 it clearly refers to the return for the *Terra regis* in Ch. 1 above.

E 8   MARTLEY, SUCKLEY. See 1,39;47 above.
      PAY TAX HERE. That is, in Doddingtree Hundred.

E 9   EARL ROGER. Roger of Montgomery, Earl of Shrewsbury from 1074 until his death in 1094; see J. F. A. Mason in TRHS (fifth series) vol. 13 (1963). DB Shrops. Ch. 4 is arranged by sub-tenants because of its size, hence the references contain three figures (as in DB Cornwall Ch. 5, land of the Count of Mortain). 4,28 largely consists of additional lands held in lordship by Earl Roger, not entered in 4,1.
      FARLOW. See 1,10a note.

ES 5 'STANWAY'. A place, now lost, in Winforton. It survived to be recorded on the 1st edition OS map of 1832 (sheet 55; reprinted 1970 as sheet 50).

ES 9 LYE. See 1,10c note.

ES 10 *TUMBELAWE*. The place has not been identified but is here assumed to have lain in that part of Leintwardine Hundred transferred to Herefordshire, like those places surrounding it in the Survey.

INDEX OF PERSONS

Familiar modern spellings are given when they exist. Unfamiliar names are usually given in an approximate late 11th century form, avoiding variants that were already obsolescent or pedantic. Spellings that mislead the modern eye are avoided where possible. Two, however, cannot be avoided: they are combined in the name of 'Leofgeat', pronounced 'Leffyet' or 'Levyet'. The definite article is omitted before bynames, except where there is reason to suppose that they described the individual's occupation. The chapter numbers of listed landholders are printed in italics. It should be emphasised that this is essentially an index of personal names, not of persons; it is probable that in the case of some entries of simple names more than one person bearing the same name has been included. Likewise, a person who elsewhere bears a title or byname may be represented under the single name; e.g., here many of the references to plain Edwy are probably to Edwy Young (see 2,58 note).

CHURCHES AND CLERGY

Abbess	(of Leominster)	1,14;38
Abbot	of Cormeilles	E 1
Bishops:	of Hereford	2. See also Askell
	(of Hereford)	C 9
	see Aethelstan, Brictric, Leofing, Robert, Walter	
Canons:	of St. Albert's (Aethelbert's)	2,13
	of St. Guthlac's	19,8
	of Hereford	2
	see Estan	
Chaplains:	of the Bishop (of Hereford?)	2,21;57
	see Ralph	
Churches:	of St. Guthlac (of Hereford)	6
	of Hereford	2
	of St. Mary, Cormeilles	3
	of St. Mary, Lyre	4
	of St. Mary, Pershore	E 5
	of St. Peter, Gloucester	5. 15,1
	of St. Peter, Hereford	2,58
	see also under **Saints** below	
Clerks:	of St. Guthlac's	14,2
Monks:	of Lyre	1,44
Nuns:	of Hereford	2,17
Saints:	St. Florent's of Saumur	1,48
	St. Guthlac's (of Hereford)	6. 7,1;5;7. 19,8
	St. Mary's of Cormeilles	3. 1,1-3;6-9;39. 10,50
	St. Mary's (of Cormeilles)	1,47
	St. Mary's of Lyre	4. 1,45;62
	St. Mary's (of Lyre)	1,40;43;46
	St. Mary's of Pershore	E 5
	St. Peter's of Castellion	8,2
	St. Peter's of Gloucester	5. 1,61
	St. Peter's of Hereford	10,5
	St. Peter's (of Hereford)	10,37;48
	St. Peter's (of Hereford?)	1,10c. 10,75
	see also under **Churches** above	
Priests:	of 3 churches in Archenfield	A 1
	see Brictwold, Spirtes, Wulfward	

SECULAR TITLES AND OCCUPATIONAL NAMES

Chamberlain (*camerarius*) ... Humphrey
Chancellor (*canceler*) ... Reinbald
Doctor (*medicus*) ... Nigel
Earl (*comes*) ... Algar, Edwin, Godwin, Harold, Morcar, Oda, Roger, William
Queen (*regina*) ... Edith
Sheriff (*vicecomes*) ... Alwin, Durand, Gilbert, Ilbert, John, Ralph of Bernay

INDEX OF PLACES

The name of each place is followed by (i) the number of its Hundred and its numbered location on the maps in this volume; (ii) its National Grid Reference; (iii) chapter and section references in DB. Bracketed figures here denote mention in sections dealing with a different place. Unless otherwise stated, the identifications of VCH and DG and the spellings of the Ordnance Survey are followed for places in England, of OEB for places abroad. Inverted commas mark lost places with known modern spelling, some no longer on modern maps, others now represented not by a building, but by a wood, hill or field name. Unidentifiable places are given in DB spelling in italics. The National Grid Reference system is explained on all Ordnance Survey maps, and in the Automobile Association Handbooks: the figures reading from left to right are given before those reading from bottom to top of the map. In this volume all mapped places are in 100 kilometre grid square SO. Places with bracketed Grid References are not found on modern 1:50,000 maps. Some places which were in Herefordshire in 1086 are now in Wales or adjacent English counties; their pre-1974 county is given in brackets after the place-name. The Herefordshire Hundreds are listed at the beginning of the maps and map-keys. Within each Hundred, places are numbered geographically west–east working southwards. Where the Hundred number is enclosed in brackets, this indicates that the place is not specifically said to be in that Hundred in the text of DB. 'C' in the Hundred column indicates an extra-Hundredal castle; 'W' or 'S' places in Worcestershire or Shropshire respectively in 1086 which were subsequently transferred to Herefordshire. A name in brackets following a place-name is that of a parish or adjacent major settlement, given to distinguish this place from others of the same name.

	Map	Grid	Text
Acton Beauchamp	W-2	67 50	EW 1
Adforton	S-6	40 71	ES 6
Adley	S-1	37 74	ES 3;19–20
Ailey	4-19	34 48	25,9
Alac	3- —	— —	1,(5);34
Alcamestune	(13- —)	— —	29,10
Almeley	4-15	33 51	6,8
Almundestune	(13- —)	— —	29,9
Alton	(6a-2a)	42 53	10,52
Alvington (Glos.)	20-22	60 00	17,1
Amberley	10-12	54 47	21,5
Ashe Ingen	18-7	58 26	1,(8);57
Ashperton	11-16	64 41	8,9. 15,8. 22,1. 36,1
Ashton	3d-2	51 64	1,10a
Aston (near Wigmore)	(1-3)	46 71	9,4
Aston Ingham	20-12	68 23	21,3
Avenbury	(7-16)	(66 53)	7,9
Aymestrey	3c-1	42 65	1,10a;10c
Bacton	13-12	37 32	10,16
'Bagburrow'	(12-3)	(74 45)	2,28
The Bage	13-4	29 43	25,4
'Baldenhall' (Worcs.)	— —	— —	(1,42)
Bartestree	15-2	56 40	7,1
'Barton' (in Hereford)	14-1	(49 39)	2,11
Barton (in Kington)	(4-3)	30 57	1,69
Baysham	18-5	57 27	1,54
Beltrou	13- —	— —	29,6
'Bernaldeston'	1- —	— —	29,16
Bickerton	(12-12)	65 30	15,5
Birch	18-2	50 30	1,58
Birley	6a-4	45 53	9,16–17. 10,51
Bishopstone	(8-9)	41 43	2,46
Bodenham	10-5	53 51	10,9. 24,9
Bollingham	(4-12)	30 52	1,69
Bosbury	(12-4)	69 43	2,29
Bowley	10-3	53 53	7,2
Bradley	(1-20)	(32 61)	24,3

	Map	Grid	Text
Little Brampton	(1-19)	30 61	24,3
Brampton Abbotts	20-5	60 26	5,1. 6,1
Brampton Bryan	S-4	37 72	ES 15
Breadward	(4-7)	28 55	1,69
Bredenbury	(7-8)	60 56	10,69
Bredwardine	(13-2)	33 44	19,5
Bridge Sollers	(8-12)	41 42	2,48;(50)
Brierley	3d-19	49 56	1,10a
Brimfield	3d-1	52 67	1,10a;20
Brinsop	(9-4)	43 44	19,3
Broadfield	3d-24	54 53	1,21
Broadward	(10-1)	49 57	1,28. 14,3
Brobury	8-8	34 44	10,54
Brockhampton	(15-9)	58 31	2,15
Brockmanton	3d-11	54 59	1,10c
Bromyard	7-15	65 54	2,49
Buckton	S-3	38 73	ES 14
Bullingham, see Bullinghope			
Bullinghope	14-3	51 37	10,19. 21,6. 25,2
Bunshill	8-13	43 42	31,3
Burcstanestune	(13- —)	— —	23,3
Burghill	9-5	47 44	19,2
Burlingjobb (Wales)	1-32	25 58	1,64
Burrington	(1-2)	44 72	9,3
Bushley (Worcs.)	— —	— —	1,44
Butterley	(7-7)	61 57	1,13. 10,70
Byford	(8-11)	39 42	10,60
Byton	(1-14)	37 64	24,2
Caerleon (Wales)	— —	— —	(14,1)
How Caple	(15-10)	61 30	2,14
Kings Caple	18-4	56 28	1,55
Cascob (Wales)	(1-9)	23 66	24,3
Chadnor	6a-5	43 52	8,5
Chetestor	7- —	— —	25,8
Chickward	(4-11)	28 53	1,69. 29,18
Cholstrey	3d-8	46 59	1,10a
Clatterbrune (Wales)	(1-13)	(31 64)	24,3
Cleeve	20-10	(59 23)	1,8
Clehonger	6b-7	46 37	21,7. 26,2
Clifford Castle	(C-1)	24 45	8,1. (10,3)
Cobhall	(14-7)	45 35	10,20
Coddington	(12-5)	71 42	2,32
Coldborough	(20-2)	63 28	22,4
Collington	(7-5)	64 59	2,50. 10,64
Colwall	(12-6)	73 42	2,31
Covenhope	(1-15)	40 64	9,9
Little Cowarne	7-17	60 51	7,8
Much Cowarne	11-4	62 47	19,10
Cradley	(12-1)	73 47	2,30;(31)
Credenhill	9-7	45 43	2,53. 29,12
Croft	2-7	44 65	14,5
'Cuple'	(7- —)	— —	10,74
Curdeslege	(4- —)	— —	31,2
Cusop	(13-6)	23 41	(1,3)
Dewsall	(17-1)	48 33	1,62
Didley	(6b-12)	45 32	2,2
Dilwyn	(4-9)	41 54	1,26;32. 14,8–9
Dinedor	14-6	53 36	8,7
Discoed (Wales)	(1-12)	27 64	24,3
Donnington	12-10	70 33	2,19
Dormington	15-3	58 40	6,2

	Map	*Grid*	*Text*
Dorstone	(13-8)	31 41	23,2
Downton on the Rock	1-1	42 73	9,2
Droitwich (Worcs.)	– –	– –	(1,4;7;8;10a;40–41. 2,18;20; 26–28;34. 29,11). E 6
Eardisland	5-1	41 58	1,6
Eardisley	4-17	31 49	1,68. 10,46. 29,17
Eastnor	(12-8)	73 37	2,27
Hill of Eaton	20-3	60 27	19,7
Eaton (near Leominster)	3d-14	50 58	1,22
Eaton Bishop	6b-5	44 39	2,8
Edvin Loach	W-1	66 58	(E 1). EW 2
Edwardestune	13- –	– –	10,18
Edwyn Ralph	3e-1	64 57	1,10a;10c
Eldersfield (Worcs.)	– –	– –	1,46
Elnodestune	13- –	– –	10,17
Elton	(1-4)	45 70	9,5
Evesbatch	(11-3)	68 48	10,34
Ewias Lacy, see Longtown			
Ewyas Harold	(C-2)	38 28	(2,2. 10,1. 13,2). 19,1
Eyton	3d-7	47 61	1,10c
Farlow (Shrops.)	3a-1	64 80	1,10a. E 9
Feckenham (Worcs.)	– –	– –	1,40;(41). E 7
Felton	(10-10)	57 48	6,6
Fencote	3d-13	59 59	1,14
Fernhill	(6a-8)	(39 49)	10,49
Ford	3d-21	51 55	1,21
Forthampton (Glos.)	– –	– –	1,43. E 3
Fownhope	15-7	58 34	29,2
Bishops Frome	11-2	66 48	2,21. 10,67
Canon Frome	(11-11)	65 43	10,33
Castle Frome	(11-6)	66 45	10,30
Halmonds Frome	(11-5)	67 47	10,29
Priors Frome	15-4	57 39	2,58. 13,1. 26,1
Garway	18-8	45 22	1,50
Gattertop	3d-23	48 53	1,18
Grendon	(7-14)	59 54	10,72
Hamnish	3d-10	53 59	1,30
Hampton (in Hope under Dinmore)	3d-25	52 52	1,16;29
Hampton Bishop	9-18	55 38	2,33
Hampton Wafre	3d-15	57 57	1,15
Hanley (Worcs.)	(7-1)	67 65	10,75
Hanley Castle (Worcs.)	– –	– –	1,42;(44). E 2
'Hanleys End' (in Cradley)	12-2	(69 46)	23,5
Harewood	13-5	(25 42)	25,6
Harpton (Wales)	(1-28)	23 59	9,13. 24,3
Lower Harpton	(1-22)	27 60	24,3
Hatfield	3d-12	57 59	1,11;27
Hazle	(12-9)	70 36	2,26
Heath	(2-10)	55 62	10,13
Little Hereford	2-3	55 68	2,51
Hereford	(9-16)	51 39	C 1;14–15. (1,3;4;7;39;41;47). 2,1;17;57. (10,7. 13,1. 19,2. E 2;4;6–8)
Hergest	(4-6)	27 55	1,69
Hill of Eaton, see Eaton			
Hinton	(10-14)	57 47	6,3
Hollow Court (Worcs.)	– –	– –	1,41. E 7
Holme Lacy	(14-8)	55 35	2,12
Holmer	(9-12)	50 42	2,41
Miles Hope	3d-4	57 64	1,10a
Sollers Hope	15-8	61 33	21,4

	Map	Grid	Text
Hope Mansell	20-16	62 19	15,1
Hope under Dinmore	(10-4)	51 52	6,5
Hopleys Green	4-13	34 52	(1,5). 10,43
Hopton Sollers	7-20	63 49	16,2
Howle Hill	18-9	60 20	1,60
Humber	3d-18	53 56	1,10c
Huntington (near Hereford)	(9-13)	48 41	2,40
Huntington (near Kington)	(4-10)	24 53	1,69
Ivington	3d-16	47 56	1,10a
Kenchester	8-14	43 42	29,1
Kilpeck	18-1	44 30	1,53
Kingsland	(1-21)	44 61	1,5
Kingstone (near Hereford)	(6b-8)	42 35	1,3.
Kingstone (in Weston under Penyard)	20-7	63 24	3,1. (E 1)
Kington	(4-5)	29 56	1,69
Kinnersley	4-18	34 49	9,15
Knill	(1-23)	29 60	24,3
Lawton	1-31	44 59	(1,5). 10,40
Laysters	2-9	56 63	11,2. 22,6. 36,2
Lea	(20-14)	66 21	5,2
Leadon	(11-5a)	68 46	10,37–38
Ledbury	12-7	71 37	2,26
Ledicot	(1-18)	41 62	9,12. 10,42
Lege	(4- –)	– –	29,19
Leinthall	(1-10)	44 67	1,10a;10c. 9,6–7
Leintwardine	S-2	40 74	ES 1–2;4
Leominster	3d-9	49 59	1,10a;10c;37;(70). E 9
Letton (near Clifford)	(4-23)	33 46	10,47
Letton (near Wigmore)	S-8	37 70	ES 11
Lincumbe	11- –	– –	29,15
Lingen	S-10	36 67	ES 7
Linton	20-6	66 25	1,1. 15,3
Litley	9-17	53 39	22,8
Llanwarne	(18-3)	50 28	2,12
Longdon (Worcs.)	– –	– –	(1,44)
Longtown (formerly Ewias Lacy)	(16-1)	32 29	10,2
Ludford (Shrops.)	(2-1)	51 74	24,12
Lugwardine	15-1	55 41	1,2
Lulham	6b-3	40 41	2,4
Luntley	3f-1	39 55	1,33
Luston	3d-5	48 63	1,10a
Lyde	9-8	51 43	2,44. 10,25–26. 24,11
Lydney (Glos.)	– –	– –	(2,8)
Lower Lye	1-11	40 66)	
Upper Lye	S-11	39 65)	1,10c. 9,8;14. 24,4. 31,7. ES 9
Lyonshall	(4-8)	33 55	10,44
Madley	6b-6	41 38	2,9
Mansell, see also Bishopstone			
Mansell Gamage	(8-6)	39 44	10,56
Mansell Lacy	(8-7)	42 45	31,4–5
Little Marcle	11-21	67 36	10,32. 17,2
Much Marcle	12-11	65 32	1,7;(10c). 4,1. 15,4
Marden	10-11	51 47	C 3. 1,4. 10,11. (16,4). 35,1
Marston (in Pembridge)	(4-4)	36 57	27,1
Marston Stannett	7-10	57 55	1,10a. 10,71. 14,12. 32,1
Martley (Worcs.)	– –	– –	1,39. E 8
Mateurdin	4- –	– –	1,67. 31,1
Mathon	W-3	73 45	10,39. 23,6. E 5
Maund	10-7	56 50	7,5. 10,6;8. 14,2
Mawfield	(14-5)	45 36	10,21
Merestone/Merestun (Wigmore Castle)	(1-6)	40 69	(1,5. 9,1)

	Map	Grid	Text
Middleton (in Lower Harpton)	(1-30)	(27 59)	9,13
Middleton on the Hill	3d-3	54 64	1,31
Middlewood (in Clifford)	13-1	28 44	25,5
'Middlewood' (in Winforton)	(4-24)	(30 45)	6,9
Milton	1-26	38 60	24,1
Moccas	6b-1	35 42	6,7. 7,7
Monkhide	(11-10)	61 43	10,35
Monkland	1-33	45 57	8,2
Monmouth (Wales)	(C-3)	50 12	1,48
Monnington (in Vowchurch)	13-11	38 36	19,(1);4
Monnington on Wye	8-10	37 43	8,6
The Moor	13-3	(24 43)	2,54
Moreton Jeffries	11-1	60 48	2,20
Moreton on Lugg	(9-3)	50 45	2,42
Munsley	11-19	66 40	10,31. 15,10. 16,1. 28,2
Mynyddbrydd	(13-7)	28 41	23,4
Nash	(1-16)	30 62	24,3
'Newarne' (Glos.)	20-20	(60 11)	1,72
Newton (near Weobley)	6a-2	39 53	24,7
Newton (near Leominster)	(10-2)	50 53	1,25. 14,4
Noakes	(7-13)	63 55	2,3. 33,1
Norton Canon	8-1	38 47	2,45
Ocle Pychard	10-16	59 46	10,5
Orleton	2-5	49 67	9,19
Pedwardine	S-7	36 70	ES 16–18
Pembridge	(4-2)	39 58	19,8
Penebecdoc	18- —	— —	1,59
Pilleth (Wales)	(1-8)	25 68	9,13
Pipe and Lyde, see Pipe, Lyde			
Pipe	(9-6)	50 44	2,43
Pixley	11-20	66 38	21,2. 28,1
Pontrilas	18-6	39 27	1,56
Pontshill	20-13	63 21	22,2
Poston	13-10	36 37	14,6
Preston on Wye	6b-2	38 42	2,5
Preston Wynne	10-13	55 47	2,16
Pudleston	(2-13)	56 59	10,14
Pull Court (Worcs.)	— —	— —	1,44
Putley	15-5	64 37	10,4
Canon Pyon	(9-1)	46 48	2,39
Kings Pyon	(6a-7)	43 50	10,50
Querentune	(1- —)	— —	24,3
Queenhill (Worcs.)	— —	— —	1,45
Old Radnor (Wales)	(1-29)	24 59	1,65
Redbrook (Glos.)	(20-21)	53 09	1,73
Richards Castle	(2-2)	48 70	(12,2). 24,13
Risbury	3d-22	54 55	1,23
Rochford (Worcs.)	2-4	63 68	22,5. 23,1
Rosemaund, see Maund			
Ross on Wye	(20-9)	59 24	2,24;(25)
Rotherwas	14-2	53 38	25,1
Rowden	7-9	63 56	1,71. 34,2
Ruardean (Glos.)	(20-17)	62 17	15,2
Rushock	4-1	30 58	1,69. 14,7
Sarnesfield	3g-1	37 50	1,17;21
Sawbury Hill	(7-12)	62 55	2,3. 10,65
Shelwick	(9-10)	52 43	2,35–36
Shirley	S-12	38 65	ES 8
Shobdon	(1-17)	40 62	9,10
Stane	(6b-—)	— —	2,2
Stanford	7-18	68 51	1,9;(10c). 10,73

	Map	Grid	Text
'Stanway'	S-9	(40 70)	ES 5
Staunton (Glos.)	(20-19)	55 12	1,74
Staunton on Arrow	(1-25)	36 60	9,11. 24,8
Staunton on Wye	8-5	36 45	10,55;57
Stockton	3d-6	52 61	1,10a
Stoke Bliss (Worcs.)	7-2	65 62	31,6
Stoke Edith	(11-17)	60 40	8,10
Stoke Lacy	7-19	62 49	10,63
Stoke Prior	3d-17	52 56	1,10a
Strangford	19-1	58 28	29,20
Street	(1-27)	42 60	(1,5). 10,41
Stretford	6a-1	44 55	19,9
Stretton Sugwas, see Stretton, Sugwas			
Stretton (in Stretton Sugwas)	9-9	46 42	10,24. 29,13
Stretton Grandison	11-9	63 44	15,6
Suckley (Worcs.)	— —	— —	1,47. E 4;8
Sugwas (in Stretton Sugwas)	(9-11)	45 42	2,37
Sutton	(10-15)	53 45	7,3–4. 29,5
Swanstone	(6a-3)	44 53	10,53
Tarrington	11-18	61 40	10,36. 21,1
Tedstone	(7-6)	69 58	2,3. 10,68
Thinghill	10-17	56 44	6,4. 7,6
Thornbury	7-4	62 59	20,1–2
Thruxton	6b-9	43 34	22,7
Titley	(1-24)	33 60	24,3;6
Treville Wood	(6b-11)	(42 32)	1,3
Tumb elawe	S- —	— —	ES 10
Tupsley	(9-14)	53 40	2,34
Turlestane	(12- —)	— —	1,7
Tyberton	6b-4	38 39	2,6
Ullingswick	(10-8)	59 49	2,18
Upleadon	11-14	67 42	18,1
Upton (in Brimfield)	2-6	54 66	1,10a. 11,1
Upton Bishop	(20-4)	64 27	2,25
Venns Green	10-9	53 48	16,3
The Vern	(10-6)	51 50	16,4
Wadetune	13- —	— —	10,16
Walford (near Leintwardine)	S-5	39 72	ES 12–13
Walford (near Ross)	(20-15)	58 20	2,23;(25)
Walsopthorne	(11-13)	65 42	15,9
Wapleford	(6b-—)	— —	(1,3)
Wapley	3b-1	34 62	1,12
Warham	(9-15)	48 39	2,38
Webton	(14-4)	42 36	10,22–23
Wellington	9-2	49 48	29,11;14
Welson	(4-16)	29 50	1,69
Weobley	6a-6	40 51	10,48
Westelet	2- —	— —	6,11
Westhide	11-8	58 44	8,8
Weston (in Llangunllo) (Wales)	(1-5)	21 70	9,13
Weston Beggard	11-15	58 41	10,27
Weston under Penyard	(20-11)	63 23	22,3
'Westwood'	17- —	— —	1,61
Wharton	3d-20	50 55	1,24
Whitney	4-20	26 47	1,66. 6,10
'Whippington' (Glos.)	20-18	(56 14)	2,22
Whitwick	(11-7)	61 45	15,7
Whyle	2-12	55 60	24,10
Wicton	7-11	62 55	30,1
Wigmore	1-7	41 69	1,19. 9,1
Willersley	4-22	31 47	8,3–4

	Map	Grid	Text
Wilmastone	(13-9)	34 40	29,8
Wilton	(20-8)	58 24	1,8
Winetune	(2- —)	— —	2,52
Winforton	4-21	29 47	8,3-4
Winnall	6b-10	45 34	25,3
Withington	(10-18)	56 43	2,17
Wluetone	(13- —)	— —	29,7
Wolferlow	7-3	66 61	9,18. 10,66
Woolhope	15-6	61 35	2,13
Woonton (in Almeley)	4-14	35 52	1,70. 10,45
Woonton (in Laysters)	2-11	54 62	10,12
Worcester (Worcs.)	— —	— —	(1,39;41;44;47. 2,32)
Wormelow Tump	(17-2)	49 30	C 3
Wormsley	(8-3)	42 47	2,47. 10,61-62
The River Wye	— —	— —	10,7
Yarkhill	(11-12)	60 42	10,28
Yarpole	2-8	47 64	1,10a;36. 12,1
Yarsop	8-2	40 47	2,3. 10,59. 14,10-11. 34,1
Yatton	(20-1)	63 30	1,75
Yazor	(8-4)	40 46	10,58

Places not Named (Main entries only are included, not sub-divisions of a named holding. Identifications provided by the Herefordshire Domesday (DBH) are given in brackets)

1,35	In Leominster 'Hundred'
1,51	In Archenfield (Ballingham GR SO 5731)
1,52	In Archenfield (Harewood GR SO 5226)
1,64	9 waste manors
2,7	In Stretford Hundred
2,10	In Stretford Hundred
2,55-56	In the Golden Valley
2,57	Lands around Hereford
10,1	In Cutsthorn Hundred in the castlery of Ewyas Harold
10,3	In the castlery of Clifford Castle
10,7	A fishery in the Wye (*Hodenac*)
10,10	In Thornlaw Hundred
10,11	In Thornlaw Hundred (Burghope GR SO 5050)
10,15	In Wolphy Hundred
12,2	In Cutsthorn Hundred, in the castlery of Richards Castle
13,2	In Cutsthorn Hundred in the castlery of Ewyas Harold
14,1	In the castlery of Caerleon
19,6	In Thornlaw Hundred (Pencombe GR SO 5952)
29,3	In Thornlaw Hundred (Livers Ocle GR SO 5746)
29,4	In Thornlaw Hundred (Westhide GR SO 5844)
36,3	In Wolphy Hundred

Additional Place-names (of DB holdings or parts of holdings) supplied by DBH. A star indicates that the place is named elsewhere in DB.

Arkstone	10,20 note
Aylton	17,2 note
Ballingham	1,51 note
Burghope	1,4. 10,11 notes
*Kings Caple	1,8 note
*Dormington	7,1 note
'Draycott'	1,10b note
Gatsford	1,1. 6,1 notes
Harewood	1,52 note

Hodenac	10,7 note
Hundeslawa	15,10 note
Hungerstone	1,3 note
Longworth	1,2 note
Mowley	24,8 note
Livers Ocle	29,3 note
Pencombe	19,6 note
*Staunton on Wye	10,56 note
*Stretton Grandison	15,8 note
Underley	9,18. 10,66 notes
Upcott	6,8 note
Villa Asmacun	1,61 note
*Westhide	29,4 note
*Wilton	1,8 note
'Wormington'	1,61 note

Places not in Herefordshire

Names starred are in the Index of Places above; others are in the Indices of Persons or of Churches and Clergy.

Elsewhere in Britain

GLOUCESTERSHIRE ...   *Alvington. *Forthampton. Gloucester, see Durand, St. Peter's Church. *Lydney. *'Newarne'. *Redbrook. *Ruardean. *Staunton. *'Whippington'.

SHROPSHIRE ...   *Farlow. *Ludford.

WILTSHIRE ...   Marlborough, see Alfred.

WORCESTERSHIRE ...   *'Baldenhall'. *Bushley. *Droitwich. *Eldersfield. *Feckenham. *Hanley. *Hanley Castle. *Hollow Court. *Longdon. *Martley. *Pull Court. *Queenhill. *Rochford. *Stoke Bliss. *Suckley. *Worcester, see also Bishop Leofing.

WALES ...   see Rhys of.

MONMOUTHSHIRE ...   *Caerleon. *Monmouth.

RADNORSHIRE ...   *Burlingjobb. *Cascob. *Clatterbrune. *Discoed. *Harpton. *Pilleth. *Old Radnor. *Weston.

Outside Britain

Abetot ... Urso. Bernay ... Ralph. Bouville ... Humphrey. Castellion ... St. Peter's Church. Cormeilles ... Ansfrid, St. Mary's Church. Dreux ... Herman. Écouis ... William. Ferrers ... Henry. Flanders ... Thurstan. Lacy ... Roger, Walter. Lorraine ... Albert. Lyre ... St. Mary's Church, monks. Mortimer ... Ralph. Mussegros ... Roger. Pîtres ... Roger. Sacey ... Ralph. Saumur ... St. Florent's Church. 'Spain' (Épaignes) ... Alfred. Tosny ... Ralph.

MAPS AND MAP KEYS

Places are mapped in their 1086 Hundreds as evidenced in the text. On the maps and in the map-keys, separated parts of Hundreds are distinguished by letters (a, b, c, etc.) after the Hundred figure. Where possible, single detached places are directed by an arrow to the main body of their Hundred and numbered with it. The Herefordshire Hundreds are:

1	Hazeltree	11	Radlow
2	Wolphy	12	Winstree
3	Leominster (Manor)	13	Golden Valley
4	Elsdon	14	Dinedor
5	Lene	15	Greytree
6	Stretford	16	Ewias
7	Plegelgate	17	Wormelow
8	Staple	18	Archenfield
9	Cutsthorn	19	Sellack
10	Thornlaw	20	Bromsash

The relation of the 1086 Hundreds to the later ones is discussed in Introductory Note 7.

Apart from dots, the following symbols indicate places on the map:

O a place in another County in 1086, later transferred to Herefordshire;

Δ places said to be on the 'Welsh March', all apparently in Hazeltree Hundred. The symbol is also marked beside such places in the map-key;

+ members of the great manor of Leominster. Those villages that are shared with other Hundreds are mapped and indexed in those Hundreds, but marked on the maps by a cross and in the map-keys by a (3);

□ castles. Those preceded by the letter 'C' on the map are extra-hundredal.

In the map-keys, an asterisk before a place-name indicates that the name occurs immediately under a Hundred head in the text or is otherwise confirmed as being in this Hundred by the text.

Within each Hundred, places are numbered from west to east working southwards, but they are keyed in alphabetical order.

A bracketed figure after a place-name shows that another part of the village was in a different Hundred bearing that number. The village is mapped in the Hundred that contains its larger portion.

County names in brackets after a place-name in the map keys are those of the modern (pre-April 1974) counties to which places that were a part of Herefordshire in 1086 were subsequently transferred.

The County boundary is marked on the map by thick lines, continuous for 1086, broken where uncertain, dotted for the pre-1974 boundary. Hundred boundaries are marked by thin lines. They follow parish boundaries or geographical features where possible, but because the later reorganisation has masked the 1086 boundaries, they should be regarded as conjectural. Until the 19th century, Herefordshire had two detached portions, Litton near Presteigne and Ffwddog near Llanthony (marked A and B respectively on the maps); if they were part of the County in 1086, their details are concealed in some other entry. The presumed course of Offa's dyke is marked ⊔⊔⊔⊔ on the maps, and the River Wye by parallel lines. In most parts of its course, the River is a Hundred boundary.

The modern boundary with Wales is marked on the maps by dotted lines. In the late 11th century, the boundary was a fluctuating frontier, laid down by the thrusts and retreats of English and Welsh armies. Thus no attempt has been made to mark the western limit of the 1086 County.

National Grid 10-kilometre squares are shown on the map borders. Each four-figure square covers one square kilometre or 247 acres, approximately 2 hides at 120 acres to the hide.

HEREFORDSHIRE: NORTHERN HUNDREDS

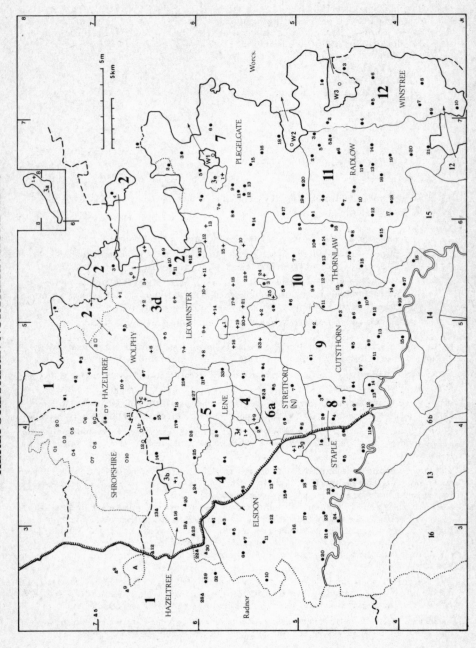

HEREFORDSHIRE: SOUTHERN HUNDREDS

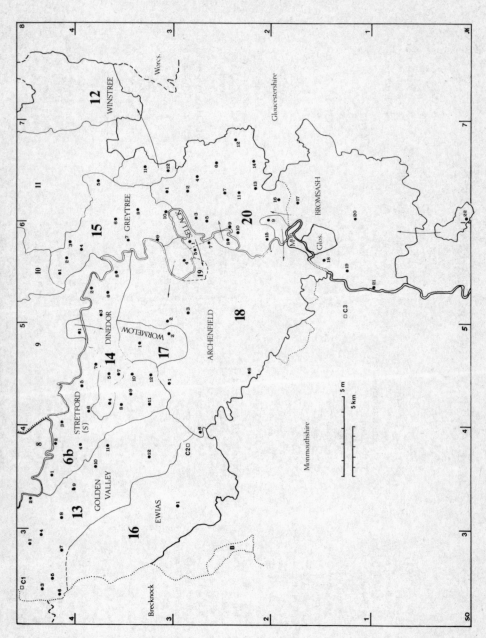

HEREFORDSHIRE HUNDREDS AND MAP KEYS

1 Hazeltree
3 Aston
'Bernaldeston'
20 Bradley △
19 Little Brampton △
32 *Burlingjobb (Wales)
2 Burrington
14 Byton
9 Cascob (Wales) △
13 Clatterbrune (Wales) △
15 Covenhope
12 Discoed (Wales) △
1 *Downton on the Rock
4 Elton
28 Harpton (Wales) △
22 Lower Harpton △
21 Kingsland
23 Knill △
31 *Lawton
18 Ledicot
10 Leinthall (3)
11 ?*Lower Lye (3)
6 *Merestun/Merestone* (Wigmore Castle)
30 Middleton △
26 *Milton
33 *Monkland
16 Nash △
8 Pilleth (Wales) △
Querentune △
29 Old Radnor (Wales)
17 Shobdon
25 Staunton on Arrow
27 Street
24 Titley (4)
5 Weston (Wales) △
7 *Wigmore (3)

2 Wolphy
7 *Croft
10 Heath
3 *Little Hereford
9 *Laysters
1 Ludford (Shropshire)
5 *Orleton
13 Pudleston
2 Richards Castle
4 *Rochford (Worcs.)
6 *Upton (3)
Westelet
12 *Whyle
Winetune
11 *Woonton
8 *Yarpole (3)

3 Manor of Leominster
3a 1 *Farlow (Shropshire)
3b 1 *Wapley
3c 1 *Aymestrey
3d 2 *Ashton
19 *Brierley
1 *Brimfield
24 *Broadfield
11 *Brockmanton
8 *Cholstrey
14 *Eaton
7 *Eyton
13 *Fencote
21 *Ford
23 *Gattertop
10 *Hamnish
25 *Hampton
15 *Hampton Wafre
4 *Hatfield
2 *Miles Hope
18 *Humber
16 *Ivington
9 *Leominster
5 *Luston
3 *Middleton on the Hill
22 *Risbury
6 *Stockton
17 *Stoke Prior
20 *Wharton
3e 1 *Edwyn Ralph
3f 1 *Luntley
3g 1 *Sarnesfield

Alac

4 Elsdon
19 *Ailey
15 *Almeley
3 Barton
12 Bollingham
7 Breadward
11 Chickward
Curdeslege
9 Dilwyn (3)
17 *Eardisley
6 Hergest
13 *Hopleys Green
10 Huntington
5 Kington
18 *Kinnersley
Lege
23 Letton
8 Lyonshall
4 Marston
Mateurdin
24 'Middlewood'
2 Pembridge
1 Rushock

5 Lene
1 *Eardisland

6 Stretford (North)
6a 2a Alton
4 *Birley
5 *Chadnor
8 Fernhill
2 *Newton
7 Kings Pyon
1 *Stretford
3 Swanstone
6 *Weobley

Stretford (South)
6b 7 *Clehonger (14)
12 Didley
5 *Eaton Bishop
8 Kingstone
3 *Lulham
6 *Madley
1 *Moccas (14)
2 *Preston on Wye
Stane
9 *Thruxton
11 Treville Wood
4 *Tyberton
Wapleford
10 *Winnall
16 Welson
20 *Whitney
22 *Willersley
21 *Winforton
14 *Woonton

HEREFORDSHIRE HUNDREDS AND MAP KEYS

7 Plegelgate
16 Avenbury
8 Bredenbury
15 *Bromyard
7 *Chetestor
5 Collington
17 *Little Cowarne
'Cuple'
14 Grendon
1 Hanley (Worcs.)
20 *Hopton Sollers
10 *Marston Stannett (3)
13 Noakes
9 *Rowden
12 Sawbury Hill
18 *Stanford
2 *Stoke Bliss (Worcs.)
19 *Stoke Lacy
6 Tedstone
4 *Thornbury
11 *Wicton
3 *Wolferlow

8 Staple
9 Bishopstone
12 Bridge Sollers
8 *Brobury
13 Bunshill
11 Byford
14 *Kenchester
6 Mansell Gamage
7 Mansell Lacy
10 *Monnington on Wye
1 *Norton Canon
5 *Staunton on Wye
3 Wormsley
2 *Yarsop
4 Yazor

9 Cutsthorn
4 Brinsop
5 *Burghill
7 *Credenhill
18 *Hampton Bishop
16 Hereford
12 Holmer
13 Huntington
17 *Litley
8 *Lyde
3 Moreton on Lugg
6 Pipe
1 Canon Pyon
10 Shelwick
9 *Stretton
11 Sugwas
14 Tupsley
15 Warham
2 *Wellington

10 Thornlaw
12 *Amberley
5 *Bodenham
3 *Bowley
1 Broadward (3)
10 Felton
14 Hinton
4 Hope under Dinmore
11 *Marden
7 *Maund
2 Newton (3)
16 *Ocle Pychard
13 *Preston Wynne
15 Sutton
17 *Thinghill
8 Ullingswick
9 *Venns Green
6 The Vern
18 Withington

11 Radlow
16 *Ashperton
4 *Much Cowarne
3 *Evesbatch
2 *Bishops Frome (7)
11 Canon Frome
6 Castle Frome
5 Halmonds Frome
5a Leadon
*Lincumbe
21 *Little Marcle
10 Monkhide
1 *Moreton Jeffries
19 *Munsley
20 *Pixley
17 Stoke Edith
9 *Stretton Grandison
18 *Tarrington
14 *Upleadon
13 Walsopthorne
8 *Westhide
15 *Weston Beggard
7 Whitwick
12 Yarkhill

12 Winstree
3 'Bagburrow'
12 Bickerton
4 Bosbury
5 Coddington
6 Colwall
1 Cradley
10 *Donnington
8 Eastnor
2 *'Hanleys End'
9 Hazle
7 *Ledbury
11 *Much Marcle
Turlestane

13 Golden Valley (Dore Valley or Straddle Hundred)
Alcamestune
Almundestune
12 *Bacton
4 *The Bage
*Beltrou
2 Bredwardine
Burcstanestune
6 Cusop
8 Dorstone
*Edwardestune
*Elnodestune
5 *Harewood
11 *Middlewood
1 *Monnington
3 *The Moor
7 Mynyddbrydd
10 *Poston
*Wadetune
9 Wilmastone
Whuetone

14 Dinedor
1 *'Barton'
3 *Bullinghope
7 Cobhall
6 *Dinedor
8 Holme Lacy
5 Mawfield
2 *Rotherwas
4 Webton

HEREFORDSHIRE HUNDREDS AND MAP KEYS

15 Greytree
2 *Bartestree
9 Brockhampton
10 How Caple
3 *Dormington.
7 *Fownhope
4 *Priors Frome
8 *Sollers Hope
1 *Lugwardine
5 *Putley
6 *Woolhope

16 Ewias
1 Longtown

17 Wormelow
1 Dewsall
*'Westwood'
2 Wormelow Tump

18 Archenfield
7 *Ashe Ingen
5 *Baysham
2 *Birch
4 *Kings Caple

8 *Garway
9 *Howle Hill
1 *Kilpeck
3 Llanwarne
*Penebecdoc
6 *Pontrilas

19 Sellack (see 29,20 note)
1 *Strangford

20 Bromsash
22 *Alvington (Glos.)
12 *Aston Ingham
5 *Brampton Abbotts
10 *Cleeve
2 Coldborough
3 *Hill of Eaton
16 *Hope Mansell
7 *Kingstone
14 Lea
6 *Linton
20 *'Newarne' (Glos.)
13 *Pontshill
21 Redbrook (Glos.)
9 Ross on Wye
17 Ruardean (Glos.)
19 Staunton (Glos.)
4 Upton Bishop
15 Walford

11 Weston under Penyard
18 *'Whippington' (Glos.)
8 Wilton
1 Yatton

C Castles (extra-Hundredal)
1 Clifford
2 Ewyas Harold
3 Monmouth (Wales)
(For Richards Castle see Wolphy
Hundred; for Wigmore, Hazeltree
Hundred; for Caerleon (GR SO 3490)
see 14,1 note)

Places in other counties in 1086

S In Shropshire
6 Adforton
1 Adley
4 Brampton Bryan
3 Buckton
2 Leintwardine
8 Letton
10 Lingen
11 Upper Lye
7 Pedwardine
12 Shirley
9 'Stanway',
Tumbelawe
5 Walford

W In Worcestershire
2 Acton Beauchamp
1 Edvin Loach
3 Mathon

SYSTEMS OF REFERENCE TO DOMESDAY BOOK

The manuscript is divided into numbered chapters, and the chapters into sections, usually marked by large initials and red ink. Farley did not number the sections and later historians, using his edition, have referred to the text of DB by folio numbers, which cannot be closer than an entire page or column. Moreover, several different ways of referring to the same column have been devised. In 1816 Ellis used three separate systems in his indices: (i) on pages i–cvii, 435–518, 537–570; (ii) on pages 1-144; (iii) on pages 145-433 and 519-535. Other systems have since come into use, notably that used by Vinogradoff, here followed. The present edition numbers the sections, the normal practicable form of close reference; but since all discussion of DB for two hundred years has been obliged to refer to folio or column, a comparative table will help to locate references given. The five columns below give Vinogradoff's notation, Ellis's three systems, and that used by Welldon Finn and others. Maitland, Stenton, Darby, and others have usually followed Ellis (i).

Vinogradoff	Ellis (i)	Ellis (ii)	Ellis (iii)	Finn
152 a	152	152 a	152	152 ai
152 b	152	152 a	152.2	152 a2
152 c	152 b	152 b	152 b	152 bi
152 d	152 b	152 b	152 b2	152 b2

In Herefordshire, the relation between the Vinogradoff column notation, here followed, and the chapters and sections is

179a	C 1-15			183a	7,1	—	7,9
b	A 1-10.	Landholders		b	8,1	—	8,8
c	1,1	—	1,4	c	8,9	—	9,10
d	1,5	—	1,8	d	9,10	—	9,19
180a	1,8	—	1,10c	184a	10,1	—	10,5;7-15;6
b	1,11	—	1,32	b	10,16	—	10,30
c	1,33	—	1,41	c	10,31	—	10,38;40-44;39
d	1,42	—	1,48	d	10,45	—	10,57
181a	1,49	—	1,61	185a	10,57	—	10,70
b	1,61	—	1,75	b	10,71	—	13,2
c	2,1	—	2,11	c	14,1	—	15,3
d	2,12	—	2,21	d	15,4	—	17,2
182a	2,21	—	2,31	186a	18,1	—	19,8
b	2,31	—	2,42	b	19,8	—	21,6
c	2,43	—	2,56	c	21,7	—	23,6
d	2,57	—	6,4;6-10;5;11	d	24,1	—	25,2
				187a	25,3	—	29,1
				b	29,1	—	29,20
				c	30,1	—	36,3
				d	Blank Column		

TECHNICAL TERMS

Many words meaning measurements have to be transliterated. But translation may not dodge other problems by the use of obsolete or made-up words which do not exist in modern English. The translations here used are given in italics. They cannot be exact; they aim at the nearest modern equivalent.

BEREUUICH, BEREWIC. An outlying place, attached to a manor. *o u t l i e r*

BERTONA. A corn-farm or lordship farm, often associated with a monastic or church holding, (2,7 note). *b a r t o n*

BORDARIUS. Cultivator of inferior status, usually with a little land. *s m a l l h o l d e r*

BOVARIUS. A man who looked after the plough-oxen (1,4 note). *p l o u g h m a n*

CARUCA. A plough, with the oxen that pulled it, usually reckoned as 8. *p l o u g h*

CARUCATA. Normally the equivalent of a *hide* in former Danish areas, but elsewhere, especially in the south-west counties, the equivalent of 'land for so many ploughs' (see 1,48 note). *c a r u c a t e*

COLIBERTUS. A continental term, rendering Old English *(ge)bur* (1,4 note), a freedman, sometimes holding land and ploughs. *f r e e d m a n*

COTARIUS. Inhabitant of a *cote*, cottage; often without land (see 6,3 note). *c o t t a g e r*

DOMINICUS. Belongin gto a lord or lordship. *t h e   l o r d ' s* or *l o r d s h i p*

DOMINIUM. The mastery or dominion of a lord (*dominus*) including ploughs, land, men, villages, etc., reserved for the lord's use; often concentrated in a *home farm* or *demesne*, a 'Manor Farm' or 'Lordship Farm'. *l o r d s h i p*

FIRMA. Old English *feorm*, provisions due to the King or lord; a fixed sum paid in place of these and of other miscellaneous dues (see 1,1 notes). *r e v e n u e*

GELDUM. The principal royal tax, originally levied during the Danish wars, normally at an equal number of pence on each *hide* of land. *t a x*

HIDA. A unit of land measurement, generally reckoned at 120 acres, but often different in practice; a measure of tax liability, often differing in number from the hides actually cultivated (see 1,1 note). *h i d e*

HUNDREDUM. A district within a Shire, whose assembly of notables and village representatives usually met about once a month. *H u n d r e d*

LEUGA, LEUUA. A measure of length, usually of woodland, generally reckoned at a mile and a half, possibly shorter (1,10a note). *l e a g u e*

M. Marginal abbreviation for *manerium*, 'manor'. *M*

MITTA. A 'mit' or measure, usually of salt, generally reckoned at 8 bushels (1,7 note). *m e a s u r e*

PRAEPOSITUS, PRAEFECTUS. Old English *gerefa*, a royal officer (see C 2 and 1,3 notes). *r e e v e*

QUARENTINA. A furlong, sometimes used as a square measure (1,10a note). *f u r l o n g*

RADMAN, RADCHENISTRE. A sub-group of the *liberi homines*, 'free men', of higher status than a villager; originally a man who rode with messages, or on escort-duty (1,4 note). Respectively *r i d e r ,   r i d i n g - m a n*

r., rq. Marginal abbreviation for *require*, 'enquire', occurring when the scribe has omitted some information.

SACA. German *Sache*, English *sake*, Latin *causa*, 'affair', 'lawsuit'; the fullest authority normally exercised by a lord (C 9 note). *f u l l   j u r i s d i c t i o n*

SEXTARIUM. A liquid or dry measure of uncertain size, reckoned at 32 oz. for honey (see A 6 note). *s e s t e r*

SOCA. 'Soke' from Old English *socn*, 'seeking', comparable with Latin *quaestio*. Jurisdiction, with the right to receive fines and other dues; also the district in which such *soca* was exercised (see C 9 note). *j u r i s d i c t i o n*

STICHA. A measure, usually of eels, at 25 to the *sticha*. *s t i c k*

SUMMA. A dry measure, usually of salt, corn and fish (see 1,4 note). *p a c k l o a d*

TAINUS, TEINUS. Person holding land from the King by special grant; formerly used of the King's ministers and military companions. *t h a n e*

T.R.E. *tempore regis Edwardi*, in King Edward's time. *b e f o r e   1 0 6 6*

VILLA. Translating Old English *tun*, 'town'. The later distinction between a small *village* and a large *town* was not yet in use in 1086. *v i l l a g e* or *t o w n*

VILLANUS. Member of a *villa*, usually with more land than a *bordarius*. *v i l l a g e r*

VIRGATA. A fraction of a *hide*, usually a quarter, notionally 30 acres. *v i r g a t e*